Becoming a European Homegrown Jihadist

Becoming a European Homegrown Jihadist

A Multilevel Analysis of Involvement in the Dutch Hofstadgroup, 2002-2005

Bart Schuurman

Amsterdam University Press

Parts of this research were supported by grants from the Prins Bernhard Cultuurfonds and the Fulbright Visiting Scholar program.

Cover illustration: Ten years after the murder of Theo van Gogh by Mohammed Bouyeri, the bullet holes are still visible in the bicycle lane in front of Linnaeusstraat 22, Amsterdam.
Source: Wikimedia Commons

Cover design: Coördesign, Leiden
Lay-out: Crius Group, Hulshout

Amsterdam University Press English-language titles are distributed in the US and Canada by the University of Chicago Press.

ISBN	978 94 6298 693 0
e-ISBN	978 90 4853 830 0 (pdf)
DOI	10.5117/9789462986930
NUR	686 / 717 / 754

© Bart Schuurman / Amsterdam University Press B.V., Amsterdam 2018

All rights reserved. Without limiting the rights under copyright reserved above, no part of this book may be reproduced, stored in or introduced into a retrieval system, or transmitted, in any form or by any means (electronic, mechanical, photocopying, recording or otherwise) without the written permission of both the copyright owner and the author of the book.

For Marlies, Willem & Claire

Contents

Acknowledgments		11
1	**Introduction**	13
1.1	Studying involvement in European homegrown jihadism	15
1.2	Existing literature on the Hofstadgroup	18
	1.2.1 Journalistic accounts of the Hofstadgroup	18
	1.2.2 Primary-sources-based academic research on the Hofstadgroup	19
	1.2.3 Secondary-sources-based academic research on the Hofstadgroup	21
	1.2.4 Insights by proxy	22
	1.2.5 Research on the Hofstadgroup by government agencies	23
1.3	Claim to originality	24
1.4	Research questions	24
1.5	Research method	25
1.6	Sources of information	27
	1.6.1 Using police files to study terrorism	27
	1.6.2 Using interviews to study terrorism	29
1.7	Ethical guidelines	31
1.8	A note on terminology	32
1.9	Outline	32
2	**Studying involvement in terrorism**	35
2.1	Issues in terrorism research	35
	2.1.1 An overreliance on secondary sources	36
2.2	Making sense of involvement in terrorism	39
	2.2.1 Structural-level explanations for involvement in terrorism	42
	2.2.2 Group-level explanations for involvement in terrorism	44
	2.2.3 Individual-level explanations for involvement in terrorism	45
	2.2.4 Interrelated perspectives	47
2.3	Limitations	47
2.4	A definitional debate	49
	2.4.1 Terrorism	49
	2.4.2 Radicalism and extremism	51
	2.4.3 Jihad and homegrown jihadism	52
2.5	Conclusion	53

3 A history of the Hofstadgroup — 55
- 3.1 The emergence of homegrown jihadism in the Netherlands — 55
- 3.2 2002: The Hofstadgroup's initial formation — 56
- 3.3 2003: Would-be foreign fighters and international connections — 57
- 3.4 2004: Individualistic plots and the murder of Theo van Gogh — 60
  - 3.4.1 Towards the murder of Theo van Gogh — 63
  - 3.4.2 Violent resistance to arrest — 67
- 3.5 2005: From 'Hofstad' to 'Piranha' — 68
  - 3.5.1 Spring and summer 2005: Renewed signs of terrorist intentions — 69
  - 3.5.2 The second and third potential plots come to light — 71
- 3.6 An overview of the court cases — 74
- 3.7 Conclusion — 75

4 The ideological and organizational nature of the Hofstadgroup — 77
- 4.1 Drawing the Hofstadgroup's boundaries — 77
- 4.2 Homegrown jihadism — 78
  - 4.2.1 The Hofstadgroup's homegrown aspects — 78
- 4.3 Ideology and terrorism — 79
  - 4.3.1 The Hofstadgroup's ideology — 82
- 4.4 Defining terrorist organizations — 87
  - 4.4.1 The Hofstadgroup's organizational structure — 88
- 4.5 Group involvement in terrorism? — 92
- 4.6 Conclusion — 94

5 Structural-level factors: Facilitating and motivating involvement — 97
- 5.1 Structural-level factors influencing involvement in terrorism — 97
- 5.2 Preconditions: Providing opportunities for terrorism — 99
  - 5.2.1 The Internet — 99
  - 5.2.2 Popular support for terrorism — 101
  - 5.2.3 External assistance — 102
  - 5.2.4 Social or cultural facilitation of violence — 106
  - 5.2.5 Ineffective counterterrorism — 107
  - 5.2.6 Political opportunity structure — 109
- 5.3 Preconditions: Providing motives for terrorism — 112
  - 5.3.1 (Relative) deprivation and intergroup inequality — 112
  - 5.3.2 Political grievances — 116
  - 5.3.3 A clash of value systems? — 118
- 5.4 Structural-level precipitants: Submission, part 1 — 120
- 5.5 Conclusion — 120

6	**Group dynamics I: Initiating and sustaining involvement**	123
	6.1 Group dynamics and involvement in terrorism	123
	6.2 Terrorist group formation	125
	6.3 Social identity and the benefits of group membership	129
	6.4 Socialization into a worldview conducive to terrorism	132
	6.5 The underground life	133
	6.6 Social learning theory	136
	6.7 The influence of leaders	139
	6.8 Peer pressure	141
	6.9 Conclusion	145
7	**Group dynamics II: Involvement in acts of terrorist violence**	147
	7.1 Group-level explanations for terrorist violence	147
	7.2 Organizational structure and lethality	148
	7.3 Group influences that lower barriers to violent behavior	149
	7.3.1 Diffusion of responsibility and deindividuation	149
	7.3.2 Authorization of violence	150
	7.4 The rationality of terrorism	154
	7.5 Terrorism as the result of strategic considerations	156
	7.6 Terrorism as the result of organizational dynamics	159
	7.6.1 The group as a vehicle for redemptive violence	161
	7.6.2 The influence of role models on the use of violence	162
	7.6.3 Interaction with the Dutch authorities	163
	7.6.4 Competition with other extremist groups	164
	7.7 Conclusion	166
8	**Individual-level analysis I: Cognitive explanations**	169
	8.1 Structuring the individual-level of analysis	169
	8.2 Radicalization	171
	8.3 Fanaticism	177
	8.4 Cognitive openings and unfreezing	181
	8.5 Cognitive dissonance and moral disengagement	185
	8.6 Conclusion	191
9	**Individual-level analysis II: Terrorists as psychologically distinctive**	195
	9.1 Terrorists as psychopaths	196
	9.2 Psychoanalysis	198
	9.3 Significance quests and identity-related alienation	200
	9.4 The terrorist personality or profile	204

9.5	The role of emotions: anger	209
9.6	Mortality salience	212
9.7	Conclusion	214

10 Conclusion — 217

- 10.1 Key findings — 218
- 10.2 Implications for research on European homegrown jihadism — 222
  - 10.2.1 The 'driving force' of involvement processes is liable to change — 223
  - 10.2.2 Involvement in extremist and terrorist groups takes various forms — 224
  - 10.2.3 The nature of the group shapes the involvement experience — 225
  - 10.2.4 Fanaticism rather than radicalization — 226
  - 10.2.5 Involvement as personal expression rather than strategic calculation — 227
  - 10.2.6 Neither victims nor psychopaths — 228
  - 10.2.7 The often-overlooked role of chance — 228
- 10.3 Policy-relevant implications — 229
- 10.4 Limitations and future research — 230
- 10.5 Toward a more empirical study of terrorism — 232

Abbreviations — 233

Bibliography — 235

Index — 259

Acknowledgments

My research into the Hofstadgroup began in late 2011, when I was fortunate enough to come into contact with the Dutch police files on this group through a research project that my employer Leiden University had been asked to conduct. Had anyone told me at the time that this first encounter would lead to a PhD thesis and ultimately this book, I would have raised my eyebrows in considerable skepticism. These pages speak to the ability to find academic interest and challenge in unexpected places. While this book marks the end of my study of the Hofstadgroup, I hope to be able to continue exploring what drives people to become and remain involved in extremism and terrorism.

The findings presented in this book, and any errors they might contain, are mine alone. Yet I received a great deal of help, inspiration and encouragement during the years of research and writing that led to this point. Above all, I would like to thank my colleagues and supervisors Edwin Bakker and Quirine Eijkman for their feedback over the years and for believing that completing a PhD thesis in part-time was realistic to begin with. I am also grateful for the support provided by John Horgan. It was an honor to be able to learn from you at UMass Lowell during the fall of 2014. Thank you to the Fulbright Committee and the Prins Bernhard Cultuurfonds for making that research stay possible. I would also like to acknowledge the very insightful feedback provided on my PhD work by the reading committee; Beatrice de Graaf, Isabelle Duyvesteyn, John Horgan, Alex Schmid, Bernard Steunenberg and Kutsal Yesilkagit. That gratitude extends to Marc Sageman, who was kind enough to offer detailed feedback on the present manuscript which I did my best to incorporate. I am honored to have your endorsement on the cover.

While working on this manuscript, I became indebted to numerous colleagues, journalists and Dutch government employees who were kind enough to share their insights into the Hofstadgroup with me. Thanks in particular to Paul Abels, Joop Bijen, Beatrice de Graaf, Martijn de Koning, Christianne de Poot, Isabelle Duyvesteyn, Arjan Erkel, Janny Groen, Ahmet Olgun, Ruud Peters, Alex Schmid, Marije Veerman, and Anton Weenink. Particular thanks are due to the Dutch Ministry of Security and Justice, the Dutch Public Prosecution Service and the Dutch National Police for making it possible to utilize the police files on the Hofstadgroup. To all the interviewees who assisted me; your help was crucial to the success of this project and I am grateful that you trusted me with information that was always sensitive and at times deeply personal.

To friends, family, and colleagues both in the Netherlands and abroad: thank you for enduring years of Hofstadgroup anecdotes. Special mention goes to Maarten, Joost, Sander, and Jasper for a friendship that borders on family and for which I am profoundly grateful. I would also like to specifically thank Nora, Mary, and Charles, Wouter, Joris, Erik, Liesbeth, Sergei, Wietse, Constant, Isabelle, Alastair, Carl, and Lisa; here is to the future. To my family; you have been a tremendous source of support throughout this process. Thank you for your encouragement, patience, and for always allowing me to find my own way. This book is dedicated to you.

Finally, if it weren't for the encouragement and help of Paul Abels and Michael Kowalski at the Dutch National Coordinator for Security and Counterterrorism (NCTV), as well as the support of professor Edwin Bakker, this book would never have materialized. I gratefully acknowledge your help.

Bart Schuurman
Utrecht, March 2018

1 Introduction

The Hofstadgroup – Islamist terrorism in the Netherlands

On 2 November 2004, Dutch filmmaker and publicist Theo van Gogh was shot and stabbed to death in broad daylight while cycling through Amsterdam. Shortly after 9 am, a twenty-six-year-old man approached Van Gogh, emptied a 9 mm pistol at him and then attempted to sever his head as he lay dead or dying on the sidewalk. Without fully accomplishing this task, the assailant stuck his knife in Van Gogh's chest. He also left behind a note in which he threatened Dutch politician Ayaan Hirsi Ali by stabbing it onto his victim's body with a second blade. The attacker then calmly reloaded the magazine of his firearm and walked towards a nearby park, where a shootout with police officers ensued. Several minutes later he was taken into custody after suffering a bullet wound to the leg. As he was taken away, a policeman told him he was lucky to be alive. Van Gogh's murderer replied that he did not agree; he had intended to die during the firefight.[1]

Van Gogh's assailant was no stranger to the Dutch police or the General Intelligence and Security Service (AIVD). Since the fall of 2003, both organizations had come across this individual during their investigations into a group of young Dutch Muslims believed to be involved in terrorist activities. Because some of them lived and met each other in The Hague, a city also known in Dutch as the *Hofstad* (Court city), the AIVD began referring to these individuals as the 'Hofstadgroup' from October 2003 onward.[2] The name has stuck, even though the group's alleged members did not use it themselves.[3] Until the day of the murder, however, the AIVD had not estimated that Van Gogh's assailant was preparing a violent crime. In fact, it had regarded him as a peripheral member of the group.[4] Moving swiftly on information provided by the AIVD after the attack on Van Gogh, the police arrested the other individuals thought to be part of this terrorist organization.[5] Although most suspects were apprehended without incident, two resisted violently.

---

1   Donner and Remkes, 'Kamerstukken 2, 2004-2005, 29854, Nr. 1', 1-2; Van Straelen, 'Requisitoir in De Strafzaak Tegen Mohammed B.', 10-27.
2   Donner and Remkes, 'Kamerstukken 2, 2004-2005, 29854, Nr. 3', 3, 5.
3   Groen and Kranenberg, *Women Warriors*, 48-49.
4   Commissie van Toezicht betreffende de Inlichtingen- en Veiligheidsdiensten, 'Toezichtsrapport Met Betrekking Tot Mohammed B.', 2, 17.
5   Police Investigator 1, 'Personal Interview 6', 4.

In the early hours of 11 November, a police arrest squad approached an apartment in The Hague where two suspects were staying. After making their presence known, the officers rammed the door only to find that it had been barricaded. Within moments, one of the occupants responded by throwing a hand grenade through the slender crack between door and door frame and was in turn shot at by the police. Both bullets missed their mark, but the grenade exploded on the street where it injured five policemen, one of whom seriously. Throughout the day that followed, the two suspects called for the police to come and get them and threatened to blow up the house. The standoff ended late in the afternoon when both individuals were induced to surrender after one of them had been shot in the shoulder by members of a military special forces unit. At the time of their arrest, both suspects were carrying additional hand grenades.[6]

It was quickly apparent that both Van Gogh's murderer and the hand-grenade wielding individuals adhered to an extremist interpretation of Islam. The note that the murderer left on Van Gogh's body and the will he had carried with him, titled 'Baptized in Blood', left little doubt that the attack had been inspired by his beliefs and that the perpetrator had hoped to die as a martyr for his cause.[7] The two suspects in The Hague hastily wrote a will during the 'siege' of their apartment that similarly set out their wish to die fighting for Allah. Because their apartment had been wired by the AIVD, there are records of the various phone calls they made to friends and relatives announcing their imminent martyrdom.[8] In fact, almost all of the other people arrested in connection with the Van Gogh killing were to a greater or lesser extent found in possession of documents, audiotapes, videos, and Internet materials espousing radical and extremist views of Islam and glorifying terrorism.[9]

These signs of an extremist ideology and the gruesome nature of Van Gogh's death, led the events of November 2004 to have an impact on Dutch society and politics that is felt to this day.[10] They fueled an already heated

---

6 Dienst Nationale Recherche, 'RL8026', 01/13: 95-96; AHA07/24: 3087-127; AGV01/62: 17969-8005; GET: 8235-8237; The Hague Court of Appeal, 'LJN BC2576', 26-29; De Weger, 'Continuïteit En Verandering', 630.

7 Peters, 'De Ideologische En Religieuze Ontwikkeling', 18; appendix: Overzicht teksten geschreven of vertaald door Mohammed B., 46-47; Dienst Nationale Recherche, 'RL8026', 01/01: 65.

8 Dienst Nationale Recherche, 'RL8026', AHA07/24: 3088-91, 3093-103, 3107, 3124; AHB01/25: 139-142; GET: 18235-37.

9 Ibid., 01/01: 131, 134, 142-47, 160-61, 171-72; 01/13: 47.

10 De Koning and Meijer, 'Going All the Way', 221; 'T Sas and Born, 'Hoofdofficier: Mohammed Bouyeri Handelde Niet Alleen'.

debate about multiculturalism and the integration of Muslim minorities.[11] But instead of being seen as a purely domestic affair, the Hofstadgroup was quickly interpreted within the context of the global 'jihadist' terrorist threat that had manifested itself with the 9/11 attacks on the United States orchestrated by Osama bin Laden's al-Qaeda organization.[12] More specifically, Van Gogh's assassin, his associates and the apparent 2005 attempts by some of the Hofstadgroup's remnants to plot additional attacks, came to be viewed as prime examples of the rise of a new 'homegrown' dimension of jihadist terrorism in Europe.[13]

Homegrown jihadist terrorism first appeared in Europe in March 2004, when bombs exploded on commuter trains in Madrid, killing 191 people and injuring 1500.[14] Almost a year and a half later, suicide bombers targeted London's public transportation system, causing the deaths of 52 victims.[15] What the attacks in Madrid, Amsterdam, and London had in common was that they were carried out by Islamist terrorists who lived, worked, and, albeit to varying degrees, belonged to the countries they attacked. The perpetrators of the Madrid attacks were largely first-generation immigrants; many of those involved in the Amsterdam and London attacks had been born and raised there.[16] Whereas previously jihadist terrorism had emanated from places like Afghanistan, the tragedies in Madrid, Amsterdam, and London revealed dangers much closer to home.

1.1 Studying involvement in European homegrown jihadism

More than a decade after Van Gogh's murder, jihadist terrorism continues to pose a threat to European societies.[17] In 2011, American forces completed their withdrawal from Iraq while neighboring Syria fell into civil war. These events created opportunities for al-Qaeda and its affiliates, but especially

11   Buijs and Demant, 'Extremisme En Radicalisering', 170-71.
12   'Spanje Ziet Band Met Nederland'; Coolsaet, 'EU Counterterrorism Strategy', 867-69; De Graaf and Eijkman, 'Terrorismebestrijding En Securitisering', 33; General Intelligence and Security Service, 'From Dawa to Jihad: The Various Threats from Radical Islam to the Democratic Legal Order', 5.
13   Sageman, 'The Next Generation of Terror', 37-39; General Intelligence and Security Service, 'Violent Jihad in the Netherlands', 29; Kirby, 'The London Bombers', 415.
14   Rose, Murphy, and Abrahms, 'Does Terrorism Ever Work?', 186.
15   Silke, 'Holy Warriors', 99.
16   Nesser, *Jihad in Europe*, 314, 333, 394, 397-405.
17   EUROPOL, *TE-SAT 2014*, 21-22; Nesser, 'Toward an Increasingly Heterogeneous Threat', 440-56.

for the so-called 'Islamic State', to make considerable gains in both countries. Thousands of European men and women have joined these groups as 'foreign fighters'.[18] The risk that battle-hardened, paramilitary trained, and ideologically extremist returnees will commit attacks in their countries of origin has become a prime concern for European authorities.[19] In addition, there is the threat posed by extremists who chose to stay at home and by the relatively large, and apparently growing, circle of radical and extremist sympathizers that surround this militant core.[20] Given this context, it is clear that research on (homegrown) jihadist terrorism in Europe continues to be relevant not just for academics, but also for those working to prevent attacks and reduce societal polarization.[21]

Using an in-depth case study, this book asks how and why people become involved in European homegrown jihadist groups. As Sageman lamented in 2014, it is a question we are still unable to conclusively answer.[22] For a topic as academically and societal relevant as terrorism this is a surprising state of affairs. After the 9/11 attacks, considerable new sources of funding became available and a large number of new researchers began studying terrorism, which led to a tremendous increase in research output.[23] Why is a comprehensive understanding of what drives people to participate in this particular form of political violence still so far off?

The slow progress towards understanding how and why involvement in terrorism occurs is in fact not so surprising. 'Terrorism' continues to lack a commonly accepted definition, frustrating comparative research and theoretical development.[24] The diversity in terms of terrorists' goals, means, organizational structures, and guiding ideologies imply that factors relevant to involvement in one typology of terrorism might be less salient in others.[25] Crucially, while there are almost fifty separate hypotheses about how and why involvement in terrorism occurs, most of them lack

---

18 General Intelligence and Security Service, 'The Transformation of Jihadism', 5; Neumann, 'Foreign Fighter Total in Syria/Iraq'.
19 Vidino, 'European Foreign Fighters', 217-19.
20 Algemene Inlichtingen- en Veiligheidsdienst, 'Jaarverslag 2014', 18-20; General Intelligence and Security Service, 'The Transformation of Jihadism', 28-34.
21 Abels, 'Het Nederlandse Contraterrorisme Beleid', 127; Cliteur, 'Waarom Terrorisme Werkt', 308.
22 Sageman, 'The Stagnation in Terrorism Research', 569.
23 Silke, 'Contemporary Terrorism Studies', 34-35; Schmid, 'The Literature on Terrorism', 458-60.
24 Sánchez-Cuenca, 'Why Do We Know So Little?', 594-95.
25 McAllister and Schmid, 'Theories of Terrorism', 202.

the empirical verification necessary to fully determine their validity.²⁶ This is due in large part to one of the most enduring problems in the study of terrorism; the scarcity of primary sources.²⁷ The secondary literature and media reports, still the most prevalent sources in terrorism research, are generally not reliable and detailed enough to function as the sole basis for academic research.²⁸

The goal of this book is to contribute to our understanding of how and why people become involved in European homegrown jihadist groups. It does so through an in-depth analysis of the structural, group-, and individual-level factors that facilitated, motivated, and sustained participants' processes of involvement in the Hofstadgroup. The Hofstadgroup has been chosen as a case study firstly because the author was able to gather extensive primary-sources-based information on the group. Access to such data is seen as a prerequisite for making an empirically substantiated contribution to the existing body of literature. Secondly, the Hofstadgroup is interesting because it was part of what could be termed the first generation of homegrown jihadism in Europe, one that gave rise to similar groups in neighboring states.²⁹ While Chapter 4 argues that past research may have overstated the representativeness of the Hofstadgroup for this broader trend, there are sufficient similarities for the case to yield generalizable insights.

At the same time, the limitations of a single-case study research design must be acknowledged from the outset. The lack of a comparative aspect means the results presented here are first and foremost applicable to the Hofstadgroup itself. Although the present author argues that the similarities between the Hofstadgroup and other European homegrown jihadist entities that arose in the early 2000s allow the case to provide insights relevant to understanding this broader typology as well, it cannot simply be assumed that the explanations for involvement in the Hofstadgroup will all be equally relevant to European homegrown jihadism as a whole. However, although 'n=1' in terms of the number of *groups* studied, this book takes an in-depth look at the involvement pathways of dozens of Hofstadgroup participants. There is therefore an element of comparison and generalizability present within this study despite its focus on a single case study.

26 Ibid., 261.
27 Silke, 'The Impact of 9/11', 76-80.
28 Silke, 'The Devil You Know', 5-6.
29 Nesser, 'Chronology of Jihadism', 934-40; Nesser, 'Toward an Increasingly Heterogeneous Threat', 441-49.

This chapter presents the research questions, the methodology and sources used to address them, and concludes by setting out the book's structure. First of all, however, it is necessary to explicate how this study of the Hofstadgroup case can yield new insights. Has more than a decade of research on this group not sufficiently addressed how and why its participants became involved?

1.2 Existing literature on the Hofstadgroup

The Hofstadgroup has been the subject of a wide variety of publications, ranging from academic works to journalistic accounts and government documents. Within this literature, four issues are identified that legitimize the present in-depth analysis of the group. First and foremost, existing publications on the group reflect the broader trend in research on terrorism in their heavy reliance on secondary sources. Furthermore, research on the Hofstadgroup has tended to be *descriptive* rather than *explanatory*. It has also predominantly been focused on a small number of participants, leaving the backgrounds and motives of the wider group relatively untouched. Finally, there has been a tendency to use singular theoretical perspectives that focus only on one of the many potential factors influencing involvement in terrorism identified in the literature. In short, the Hofstadgroup's considerable potential to inform the debate on how and why involvement in European homegrown jihadism occurs has not been fully realized.

1.2.1 Journalistic accounts of the Hofstadgroup

Several journalists have provided descriptions and initial analyses of the main events and actors in the Hofstadgroup timeline.[30] Others have produced in-depth biographies and background pieces on particular participants.[31] Most of these publications utilize at least some primary sources, such as interviews with former participants or their acquaintances,[32] information derived from court cases,[33] or even data from police files.[34] Particularly

---

30   Chorus and Olgun, *In Godsnaam*; Groot Koerkamp and Veerman, *Het Slapende Leger*; Derix, 'Hoe Kwam Toch'; Alberts and Derix, 'Het Mysterie'; Vermaat, *De Hofstadgroep*.
31   Chorus and Olgun, *Broeders*; 'Op De Thee'; Erkel, *Samir*; Alberts et al., 'De Wereld Van Mohammed B.'; Calis, 'Iedereen Wil Martelaar Zijn'.
32   Chorus and Olgun, *In Godsnaam*; Groot Koerkamp and Veerman, *Het Slapende Leger*.
33   Vermaat, *De Hofstadgroep*; Vermaat, *Nederlandse Jihad*.
34   Eikelenboom, *Niet Bang Om Te Sterven*, 10-11.

noteworthy is Groen and Kranenberg's groundbreaking book on the various women in and around the Hofstadgroup. Based on interviews collected over two years, it offers invaluable first-hand perspectives on what drove these individuals to become involved.[35] Similarly, Vermaat's account of the trials against Hofstadgroup participants is especially valuable for its inclusion of verbatim transcripts of what was said during the proceedings.[36]

Many of these accounts provide informative introductions to the Hofstadgroup. Yet on the whole, the journalistic literature on the Hofstadgroup is unable to provide a comprehensive explanation of the factors that governed the processes by which its participants became involved. Owing to their journalistic rather than academic point of departure, these publications tend to focus on description instead of systematic and theoretically grounded analysis. Furthermore, the empirically most valuable works have limited their focus to specific individuals or segments of the group. Erkel's biography of a leading participant, which mixes information derived from interviews with fiction, is a case in point. As is Groen and Kranenberg's book; while it utilizes extensive interviews, it focuses almost exclusively on the women in the group. The journalistic literature offers a springboard into the Hofstadgroup's world, but leaves considerable uncharted territory.

1.2.2 Primary-sources-based academic research on the Hofstadgroup

Within the academic literature on the Hofstadgroup, a general distinction can be made between studies that utilize primary sources and those that do not. The use of interviews or materials produced by participants makes works in the first category especially valuable. Peters, for instance, has used the texts written and translated by Van Gogh's killer to write an in-depth analysis of the latter's ideological development.[37] Several other authors have used interviews to produce biographies of people in and around the Hofstadgroup that provide insights into how and why they became involved.[38] There are also numerous descriptive and historical studies based on a mix of secondary sources and primary ones.[39] Silber's chapter on the Hofstadgroup

---

35 Groen and Kranenberg, *Women Warriors*, 17.
36 Vermaat, *Nederlandse Jihad*.
37 Peters, 'De Ideologische En Religieuze Ontwikkeling', 1-87; Peters, 'Dutch Extremist Islamism', 145-59.
38 De Graaf, *Gevaarlijke Vrouwen*, 249-90; De Koning, 'Changing Worldviews and Friendship', 372-92; Van San, Sieckelinck, and De Winter, *Idealen Op Drift*, 44-53.
39 Benschop, 'A Political Murder Foretold'; De Goede and De Graaf, 'Sentencing Risk', 319-23; De Graaf, 'The Nexus between Salafism and Jihadism', 18-20; De Graaf, 'The Van Gogh Murder', 101-42.

is a good example in this regard, providing a detailed overview of events and participants.[40]

De Koning et al. have produced three publications that are notable for utilizing primary sources, looking at the Hofstadgroup in its entirety and being explanatory rather than descriptive in focus. One uses social movement theory to argue that the Hofstadgroup's development was influenced by the increasingly strident debate on the role of Islam in the Netherlands and the accommodating response of Dutch Salafist mosques.[41] Another relies on the concept of governmentality to make a similar point and interprets the group as a rebellious response to the Dutch government's integration and counter-radicalization efforts.[42] A third contribution, based on the idea of transnationalism, posits that the behavior of Hofstadgroup participants reflected the transposition of global conflicts, in this case a presumed Western war against Islam, to a local setting.[43]

All of these primary-sources-based academic studies have made valuable contributions to understanding the Hofstadgroup. But like the journalistic accounts discussed earlier, they cannot provide a comprehensive account of participants' involvement processes. First of all because none of these works explicitly focus on this question. The publications that provide an overview of events are good at detailing *what* happened, but their descriptive focus means that they can only partially explain *why* or *how* the group came to be. In-depth studies of particular participants reveal a lot about these individuals' motivations, their worldviews, and involvement processes, but little about the rest of the group. The contributions of De Koning et al. usefully demonstrate the influence that particular factors had in bringing about involvement in the Hofstadgroup, yet as Chapter 2 details, the factors that influence how and why people become involved in terrorism are interrelated and spread over several levels of analysis.[44] While singular theoretical perspectives can illuminate the influence of a particular variable, they leave the potential influence of many others unaddressed.[45]

---

40 Silber, *The Al Qaeda Factor*, 206-23.
41 De Koning and Meijer, 'Going All the Way', 234-35; De Koning, '"Moge Hij Onze Ogen Openen"', 54-55.
42 De Koning, '"We Reject You"', 105.
43 Bartels and De Koning, 'Submission and a Ritual Murder', 30-31, 33.
44 E.g. Veldhuis and Staun, *Islamist Radicalisation*, 21-27.
45 Eyerman does use multiple theoretical perspectives to study the murder of Van Gogh but his work is not concerned with studying how involvement in the Hofstadgroup came about, nor does it utilize primary-sources-based data: Eyerman, *The Assassination of Theo Van Gogh*.

1.2.3 Secondary-sources-based academic research on the Hofstadgroup

Only a small number of academic studies on the Hofstadgroup use primary sources. For the most part, this literature relies on newspaper articles or existing publications to substantiate the arguments being put forward. The uncertain reliability of media reporting on terrorism, which is discussed in detail in Chapter 2, has had the unfortunate result of casting doubt on the accuracy and completeness of at least some of the information on the Hofstadgroup found in this category. This problematizes how much we can confidently assert to know about what the Hofstadgroup was, what it did, and what led its participants to become involved.[46]

The benefits of hindsight and access to primary sources reveal that numerous secondary-sources-based explanations for the Hofstadgroup contain inaccuracies. This is a particularly prevalent issue in early studies of the group, where authors had little choice but to rely on media reports. For example, there is no reliable basis for the idea that Van Gogh's murderer was directly motivated to kill by the escalation of the Iraq war,[47] Dutch counterterrorism measures,[48] or European immigration policies.[49] It is also disputable that the group was led by Van Gogh's killer,[50] that it had a distinct organizational structure,[51] planned to assassinate Portuguese Prime Minister José Barroso,[52] or had links to al-Qaeda.[53] Similarly, the claims that Van Gogh's assailant became violent after being turned down by a girl,[54] that his violent act followed unsuccessful attempts to carve out a place in Dutch society,[55] or that two individuals arrested in June 2005 were on their way to kill a Dutch politician, lack a reliable empirical basis.[56]

---

46 Egerton, 'The Internet and Militant Jihadism', 116-21; Egerton, *Jihad in the West*, 75-83, 114, 121, 125, 129, 150-51; Eyerman, *The Assassination of Theo Van Gogh*, 5; Likar, *Eco-Warriors*, 107-08, 113-15, 228-29; McCauley and Moskalenko, *Friction*, 85-88; Rabasa and Benard, *Eurojihad*, 78, 130; Silber and Bhatt, 'Radicalization in the West', 24-25, 32-33, 38, 40, 47-48; Van der Hulst, 'Terroristische Netwerken', 14-15.
47 Nesser, 'The Slaying of the Dutch Filmmaker', 8-9, 20, 22, 24-25; Nesser, 'Jihadism in Western Europe', 332-37.
48 Nesser, 'The Slaying of the Dutch Filmmaker', 8, 20, 24.
49 Nesser, 'Lessons Learned', 3.
50 Nesser, 'Europe's Global Jihadis', 246.
51 Nesser, *Jihad in Europe*, 337-38, 340.
52 Vidino, 'The Hofstad Group', 583; Leiken, 'Europe's Mujahideen', 5; Vidino, *Al Qaeda in Europe*, 344-45.
53 Wilkinson, 'International Terrorism', 22-23.
54 Transnational Terrorism Security & the Rule of Law Project, 'The "Hofstadgroep"', 6.
55 Buruma, *Murder in Amsterdam*, 22-23; Jacobson, *The West at War*, 6.
56 Von Knop, 'The Female Jihad', 405.

Of course, none of this is to say that the secondary-sources-based literature on the Hofstadgroup should be dismissed out of hand. It includes many insightful overviews of events and interesting hypotheses on how and why involvement came about. This segment of the literature also encompasses publications whose value is primarily their ability to be thought-provoking. For instance, Cliteur has argued that excessive political correctness has prevented a full appreciation of the group's Islamist motivations.[57] Likewise, there are various pieces that assert[58] or dispute[59] that the Hofstadgroup can be linked to the failure of multiculturalism that are essentially societal critiques. Nevertheless, moving towards a more complete and accurate understanding of the various factors that underlay the involvement processes of its participants necessitates the use of more reliable sources of information.

1.2.4 Insights by proxy

A third set of publications provides insights by proxy. De Poot et al. have conducted a study on the various homegrown jihadist networks active in the Netherlands between 2001 and 2005, of which the Hofstadgroup was one.[60] These authors use police files to provide insights into a range of factors relevant to these groups, such as their members' socioeconomic backgrounds or their daily routines. However, because such findings are agglomerated and completely anonymized, it is difficult to isolate which are specific to the Hofstadgroup. A similarly indirect perspective is offered by the autobiography of Yehya Kaddouri. While Kaddouri was not a Hofstadgroup participant, his September 2004 arrest on suspicion of preparing a terrorist attack allows the book to provide an interesting first-hand impression of how a young Dutch Muslim could become involved in militant Islamism in the early 2000s.[61] It draws particular attention to the role of the Internet, news of violence perpetrated by and against Muslims, and feelings of discrimination as facilitating and motivating such involvement.[62]

57　Cliteur, 'De "Eigen-Schuldtheorie"', 185-97; Cliteur, 'De Lankmoedige Elite', 207-35; Cliteur, 'Waarom Terrorisme Werkt', 307-45.
58　Carle, 'Demise of Dutch Multiculturalism', 68-74; Spruyt, 'Liberalism and the Challenge of Islam', 320-21; Leiken, 'Europe's Angry Muslims', 120-26; Leiken, 'Europe's Mujahideen', 3-6; Esman, *Radical State*; Wessels, *De Radicaal-Islamitische Ideologie Van De Hofstadgroep*, 24; Mak, *Nagekomen Flessenpost*, 34-37.
59　Aarts and Hirzalla, 'Lions of Tawhid', 18-23; Mak, *Gedoemd Tot Kwetsbaarheid*, 20.
60　De Poot et al., *Jihadi Terrorism in the Netherlands*.
61　Kaddouri, *Lach Met De Duivel*.
62　Ibid., 10-34.

INTRODUCTION

Several scholars have undertaken empirical studies of the Dutch Muslim community from which useful parallels with the Hofstadgroup can be drawn. Because the group's participants were ideologically strongly influenced by the fundamentalist 'Salafist' interpretation of Islam, the in-depth analysis by Roex et al. of the Dutch Salafism provides several informative insights.[63] In particular, fieldwork derived information on Dutch Salafists' attitudes towards democracy, and the degree to which they support violence.[64] Buijs et al. investigated how the convictions of 'democratic' and 'radical' Dutch Muslims differed and what drove the latter to become radicalized.[65] Among their conclusions are the findings that radicalization can be the result of a reaction to perceived injustice, a search for meaning in life, or a desire for social solidarity.[66]

Slootman and Tillie conducted a study on why some Dutch Muslims in Amsterdam became radicalized. Their research is based partly on interviews with twelve young men in the 'periphery' of the Hofstadgroup.[67] 'Periphery', however, does not appear to mean that these individuals actually participated in any direct sense in the Hofstadgroup but, rather, that they shared its interpretation of Islam. Their conclusions that radicalization is tied to very orthodox religious convictions, the perception that Muslims are treated unjustly, and that Islam as a whole is threatened, are valuable nonetheless.[68] The main benefit of these and the other 'insights by proxy' is that they draw attention to factors that influenced the radicalization of groups and individuals quite similar to the Hofstadgroup, thus hinting at factors with above-average explanatory potential.

1.2.5   Research on the Hofstadgroup by government agencies

Reports written by the AIVD, the National Coordinator for Security and Counterterrorism (NCTV), and the Dutch Review Committee on the Intelligence and Security Services (CTIVD) constitute the last category of publications on the Hofstadgroup. Although the AIVD report on the Hofstadgroup is largely descriptive, it does raise several potential explanations for involvement, such as peer pressure and the influence of a charismatic

---

63   Roex, Van Stiphout, and Tillie, 'Salafisme in Nederland'.
64   Ibid., 274-76, 280-82.
65   Buijs, Demant, and Hamdy, *Strijders Van Eigen Bodem*, 18.
66   Ibid., 251.
67   Slootman and Tillie, 'Processen Van Radicalisering', 3, 85-106.
68   Ibid., 4.

religious authority figure.[69] These hypotheses are worthy of further investigation not in the least because the conclusions are drawn from information collected by the agency itself. The NCTV study is concerned with Internet usage by jihadists in general, but provides some relevant information on the Hofstadgroup in this regard.[70] The CTIVD reports are arguably the most useful of the three, as they detail when the AIVD began collecting intelligence on the Hofstadgroup and what it knew of Van Gogh's murderer and possible accomplices.[71]

1.3   Claim to originality

From journalistic accounts to government reports, while the best studies on the Hofstadgroup provide key *parts* of the overall puzzle, a comprehensive and robustly empirical account that explains how and why participants became involved in the group is lacking. This knowledge gap provides the primary rationale for the current study, which makes a threefold contribution to the existing literature. First of all, it aims to improve our understanding of the factors that governed involvement in the Hofstadgroup. Secondly, because this group was not a unique phenomenon but one example of the broader European homegrown jihadist trend, the research will also provide insights into processes of involvement in this typology of terrorism in a more general sense. Finally, by utilizing extensive primary sources, this book aims to contribute to moving terrorism research toward a more empirically robust basis.

1.4   Research questions

Two important premises drawn from the literature on terrorism form the foundation of this book. Explained in detail in Chapter 2, the first of these is that involvement in terrorism is best understood as the end-result of a complex process rather than a sudden or clearly made decision. Secondly,

---

69   General Intelligence and Security Service, 'Violent Jihad in the Netherlands', 9, 37, 39-41. See also: Algemene Inlichtingen- en Veiligheidsdienst, 'Jihadistisch Terrorisme in Nederland', 88.
70   National Coordinator for Security and Counterterrorism, 'Jihadists and the Internet: 2009 Update', 69.
71   Commissie van Toezicht betreffende de Inlichtingen- en Veiligheidsdiensten, 'Toezichtsrapport Met Betrekking Tot Mohammed B.,' 8-24; Commissie van Toezicht betreffende de Inlichtingen- en Veiligheidsdiensten, 'Toezichtsrapport over Eventuele Handlangers', 1-41.

the involvement process is itself predicated on multiple factors that reside at the structural, group, and individual levels of analysis.[72] Structural-level analyses focus on the broader social, political, and economic influences that shape motives and opportunities for engaging in terrorism. Group-level explanations focus on how small-group dynamics influence group formation and the establishment of a social reality conducive to the adoption of extremist worldviews and violent behavior. Individual-level accounts for terrorism examine the personal histories of terrorists and assess whether mental health issues or personality profiles offer explanations for their involvement in violence.

The overarching question that this book poses is: What factors governed the involvement processes of participants of the Hofstadgroup during its 2002-2005 existence? Based on the premises outlined in the previous paragraph, three subsidiary research questions are formulated which function as stepping-stones towards addressing the main research question. These are: How did 1) structural-level factors, 2) group-level factors, and 3) individual-level factors influence involvement in the Hofstadgroup? It should be noted that the emphasis is on understanding processes of involvement rather than a singular process. It is apparent from the outset that even within this one particular group, not all participants thought and acted similarly. The fact that only a minority of Hofstadgroup participants actually planned or perpetrated acts of terrorist violence, is the most obvious example of this fact. The discussion that follows thus looks at how such different forms of involvement can be explained.

1.5 Research method

This book combines the author's background in history with the interdisciplinary nature of the study of terrorism. The historical method is reflected in the emphasis placed on analyzing primary sources; Dutch police files on the Hofstadgroup and interviews with former participants as well as Dutch government employees involved in the case. Rather than letting these materials speak for themselves, however, the author examines this material by drawing on insights from the literature on terrorism. Essentially, existing explanations for involvement in terrorism are used as 'lenses' through which to study the available empirical data. Over the course of five chapters,

---

72 Borum, *Psychology of Terrorism*, 23; Horgan, *Walking Away from Terrorism*, 7-10; Taylor and Horgan, 'A Conceptual Framework', 586.

structural-, group-, and individual-level explanations for involvement in terrorism are applied to the Hofstadgroup to see whether they can illuminate distinct explanatory variables. Each relevant explanation is briefly introduced, its main assumptions are identified and then applied to the Hofstadgroup to see if it offers meaningful insights.

This methodological approach has three distinct benefits. First, it allows for a theoretically guided and robustly empirical understanding of the factors that influenced involvement in the Hofstadgroup to emerge. Second, it enables a reflection on the applicability of the various hypotheses on involvement in terrorism to European homegrown jihadism as represented by the Hofstadgroup. Although single-case studies cannot provide conclusive evidence of a theory's explanative potential or lack thereof, they can provide important empirical evidence relevant to those theories. This form of theory testing is especially important in the context of terrorism studies, as various authors have pointed to the field's tendency to develop explanations without sufficiently assessing their empirical validity.[73] A third benefit of this approach is that it can highlight hypotheses of above-average explanatory potential. What were the most salient factors that led to involvement in the Hofstadgroup? Conversely, the methodological approach followed here can help *disprove* the applicability of hypotheses thought to be of general relevance.

No research method is without its drawbacks. The most salient one here being the deliberate choice to focus on breadth rather than depth. By using existing insights as analytical tools to better understand the processes that led to involvement in the Hofstadgroup, a broad perspective is gained on the variety of factors on which individuals' participation was based. A downside is that no single explanatory variable is studied exhaustively. Many of the explanations used in this book are at the heart of decades of debate and research. The multicausal approach utilized here requires reducing the complexity of individual theories to a short summary of their constituting elements and the main lines of scholarly argument for the sake of clarity and space. An in-depth and empirically grounded analysis of the many theories discussed in these pages would undoubtedly be a fruitful avenue for future research on involvement in European homegrown jihadism, but falls outside of the scope of the present undertaking.

---

73   Aly and Striegher, 'Examining the Role of Religion', 849-50; King and Taylor, 'The Radicalization of Homegrown Jihadists', 616; Lia and Skjølberg, 'Why Terrorism Occurs', 28; McAllister and Schmid, 'Theories of Terrorism', 261.

Following the main research question's focus on the factors that brought about involvement in the Hofstadgroup, the unit of analysis is the individual participant. Whether the discussion is on the structural-level influences such as poverty or on group-based processes such as peer pressure, the (implicit) question is always to what degree these factors exerted an influence on the young men and women who constituted the Hofstadgroup. After all, it was these individuals' convictions, their backgrounds, their actions, and their interactions with each other and the world outside of the group that made the Hofstadgroup what it was. This study is thus primarily concerned with charting the processes that led these people to become interested in a radical or extremist interpretation of Islam, brought them together with like-minded individuals and, in a small number of cases, motivated them to commit or plan an act of terrorism.

1.6 Sources of information

Two types of primary sources are utilized in this book. The most important of these in terms of the amount of information they contain and the frequency with which they are referenced are the files that the Dutch National Police Services Agency (*Korps Landelijke Politiediensten*, KLPD) assembled during its various investigations of Hofstadgroup suspects.[74] Permission to use this material was granted following the submission of a formal written request to the office of the Prosecutor General.[75] This data is supplemented with semi-structured interviews with Dutch government officials who were involved in the Hofstadgroup investigation and former participants in the Hofstadgroup itself. The following paragraphs provide further information on these sources and a critical assessment of their utility.

1.6.1 Using police files to study terrorism

The police files contain thousands of pages of information obtained in a variety of ways. Principally, these are the police's interrogation of suspects and witnesses, the results of house searches, phone and Internet taps, and a

---

74 The various police investigations were collated into two dossiers; 2004's 'RL8026' and 2005's 'Piranha'. References to these files always list one of these dossiers, followed by a section reference if applicable, and a page number. In 2013, the KLPD was renamed the National Unit (LE).
75 The Ministry of Security and Justice gave written permission to use the files for research purposes on 8 March 2013.

limited degree of information provided by the AIVD. Much of this material can be considered a primary source of information as it is a verbatim record of what Hofstadgroup participants said, wrote, and did. Particularly useful are wiretapped phone calls and transcripts of online chat conversations as they are unaffected by the wish to downplay culpability or provide post-event rationalizations, factors that may diminish the reliability of police interrogations and interviews with researchers.[76]

Another benefit of the police files is that they represent the totality of information gathered during the investigations into the Hofstadgroup's participants that followed the various arrests in 2003, 2004, and 2005. This makes them less subjective than the easier to find public prosecutors' indictments, which only contain that information best thought to fit the prosecution's case against the suspects. The quantity and quality of the information in the police files means that they provide researchers with valuable data on Hofstadgroup participants' backgrounds, worldviews, and actions, as well as intragroup dynamics. Yet care must be taken not to see these files as a 'holy grail' for terrorism researchers. There are distinct drawbacks to their use that must be acknowledged if they are to contribute to a well-balanced analysis.

Police investigations are intended to gather evidence that can be used to charge suspects. This means that there can be a certain bias in the way information is collected and presented.[77] It also means that the questions investigators posed to suspects and witnesses often differ from what a researcher would have liked to address. There is more emphasis on potential criminal offenses than on, for instance, group dynamics or the why of how of involvement. A related problem is the questionable reliability of statements derived from the interrogation of suspects and witnesses. Suspects in particular are liable to deny the allegations leveled at them, to distort the truth, or to tell outright lies in order to escape sentencing. These limitations necessitate a critical attitude towards the files and the use of complementary sources where possible.

A second limitation of using these police files is that, despite their considerable size, they still provide only glimpses into the Hofstadgroup phenomenon. The files are based on criminal investigations and therefore primarily illuminate those events that occurred around the various arrests of group participants in October 2003, June 2004, November 2004, and June

---

76 Cottee, 'Jihadism as a Subcultural Response', 743; Harris-Hogan, 'Australian Neo-Jihadist Terrorism', 298-314; Lentini, '"If They Know Who Put the Sugar"', 1-12; Sageman, *Leaderless Jihad*, 76.
77 Lentini, '"If They Know Who Put the Sugar"', 6-7.

and October 2005. The details of what happened before or between these dates are much less well covered, underlining the need to complement the files with information derived from other sources.

Perhaps most problematic of all is the fact that the police files used here are not publicly accessible. This is a serious shortcoming with regard to transparency. Crucially, however, the files are not a *secret* source. Although the application process is lengthy and cumbersome, researchers and other interested parties can apply for access to the very same materials that the author used and thus assess the claims made in these pages. To further avoid the appearance of 'masquerading behind a thin façade of privileged access to secret sources',[78] and to increase the reliability of the analysis, references to the files are complemented with publicly available sources wherever possible.[79] Additionally, it should be noted that the use of confidential data is quite common in the social sciences; full interview transcripts, or information about the interviewees themselves, are seldom provided to readers. Finally, many pieces of information from the police files on the Hofstadgroup have been leaked to the press over the years and can be easily found online.

1.6.2   Using interviews to study terrorism

Twelve semi-structured interviews were carried out for this study. Seven of these were held with Dutch government employees involved in the Hofstadgroup case in some capacity and five were held with former Hofstadgroup participants. The government employees comprised of two public prosecutors, two police investigators, one NCTV analyst, one AIVD analyst, and one community policing officer. In addition to these interviews, the author also spoke on a more informal basis with academics and journalists who had previously conducted work on the Hofstadgroup, and with defense attorneys involved in the case. It should be noted that another nine former Hofstadgroup participants were also approached for an interview but declined, did not reply, or were not allowed to speak with the author due to the terms of their release on probation. One former participant could not be contacted because the Dutch prison authorities declined the request for an interview. One government employee involved in the case also declined to be interviewed. Unless explicitly stated otherwise, 'interviews' always refer to data collected by the author and not to police interrogations of suspects or

---

78   Ranstorp, 'Mapping Terrorism Studies', 26.
79   See also: Horne and Horgan, 'Methodological Triangulation', 182-92.

witnesses. All the interviews were held in Dutch, which means that all direct quotations encountered in these pages have been translated to English by the author. The verbatim Dutch version of quotations is given in the notes.

The semi-structured interview format used here has several advantages. The interviewer decides beforehand the topics he or she wishes to discuss but, in contrast to the more formal fully-structured interview, leaves room for the interview to develop in unforeseen directions.[80] This allows semi-structured interviews to generate information that the interviewer had not anticipated beforehand. By coming across more as a conversation than as a formal, question-by-question interrogation, semi-structured interviews can also help make interviewees feel more comfortable.[81] This is especially beneficial when sensitive or controversial topics are discussed, such as someone's past involvement in extremism or terrorism.

Interviewees were approached in several ways. The Dutch government employees were either contacted via publicly available e-mail addresses or introduced to the author via his professional network. The majority of former Hofstadgroup participants were found through the Internet and social media websites in particular. Contacts with two of them were established through introductions. None of the interviewees were under any kind of obligation to speak with the author. Most seemed motivated by a simple willingness to help, a chance to speak about a formative period in their lives or professional careers, or the ability to contribute to a more nuanced understanding of the Hofstadgroup. As most interviewees did not allow a recording device to be used, the author largely relied on handwritten notes.

Information gathered through interviews was utilized in several ways. The government employees were closely involved in investigating, monitoring, or prosecuting the Hofstadgroup. Interviews with these individuals primarily served to establish a detailed chronology of events and to assess the validity of information found in other sources.[82] Interviews with former Hofstadgroup participants were also used for these purposes, but held two additional benefits. Of particular importance was their ability to act as a counterweight to the 'official' take on events represented by the police files. Interviews with former participants restored a degree of balance to what would otherwise have been an almost total reliance in terms of primary data on materials produced by the Dutch authorities. These interviews were also an ideal way of gaining more information on participants' personal

---

80 Zhang and Wildemuth, 'Unstructured Interviews', 222.
81 Post and Berko, 'Talking with Terrorists', 147.
82 Tansey, 'Process Tracing and Elite Interviewing', 766.

INTRODUCTION   31

backgrounds and motives, as well as an insiders' perspective on the group's functioning and internal dynamics.[83]

Like the police files, the use of interviews poses several concerns. One is their representativeness. Because most former Hofstadgroup participants were not willing to be interviewed or could not be found, the author essentially utilized 'opportunity sampling', interviewing only those who happened to be accessible and willing to talk.[84] This means that it is unclear how representative these interviewees are for the group as a whole. Another issue with using interviews is assessing their reliability. Ulterior motives such as the wish to justify past conduct or to avoid admitting mistakes can degrade the truthfulness of interviewees' accounts. Furthermore, to what degree can people be expected to accurately recall what they thought or how they felt many years ago?[85] While interviews can afford unique insights, these issues underline the need to remain critical of data gathered using this method. Wherever possible, information derived from the interviews was complemented with or checked against other (publicly available) sources.

1.7   Ethical guidelines

The use of interviews and data taken from police files posed several privacy and security-related concerns. The author followed the guidelines for the use of personal data set out by the Royal Netherlands Academy of Arts and Sciences.[86] In addition, the Dutch Ministry of Security and Justice, the police files' owner, stipulated several conditions for their use. The most important measure taken to ensure the privacy and safety of the individuals discussed in this book is anonymization. No interviewee or Hofstadgroup participant is referred to by their actual name. Although this measure negatively affects the book's readability, it is a drawback that is outweighed by the benefits in terms of reliability and detail that access to these sources provides. The one partial exception is a Syrian preacher, who is referred to by his *nom de guerre* 'Abu Khaled'. As a central figure in the group, using this moniker ensures a balance between anonymity and readability.

---

83   Horgan, 'Interviewing the Terrorists', 198-99; Post and Berko, 'Talking with Terrorists', 146.
84   Silke, 'The Devil You Know', 8.
85   Tansey, 'Process Tracing and Elite Interviewing', 767.
86   Royal Netherlands Academy of Arts and Sciences, *Gedragscode Voor Gebruik Van Persoonsgegevens*.

1.8 A note on terminology

Terrorism is a complex phenomenon that cannot be reduced to one or even a handful of causes. To avoid the implied causality attached to the word 'causes', this book prefers to use the term 'factor'. However, because the literature on involvement in terrorism itself frequently uses the word 'causes', this term will still be encountered during discussions of existing explanations. With regard to 'involvement', this book utilizes a broad definition that sees it as the process of becoming a participant in an extremist or terrorist group in some capacity. As such, involvement encompasses a spectrum of activities, ranging from the relatively benign, such as attending group gatherings, to the clearly violent, such as planning or perpetrating acts of terrorism. Chapter 2 discusses these and other core concepts in more detail.

1.9 Outline

This book consists of ten chapters, including this introduction. Chapter 2 presents a theoretical perspective on researching terrorism. It underlines the need for a primary-sources-based approach and details why three levels of analysis are used to study the factors that governed involvement in the Hofstadgroup. Chapter 3 and Chapter 4 provide the necessary background on the group. The first presents a chronological overview of the most important events in the Hofstadgroup's timeline to familiarize readers with what happened. The second contextual chapter takes a critical look at what the group was; to what extent are the labels 'homegrown', 'jihadist', and 'terrorist' actually applicable to the Hofstadgroup and how can it be characterized organizationally?

The empirical analysis is presented in Chapters 5 through 9. The first of these looks at structural factors influencing involvement in terrorism, such as poverty, geopolitics, and intergroup inequality. Because of the large number of group-level hypotheses relevant to the Hofstadgroup, that analysis is spread over Chapters 6 and 7. The former deals with group formation whereas the latter looks at group-based motives for terrorist violence. The individual level of analysis is also spread over two chapters; Chapter 8 focuses on cognitive explanations for involvement in terrorism, essentially studying how distinct ways of thinking about and perceiving the world can contribute to involvement in terrorism. Chapter 9 utilizes numerous theories that relate involvement in terrorism to psychological characteristics such as mental illness, or to the influence of emotions such as frustration, anger, and fear of death. Chapter 10 concludes the book by drawing together the main findings, assessing their implications for academics and policy makers, and looking ahead to fruitful avenues for future research.

2 Studying involvement in terrorism

This chapter details the theoretical and methodological underpinnings of the multicausal framework used to study involvement in the Hofstadgroup. This discussion is preceded by a look at the various issues affecting research on terrorism in order to underline the importance of using primary-sources-based data. What are their benefits compared to secondary sources and why have terrorism researchers found it so difficult to incorporate them into their work? The chapter closes by providing definitions for commonly used but highly-debated terms such as 'terrorism', 'radicalism', and 'extremism'.

2.1 Issues in terrorism research

Research on terrorism has a strong multidisciplinary character. Academic perspectives used to study this form of political violence range from psychology, sociology, political science, history, economics, criminology, and anthropology to international relations, law, the military sciences, and critical theory.[1] Given this diversity in terrorism researchers' backgrounds, the associated differences in the methodologies used, and the thus far limited attempts at integrating these perspectives, it is not surprising to find scholarship on terrorism spread over several subfields.[2] However, the absence of a single field of terrorism studies is not necessarily an impediment to academic progress. As Schmid concludes his 2011 review of the literature on terrorism; a 'fairly solid body of consolidated knowledge has emerged'.[3] More worrying are the various and longstanding concerns over the empirical quality of this research.

Contrary to the claims of the recently created discipline of Critical Terrorism Studies,[4] there is a long history of critical reflection among established terrorism scholars.[5] In the 1980s, authors like Crenshaw, Reich, and Schmid and Jongman critiqued existing research for being unsystematic, ahistorical

---

1 Schmid, 'The Literature on Terrorism', 458; Duyvesteyn, 'The Role of History and Continuity', 51-75; Jackson, Smyth, and Gunning, *Critical Terrorism Studies: A New Research Agenda*; Sluka, *Hearts and Minds*.
2 Reid and Chen, 'Mapping the Contemporary Terrorism Research Domain', 44, 53; Sinai, 'New Trends in Terrorism Studies', 32.
3 Schmid, 'The Literature on Terrorism', 470.
4 Jackson, 'The Core Commitments', 244-46.
5 Horgan and Boyle, 'A Case against "Critical Terrorism Studies"', 51-53.

or alarmist,[6] prone to unwarranted overgeneralizations and attempts to explain complex behavior in monocausal terms,[7] as well as impressionistic, superficial, and pretentious.[8] More recently, critics have pointed to the discrepancy between the small number of dedicated terrorism scholars and the multitude of one-time contributors, many of whom are non-academics or lack terrorism-related expertise.[9] This critical perspective on the field is perhaps best summarized by Sageman's 2014 claim that research on terrorism had 'stagnated'.[10]

Fortunately, research on terrorism has also seen important signs of progress and maturation in recent years.[11] Improvements include an increase in collaborative research, a broadening of scholars' interest beyond topics related to Islamist terrorism or weapons of mass destruction, a greater number of dedicated researchers and more variety in methodological approaches.[12] Scholars have also drawn attention to the valuable knowledge gained since 9/11, for instance on risk factors for the occurrence of terrorism or the finding that radical beliefs alone are insufficient to explain involvement in this form of violence.[13] Given these encouraging signs, claims of a stagnant field seem overly pessimistic.[14] Yet, a core issue among these various concerns, namely that terrorism research has been too heavily reliant on secondary sources of information for too long, cannot be overlooked.

2.1.1 An overreliance on secondary sources

In 1988, Schmid and Jongman remarked that 'there are probably few areas in the social science literature in which so much is written on the basis of so little research'.[15] They were referring to the fact that very few terrorism researchers actually collected new data on their subject. Instead, most of them used the existing secondary literature, consisting of other academic works on terrorism but also media reports, as the basis for their own conclusions.

---

6   Crenshaw, 'The Psychology of Political Terrorism', 381.
7   Reich, 'Understanding Terrorist Behavior', 261-71.
8   Ranstorp, 'Mapping Terrorism Studies', 14.
9   Ibid., 14-15; Silke, 'An Introduction', 1-2; Stampnitzky, *Disciplining Terror*, 7, 12-13, 44, 46.
10 Sageman, 'The Stagnation in Terrorism Research', 569-72.
11 Smith, 'William of Ockham, Where Are You?', 334.
12 Silke, 'Contemporary Terrorism Studies', 39-41, 46-47; Dolnik, *Conducting Terrorism Field Research*.
13 Stern, 'Response to Marc Sageman', 608; McCauley and Moskalenko, 'Some Things We Think We've Learned', 602; Schanzer, 'No Easy Day', 598.
14 Sageman, 'The Stagnation in Terrorism Research', 569.
15 Schmid and Jongman, *Political Terrorism*, 179.

More than a decade later, Silke found that little had changed; publications on terrorism were still characterized by an overreliance on secondary sources and the predominance of literature-review-based methods.[16] There has been little improvement since; a 2006 study found that just 3% of research on terrorism was based on empirical analysis.[17] A 2008 publication reached the conclusion that only 20% of articles provided previously unavailable data.[18] More recently, Sageman's 2014 piece lamented that terrorism researchers were still largely unable to access and utilize primary sources.[19]

An almost exclusive reliance on secondary sources means that researchers run the risk of developing theories that are insufficiently rooted in empirical evidence or rehashing existing findings rather than adding new insights. A second potential problem is that there is often a marked qualitative difference between secondary and primary sources, especially when those secondary sources are newspaper articles rather than academic publications. Whereas primary sources typically provide information based on the direct observation of, or participation in, a certain subject, secondary sources relate information indirectly. The lack of a first-hand perspective may introduce inaccuracies and the subjectivity inherent in the act of relaying information may have diminished its reliability.[20] The qualitative differences between primary and secondary sources become all the more pronounced when the complexity of the subject of study increases.

There is little room for a reporter to make factual errors or misinterpret what happened when reporting on something as straightforward as a car crash. But the chances of this occurring when covering terrorism are considerably greater. The illegal and secretive nature of terrorism means that even such an ostensibly straightforward task as establishing a chronology of events can be a difficult undertaking. Journalists are often among the first to tackle these questions, a fact well illustrated by the numerous books on al-Qaeda written by investigative journalists shortly after the 9/11 attacks.[21] When such accounts are well researched, they can form invaluable sources of information. The more problematic aspect of relying on the journalistic literature is terrorism scholars' heavy use of much shorter and less extensively researched newspaper articles, which are frequently published mere hours after the events they relate transpired and thus raise

---

16 Silke, 'The Devil You Know', 4-9.
17 Lum, Kennedy, and Sherley, 'The Effectiveness of Counter-Terrorism Strategies', 8.
18 Silke, 'Holy Warriors', 101.
19 Sageman, 'The Stagnation in Terrorism Research', 569-72.
20 Stewart and Kamins, 'Evaluating Secondary Sources', 17-32.
21 E.g. Bergen, *Holy War*; Burke, *Al-Qaeda*.

critical questions concerning their accuracy and the comprehensiveness of the account presented.

On the one hand, media sources are a necessary staple in terrorism research as they are often the only readily available type of information. Yet assessments of their usefulness should take into account several potential concerns. First of all, newspapers and their reporters are selective in the stories they pursue.[22] For instance, they tend to under-report or simply ignore failed or foiled terrorist attacks.[23] Secondly, newspapers and other media outlets may be of questionable objectivity, colored by political leanings, or a desire to attract readership through sensationalist reporting. Furthermore, the reliability and objectivity of reporters' sources can be hard to ascertain.[24] Perhaps most problematic of all, media sources too frequently contain factual errors.[25] In sum, these problems make media sources ill-suited to functioning as the main, let alone the *only* source of data used in academic research on terrorism.

Recent years have seen signs of a broadening of methodological approaches and indications that the overreliance on secondary sources may not be as pronounced in every subfield of terrorism research.[26] These are promising trends, yet the scarcity of primary-sources-based research remains a key concern in the academic study of terrorism.[27] Given that most publications cite secondary literature that, in turn, refers to yet another set of academic works, and that at the end of this referral chain the empirical data often consists of media accounts, a worrisome situation has developed. Much research on terrorism resembles a 'highly unreliable closed and circular research system, functioning in a constantly reinforcing feedback loop'.[28] More empirical work that utilizes high-quality sources is needed to move the study of terrorism forward.[29]

Why has this lack of primary-sources-based research persisted? Crucially, terrorism is a difficult subject to study empirically.[30] One way to gather

---

22 Franzosi, 'The Press as a Source of Socio-Historical Data', 6.
23 Schmid, 'The Literature on Terrorism', 461.
24 Silke, 'The Devil You Know', 6; Franzosi, 'The Press as a Source of Socio-Historical Data', 6.
25 Silke, 'The Devil You Know', 5-6; Quiggin, 'Words Matter', 71-81; Schulze, 'Breaking the Cycle', 163.
26 Silke, 'Contemporary Terrorism Studies', 40-41, 48; Neumann and Kleinmann, 'Radicalization Research', 372.
27 Schmid, 'The Literature on Terrorism', 460; Sageman, 'The Stagnation in Terrorism Research', 565-80; Sageman, *Turning to Political Violence*, xv.
28 Dolnik, 'Conducting Field Research', 5.
29 Schuurman and Eijkman, 'Moving Terrorism Research Forward', 1-13.
30 Horgan, 'The Case for Firsthand Research', 30; Silke, 'The Devil You Know', 2.

primary sources is through interviews with (former) terrorists. While these are more common than might be assumed,[31] finding and gaining access to individuals that engage(d) in illegal and violent activities is time-consuming and by no means guaranteed to succeed.[32] All the more so when interviews are undertaken during fieldwork abroad. Although the potential dangers of fieldwork are generally described as manageable, they cannot be overlooked.[33] Fieldwork or interviews also require ethics approval, which may form a considerable obstacle in itself.[34] Especially after the 2014 Boston College controversy, where researchers were forced to hand over interviews with members of the Irish Republican Army to the Northern Irish police, breaching the interviewees' confidentiality and leading to the arrest of Sinn Féin leader Gerry Adams.[35]

Government organizations such as law enforcement and intelligence agencies are another potential source of primary data on terrorism. However, most researchers lack security clearances and organizations involved in counterterrorism are generally reluctant to share their information for security and privacy-related reasons.[36] Databases with information on terrorists and terrorist events constitute a third source of empirical data.[37] However, the media-based foundation of many databases raises important questions about their reliability.[38] Gaining primary-sources-based data on terrorism is certainly not impossible, but these obstacles go some way towards explaining its scarcity.

2.2 Making sense of involvement in terrorism

No less important than high quality-data is making sense of it.[39] The rationale behind the multicausal approach to understanding involvement in the Hofstadgroup stems from a review of the literature on involvement in

---

31 Horgan, 'Interviewing the Terrorists', 195-211.
32 Orsini, 'A Day among the Diehard Terrorists', 337-51; Toros, 'Terrorists, Scholars and Ordinary People', 279-80, 286-90.
33 Dolnik, 'Conducting Field Research', 4; Horgan, 'The Case for Firsthand Research', 48-50; Schulze, 'Breaking the Cycle', 181-82.
34 Dolnik, 'Conducting Field Research', 7-14.
35 Marcus, 'Oral History'.
36 Lentini, '"If They Know Who Put the Sugar"', 7; Sageman, 'Low Return', 616; Horgan, 'Issues in Terrorism Research', 193.
37 Bowie and Schmid, 'Databases on Terrorism', 294-340.
38 Silke, 'Contemporary Terrorism Studies', 40-41; Weenink and Cohen, 'Trends in Terrorisme'.
39 Taylor, 'If I Were You', 583.

terrorism,[40] which revealed four key insights. First of all, there is no single, generally applicable 'theory of terrorism'.[41] Instead, with regard to its causes alone the literature is able to identify almost fifty separate hypotheses.[42] Secondly, most of these explanations lack robust empirical verification.[43] Both issues make it difficult to choose one particular theoretical approach to study involvement in the Hofstadgroup. After all, how to justify choosing one out of dozens of possible approaches, particularly when the validity of many of them has not been adequately ascertained?

Thirdly, studies that emphasize one particular hypothesis, such as a presumed link between poverty or discrimination and involvement in terrorism, tend to be unable to explain why only a minority of the individuals exposed to such factors turn to terrorism.[44] Vice versa, monocausal approaches find it difficult to account for why not all of the people who *do* become involved in terrorism were exposed to the factor in question. For example, the ubiquitous use of 'radicalization' as an explanation for terrorism obscures the fact that the majority of individuals with 'radical' ideas never act on them, and that not all terrorists are strongly ideologically motivated.[45] Because no single factor has been found that is both *necessary* and *sufficient* to explain involvement in terrorism, the potential factors underlying involvement in this phenomenon should be assessed in conjunction with one another, rather than independently or as mutually exclusive competitors.[46]

A fourth reason for choosing a multicausal analytical framework is that it is well-established that involvement in terrorism is best understood as the result of a complex process in which multiple factors play a role.[47] Not only that, but these causative factors can reside at different levels of analysis and their relative importance may change over time.[48] In other words, although a particular factor may convincingly explain why someone became involved

---

40 As there presently does not exist a specific set of explanations for the homegrown jihadist typology of terrorism, a wide net was cast that focused on terrorism in general.
41 Crenshaw, 'Terrorism Research', 557; McAllister and Schmid, 'Theories of Terrorism', 202, 261.
42 McAllister and Schmid, 'Theories of Terrorism', 261.
43 Aly and Striegher, 'Examining the Role of Religion', 849-50; King and Taylor, 'The Radicalization of Homegrown Jihadists', 616; Lia and Skjølberg, 'Why Terrorism Occurs', 28; McAllister and Schmid, 'Theories of Terrorism', 261.
44 Newman, 'Exploring the "Root Causes"', 756.
45 Abrahms, 'What Terrorists Really Want', 78-105; Borum, 'Rethinking Radicalization', 1-2.
46 Borum, *Psychology of Terrorism*, 10; Dalgaard-Nielsen, 'Violent Radicalization in Europe', 810.
47 Bjørgo, 'Conclusions', 257; Horgan, 'Understanding Terrorist Motivation', 111-14; Taylor and Horgan, 'A Conceptual Framework', 586-87.
48 Bjørgo, 'Conclusions', 260; Della Porta, *Social Movements*, 9-10; Horgan, *Walking Away from Terrorism*, 7-10.

in a terrorist group in the first place, it may lose its explanatory potential when it comes to ascertaining how or why that person came to commit an actual act of violence. As Della Porta states, 'different analytical levels may dominate different stages of the evolution of radical groups'.[49]

For these reasons, it would be difficult to justify using a single theoretical perspective to study involvement in the Hofstadgroup. An alternative is to use a multicausal approach. Not only does this reflect the complexity of terrorism, it also utilizes the explanatory power of the body of literature on the various factors relevant to understanding involvement in this phenomenon to its fullest potential. Such an approach can count on considerable support from the literature.[50] In the words of Borum, '[a]ny useful framework [to understand radicalization] must be able to integrate mechanisms at micro (individual) and macro (societal/cultural) levels'.[51] Similarly, Stern argues that '[humans] catch the fire of terrorism in myriad ways – some environmental, some individual (or more likely, in most cases, a mix of the two)'.[52]

Many authors referenced in the previous paragraphs (implicitly) utilize three 'levels of analysis'. A concept borrowed from the field of international relations, which commonly distinguishes between individual, state, and international system perspectives.[53] The study of terrorism similarly utilizes a distinction between micro, meso, and macro perspectives, but generally translates these as the individual, the group, and structural, or environmental conditions in which they operate.[54] That is not to say that there are no other useful analytical divisions that could be made.[55] But it is this tripartite distinction that is most commonly used to capture the myriad potential factors that may lead to involvement in terrorism, making it most suited for the goals of this book. Its utility is also well demonstrated by Della Porta's work on post-1945 left-wing terrorism in Italy and Germany, which shows that by studying these three levels in conjunction with each other,

---

49   Della Porta, *Social Movements*, 10.
50   Crenshaw, 'The Psychology of Political Terrorism', 380; Dalgaard-Nielsen, "Violent Radicalization in Europe', 810; Horgan, 'Understanding Terrorist Motivation", 109, 113-14; Hudson, 'The Sociology and Psychology of Terrorism', 15, 23; McCauley and Moskalenko, 'Mechanisms of Political Radicalization', 429; Miller, 'Rationality, Decision Making', 3-4; Ross, 'A Model of the Psychological Causes', 129; Sinai, 'New Trends in Terrorism Studies', 36-37; Veldhuis and Staun, *Islamist Radicalisation*, 21-26.
51   Borum, 'Radicalization into Violent Extremism I', 8.
52   Stern, 'Response to Marc Sageman', 607.
53   Rourke, *International Politics*, 65.
54   See also: Lia and Skjølberg, 'Causes of Terrorism', 1-82; Sageman, *Leaderless Jihad*, 13-16.
55   Oleson and Khosrokhavar, *Islamism as Social Movement*, 10; McAllister and Schmid, 'Theories of Terrorism', 255-60.

a fuller understanding can be generated of how and why people become and remain involved in such groups.[56]

2.2.1 Structural-level explanations for involvement in terrorism

Structural-level factors relate to specific characteristics of the social, cultural, economic, and (geo)political *environment* that are seen as potential enablers, motivations, or triggers for involvement in terrorism.[57] Examples include widespread poverty, profound social inequality, war or regional instability, and lack of political freedoms.[58] In addition to forming environmental characteristics that can exert their influence over a longer period of time, structural factors can also relate to specific events in which people become embroiled. A government's violent crackdown on a protest can be considered an example of such an event as it leaves a significant number of people with little choice but to undergo the violence that has suddenly become a part of their surroundings. Such events, and the grievances they may feed or form, can potentially form decisive moments in people's lives that may set them on a path towards militancy and terrorism.

The above discussion is inspired by Crenshaw's influential 1981 article on the causes of terrorism, in which she distinguishes between structural factors that function as preconditions and those that act as precipitants.[59] Preconditions can provide both opportunities and motives for involvement in terrorism.[60] With access to the Internet, for instance, people can easily find information on how to construct explosives, facilitating the acquisition of violent means. Ability alone, however, is unlikely to lead to an act of terrorism unless it is matched by a willingness to do harm. Structural factors that can *motivate* involvement in terrorism include widespread grievances against the government and intergroup inequality.[61] The onset of Northern Ireland's violent 'Troubles' in 1968, for instance, was influenced by the Catholic population's political underrepresentation and socioeconomic disadvantagement vis-à-vis their Protestant neighbors.[62]

---

56 Della Porta, *Social Movements*, 9-10.
57 Lia and Skjølberg, 'Causes of Terrorism', 17-63; Ross, 'Structural Causes', 317.
58 Newman, 'Exploring the "Root Causes"', 749-72.
59 Crenshaw, 'The Causes of Terrorism', 379-99.
60 Ibid., 381.
61 Lia and Skjølberg, 'Causes of Terrorism', 17-63.
62 Kennedy-Pipe, *The Origins*, 39-41.

Precipitants are what Crenshaw identifies as 'specific events that immediately precede the occurrence of terrorism'.[63] Excessive use of force by the authorities can instigate a violent response, but precipitants need not be violent in nature. As Chapter 5 discusses in more detail, the broadcast of a controversial short film criticizing Islam was a key structural-level event for the Hofstadgroup as it exposed its participants to criticism of very closely held beliefs, triggering a violent response from one participant that led to the murder of Van Gogh. In more recent publications, the basic distinction between preconditions and precipitants that Crenshaw suggested in 1981 has been maintained, making this a valuable way of structuring the various explanations found at the structural level of analysis.[64] Table 1 provides an overview of the most commonly encountered structural-level explanations for terrorism found in the literature, divided over the three categories described here.

Table 1 Structural-level explanations for involvement in terrorism

Preconditions: Opportunities	Preconditions: Motives	Precipitants
The Internet	(Relative) Deprivation	Government's excessive use of force
Popular support for terrorism	Intergroup inequality	Government attempts reforms
External assistance	Political grievances	
Social/ cultural facilitation of violence	Clash of value systems	
Ineffective counterterrorism	Economic globalization	
Political opportunity structure	Cultural globalization	
Modernization	Urbanization	
Population growth/ youth bulge	Modernization	
Shifts ethnic/ religious balance society	Spillover from other conflicts	
Urbanization	State sponsorship of terrorism	
Mass media	Power structure international system	
Organized crime – terrorism nexus	Failed/ failing states	
	Armed conflict	

63 Crenshaw, 'The Causes of Terrorism', 381.
64 Bjørgo, 'Conclusions', 258; Newman, 'Exploring the "Root Causes"', 751.

2.2.2 Group-level explanations for involvement in terrorism

As a form of 'organized violence', considerable attention has been paid to the role of group dynamics in initiating, sustaining, and precipitating involvement in terrorism.[65] Indeed, some authors believe this level of analysis to be an especially salient lens through which to study the phenomenon.[66] In this book, explanations are categorized as belonging to the group level of analysis when they have their basis in the interaction between individuals or in the tangible and intangible attractions that group participation offers. Peer pressure, which under specific circumstances can push individuals towards participation in a terrorist group, is an example of the former.[67] The possibility to acquire status, increased self-esteem, and a sense of belonging are some examples of the latter.[68] Most explanations at this level of analysis focus on person-to-person interactions within the terrorist group itself. However, group effects can also stem from virtual social connections enabled by the Internet.[69]

A literature review of group-level factors relevant to involvement in terrorism identified a wide variety of possible explanations. Some of these account for the formation of terrorist groups; how and why do people become involved in these violent organizations? Research indicates that preexisting social ties are especially important in this regard.[70] Other explanations focus on how an actual act of terrorism comes about. What rationales underlie the decision of terrorist groups to commit attacks? One thing that this level of analysis lacks, however, is a broadly accepted way of distinguishing between the various explanations. Unlike the structural level of analysis, which could build on Crenshaw's distinction between preconditions and precipitants, there is no common way of categorizing the various hypotheses to make for a more structured overview.

Instead, the author relies on work by Taylor and Horgan because it convincingly argues that the factors influencing people's *involvement* in terrorist groups are distinct from those that govern a group's decision to

---

65 Crenshaw, *Explaining Terrorism*, 69.
66 Kleinmann, 'Radicalization of Homegrown Sunni Militants,' 288; Sageman, *Leaderless Jihad*, 22.
67 Della Porta, 'Recruitment Processes', 310.
68 McCauley and Segal, 'Social Psychology of Terrorist Groups', 336.
69 Oleson and Khosrokhavar, *Islamism as Social Movement*, 19.
70 Della Porta, 'Recruitment Processes', 309-10.

commit a terrorist *attack*.⁷¹ In other words, joining a terrorist group does not automatically lead to involvement in (preparations for) an act of terrorist violence. As a result, explanations for the former do not necessarily extend to cover the latter. The distinction between group-level factors that can account for the process of becoming and remaining involved in a terrorist group, and those that can contribute to the rationale for committing an act of terrorist violence, forms the overarching structure for the group level of analysis. Because both subjects cover a large number of relevant explanations, they have been turned into separate chapters (see Tables 2 and 3). The second of these has been subdivided further based on the themes to emerge from the review of the relevant literature.

Table 2   Group dynamics I: Becoming and staying involved in terrorist groups

Terrorist group formation
Social identity and the benefits of group membership
Socialization into a worldview conducive to terrorism
The underground life
Social learning theory
The influence of leaders
Peer pressures
Brainwashing

Table 3   Group dynamics II: Committing acts of terrorist violence

Organizational lethality	Overcoming barriers to violence	Rationales for terrorism
Organizational lethality	Diffusion of responsibility	Strategic
	Deindividuation	Organizational
	Authorization of violence	

2.2.3   Individual-level explanations for involvement in terrorism

The individual level of analysis seeks explanations for terrorism in the distinct psychological characteristics and ways of thinking of the terrorists themselves.⁷² During the 1970s and 1980s, as research on terrorism was emerging as a distinct subject of academic study, there was a strong focus on explaining terrorism as stemming from some form of psychopathology

---

71   Horgan, *Walking Away from Terrorism*, 13, 142-46; Taylor, 'Is Terrorism a Group Phenomenon?', 125-26; Taylor and Horgan, 'A Conceptual Framework', 592.
72   Della Porta, *Social Movements*, 9, 12-13; Victoroff, 'The Mind of the Terrorist', 3-42.

or as a result of psychological trauma incurred during childhood and adolescence.[73] More recently, individual-level explanations have been particularly strongly wedded to the concept of 'radicalization'. This is the idea that involvement in terrorism stems from the adoption of increasingly extremist political or religious worldviews.[74]

Of the three levels of analysis, the individual one has arguably been affected most by the difficulties of gaining reliable data on terrorism. For instance, sound empirical evidence for serious mental health issues among terrorists has generally been lacking.[75] Nevertheless, the individual perspective is a crucial complement to the other analytical lenses. As Crenshaw remarks, 'terrorism is not the direct result of social conditions but of individual perceptions of those conditions'.[76] Although a host of factors may exert an influence, involvement in terrorist groups and terrorist violence is still predicated on the deliberations and decisions of individuals.

The literature on individual-level explanations for involvement in terrorism is extensive. In keeping with this study's goals, only those hypotheses that focus directly on involvement in terrorism have been included for analysis. Publications on, for instance, the psychological impact of terrorism, biological explanations for violent behavior, or evolutionary psychological accounts for why certain behaviors exist in the first place, are not taken into consideration. In the end, two main areas of inquiry were identified that, because of their size, formed the basis for two separate chapters. The first of these deals with cognitive explanations for involvement in terrorism (Table 4). It essentially looks at how particular ways of thinking about and perceiving the world can make it more likely that someone becomes involved in extremism and terrorism. The second chapter discusses explanations for involvement that center on terrorists' presumed distinctiveness in terms of psychology, character, or emotional state (Table 5).

Table 4 Individual-level analysis I: Cognitive explanations

Radicalization
Fanaticism
Cognitive openings and 'unfreezing'
Cognitive dissonance and moral disengagement

---

73 Crenshaw, 'The Psychology of Political Terrorism', 384-90; Victoroff, 'The Mind of the Terrorist', 23-24.
74 Schmid, 'Radicalisation, De-Radicalisation', 1-91.
75 Victoroff, 'The Mind of the Terrorist', 31-32.
76 Crenshaw, 'Questions to Be Answered', 250.

Table 5 Individual-level analysis II: Terrorists as psychologically distinctive

Psychopathology
Psychoanalysis, significance loss and identity-related alienation
Terrorist personality or profile
Anger and frustration
Mortality salience

2.2.4   Interrelated perspectives

Each level of analysis offers unique explanations for involvement in terrorism. Although they are each treated in separate chapters, the distinctions between these various perspectives is in reality quite artificial. Structural, group, and individual-level factors do not exert their influence independent of one another, but frequently operate in an interdependent and interrelated fashion. To gain a comprehensive understanding of involvement in the Hofstadgroup, these various perspectives separately must also be discussed in relation to each other. Although each chapter refers to other levels of analysis where relevant, drawing together the various explanatory strands is the primary purpose of the concluding chapter.

2.3   Limitations

By studying the available empirical data on the Hofstadgroup through the various lenses provided by these three levels of analysis, a comprehensive understanding of how and why involvement in this group came about can be realized. However, several limitations should be acknowledged. A general first point is that, while the author has tried to be comprehensive in his approach, he does not claim to have found and utilized *all* possible explanations for terrorism. Undoubtedly, readers will remark upon omissions. Partly this may be because in the absence of clear naming conventions, the author has used unfamiliar designations, or because similar explanations have been grouped together under a single heading. Given the large amount of literature on, or relevant to understanding involvement in terrorism, a truly exhaustive overview is practically unfeasible.

A more specific limitation is the omission of social movement theory as a potential explanation for involvement in terrorism. According to Tarrow, social movements are 'collective challenges, based on common purposes and social solidarities, in sustained interaction with elites, opponents, and authorities'.[77] While the Hofstadgroup's adoption of a militant interpretation of Islam could be seen as a collectively mounted form of contention targeted at both the Dutch authorities, non-militant Muslims, and unbelievers, a clearly defined common purpose was strikingly absent. This finding, which is discussed in considerable detail in later chapters, forms an impediment to viewing the Hofstadgroup from a social movement perspective.

In addition to lacking collective goals, the Hofstadgroup also failed to engage in collective action. According to Beck, terrorism can be seen as a form of collective action focused on making political claims and seeking political influence, which in turn allows terrorist groups to be studied as movements with political goals.[78] The very absence of such claims and the associated instrumental use of violence problematizes seeing the Hofstadgroup's activities in this light. The only terrorist attack to actually materialize was the murder of Van Gogh, which was not the result of a collective effort but the work of one man. Furthermore, there are no indications that the killer was pursuing political goals. While there were some signs that the Hofstadgroup was beginning to undertake collective efforts towards the end of its existence in 2005, later chapters will demonstrate that collective action, like a common purpose, was for all intents and purposes not part of the group's repertoire.

A final reason why social movement theory is not used to study involvement in the Hofstadgroup is its emphasis on contention and social interactions, which leaves only a secondary role for the explanatory potential of ideas, beliefs, and the biographies or characteristics of individuals.[79] This comes back to the assumption that involvement in terrorism is a multicausal process with explanations at the structural, group, and individual levels of analysis. Focusing on one of these at the expense of another would go against the central aim of constructing a multifaceted understanding of involvement in the Hofstadgroup. None of this means, however, that social movement theory is abandoned altogether. Various elements, such as political-opportunity structure and the importance of looking at how terrorist groups frame their causes and their justifications for violence are discussed in the relevant chapters.

77 Tarrow, *Power in Movement*, 4, italics removed from original.
78 Beck, 'The Contribution of Social Movement Theory', 1566.
79 See, for instance: Tilly, *The Politics of Collective Violence*, 7-8.

2.4 A definitional debate

The terms 'terrorism', 'radical', 'extremist', and 'jihad' are used throughout these pages. Virtually all of them can be interpreted in multiple ways and constitute subjects of an ongoing and sometimes controversial definitional debate. To avoid confusion, it is therefore important to make clear at the outset how these terms are understood here. On account of its especially divisive nature, 'terrorism' is discussed at some length whereas the other terms are introduced more succinctly.

2.4.1 Terrorism

The debate on what constitutes 'terrorism' and when individuals or groups become 'terrorists', is a contentious one. After decades of discussion, a broadly accepted definition is still not at hand.[80] Some authors believe that such efforts are futile because terrorism 'is a term like *war* or *sovereignty* that will never be defined in words that achieve full international consensus'.[81] This quote suggests that the study of terrorism is not the only discipline to be affected by definitional quandaries. But that does little to diminish the adverse effects produced by the absence of a clear understanding of what 'terrorism' is. This issue has stood in the way of the development of a general theory of terrorism, 'scattered and fragmented' the focus of research efforts and complicated the comparison of research results.[82] Some scholars have even argued that 'it is time to stop using the "t word"' altogether.[83] Why has achieving consensus on the meaning of terrorism proven so difficult?

An immediate problem with the word 'terrorism' is that it has strong negative connotations, conjuring an image of 'cowardly violence, fear, and intimidation'.[84] A closely related second issue is the politicized nature of the term. The 'terrorism' descriptor is frequently used to delegitimize an oppositional regime, movement, or organization while simultaneously legitimizing violence against that opponent.[85] Used in this fashion, the term terrorism becomes part of a 'war of words', aimed at condemning rather

---

80 Schmid, 'The Definition of Terrorism', 39; Toros, '"We Don't Negotiate with Terrorists!"', 408-09.
81 Cronin, *How Terrorism Ends*, 7, italics in original.
82 Sánchez-Cuenca, 'Why Do We Know So Little?', 594-95; Schmid, 'The Definition of Terrorism', 43; Silke, 'An Introduction', 3-4.
83 Bryan, Kelly, and Templer, 'The Failed Paradigm', 94.
84 Kiras, 'Terrorism and Irregular Warfare', 210.
85 Kruglanski and Fishman, 'The Psychology of Terrorism', 201.

than understanding a certain form of violent behavior.[86] Such definitions are essentially political tools that serve the defining party's interests, for instance by limiting the scope of 'terrorism' to an activity only non-state actors can engage in, even though states can and have used terror on a much larger scale than most non-state groups are capable of.[87] The biases inherent in such definitions make them unsuitable for research purposes.

A third obstacle is that the interpretation of what constitutes terrorism is highly subjective. This is best represented by the classic dichotomy between freedom fighters and terrorists, with the choice for one or the other depending on the observer's perspective and his or her stake in the conflict.[88] Tellingly, few violent oppositional groups call themselves terrorists and most prefer to describe their activities in much more neutral terms such as 'liberation' or 'resistance'.[89] Delineating where terrorism begins and ends constitute a fourth stumbling block. How to disentangle terrorism from insurgency, two forms of political violence that are often used in conjunction with one another?[90] Similarly, how is terrorism different from organized crime? Criminals and terrorists both place a premium on secrecy, they both use force and intimidation against civilians to achieve their aims, and both exert strong control over group members.[91]

These obstacles have not prevented the creation of many different legal, government, and academic definitions of terrorism.[92] Of these three types of definitions, only academic ones are expressly intended to guide non-partisan analysis, making them most suited to the task at hand.[93] Within the subset of academic definitions of terrorism, it is hard to overlook the pioneering work of Alex Schmid, who has been working on the definitional question for decades.[94] This book utilizes Schmid's 2011 'revised academic consensus definition' because it convincingly addresses the issues raised above.[95] Its neutral wording avoids issuing a value judgment on terrorism. By being applicable to state as well as non-state actors, Schmid's definition offers some protection against an overly politicized view of terrorism.

86 Turk, 'Sociology of Terrorism', 271-73.
87 Schmid, 'The Definition of Terrorism', 40.
88 Martin, *Understanding Terrorism*, 34-36.
89 Ibid., 35-36.
90 Duyvesteyn and Fumerton, 'Insurgency and Terrorism', 27-41.
91 Schmid, 'The Definition of Terrorism', 64-67.
92 Ibid., 44-60; Weinberg, Pedahzur, and Hirsch-Hoefler, 'Challenges of Conceptualizing Terrorism', 780.
93 Hoffman, *Inside Terrorism*, 31-33.
94 See, for instance: Schmid and Jongman, *Political Terrorism*, 1-38.
95 Schmid, 'The Definition of Terrorism', 39-98.

Furthermore, its detailed nature allows it to differentiate terrorism from other forms of organized violence.

In these pages, therefore,

> [t]errorism refers on the one hand to a *doctrine* about the presumed effectiveness of a special form or tactic of fear-generating, coercive political violence and, on the other hand, to a conspiratorial *practice* of calculated, demonstrative, direct violent action without legal or moral restraints, targeting mainly civilians and non-combatants, performed for its propagandistic and psychological effects on various audiences and conflict parties.[96]

2.4.2 Radicalism and extremism

The terms 'radical' and 'extremist' are repeatedly used to describe the convictions of Hofstadgroup participants. Because both are inherently subjective and frequently used interchangeably, clear definitions are in order.[97] Schmid once again provides a thoroughly researched and well-reasoned definition of both terms. Radicalism comprises

> two main elements reflecting thought/attitude and action/behaviour respectively: 1. Advocating sweeping political change, based on a conviction that the status quo is unacceptable while at the same time a fundamentally different alternative appears to be available to the radical; 2. The means advocated to bring about the system-transforming radical solution for government and society can be non-violent and democratic (through persuasion and reform) or violent and non-democratic (through coercion and revolution).[98]

Radicals may hold views that are deemed inappropriate, offensive, or disagreeable for other reasons, but they do not *necessarily* justify or support the use of violence. This marks an important difference with extremists.[99]

---

96 Ibid., 86-87, emphases in original.
97 Schmid, 'Radicalisation, De-Radicalisation', 11; Downs, *Political Extremism in Democracies*, 13.
98 Schmid, 'Radicalisation, De-Radicalisation', 8.
99 Bartlett and Miller, 'The Edge of Violence', 1-21.

> While radicals might be violent or not, might be democrats or not, extremists are never democrats. Their state of mind tolerates no diversity. They are also positively in favour of the use of force to obtain and maintain political power [...]. Extremists generally tend to have inflexible 'closed minds', adhering to a simplified mono-causal interpretation of the world where you are either with them or against them, part of the problem or part of the solution.[100]

For extremists, violence constitutes *the* preferred means to an end. This distinction is important, as it allows for a nuanced discussion of the beliefs held by Hofstadgroup participants and their views on the use of violence. It should be noted that some scholars refer to these dispositions using the terms 'non-violent extremism' and 'violent extremism'.[101] The author finds that 'radical' and 'extremist' better convey the different mindsets associated with these positions which, as Schmid's definitions make clear, encompass more than differing views on the use of violence alone.

2.4.3 Jihad and homegrown jihadism

Islam, which translates as 'submission to the will of God', constitutes one of the world's three great monotheistic religions.[102] There is, however, no singular way in which Islam is interpreted or practiced. This is reflected, for instance, in the division of the global community of believers, known as the 'ummah', between Sunnis and Shiites, a rift with its origins in a centuries-old debate over the rightful successor to the Prophet Muhammad. Sunnis, who constitute the largest denomination within Islam, believe that essentially anyone can be proclaimed heir to the prophet. Shiites, on the other hand, accept only Muhammad's descendants, specifically the progeny of the prophet's son-in-law Ali and his wife Fatima, who was Muhammad's daughter. The Sunni-Shia divide is Islam's most well-known internal division. But there are a multitude of other, smaller, denominations such as the Druze and the Alawis, as well as the more mystical approach to Islam known as Sufism, that further undermine the idea of Islam as a homogeneous religion.[103]

---

100 Schmid, 'Radicalisation, De-Radicalisation', 10.
101 Neumann, 'The Trouble with Radicalization', 873-93.
102 Esposito, *Islam*, 85.
103 Douwes, 'Richtingen En Stromingen', 162; Esposito, *Islam*, 2, 42-43, 47-48, 124-26, 291-94.

Just as there is no one Islam, there is no one view on the conditions under which Muslims are allowed or required to use violence, who and what can justifiably be targeted, and which means and methods of war are permitted.[104] The use of violence by Muslims has been closely linked to the concept of 'jihad', the Arabic word for struggle or effort.[105] As a contested concept that has been the subject of centuries of debate and varying interpretations, there is not one clear way to define jihad.[106] Moghadam notes that the Quran's coverage of jihad allows a broad distinction to be made between a peaceful and an aggressive interpretation.[107] The first form, which has also been called the 'greater' jihad, refers to an individual believer's personal struggle against temptation and sin, his or her quest to live in accordance with god's will, or a community's efforts to better themselves.[108] The aggressive or 'lesser' interpretation of jihad sees it as religiously sanctioned or mandated warfare.[109]

Jihad is therefore not necessarily a violent undertaking. Unless specified otherwise, however, the use of the term jihad in this book refers to the 'lesser' or militant variety. Jihadist groups or individuals are thus those that believe their religious beliefs necessitate or sanction the use of violence against perceived enemies. Following Crone and Harrow's definition, jihadists can be labeled 'homegrown' when they display a high degree of autonomy from internationally operating terrorist networks such as al-Qaeda, and a strong sense of belonging, e.g. through citizenship, to the countries they target.[110]

2.5 Conclusion

This chapter began by highlighting several issues that have affected research on terrorism. In particular, the qualitative difference between primary and secondary sources and the longstanding scarcity of the former in existing research on terrorism. Given that terrorism is in many ways a difficult subject to study empirically, this situation is perhaps not that

---

104 Moghadam, 'Mayhem, Myths, and Martyrdom', 126-29. Turner, 'From Cottage Industry to International Organisation', 544; Egerton, *Jihad in the West*, 17-21.
105 Knapp, 'Concept and Practice of Jihad', 82.
106 Turner, 'From Cottage Industry to International Organisation', 544.
107 Moghadam, 'Mayhem, Myths, and Martyrdom', 126.
108 Ibid.; Turner, 'From Cottage Industry to International Organisation', 544.
109 Turner, 'From Cottage Industry to International Organisation', 544; Moghadam, 'Mayhem, Myths, and Martyrdom', 126.
110 Crone and Harrow, 'Homegrown Terrorism in the West', 521-36.

surprising. Nevertheless, it has had serious consequences. There exist many explanations for involvement in terrorism whose accuracy and reliability have been insufficiently ascertained due to the difficulties of gathering the high-quality data required to do so. Consequently, this book sees the use of primary sources as a prerequisite for making a contribution to existing knowledge on the Hofstadgroup and understanding involvement in homegrown jihadism more broadly.

The bulk of this chapter was dedicated to explaining the decision to use a multicausal analytical framework for studying involvement in the Hofstadgroup. Using literature reviews, a comprehensive inventory was made of the various explanations for involvement in terrorism at the structural, group, and individual levels of analysis. Applying these to the available data on the Hofstadgroup will enable a multifaceted and detailed understanding of the factors that shaped participants' involvement in this group to emerge. Following this discussion, the chapter concluded with an overview of several key terms that are used throughout the text.

One task remains before it is possible to move on to the analysis of the factors that influenced involvement in the Hofstadgroup proper. That is to familiarize readers with the Hofstadgroup and its activities. The next chapter provides a detailed chronology of the most important events in the group's 2002-2005 existence in order to create the necessary factual background for the analysis that is to follow. Chapter 4 then rounds off the introductory section of this book by discussing the Hofstadgroup's organizational and ideological characteristics, and assessing to what extent it can be considered a group that engaged in (preparations for) acts of terrorist violence.

3 A history of the Hofstadgroup[1]

This chapter provides a chronological description of the Hofstadgroup's 2002-2005 lifespan and concludes with a brief overview of the court cases against the group's participants. This discussion will familiarize readers with the group and act as a reference for the analytical chapters that follow. Although several good overviews of the Hofstadgroup exist, none are as strongly embedded in primary sources as the present account.[2]

3.1 The emergence of homegrown jihadism in the Netherlands

Developments both within the Netherlands and beyond its borders created conditions favorable to the emergence of homegrown jihadism. Some of these began many years before the Hofstadgroup's emergence, such as the growing influence of the fundamentalist Salafist interpretation of Islam, or the presence of small networks of veterans of jihadist conflicts in Afghanistan and Bosnia.[3] Other underlying factors were rooted in the increasingly sharp and polarizing debates about immigration and Islam which came to dominate media headlines in the late 1990s and early 2000s, especially after the rise of populist politicians such as Pim Fortuyn and Geert Wilders.[4] Such tensions became more palpable after the 9/11 attacks, as immigrant communities were increasingly framed as 'Muslims' and sometimes even held responsible for jihadist attacks.[5]

As later chapters will explore in detail, the 9/11 attacks, the ensuing 'War on Terror', and the Dutch government's decision to lend assistance to that fight were key geopolitical developments underlying the development of jihadism in the Netherlands. They drew attention to the ideas, ideologues, and propaganda of terrorist organizations such as al-Qaeda, especially so among some young Muslim citizens. Together, these factors created

---

1 This chapter has been published in amended form as: Schuurman, Eijkman, and Bakker, 'A History of the Hofstadgroup'.
2 Silber, *The Al Qaeda Factor*, 206-23; Vidino, 'The Hofstad Group', 579-92.
3 De Poot et al., *Jihadi Terrorism in the Netherlands*, 42-43; General Intelligence and Security Service, 'Violent Jihad in the Netherlands', 15-16.
4 De Koning and Meijer, 'Going All the Way', 223-24; De Koning, '"Moge Hij Onze Ogen Openen"', 52-53.
5 De Graaf, 'The Nexus between Salafism and Jihadism', 18.

conditions favorable to the emergence of Islamist radicalism and extremism. In early 2002, two Dutch citizens of Moroccan descent were killed in Kashmir by Indian security forces, ostensibly after having been recruited by Islamist militants at a mosque in the Netherlands.[6] That same year, dozens of people were arrested on suspicion of involvement in providing recruitment, financial, and logistical support to internationally operating jihadist terrorist groups.[7] Although the Hofstadgroup was the most infamous entity to arise in the Netherlands in the early 2000s, it was certainly not the only exponent of this broader trend.

3.2   2002: The Hofstadgroup's initial formation

The earliest reference to the Hofstadgroup stems from 2002. Over the course of that year, a group of increasingly radical Muslims began to draw the attention of the Dutch General Intelligence and Security Service (AIVD).[8] It was not until September 2003, however, that the Service began to label this particular set of people as the 'Hofstadgroup'.[9] The name refers to The Hague, a city colloquially known in Dutch as the *Hofstad* (court city) and one of the places in which the group gathered. Little is known about the group's activities in 2002, although it appears that regular gatherings began taking place by the end of the year. A middle-aged Syrian asylum seeker known by the moniker of Abu Khaled occupied a prominent position during these so-called 'living room meetings' as a religious instructor.[10] While he does not appear to have spoken of the use of violence or participation in jihad directly, his teachings conferred a dogmatic and fundamentalist interpretation of Islam. This formed a fertile base for some participants' subsequent adoption of a decidedly extremist, pro-violence, interpretation of Islam.[11]

The group's meetings were held in a variety of locations in addition to The Hague, with an Internet café in Schiedam and the Amsterdam residence of the Hofstadgroup participant who would go on to murder Dutch filmmaker

---

6   Ibid., 18-19.
7   Algemene Inlichtingen- en Veiligheidsdienst, 'Jaarverslag 2002', 21.
8   Donner and Remkes, 'Kamerstukken 2, 2004-2005, 29854, Nr. 3', 5.
9   Ibid., 18.
10 General Intelligence and Security Service, 'Violent Jihad in the Netherlands', 37.
11 Dienst Nationale Recherche, 'RL8026', 01/17: 4095; VERD: 19480, 19705-706, 19747; NCTV Employee 1, 'Personal Interview 1', 2; Public Prosecutor 1, 'Personal Interview 1', 8.

Theo van Gogh being used regularly.[12] A first hint that elements within the group were developing extremist views manifested itself towards the end of 2002. Information provided to the police by the AIVD suggests that in November of that year, one person who would feature prominently in the group's extremist core spoke out in favor of a mass-casualty bombing.[13] Regarding the group's organizational development, it is interesting to note that initial group formation appears to have been based primarily on preexisting social bonds. Many participants had grown up in the same neighborhoods, attended the same schools, or knew each other through their local mosques.[14] In the words of one former participant, the Hofstadgroup was a 'circle of acquaintances'.[15]

3.3 2003: Would-be foreign fighters and international connections

At the start of 2003, a prominent Hofstadgroup participant together with a friend of his who does not appear to have been involved in the group, made an attempt to join Islamist rebels in Chechnya. They were arrested by the Russian authorities just after they left Ukraine and were sent back home after questioning. Upon return to the Netherlands they were interrogated further by both the Dutch police and the AIVD.[16] That summer, two other participants separately undertook travel to Pakistan where they allegedly met each other for the first time at a Quran school. Their travels appear to have been facilitated through another Hofstadgroup participant.[17] Messages written after their return and intelligence information imply that both underwent or at least sought paramilitary training in Pakistan or Afghanistan.[18] That this trip was more than an opportunity to study Islam

---

12 Dienst Nationale Recherche, 'RL8026', AHA 01/18: 89-90.
13 Ibid., AHA 02/19: 100.
14 Ibid., VERD: 19444, 19459, 19675, 19717, 19858-860, 19877, 19916, 19980, 19994, 20079, 20112, 20115, 20174; GET: 18215, 18312-313, 18374-375, 18414, 20348; 01/17: 4176; AHA03/20: 1227; Erkel, *Samir*, 78-79.
15 'een vriendenkring': Former Hofstadgroup Participant 3, 'Personal Interview 1', 4.
16 Dienst Nationale Recherche, 'RL8026', 01/01: 33; GET: 18061-62; Calis, 'Iedereen Wil Martelaar Zijn'.
17 Erkel, *Samir*, 195; Vermaat, *Nederlandse Jihad*, 33.
18 Dienst Nationale Recherche, 'RL8026', 01/13: 140-41; AHA04/21: 1657, 1666; AHA05/22: 2176; AHD07/36: 8401-02; AHD08/37: 569-571, 595-597, 618-619, 635-637, 715-717, 767-769, 773-775, 880, 919-931; AHD09/38: 9049, 9054-56.

abroad is underlined by a farewell letter one of the two men left his family, in which he expressed a desire to remain in the 'land of jihad'.[19]

These two men returned from Pakistan separately in September. Later that month, AIVD intelligence revealed that one of the Pakistan-goers may have returned on the instigation of an unnamed 'emir' who tasked him with 'collecting balloons'.[20] According to the AIVD's information, a fellow Hofstadgroup participant had mentioned that this particular traveler had returned to 'play a match' before Ramadan that year (which began on 27 October). Around the same time, it was also discovered that this individual, together with the person who had tried to reach Chechnya and a third Hofstadgroup participant, were in contact with a Moroccan man living in Spain who was sought by the Moroccan authorities for his suspected involvement in the 2003 Casablanca bombings and for his membership of the Moroccan Islamic Combatant Group (GICM).[21]

The Hofstadgroup participant who may have been in touch with the unknown emir traveled to Barcelona in the first week of October to meet the Moroccan man, returning to Amsterdam on 8 October. While in Spain, he also met an acquaintance of the Moroccan suspect, a man who Spanish authorities believed had ties to the Iraqi terrorist organization Ansar al-Islam. Another Hofstadgroup participant communicated with the Moroccan man via telephone from the Netherlands and apparently received instructions to procure 'a notebook' and 'credit'.[22] Other topics of conversation were 'shoes class 1 and class 2' and 'things that come from Greece or Italy'.[23] The Moroccan suspect also mentioned that he would send a man from Belgium to meet the participant he had been phoning with. Whether this meeting occurred is unclear, although two of the participants who were in telephone contact with the Moroccan individual traveled to Belgium on 15 October for unknown purposes.[24]

On 14 October, the Spanish authorities arrested the Moroccan suspect. A day later, the AIVD informed the Dutch public prosecutor's office about the travels to Pakistan or Afghanistan and the Spanish connection. The police then arrested five Hofstadgroup participants on 7 October. These included the three individuals who undertook travel abroad, two of whom were in contact with the Moroccan man, another person who was also in

19 Ibid., 01/13: 163.
20 Ibid., 01/01: 23-24.
21 Ibid.; A[.], 'Deurwaarders Van Allah', 33.
22 Dienst Nationale Recherche, 'RL8026', 01/01: 24.
23 Ibid., AHA01/18: 81.
24 Ibid., 01/01: 23-25; AHA01/18: 80-81; RHV01/66: 18845-46.

contact with the Moroccan individual and the middle-aged Syrian religious instructor Abu Khaled. House searches turned up books, tapes, and digital materials espousing an extremist interpretation of Islam, study notes on martyrdom, an at that point unknown person's will expressing a desire to die as a martyr, and, in the case of one of those arrested, materials suggestive of an interest in constructing an explosive device. However, all of the suspects were released at the end of October due to lack of evidence.[25]

The Dutch police were thus unable to substantiate the possibility that the suspects were planning a terrorist attack or assisting foreign groups or individuals in doing so. Given that two of those arrested had in September and October been trying to encourage other young Dutch Muslims to travel to Pakistan, a likely explanation for the 'emir's' task is that it was to inspire others to make a similar trip. The communication with the Moroccan suspect in Spain is harder to explain, although a source close to the investigation thought it likely that the Hofstadgroup participants were providing logistical assistance with acquiring a passport ('notebook') and money ('credit'), perhaps to help the Moroccan suspect avoid arrest.[26] What the other terms referred to, and what type of 'match' was to be played before Ramadan has remained unclear.

On the very last day of 2003, one of the Pakistan travelers undertook a second journey to that country, this time accompanied by a fellow Hofstadgroup participant who had not been there before. Scarcely more than a week later, on 9 January 2004, both of them returned. The sources provide several different explanations for this rapid return.[27] Regardless of which of these accounts is true, it is clear that this second trip abroad was not very successful, with little to indicate that the travelers were able to get any paramilitary training or make contacts with foreign jihadists.

Judging by the tone and contents of his writings and translations, 2003 also saw the man who would murder Van Gogh in November 2004 rapidly embrace more fundamentalist and radical views.[28] This process was accompanied by a withdrawal from 'mainstream' Dutch society; he quit his job, stopped volunteer work for his local community in June and distanced himself from non-religious old friends. Around the same time, he adopted the clothing and facial hairstyle of a fundamentalist Muslim, leading him to

---

25   Ibid., 01/01: 24-27; RHV01/66: 18792; Donner and Remkes, 'Kamerstukken 2, 2004-2005, 29854, Nr. 3', 25-26.
26   Police Investigator 1, 'Personal Interview 3', 1.
27   Dienst Nationale Recherche, 'RL8026', 01/13: 141-43; GET: 18840, 188452.
28   Peters, 'Dutch Extremist Islamism', 145-59.

become known as 'the Taliban' among youths in his Amsterdam neighborhood. Of particular interest is the finding that he traveled to Denmark in October. Although the available sources do not reveal what the purpose of his trip was, it is possible that he visited a Syrian preacher who lived there. This preacher was a friend of the Hofstadgroup's Syrian religious instructor Abu Khaled and occasionally traveled to the Netherlands to visit him.[29]

3.4 2004: Individualistic plots and the murder of Theo van Gogh

The Hofstadgroup appears to have undertaken few, if any, communal activities during 2004. Burgeoning collective efforts involving at least parts of the group could be identified in 2003, such as the contacts with the Moroccan suspect and the attempts to encourage other Dutch Muslims to travel to Pakistan. Yet 2004 was characterized by distinctly individualistic initiatives. When accounting for this change, the impact of the October 2003 arrests cannot be overlooked. A former participant explained that the arrests resulted in an acutely heightened sense of paranoia and a preoccupation with personal safety. This was debilitating to the point that he described the Hofstadgroup as being effectively crippled in early 2004.[30]

While the realization that they had come under surveillance dampened group-based activities, a small number of individuals were not deterred. Peters's analysis of the writings of Van Gogh's killer-to-be shows that this participant moved from radical convictions to distinctly extremist ones around March 2004.[31] His rapidly developing extremism would lead him, around the summer of that year, to embrace the view that blasphemers needed to be killed.[32] This provided him with both the ideological motive and justification for murdering writer and filmmaker Van Gogh, who was very outspoken in his criticism of Islam and Muslims and often presented his arguments in a coarse fashion intended to cause offense.[33]

---

29 Alberts et al., 'De Wereld Van Mohammed B.'; Chorus and Olgun, *In Godsnaam*, 61; Commissie van Toezicht betreffende de Inlichtingen- en Veiligheidsdiensten, 'Toezichtsrapport Met Betrekking Tot Mohammed B.', 11; Dienst Nationale Recherche, 'RL8026', 01/01: 32, 37; GET: 18349, 18415; VERD: 9754; Kranenberg, 'De Zachte Krachten Achter Mohammed B.'
30 Former Hofstadgroup Participant 3, 'Personal Interview 1', 5.
31 Peters, 'Dutch Extremist Islamism', 152-55.
32 Ibid., 155-56.
33 E.g. Chorus and Olgun, *In Godsnaam*, 33-34.

Several other notable developments took place before that time, however. On 8 April 2004, a supermarket in Rotterdam was robbed by two men armed with automatic weapons. Although the suspicion could not be substantiated by concrete evidence, it seems likely that the robbers received help getting into the store from one of its employees; the Hofstadgroup participant who tried to reach Chechnya a year earlier. Minutes after the robbers got away with approximately 700 Euros, one of them was arrested and later confirmed as an acquaintance of the store's Hofstadgroup employee.[34] Several Hofstadgroup participants have since claimed that the second robber was also involved in the group and only managed to 'evade' the police because he was in fact an AIVD informant.[35] Concrete evidence to support this claim was, however, not encountered.

On 19 May, the police received information which suggested that the supermarket employee was involved in preparations for a terrorist attack. On 7 June, that same individual was captured on security cameras walking around the AIVD's headquarters in Leidschendam, apparently measuring distances by taking equally spaced steps. These events contributed to his second arrest, on 30 June (the first was in October 2003). Among the items encountered in the ensuing house search were photographs, maps, and directions of the AIVD headquarters, the nuclear reactor in the Dutch town of Borssele, the House of Representatives, the Ministry of Defense, Amsterdam Schiphol airport, and the barracks of the Dutch commandos in Roosendaal. Other finds included a bulletproof vest, two magazines, and a silencer that could be fitted to the weapons used in the supermarket robbery, electrical circuits, night-vision goggles, household chemicals, fertilizer, documents espousing an extremist interpretation of Islam, jihad 'handbooks', and a hand-written will in the suspect's name.[36]

While indicative of an interest in improvised explosive devices (IEDs), it should be noted that the electrical circuits and chemicals were everyday, over-the-counter items that had not (yet) been combined into an explosive device or its precursor components. It should also be emphasized that the particular type of fertilizer found turned out to be unsuitable for making an explosive substance.[37] Hence, the individual in question does not appear to have had the capability to construct an actual bomb at that point in time.

---

34 Dienst Nationale Recherche, 'RL8026', 01/01: 38-39.
35 Erkel, *Samir*, 209; De Graaf, *Gevaarlijke Vrouwen*, 262; Alberts and Derix, 'Het Mysterie'; Groen and Kranenberg, '"Saleh B. Wel Terroristisch Actief"'.
36 Dienst Nationale Recherche, 'RL8026', 01/01: 38-45.
37 Ibid., 01/01: 48-49.

Interestingly, in the same month two other Hofstadgroup participants had inquired after fertilizer at a garden store. Whether this was related to an intention to construct an IED remains unclear. However, it is striking that the individual arrested on 30 June was found in possession of a list of addresses of that particular chain of stores.[38]

On 6 June, two other Hofstadgroup participants, in the company of two acquaintances who do not appear to have been directly involved in the group, traveled to Portugal. On a tip-off likely provided by the AIVD, which raised the possibility that the goal of this trip was to commit a terrorist attack during the European soccer championships or to kill Portuguese Prime Minister Barroso, the four travelers were arrested by the Portuguese police on 11 June and their whereabouts searched. No evidence was uncovered to substantiate any of the terrorism related allegations or a later claim by a witness that the trip's goal was to acquire weapons. In light of the lack of incriminating evidence, it may simply have been the case that the Hofstadgroup participant who came up with the idea for the trip in the first place, an illegal immigrant from Morocco, was telling the truth. He claims to have wanted to benefit from a Portuguese amnesty for asylum seekers. Similarly, there is little to contradict his companions' assertion that they went along to enjoy a holiday.[39]

Despite the lack of incriminating evidence, all four travelers were handed over to the Portuguese immigration police on 14 June for 'visa irregularities' and sent back to the Netherlands several days later. Upon his arrival at Schiphol airport, the trip's initiator was questioned by the Dutch police. One particularly interesting aspect of this conversation is that he warned the police about a friend of his who, he claimed, spoke a lot of jihad, adhered to the ideology of 'takfir' (declaring other Muslims apostates) and who wanted to join Islamist insurgents in Chechnya. This friend would later commit the murder of Van Gogh.[40] What exactly motivated this willingness to incriminate others is unclear, but it suggests the Hofstadgroup was not (yet) a particularly tightly-knit group of extremists.

Two other developments complete this overview of the eventful month of June 2004. On 14 June, the mother of two Hofstadgroup participants filed a report with the police declaring that she and her daughters felt

---

38 Ibid., 01/01: 40; 01/13: 175.
39 Ibid., 01/13: 104; AHA03/20: 859; GET: 18375; VERD: 20347-48; RHV02/67: 19216-18, 19291-92; Noivo, 'Jihadism in Portugal', 6; Vidino, 'The Hofstad Group', 583; Chorus and Olgun, *Broeders*; Vermaat, *Nederlandse Jihad*, 107.
40 Dienst Nationale Recherche, 'RL8026', AHA03/20: 859-61; RHV02/67: 19292.

threatened by her sons' extremist and violent behavior to the point that they moved out of their own home.[41] Investigations conducted later in 2004 also revealed 14 June to be the first day on which an AIVD interpreter leaked confidential information to two Hofstadgroup participants; one of them received a 'weekly report' on the group in June and the other a wiretap in August.[42] The leak was discovered in September 2004 when a Dutch newspaper, which had also acquired the materials, faxed a part of the weekly report back to the AIVD. The interpreter was a prior acquaintance of one of the Hofstadgroup's participants, for whom the AIVD employee had bought a ticket from Al Hoceima (Morocco) to Amsterdam in May 2003.[43] Why he leaked this information and what, if any, effect the files had on the Hofstadgroup remains unknown.

3.4.1 Towards the murder of Theo van Gogh

On 29 August 2004, the Somali-born Dutch politician Ayaan Hirsi Ali appeared for an in-depth interview on the TV-program *Zomergasten* (summer guests). As part of the show, a short Islam-critical film she had recently made with Van Gogh called *Submission, part 1* was broadcast.[44] The film contains fragments in which Quranic verses are projected on semi-naked women and was supposedly met with either disgust or indifference by the Dutch Muslim community.[45] But among the Hofstadgroup the film evoked much stronger reactions, all the more so since, having renounced her Muslim faith, Hirsi Ali was already a particularly hated public figure.[46]

A day after the film was broadcast, a message appeared on an 'MSN Group', a type of 'do-it-yourself' online message board popular at the time, called *MuwahhidinDeWareMoslims* ('Muwahhidin[47] the True Muslims'). This website was administered and frequented by Hofstadgroup participants, for instance to propagate the increasingly extremist texts written by Van Gogh's killer-to-be. The message, titled 'The unbelieving diabolical

---

41   Ibid., 01/01: 141; AHA03/20: 831.
42   Alberts and Derix, 'AIVD-Stuk Lekte Uit Naar Extremisten'.
43   Dienst Nationale Recherche, 'RL8026', 01/13: 104; AHA05/22: 837, 1811-13, 1837; Alberts and Derix, 'AIVD-Stuk Lekte Uit Naar Extremisten'; Kilcullen, 'Subversion and Countersubversion', 657.
44   The film can be viewed online: Hirsi Ali and Van Gogh, 'Submission, part 1' (YouTube). Last accessed 15 April 2014.
45   'Hirsi Ali Zoekt Tegenstanders Voor Haar Wedstrijd'.
46   Dienst Nationale Recherche, 'RL8026', 01/13: 74, 161-62; Erkel, *Samir*, 223.
47   'Muwahhidin' refers to Muslims who uphold a strict belief in the concept of tawhid (the unity of god). See: Esposito, *Islam*, 146.

mortada [apostate], Ayaan Hirsi Ali', was posted by an individual on the group's edges. In it, the author claimed that the 'Muwahhidin Brigade' had uncovered Hirsi Ali's residence, proceeded to publish that presumed address in full and also posted a picture of Van Gogh.[48] A second message followed on 4 September and was openly threatening. Writing of Hirsi Ali, the author claimed that 'wherever she hides, death shall find her!'[49] The messages' author was arrested on 14 September.

A day later, the Dutch police received an anonymous e-mail warning them that two individuals might be preparing a terrorist attack. The anonymous source had supposedly been asked by two 'terrorists' to commit attacks in the Netherlands, with the House of Representatives in The Hague and Amsterdam's red light district as possible targets. Unfortunately, the available sources divulge no further information on this potential terrorist plot.[50] Interestingly, however, one of the two supposed terrorists was an active participant in the Hofstadgroup. In September, he responded affirmatively to a question posted on his website 'TawheedWalJihad'[51] inquiring whether it was a Muslim's duty to kill those who insulted the Prophet Muhammad. To substantiate his argument, the participant relied on a translation of the influential fourteenth-century Salafist scholar Ahmad ibn Taymiyya's argument to this extent. This translation had been written by Van Gogh's killer-to-be. The individual acting as an 'online help desk' on extremist matters was arrested on 8 November because he had issued death threats to Dutch politician Geert Wilders using the aforementioned website.[52]

On 2 November 2004, Van Gogh was murdered while cycling to work in his hometown of Amsterdam. The killer cycled up alongside Van Gogh, shot him several times with a pistol and then tried to decapitate his dead or dying victim with a kukri knife. Without fully accomplishing this task, he decided to pin a note to the dead man's chest with another knife in which he threatened Hirsi Ali with death. Calmly reloading the magazine of his HS model 95 pistol, the killer then walked towards a nearby park where a

---

48 Dienst Nationale Recherche, 'RL8026', AHA04/21: 1324-39, 1342; AHA05/22: 2339; 01/17: 4002-03, 4025-26, 4047; Benschop, 'A Political Murder Foretold'.
49 'waar ze maar schuilt, de dood zal haar achterhalen!': Dienst Nationale Recherche,'RL8026', AHA04/21: 1325.
50 Ibid., 01/01: 179-80.
51 'Monotheism and Jihad', possibly a reference to a group by that name led by Abu Musab al-Zarqawi which would later become known as al-Qaeda in Iraq. See: Benschop, 'A Political Murder Foretold'.
52 Dienst Nationale Recherche, 'RL8026', 01/01: 160, 167, 200-01, 203; Benschop, 'A Political Murder Foretold'; Peters, 'Dutch Extremist Islamism', 156.

shoot-out with police officers ensued. After running out of ammunition and being shot in the leg, Van Gogh's murderer was arrested. Three other people were also hit by the killer's bullets; one bystander in the leg, another in the heel, and one police officer in his bulletproof vest. Upon being taken into custody the killer was told that he was lucky to be alive; he responded that he had hoped to die.[53]

Van Gogh's murder was a premeditated act of terrorism. The attacker utilized deadly violence against a civilian with the distinct intent of achieving propagandistic and psychological goals. For the attacker, Van Gogh's death was not just an aim in itself, but an extreme form of communication that guaranteed him the attention of those he considered Islam's enemies and those who he hoped to inspire to rise up in its defense. This follows not just from the ritualistic manner in which Van Gogh was killed in a public place in broad daylight, but also from the various letters that his assailant left behind for his compatriots to propagate. These alternately threatened death to specific Dutch politicians and the general public, and encouraged Muslim youngsters to embrace militancy.[54] According to Schmid's definition used here, this differentiation between the immediate victim and a wider target audience to whom the violent act is meant to speak is a defining characteristic of terrorism.[55]

Nine witnesses later reported having seen the killer at different locations along the route Van Gogh usually traveled to work between early October and the day of the murder. Two witnesses, independently of each other, claim to have seen the killer on the first of November standing with his bike along Van Gogh's usual route, observing passing cyclists. This implies that Van Gogh's attacker had carefully chosen where to strike and perhaps even that 2 November was not his first attempt to kill the filmmaker.[56]

There has been considerable speculation about the rest of the group's involvement in or knowledge of the attack.[57] In September 2014, a public prosecutor involved in the case voiced his suspicion, on national television,

---

53 Donner and Remkes, 'Kamerstukken 2, 2004-2005, 29854, Nr. 1', 1-2; Van Straelen, 'Requisitoir in De Strafzaak Tegen Mohammed B.', 10-27; Dienst Nationale Recherche, 'RL8026', 01/13: 95.
54 Peters, 'De Ideologische En Religieuze Ontwikkeling', appendix: Overzicht teksten geschreven of vertaald door Mohammed B., 32-46, 50-56.
55 Schmid, 'The Definition of Terrorism', 62-63.
56 Van Straelen, 'Requisitoir in De Strafzaak Tegen Mohammed B.', 9-10.
57 Derix, 'Hoe Kwam Toch'.; Former Hofstadgroup Participant 4, 'Personal Interview 2', 4-5; NCTV Employee 1, 'Personal Interview 1', 3-4; Van Straelen, 'Requisitoir in De Strafzaak Tegen Mohammed B.', 7; Public Prosecutor 2, "Personal Interview 1', 3.

that multiple people had been involved in the murder.[58] In November 2015 a new report by the Dutch Review Committee on the Intelligence and Security Services revealed that the AIVD had received ten pieces of information in the years after the murder indicating that others were aware of the murder, had assisted in preparations for it, or had even ordered it.[59] While the report is careful not to dismiss this information out of hand, nine out of ten pieces of intelligence were based on hearsay and speculation; in all, there was no *concrete evidence* to suggest the involvement of others.[60]

Consequently, this book takes the position that the *currently available evidence* indicates that the murder was planned, prepared, and executed solely by the attacker himself.[61] Based on his explanation in court, he appears to have been primarily driven by a sense that it was every individual believer's duty to behead those who insulted Allah and his prophet, as he felt Van Gogh had done with his movie and writings. He took full responsibility for his actions and claimed that he would have done exactly the same had the blasphemer been his brother or father.[62]

The authorities responded to the murder by arresting most of the suspected members of the Hofstadgroup on the day of the attack. Two, however, managed to evade apprehension. One was Abu Khaled, the middle-aged Syrian man who had provided religious instruction to the group. Aided by several acquaintances, he left for Syria the day that Van Gogh was killed, traveling via Belgium and Greece, and entering the country illegally from Turkey. Despite the striking coincidence, the police investigation was unable to ascertain whether Abu Khaled was aware of the murderer's plans. The second participant who got away was the member of the group's extremist core who featured earlier as the initiator of the trip to Portugal. Although precisely where he went after evading arrest has remained unclear, he may have traveled back to his family in Morocco in November 2004 or spent the time until his arrest in June 2005 alternately living in Brussels and possibly Luxembourg, from where he would occasionally travel to the Netherlands.[63]

---

58 'T Sas and Born, 'Hoofdofficier: Mohammed Bouyeri Handelde Niet Alleen'.
59 Commissie van Toezicht betreffende de Inlichtingen- en Veiligheidsdiensten, 'Toezichtsrapport over Eventuele Handlangers', 14-16.
60 Ibid., 16.
61 Van Straelen, 'Requisitoir in De Strafzaak Tegen Mohammed B.', 6-7.
62 NOS, 'Verklaring Mohammed B. In Tekst'; Vermaat, *Nederlandse Jihad*, 27.
63 Dienst Nationale Recherche, 'RL8026', AHA02/19: 755; GET: 4069; Public Prosecutor 1, 'Personal Interview 1', 17, 42; Groen and Kranenberg, *Women Warriors*, 84-85.

3.4.2 Violent resistance to arrest

The most dramatic episode in the arrests of alleged Hofstadgroup members occurred during the early hours of 10 November 2004. As a police arrest squad tried to force the door on the apartment of two suspects in The Hague around 02:50 in the morning, they found that it had been barricaded from within and could only be partially opened. The two men had prepared for the police's arrival and discussed beforehand how to respond to it. Mere moments after the squad's attempt to force entry to the apartment, one of its occupants threw a hand grenade through the crack between door and door frame, which passed the officers standing on the landing and bounced down an outdoor stairwell to explode on the street below. Moments after realizing a grenade had been thrown at them, one of the officers fired twice at their attacker, both shots just missing his head. The grenade's ensuing explosion injured five policemen, one of whom seriously, and forced the squad to pull back.[64]

During the day that followed, the suspects spoke on the phone with friends and family, announcing their imminent martyrdom. They hastily wrote a will and made several prank calls to the emergency services asking for the police to come and rescue them from the 'masked scary men' surrounding their home.[65] Additionally, they threatened to blow up the entire street with twenty kilograms of explosives, provoked officers to shoot them and were seen waving a sword and a firearm that would later turn out to be a fake. Towards the end of the afternoon, a military special forces unit went into action. After eighteen tear gas canisters were fired into the apartment, the two suspects clambered onto a balcony. Soldiers in an opposite building then ordered them to raise their hands and fired a warning shot. The suspects were told to undress and descend into the garden via a ladder. Instead, one of them reached into his jacket pocket, prompting him to be shot in his shoulder. Subsequently, both suspects complied with the soldiers' orders, climbed down, and were taken into custody. No explosives were found in the apartment but both suspects were found to have carried additional grenades in their pockets.[66]

---

64 Dienst Nationale Recherche, 'RL8026', 01/13: 38, 95-96, 105-06, 171; GET: 18011, 18235-237; AGV01/62: 7967-05.
65 'gemaskerde enge mannen': Ibid., AHA07/24: 3112.
66 Ibid., 01/01: 131; 01/12: 9-10; 01/13: 71; AHA02/19: 610-14; AHA07/24: 3087-127; AGV01/62: 17969-8005; GET: 8011, 8235-8237; The Hague Court of Appeal, 'LJN BC2576'.

3.5   2005: From 'Hofstad' to 'Piranha'

The November 2004 arrests ended what could be called the 'first wave' of the Hofstadgroup. Yet from approximately April 2005 onward, a small group re-emerged that, with regard to its participants, ideological convictions, and practical intentions, was a direct successor to the 2002-2004 Hofstadgroup. This 'second wave' has become known under the name of the police investigation into its activities as the 'Piranha' group. Despite the separate investigations and court cases, the Piranha group was essentially a continuation of the Hofstadgroup and is treated here as such.

The 2005 resurgence was made possible by three factors. First of all, the individual arrested in June 2004 after reconnoitering the AIVD headquarters was acquitted and released from custody in April 2005. Thus, one of the most extremist individuals in the Hofstadgroup was able to continue his activities. Secondly, another member of the Hofstadgroup's extremist core had evaded arrest in November 2004 and remained at large until his apprehension in June 2005. During this interval, he contributed to the new group's operational capabilities by procuring three firearms. These two men appear to have formed the new group's main protagonists and are referred to here as its ringleaders. Of the remaining nine individuals ultimately earmarked as alleged members of the Piranha group, all but two had been on the original Hofstadgroup's fringes. The arrest of most of the original participants seems to have brought these peripheral individuals forward into positions of increased prominence.[67]

The Piranha group displayed some interesting differences from its predecessor. Most importantly, there appeared to be a burgeoning sense of hierarchy, tenuous indications of a return to more *group-based* efforts and clearer signs that these efforts were in the service of *terrorism-related* goals.[68] Police and intelligence information reveals that as many as three tentative terrorist plots may have been considered, all three of which were being shaped under the overall guidance of the individual released in April 2005. One of these potential plots targeted Dutch politicians, with particular emphasis on Hirsi Ali. The second aimed to bring down an El-Al airplane, while the third envisioned a double strike; first against the AIVD headquarters and then targeting several Dutch politicians.

---

67   Dienst Nationale Recherche, 'RL8026', 01/17: 4085-86, 4128, 4179, 4201; Dienst Nationale Recherche, 'Piranha', REL00: 55, 62, 205; Public Prosecutor 1, 'Personal Interview 1', 42.
68   Schuurman, Eijkman, and Bakker, 'The Hofstadgroup Revisited'

A HISTORY OF THE HOFSTADGROUP

One of the first things the individual released in April 2005 did was approach an old acquaintance, someone who had been in contact with Hofstadgroup participants from approximately the end of 2003. During the trial against the Piranha suspects, this person claimed to have been coerced and threatened by the group's two ringleaders, for instance into renting a house for the group in Brussels and occasionally supplying participants with money.[69] In contrast, the other suspects in the Piranha case claimed that this individual was in fact very radical, not at all involuntarily associated with them, and purely motivated to give incriminating testimony in court to avoid being sentenced.[70] Although the currently available data does not allow these conflicting claims to be convincingly resolved, it should be noted that this was one of the witnesses whose testimony a Dutch court qualified as unreliable.[71]

Police intelligence from early April 2005 indicated that the individual recently released from detention had gathered a new group around him, that he wanted to die as a martyr and that he was driven to rectify the '1-0' in the unbelievers' favor.[72] This latter point suggests that he was at least partially motivated by a personal desire for revenge for his arrest and incarceration. This motive also appears in various writings by and about this individual, which highlight his experience of poor treatment by the Dutch justice system and police and, especially, his adversarial relationship with the AIVD.[73] Given this background, it is unsurprising that one of the three potential plots overseen by this person appears to have targeted the AIVD.

3.5.1 Spring and summer 2005: Renewed signs of terrorist intentions

May 2005 brought signs of a renewed interest in pursuing acts of terrorism in the Netherlands among some of the Piranha group's participants. For instance, the Piranha ringleader who had been a fugitive since the murder of Van Gogh allegedly told two other participants that he had a CD-ROM with instructions on how to make a suicide vest and that the required components could be bought in Germany. This person also acquired three firearms around this point in time; a CZ 'Skorpion' version 61 submachine

---

69 Dienst Nationale Recherche, 'Piranha', REL00: 61-63, 82-83, 85-86, 104-05, 158-60, 211-14.
70 'Getuige Piranha-Zaak Zelf Radicaal'; Kranenberg and Groen, 'Kroongetuigen Vallen in Eigen Kuil'.
71 Kranenberg and Groen, 'Kroongetuigen Vallen in Eigen Kuil'.
72 Dienst Nationale Recherche, 'Piranha', REL00: 29; NOVA, 'Informatie AIVD En Politie Uit Strafdossier'.
73 De Graaf, *Gevaarlijke Vrouwen*, 273; Erkel, *Samir*, 199-200, 206-08, 218-19, 227-28, 240-41.

gun (also referred to as a 'baby Uzi'), an Agram 2000 submachine gun with a separate silencer, and a .38 caliber Smith & Wesson revolver. In May, he instructed a participant to visit the group's other leader, the man released from custody in April, to pick something up. This turned out to be a piece of paper printed in an Internet café which listed the names, addresses, and telephone numbers of several Dutch politicians.[74]

Events in June provided further indications that both the intent and capability to use terrorist violence was being developed, again with a particular focus on Dutch politicians. On or around 15 June, the fugitive and his female companion took two other participants to a large park in Amsterdam to fire one of the submachine guns at a tree.[75] Several days later, on 20 June, the aforementioned companion phoned a family member who worked at a pharmacy in The Hague. She asked for the addresses of the politicians who frequented it and was particularly interested in Hirsi Ali's, but was not given the information.[76] The next day, police officers conducting surveillance in The Hague recognized the fugitive they had sought since November 2004. At the time, he had been staying with someone who appears to have been pressured into providing him and his companion with shelter and transportation.[77]

This was also the case a day later, on 22 June, when this acquaintance was instructed to drive the fugitive and his companion to Amsterdam. Both seemed tense and the fugitive twice made their driver attempt to shake off any possible tails. In Amsterdam, he took over the wheel and drove towards train station Amsterdam Lelylaan, where he and his companion got out. Upon reaching the platform, both were apprehended by a police special intervention unit. At the time, the fugitive was carrying the loaded Agram 2000 in his backpack. In the driver's home, the police found a handwritten and coded note listing the addresses of four Dutch politicians which appears to have belonged to the two people who had just been arrested. Their interest in the whereabouts of Dutch politicians and Hirsi Ali in particular, something corroborated by the statements of two inmates who met them in prison, lends further credence to the idea that they were considering plans to assassinate one or more of these individuals.[78]

74   Den Hartigh and Van Dam, 'Requisitoir "Piranha" Deel 1', 70; Dienst Nationale Recherche, 'Piranha', REL00: 61-62.
75   Dienst Nationale Recherche, 'Piranha', REL00: 213.
76   Ibid., REL00: 158-60.
77   Dienst Nationale Recherche, 'RL8026', AHA06/23: 2564-600, 2618-620.
78   Ibid., AHA06/23: 2587-89, 2596, 2610-612, 2713, 2755-756; 01/17: 4236-38, 4241; Dienst Nationale Recherche, 'Piranha', REL00: 99, 1056.

Two days after the arrests, the group's remaining ringleader phoned one of his imprisoned Hofstadgroup friends. He mentioned being unable to sleep since the arrests and that there was a story which had not yet made the newspapers which would astound his friend.[79] The next day he phoned again and cryptically talked of a 'soup' that was still boiling but would make it onto television soon.[80] Suspicions that the caller was involved in preparations for an act of terrorism were strengthened a month later. Just after midnight on 26 July, police officers observed this person enter a park in The Hague in the company of an unknown male. Not much later a bang was heard. Its source has never been discovered, leaving it uncertain whether this was potentially some kind of firearms or explosives test. Two days later the AIVD officially informed the police that they had indications that the group's remaining leader was involved in terrorist activities.[81]

3.5.2 The second and third potential plots come to light

In early August 2005, signs of a second potential terrorist plot began to manifest themselves. Police intelligence reports indicated that a group of young men of Moroccan descent in Amsterdam West, including two Piranha participants, were working on a plan to shoot down an El Al plane at Schiphol airport, possibly using some type of Rocket Propelled Grenade (RPG). The reports raised the possibility that one individual had been tasked with conducting a reconnaissance of a particular area of Schiphol airport and that the plot was being funded by a levy on the criminal proceeds of acquaintances of the remaining Piranha ringleader. The intelligence information, however, could not be marked as 'reliable'.[82] Furthermore, subsequent police investigations were unable to substantiate the intelligence. This suggests that the potential second terrorist plot attributable to the Piranha never proceeded beyond a conceptual phase.[83]

In contrast to the 'first wave' Hofstadgroup, 'living-room meetings' did not feature as prominently in its 2005 continuation. Participants did visit each other and some individuals provided religious instruction, yet relatively large-scale group meetings such as those that were held at the

---

79 Dienst Nationale Recherche, 'Piranha', REL00: 144-45.
80 Ibid.
81 Ibid., REL00: 39-40; NOVA, 'Informatie AIVD En Politie Uit Strafdossier'.
82 Dienst Nationale Recherche, 'Piranha', REL00: 40-42; NOVA, 'Informatie AIVD En Politie Uit Strafdossier'.
83 Den Hartigh and Van Dam, 'Requisitoir "Piranha" Deel 1', 5; NOVA, 'Informatie AIVD En Politie Uit Strafdossier'.

house of Van Gogh's killer were not encountered in the available sources. A likely explanation is that the Piranha group had developed a much more acute sense of safety and was wary of indoor gatherings for security reasons. This is supported by several meetings held outdoors in public places, such as on 24 August in The Hague, when four Piranha participants were observed together, on 7 September in Amsterdam, when two individuals met and exchanged a package, and on 11 October, when five suspected members of the Piranha group met in The Hague.[84]

Arguably the most interesting such meeting occurred in September 2005, when the Piranha group's principal remaining protagonist met a Belgian national of Moroccan descent at a train station in The Hague. According to police information, the Belgian man declined the protagonist's request to participate in a suicide attack against the AIVD on the grounds that he was already planning something in Morocco.[85] A different take is given by investigative journalists Groen and Kranenberg. They describe the Belgian man as a cousin of a participant of the 'original' Hofstadgroup and as supposedly offering three female suicide bombers to his Piranha contact, who declined the offer because he wanted men only for his attack on the AIVD.[86] The Belgian man was arrested in Morocco in November 2005 on charges not related to the Piranha case. The available data offers no further information on the meeting, leaving it unclear exactly what happened.

Signs of the third potential terrorist plot came to the fore in October. AIVD information from the beginning of the month indicated that the Piranha group's participants were, to differing degrees, involved in preparations for a terrorist attack. This potential attack was to occur before 31 October 2005, the date set for the main protagonist's appeal hearing. The plot was thought to consist of two parts; one group of attackers would target politicians while the second would force entry to the AIVD headquarters and blow it up. None of the perpetrators expected to survive the attacks. The AIVD information also indicated that the Piranha ringleader was looking for additional weaponry; ten AK-47 assault rifles, two silenced pistols, and ten vests containing eight kilograms of explosives each. The individual in question apparently expected a call from someone to discuss delivery of these goods. Phone intercepts revealed that a meeting between a possible supplier and the ringleader was arranged for 12 October. However, despite

---

84 Dienst Nationale Recherche, 'Piranha', REL00: 43-44; Den Hartigh and Van Dam, 'Requisitoir "Piranha" Deel 1', 7.
85 Dienst Nationale Recherche, 'Piranha', REL00: 151-52.
86 Groen and Kranenberg, *Women Warriors*, 144-45.

agreeing to a time and place over the phone, the Piranha participant did not show up.[87]

The next day, the police received additional information from the AIVD that precipitated the remaining suspects' arrest. Most important was a videotaped will in which the group's main protagonist, seated next to the Skorpion submachine gun, threatened the Dutch state and its citizens with violence for, among other things, the country's involvement in the Iraq war. Until the Dutch 'left Muslims alone and chose the path of peace' the 'language of the sword' would reign.[88] He also appeared to bid his family farewell by stating that he 'commits this deed out of fear for the punishment of Allah'.[89] In addition, he called upon the faithful to rise up in defense of oppressed Muslims worldwide and spoke out in support of his incarcerated Hofstadgroup friends.[90] Just how the AIVD got its hands on this video has remained unclear. The person seen on the video claims that an AIVD informant assisted him with the recording and then supplied it to the AIVD after staging a break-in of his home as cover for the tape's disappearance.[91]

Acting on the above information, the police arrested the remaining Piranha suspects on 14 October without incident. Among the items found during house searches were three gas masks, several balaclavas, radical and extremist materials and, notably, a document made by one of the suspects called 'lessons in safety' which underlined the Piranha group's greater awareness of and concern for the authorities' interest in them.[92] The remaining two firearms – the Skorpion and the revolver – were, however, not recovered at this time. They were found on 28 August 2006 in a cellar belonging to one of the Piranha suspects by plumbers called in to address flooding on the premises.[93] The October 2005 arrests effectively put an end to the Hofstadgroup; its most extremist elements were imprisoned and the remainder made no attempt to resuscitate the group a third time. As Chapter 5 explores in more detail, the group's lack of widespread popular support and the absence, at least at that time, of a sizeable community

---

87   Dienst Nationale Recherche, 'Piranha', REL00: 46-53; NOVA, 'Informatie AIVD En Politie Uit Strafdossier'.
88   'Ik zeg jullie dat er tussen ons en jullie alleen de taal van het zwaard zal gelden tot jullie de moslims met rust laten en de weg van de vrede kiezen': NOVA, 'Videotestament Samir A.'.
89   'weet dat ik deze daad verricht uit vrees voor de straf van Allah': Ibid.
90   Ibid.
91   De Graaf, *Gevaarlijke Vrouwen*, 273-74.
92   Dienst Nationale Recherche, 'Piranha', REL00: 57, 161; Meijer, 'Inhoud Van De Religieuze', 1-74.
93   Den Hartigh and Van Dam, 'Requisitoir "Piranha" Deel 1', 8; Groen and Kranenberg, *Women Warriors*, 134-35.

of like-minded individuals in the Netherlands, essentially prohibited the development of a successor group.

3.6   An overview of the court cases

The first decade of the 21st century saw the Dutch government enact various legal and policy measures intended to increase its counterterrorism effectiveness.[94] One of these was the Crimes of Terrorism Act, which was passed in August 2004. This Act enabled judges to pass heavier sentences on suspects if they were found to have committed their crimes *with terrorist intent*. It also specified recruitment for terrorism and membership of an organization that intended to commit terrorist crimes as distinct offenses. The latter became known as article 140a of the Dutch Criminal Code, which was based on article 140 that deals with organized crime.[95]

On 26 July 2005, Van Gogh's assassin was found guilty of, inter alia, murder with a terrorist intent, multiple counts of attempted murder on bystanders and police officers, and threatening Hirsi Ali with terrorist intent. He was sentenced to life in prison.[96] In March 2006, the first judgment was passed on whether the Hofstadgroup had constituted a terrorist organization. On 10 March, the Rotterdam District Court found nine out of fourteen suspects guilty of membership of a terrorist organization as described in the recently minted Article 140a.[97]

However, in early 2008 The Hague Court of Appeal acquitted seven of them on this particular count, arguing that '[t]he Hofstadgroup had insufficient organizational substance to warrant the existence of an organization as intended in articles 140 and 140a'.[98] This judgment was in turn revoked in February 2010, when the Supreme Court ordered a partial retrial after ruling that the Court of Appeal's grounds for acquittal had been partly based on an incorrect interpretation of the law.[99] The cases of these seven individuals were referred to the Amsterdam Court of Appeal. In December 2010, that Court ruled that the defendants had indeed participated in a criminal

---

94   Commissie Evaluatie Antiterrorismebeleid, 'Naar Een Integrale Evaluatie Van Antiterrorismemaatregelen', 16-18.
95   Donner, 'Wet Van 24 Juni 2004', 1-9.
96   Amsterdam District Court, 'LJN AU0025', 15-16.
97   Rotterdam District Court, 'LJN AV5108', 3, 42-44.
98   The Hague Court of Appeal, 'LJN BC4178', 1; 'LJN BC4183', 1; 'LJN BC4182', 1; 'LJN BC4171', 1; 'LJN BC2576', 1; 'LJN BC4129', 1; 'LJN BC4177', 1.
99   Supreme Court of the Netherlands, 'LJN BK5175', 1.

and terrorist organization.[100] After another referral to the Supreme Court, however, the Den Bosch Court of Appeal ruled in June 2015 that two of these suspects had not been members of a terrorist organization after all.[101]

The trials against the six Piranha suspects followed a similar course. On 1 December 2006, the Rotterdam District Court found five of the defendants guilty of preparation for or furtherance of a terrorist offense. However, the Court did not convict them of constituting a terrorist organization. One suspect was acquitted of the charges brought against him.[102] On the second of October 2008, however, The Hague Court of Appeal ruled that four of those convicted in 2006 had indeed been members of a terrorist organization.[103] In late 2011, the Supreme Court decreed a retrial for three of them. In one case, the Supreme Court found that the defense had not been given access to all relevant intelligence sources.[104] With regard to the other two individuals, the Court ruled that participation in a terrorist organization had been insufficiently demonstrated.[105] On 25 March 2014, the Amsterdam Court of Appeal once again convicted two of these three individuals for membership of a terrorist organization, but acquitted the third on this count.[106]

3.7 Conclusion

The preceding pages reveal more about the Hofstadgroup than simply the most prominent activities of its participants. For instance, this overview has made clear that on the whole the Hofstadgroup *did* very little that had any direct bearing on (preparations for) terrorism. Only a small inner circle of extremist participants showed signs of interest in conducting an attack or joining jihadist insurgents overseas. Secondly, even among the minority of participants who appeared to be interested in conducting acts of terrorism, there were very few indications of *communal* efforts. After initial signs of working together in 2003's trips abroad and the connections that were established with a jihadist suspect in Spain, 2004 was characterized

---

100 Amsterdam Court of Appeal, 'LJN BO7690', 35-36; 'LJN BO8032', 40-43; 'LJN BO9014', 39-40; 'LJN BO9015', 41-42; 'LJN BO9016', 36-37; 'LJN BO9017', 38; 'LJN BO9018', 41-44.
101 'Terreurverdachten Hofstadgroep'.
102 Rotterdam District Court, 'LJN AZ3589', 40, 42-44.
103 The Hague Court of Appeal, 'LJN BF3987', 1.
104 Willems, 'Zaak Tegen Terrorismeverdachte'.
105 Beentjes, 'Zaken Terreurverdachten Moeten Over'.
106 Amsterdam Court of Appeal, 'GHAMS:2014:914', 23; 'GHAMS:2014:905', 21; 'Drie Jaar Cel'.

by individual and ad hoc activities. Not until 2005's 'Piranha' continuation did the Hofstadgroup once again show signs of a communal pursuit of shared goals.

These findings thus provide some first insights into the group's organizational characteristics, providing a link to the focus of the next chapter. They also suggest that involvement in the Hofstadgroup could take on a variety of forms. Only a minority of participants actually became involved in (preparations for) acts of terrorism. This underlines the importance of keeping in mind that 'involvement', and the processes that preceded it, were distinctly heterogeneous in nature. A crucial question that this poses, is what distinguished those who planned or perpetrated acts of terrorism from those who did not. Before the analysis can turn to the factors underlying the various involvement processes, however, the descriptive part of this study needs to be completed. To that end, the next chapter delves deeper into what the Hofstadgroup was by discussing the group's ideological and organizational nature, as well as shedding further light on the degree to which it was communally involved in terrorism.

4 The ideological and organizational nature of the Hofstadgroup[1]

The Hofstadgroup is frequently described as a homegrown jihadist terrorist network[2] and has even been labeled a 'quintessential' one.[3] But to what extent is this designation justified? Before examining how and why involvement in this group came about, it must be made clear what participants were becoming involved *in*. The present chapter discusses what the Hofstadgroup was by critically examining the characteristics commonly attributed to it, beginning with its 'homegrown' dimension and continuing to its ideology. Subsequently, the chapter discusses the Hofstadgroup's organizational characteristics and finally the degree to which it was communally involved in terrorism.

4.1 Drawing the Hofstadgroup's boundaries

When discussing what the Hofstadgroup was, a first difficulty is defining the group's size; who exactly were its participants? Due to its ambiguous organizational structure and lack of anything resembling a formal list of 'members', this is a difficult question to answer. In this book, the Hofstadgroup is assumed to have encompassed approximately 38 individuals.[4] This number includes all those arrested as suspected group members during the various police investigations, witnesses who participated in group meetings at least once, as well as any individuals listed in suspects' or witnesses' statements that also matched this criterion. This definition of 'participation' is by no means definitive but it provides a basic way of demarcating the group's boundaries. It is also supported by an interviewee, who explained that the group was broader than those arrested following Van Gogh's murder.[5] It appears that the public prosecutor was aware of this, but decided to keep several individuals out of the criminal case against the Hofstadgroup in order to keep it manageable.[6]

1   This chapter has been published in amended form as: Schuurman, Eijkman, and Bakker, 'The Hofstadgroup Revisited'.
2   E.g. Nesser, *Jihad in Europe*, 332-33; Silber and Bhatt, 'Radicalization in the West', 6.
3   Vidino, 'The Hofstad Group', 579.
4   Silber, *The Al Qaeda Factor*, 206-24.
5   Former Hofstadgroup Participant 3, 'Personal Interview 1', 3-4.
6   Police Investigator 2, 'Personal Interview 1', 1.

4.2 Homegrown jihadism

What exactly makes a jihadist group a homegrown one? Crone and Harrow argue that the concept of homegrown terrorism has two dimensions; belonging, or the extent to which the terrorists are raised in or attached to the West, and their degree of operational autonomy from foreign terrorist groups.[7] The 9/11 attacks, for instance, were clearly *not* a homegrown operation, as the attackers were foreign nationals rather than U.S. citizens and because the attacks were coordinated by and executed on behalf of al-Qaeda. Seen from this perspective, how 'homegrown' was the Hofstadgroup?

4.2.1 The Hofstadgroup's homegrown aspects

Looking at 'belonging' first, the majority of the 38 participants were born in the Netherlands or held double nationalities. However, there was a sizable minority of foreigners (seven Moroccans, one Syrian). Some of these foreign nationals had spent a significant part of their lives in the Netherlands, making it likely they felt a considerable degree of belonging to the country despite not being citizens. Yet two of the foreign nationals with prominent positions in the group's radical and extremist inner circle were recent immigrants and thus unlikely to have felt strongly attached to the country; the middle-aged Syrian man known as Abu Khaled who first arrived in Germany as an asylum seeker in 1995 and a young Moroccan man who played an important role in the group's 2005 resurgence.[8] The group was thus mainly but not exclusively a Dutch phenomenon.

Similarly, the Hofstadgroup seems to have enjoyed a high, but not absolute degree of autonomy. Several participants had connections to foreign nationals whose backgrounds suggest a possible link with Islamist terrorist groups. For instance, Van Gogh's murderer was acquainted with two Chechen men, one of whose uncle was suspected by the American Federal Bureau of Investigation (FBI) of supplying Chechen jihadists with weapons.[9] In addition to Abu Khaled, the Syrian preacher mentioned above, three other middle-aged Syrian men with ties to the Muslim Brotherhood also appeared on the group's fringes.[10] Characterizing the nature of these connections is difficult as they were never investigated in detail. It appears,

---

7 Crone and Harrow, 'Homegrown Terrorism in the West', 521.
8 Chorus and Olgun, *Broeders*, 40.
9 Dienst Nationale Recherche, 'RL8026', 01/01: 93-96; Derix, 'Hoe Kwam Toch'.
10 Dienst Nationale Recherche, 'RL8026', 01/01: 32, 37; VERD: 19664-825; GET: 8349, 8415.

however, that none of these men tried to exert any kind of direct control over the Hofstadgroup, leaving its autonomy intact.

The clearest examples of foreign extremists exerting some form of operational control over (parts of) the group stem from October 2003. The first concerned an Islamist militant residing in Spain, the second centered on an unnamed Pakistani or Afghan 'emir' who had apparently instructed one of the Hofstadgroup participants to return to the Netherlands to 'collect balloons'.[11] Suspicions that these connections might be in some way related to an impending terrorist attack could not be substantiated. Instead, it seems likely that the militant in Spain sought the group's assistance with acquiring a passport and finances and that the emir's instructions revolved around trying to motivate other young Muslims to travel to Pakistan or Afghanistan. The latter point is supported by the fact that two Hofstadgroup participants undertook a 'recruitment drive' via the Internet during the fall of 2003 with precisely that purpose in mind.[12]

As detailed in the previous chapter, the first round of arrests in October 2003 and the failure of the second trip to Pakistan or Afghanistan at the end of the year made the group more cautious and inward looking. While some participants continued to have connections with foreign nationals suspected of extremist views or even terrorist intentions, there were no indications that such links impinged on the group's autonomy in any clear sense. In short, it appears that the Hofstadgroup was predominantly an autonomously operating group and that it became relatively more so from late 2003 onward. At the same time, the small number of examples of outside interference and the prominent positions held by at least two foreign nationals mean that the group was not some kind of 'ideal type' of the homegrown jihadist typology.

4.3   Ideology and terrorism

Maynard defines ideology as 'a distinctive system of normative, semantic, and/or reputedly factual ideas, typically shared by members of groups or societies, which underpins their understandings of their political world and shapes their political behavior'.[13] Ideologies are cognitive frameworks that provide a way of ordering information about the world and imbuing

---

11   Ibid., 01/01: 23.
12   Ibid., 123-26.
13   Maynard, 'Rethinking the Role of Ideology', 824.

it with meaning.¹⁴ Extremist ideologies can justify violence through their ability to provide motives, (e.g. by painting a specific group as a dangerous threat) legitimacy (e.g. by depicting the use of force as the only option) and rationalizations (e.g. utopian ideals justify using violence).¹⁵ Extremist ideological beliefs are also an effective way of attenuating individuals' inhibitions against killing or harming others by coupling an acute sense of crisis with a black and white worldview; the in-group's existence is threatened by implacable foes; exceptional circumstances that legitimize and necessitate the use of violence.¹⁶

As later chapters will explore in detail, ideological convictions alone are insufficient to explain involvement in a terrorist group or participation in an act of terrorism. Ideological beliefs *may* directly motivate such behavior, but they are generally one of many factors and not a sufficient explanation in and of themselves. That being said, ideological beliefs can play an important role in *guiding* behavior. As Sageman writes, the global jihadi movement is driven by a 'Salafi ideology [that] determines its mission, sets its goals, and guides its tactics'.¹⁷ A group's ideology can therefore provide important clues to its stance on the use of political violence, identifying perceived enemies and allies, clarifying the goals being strived for and, crucially, the conditions under which the use of violence is seen as legitimate. Examining a terrorist or extremist group's ideology is therefore a key aspect of reaching a more accurate understanding of its nature.

The Hofstadgroup is commonly designated a 'Salafi', 'jihadist', or 'Salafi-Jihadist' group.¹⁸ Salafi-Jihadists form the militant branch of the heterogeneous and international Salafist movement. Its devotees share a desire to return to a 'pure' Islam as practiced by the faith's earliest adherents (the Salafs) and place a strong emphasis on a strict and literalistic adherence to the precepts found in the Quran and the examples set by the Prophet Muhammad.¹⁹ Contemporary Salafists also share a stringent form of monotheism that stresses the concept of 'tawhid', or the oneness of god

14   Crenshaw, *Explaining Terrorism*, 90.
15   Maynard, 'Rethinking the Role of Ideology', 828-30.
16   Crenshaw, *Explaining Terrorism*, 90; Della Porta, *Social Movements*, 174-76; Juergensmeyer, *Terror in the Mind of God*, 149-63, 174-79; Neumann, 'The Message', 47-48; Pyszczynski, Motyl, and Abdollahi, 'Righteous Violence', 26.
17   Sageman, *Understanding Terror Networks*, 1.
18   Bartolo, 'Decentralised Leadership in Contemporary Jihadism', 51; Nesser, 'Lessons Learned', 3; Nesser, 'Chronology of Jihadism', 936; Noivo, 'Jihadism in Portugal', 6; Sageman, 'Confronting Al-Qaeda', 5; Silber and Bhatt, 'Radicalization in the West', 16; Vidino, 'The Hofstad Group', 587; Vidino, 'Radicalization, Linkage, and Diversity', 4.
19   Wiktorowicz, 'Anatomy of the Salafi Movement', 207, 209.

and his exclusive right to be worshiped as the sole creator and lawmaker in the universe. As such, secular laws and institutions are rejected as idolatry in the sense that they violate tawhid by worshiping the man-made instead of the divinely-inspired.[20]

Reflecting the multiple perspectives from which Islamist thinkers throughout history have looked to the Salafs for guidance on worldly problems, several key distinctions can still be drawn in today's Salafist movement. These distinctions stem not so much from key principles or the goals being pursued, but from disagreements on how to achieve them. Wiktorowicz has popularized a three-fold division of the Salafist movement into 'politicos' who strive to achieve their theocratic ideals through political participation, 'purists' who eschew politics in favor of proselytization and religious education, and 'jihadists' who believe revolutionary violence is necessary to bring about change and safeguard a community of believers beleaguered by apostasy, heresy, and the aggressive geopolitics of unbelievers such as the United States.[21]

Although their ultimate goal is to bring about change in Muslim lands, prominent Salafi-Jihadist groups such as al-Qaeda have internationalized their struggle. This development is at least partly based on the idea that the 'near enemy' of corrupt, un-Islamic Middle Eastern regimes cannot be toppled until the 'far enemy' of Western governments that support them, and which have invaded Muslim states, have been forced to withdraw their influence and presence from the Islamic regions of the world.[22] As such, Salafi-Jihadist ideology provides a justification for the use of political violence against Western targets based on a fusion of geopolitical and religious motives. A second ideological justification for violence that is important for understanding the Hofstadgroup revolves around the practice of 'takfir', or excommunication. Because apostasy is a grave offense within Islam, denouncing Muslims as unbelievers is a powerful theological weapon that legitimizes the use of violence against rulers and people who are ostensibly co-religionists.[23]

It should be pointed out that Salafi-Jihadists are themselves not a homogeneous group. Important differences in terms of strategy and principle

---

20 Ibid., 207-10; Peters, 'Dutch Extremist Islamism', 151.
21 Wiktorowicz, 'Anatomy of the Salafi Movement', 207-39. For an alternative typology, see: Maher, *Salafi-Jihadism*, 8-13.
22 Brooke, 'Jihadist Strategic Debates', 212-18; Turner, 'From Cottage Industry to International Organisation', 544-45.
23 Cozzens, 'Al-Takfir Wa'l Hijra', 500-01, 503; Wiktorowicz, 'Anatomy of the Salafi Movement', 229-30.

remain. For instance, although al-Qaeda eventually focused its efforts on fighting the 'far enemy' epitomized by the United States, the organization was initially hamstrung by internal discord over this matter. Another important distinction to keep in mind for the discussion of the Hofstadgroup's ideology is that although the principle of takfir is recognized by a broad range of radical and extremist groups, they differ in their interpretation of when the criteria for excommunication are met.[24] As the following paragraphs illustrate, many of the divisions within the contemporary Salafist movement, and discussions over the legitimate use of takfir, were mirrored among the Hofstadgroup's participants.

4.3.1 The Hofstadgroup's ideology

Shared religious beliefs were the most important factor binding Hofstadgroup participants together.[25] In a general sense, the entire group can be positioned within the broad Salafist revivalist movement. This is evidenced first and foremost by the primacy attached to a strict interpretation of tawhid and the related necessity to reject all secular governments and institutions. These themes appear to have been the most frequent subjects of group meetings, and the essence of the teachings of Abu Khaled, the middle-aged Syrian man who provided the group with religious instruction.[26] Equally revealing, one interviewee declared that the first question asked of newcomers was 'do you know what tawhid means?'[27] Many participants possessed (parts of) a large digital 'library' containing a wide range of works by Islamic scholars, jurists, and theologians representing various strands of Salafist thinking.[28] These ranged from the influential thirteenth-century jurist and Salafist scholar Ahmad Ibn Taymiyya to more contemporary and politicized authors such as Sayyid Qutb, an erstwhile militant leader of Egypt's Muslim Brotherhood.

---

24 Cozzens, 'Al-Takfir Wa'l Hijra', 500-01, 503; Wiktorowicz, 'Anatomy of the Salafi Movement', 228-34.
25 Former Hofstadgroup Participant 1, 'Personal Interview 1', 2; Former Hofstadgroup Participant 3, 'Personal Interview 1', 2; Former Hofstadgroup Participant 4, 'Personal Interview 2', 1; Former Hofstadgroup Participant 5, 'Personal Interview 1', 2.
26 Dienst Nationale Recherche, 'RL8026', 01/13: 136-40; 01/17: 4002, 4026, 4048-50, 4090-91, 4096, 98, 4129, 4179, 4146, 4201; AHB02/26: 3796-803; Former Hofstadgroup Participant 1, 'Personal Interview 1', 2-3; 'Personal Interview 2', 8-9; A[.], 'Deurwaarders', 24; Erkel, *Samir*, 190-92; Vermaat, *Nederlandse Jihad*, 140, 94.
27 'weet je wat Tawheed inhoudt?': Former Hofstadgroup Participant 3, 'Personal Interview 1', 2.
28 Dienst Nationale Recherche, 'RL8026', 01/13: 47; NCTV Employee 1, 'Personal Interview 2', 2; Wubbels, 'Mohammed B. Strijdt Verder'.

Surprisingly, however, the Hofstadgroup's participants were largely but not exclusively drawn to the Salafi-Jihadist strand of thinking.[29] For instance, two persons with misgivings about the ideas espoused by the more extreme elements within the group asked a Dutch Salafist imam loyal to the Saudi-Arabian regime for advice, thereby displaying an allegiance to such established religious authority reminiscent of 'purist' sensibilities.[30] Two others candidly declared during police questioning that they supported the introduction of Islamic law, but only if a majority of people in the Netherlands voted for it, thus hinting at opinions more in line with politicos than jihadists.[31] Another three seem to have had little interest in radical or fundamentalist interpretations of Islam altogether.[32]

Within the confines of the Hofstadgroup's largely Salafist interpretation of Islam, there appears to have been a surprising degree of tolerance for differing opinions. It seems that this was due in part to a sense among the more extremist participants that newcomers could not be expected to immediately embrace 'true' Islam.[33] Once someone was considered a true brother or sister in the Hofstadgroup's extremist views on Islam, dissension was treated with markedly less indifference and could trigger considerable verbal outrage.[34] Still, the lack of a singular, exclusively extremist, and rigorously enforced 'Hofstadgroup ideology' is striking.

These findings add a degree of nuance to discussions about the beliefs of the Hofstadgroup's participants. But they should not detract from the overarching conclusion that most of the group's participants displayed an affinity with an extremist Salafi-Jihadist interpretation of Islam. This can be gleaned from their possession of documents, videos, and audio recordings which emphasized the legitimacy and necessity of waging armed jihad and their adoration of key figures in the jihadist movement such as Bin Laden and the leader of al-Qaeda in Iraq, the outspokenly violent Jordanian militant Abu Musab al-Zarqawi.[35]

---

29 Vermaat, *Nederlandse Jihad*, 128-29, 83.
30 Dienst Nationale Recherche, 'RL8026', GET: 4018-20, 4129, 4132, 4146, 4148, 4159; Groen and Kranenberg, *Women Warriors*, 98-99.
31 Dienst Nationale Recherche, 'RL8026', VERD: 20083, 20567.
32 Ibid., VERD: 19477-78, 19480, 19597, 19654, 20522, 20535, 20566; Former Hofstadgroup Participant 2, 'Personal Interview 1', 2-4, 6-7.
33 Former Hofstadgroup Participant 4, 'Personal Interview 2', 1; Former Hofstadgroup Participant 5, 'Personal Interview 1', 3.
34 Former Hofstadgroup Participant 5, 'Personal Interview 1', 3.
35 Dienst Nationale Recherche, 'RL8026', 01/01: 131, 134, 142-47, 160-61, 171-72; 01/13: 47; Former Hofstadgroup Participant 1, 'Personal Interview 1', 6; 'Personal Interview 2', 21, 33; Former Hofstadgroup Participant 3, 'Personal Interview 1', 9; A[.], 'Deurwaarders', 7.

Although a large segment of the Hofstadgroup subscribed to an ideology that legitimizes and even calls for the use of violence against Western states and impious Muslims, this did not immediately translate into a desire to commit terrorism. Initially, the group's most militant participants took from Salafi-Jihadism the understanding that jihad was a personal duty, yet saw it as a *defensive* form of warfare against foreign aggressors. In 2003, this led four participants to attempt to reach conflict zones in Chechnya and Pakistan or Afghanistan.[36] There is little to suggest that these trips were made to prepare for a terrorist attack in the Netherlands. Instead, the available data, such as a farewell letter left by one of them, indicates they intended to stay with the insurgents.[37] Essentially, for the main part of 2003, core participants in the Hofstadgroup were would-be foreign fighters, but not yet would-be terrorists.[38]

Towards the fall of 2003, the group's most militant participants increasingly began to see jihad as something that could be waged *offensively* as well. Two developments were central to this change. In October 2003, the Dutch police arrested several participants and found one of them in possession of materials indicating an interest in constructing an improvised explosive device.[39] Based on an unfinished autobiography written while in custody and a martyr's video recorded in 2005, this individual came to justify violence against the Netherlands for its (military) support of the United States and what he saw as unwarranted aggression against Muslim countries.[40] Numerous other participants developed a strong sense of antipathy towards the Dutch government for similar reasons.[41] One interviewee explicitly named the Dutch military presence in Iraq as contributing to changing the group's focus from participation in the international jihad to using violence in the Netherlands.[42] Catalyzing this shift was the 2004 terrorist attack in Madrid. To the group's most militant participants, the bombing represented a dramatic demonstration that

36 Dienst Nationale Recherche, 'RL8026', 01/01: 33; 01/13: 140-43; GET: 18061-62, 18840, 18452; A[.], 'Deurwaarders', 10-19.
37 Dienst Nationale Recherche, 'RL8026', 01/13: 163; AHD08/37: 8571, 8767; AHD09/38: 9055-56; A[.], 'Deurwaarders', 10-11; De Graaf, *Gevaarlijke Vrouwen*, 258-59; Nesser, *Jihad in Europe*, 349.
38 Making them similar to other jihadist extremists in the Netherlands. See: De Bie, De Poot, and Van der Leun, 'Shifting Modus Operandi', 422-35.
39 Dienst Nationale Recherche, 'RL8026', 01/01: 25-26.
40 A[.], 'Deurwaarders', 4-5, 9; NOVA, 'Videotestament Samir A.'.
41 Dienst Nationale Recherche, 'RL8026', 01/01: 131; 01/13: 61; 01/17: 4069; AHA05/22: 2228; Peters, 'De Ideologische En Religieuze Ontwikkeling', Appendix: Overzicht teksten geschreven of vertaald door Mohammed B., 32-34.
42 Former Hofstadgroup Participant 1, 'Personal Interview 2', 23.

terrorism in Europe was both practically feasible and seen as permissible by the international jihadist movement.[43]

Late 2003 also saw the group's extremist inner circle begin to consider terrorism in the Netherlands for religious reasons. During the fall, one individual jubilantly chatted online about slaughtering 'all those fake Muslims' and in a later conversation claimed that Dutch Member of Parliament Geert Wilders, known for his strong criticism of Islam, should be killed for insulting the religion.[44] Another condemned 90% of the mujahedeen in Chechnya as apostates.[45] At this time, however, other participants including Abu Khaled who led many gatherings still advocated a modicum of restraint in wielding takfir as a theological weapon.[46] Based on participants' accounts, it seems that the use of takfir became increasingly indiscriminate from 2004 onward, leading to internal disagreements, and causing several participants to distance themselves from the group.[47] According to one former participant, judging whether other Muslims' actions and words were grounds for excommunication was an almost everyday practice.[48]

Some participants went so far as to excommunicate virtually everyone who was not a part of their group; one allegedly even 'did takfir' on Bin Laden while others excommunicated each other.[49] The extremes to which some took takfir problematizes the extent to which these individuals can be considered as falling within the Salafi-Jihadist ideological current. While a broad range of Islamist groups wield takfir, they usually do so to delegitimize Muslim governments in order to justify violent resistance.[50] Excommunicating vast swathes of Muslims appears to be more in line with extremist sects such as Egypt's now defunct Takfir wal Hijra.[51] There are no signs that (elements of) the Hofstadgroup ever claimed to be successors to this extremist offshoot of the Muslim Brotherhood. However, some former participants did refer to the Hofstadgroup's most avid excommunicators

---

43   Ibid., 22; Former Hofstadgroup Participant 4, 'Personal Interview 2', 5.
44   'al die nep moslims': Dienst Nationale Recherche, 'RL8026', 01/01: 125; AHD09/38: 9077; Alberts and Derix, 'Balkenende in 2003'.
45   Dienst Nationale Recherche, 'RL8026', AHD08/37: 8550.
46   Ibid., AHA05/22: 2167-68; AHA09/26: 3799-803; Former Hofstadgroup Participant 4, 'Personal Interview 1', 1.
47   Dienst Nationale Recherche, 'RL8026', 01/17: 4002-03, 4018-20, 4030, 4048-58, 4062, 4085-86, 4092, 4100, 4125-127, 4129, 4204; Former Hofstadgroup Participant 4, 'Personal Interview 1', 1; Groen and Kranenberg, *Women Warriors*, 36-37, 93.
48   Former Hofstadgroup Participant 3, 'Personal Interview 1', 2-3.
49   Ibid., 3; Groen and Kranenberg, *Women Warriors*, 166, 181.
50   Cozzens, 'Al-Takfir Wa'l Hijra', 497, 500-01.
51   Ibid., 489-510.

as 'takfiris', and one interviewee classified the group as 'sect like'.[52] Like the Salafists and jihadist that inspired it, the Hofstadgroup was clearly not an ideologically homogeneous entity, but one in which various currents of thought were reflected.

Crucial in sustaining and strengthening this trend towards a greater emphasis on religious justifications for violence, was the murderer-to-be of Van Gogh. In July 2004, he translated a section of Ibn Taymiyya's work which postulates that it is a Muslim's duty to kill anyone who insults the Prophet Muhammad.[53] This led the assassin to believe it was his personal duty to commit violence in defense of his faith. Although the murderer was the only one to act on his beliefs, his ideas on religiously justified violence were shared by at least the group's inner circle. Several other participants made explicit statements in favor of murdering Ayaan Hirsi Ali, especially after the short Islam-critical film she had made with Van Gogh, *Submission, part 1*, was broadcast at the end of August 2004.[54] Likewise, various sources suggest tacit and even outspoken support for the killing of Van Gogh on religious grounds. One inner-circle participant openly told the police that Van Gogh deserved to be executed for his offenses to Islam.[55]

Given these developments, it is interesting to note that the participants in 2005's 'Piranha' resurgence of the Hofstadgroup appear to have reverted to predominantly geopolitical justifications for terrorist attacks in the Netherlands. While the police found evidence that the suspects had been gathering information on the addresses of several Dutch politicians, most of them did not have an outspokenly 'anti-Islam' profile. More importantly, in a martyr's video recorded in late 2005, one of the ringleaders strongly condemned the Dutch government for its involvement in the Iraq war and threatened violence against the Dutch people for their complicity in this endeavor.[56] These fluctuations in the justifications for violence, from an emphasis on geopolitics in 2003, to religious motives in 2004 and back to geopolitics in 2005, indicate just how difficult it is to speak of a clearly defined or commonly shared 'Hofstadgroup ideology'.

Like the militants and scholars who inspired them, the group's most extremist participants held differing and changing views on the form jihad

---

52 Dienst Nationale Recherche, 'RL8026', 01/17: 4002-204; Former Hofstadgroup Participant 3, 'Personal Interview 1', 3.
53 Peters, 'Dutch Extremist Islamism', 155-56; Public Prosecutor 1, 'Personal Interview 1', 11.
54 Dienst Nationale Recherche, 'RL8026', 01/13: 74, 161-62.
55 Ibid., VERD: 20462; Chorus and Olgun, *Broeders*, 21; Vermaat, *Nederlandse Jihad*, 41.
56 Dienst Nationale Recherche, 'Piranha', 34-35; NOVA, 'Videotestament Samir A.'; Groen and Kranenberg, 'Samir A. In Afgesplitste Terreurgroep'.

was to take. While some were narrowly motivated to punish blasphemers, others were inspired by geopolitical events to defend the Muslim ummah; while some practiced takfir without restraint, others acknowledged at least some boundaries. While in 2003 militant participants saw jihad in a defensive light and sought to aid overseas Islamist insurgents in their fight against foreign aggressors, an 'offensive' interpretation of jihad that legitimized violence in the Netherlands began to take hold from late 2003 onward. Furthermore, while most participants adhered to the Salafi-Jihadist current, a minority more closely resembled its political and purist strands of thought, and some even appeared completely disinterested in religious matters.

These conclusions are important not just because they infuse some nuance into the debate about the group's nature. The relative 'tolerance' for views not completely in line with Salafist-Jihadist principles, the sect-like elements that took the excommunication of Muslims to extremes, and the different opinions on how to implement jihad meant that the Hofstadgroup remained an ideologically somewhat ambiguous entity. As a result, there was never a concrete blueprint for what the group hoped to achieve, no clear ideological foundation that could form the basis for communal efforts. This relative diversity of ideological views also contributed to ambiguity in an organizational sense, as at least initially it appears that essentially anyone who subscribed to basic Salafist principles could participate. Ideologically, the Hofstadgroup was largely but never exclusively wedded to views that supported the use of terrorist violence.

4.4 Defining terrorist organizations

The Hofstadgroup's organizational characteristics are assessed using three contrasting perspectives found in the literature on terrorism. The first is Crenshaw's view of terrorist groups as *organizations* characterized by a defined structure, a systematic decision-making process, clearly defined roles and tasks for members, recognized leadership and authority and, lastly, the collective pursuit of clearly defined organizational goals.[57] Second, there is Sageman's concept of contemporary jihadist groups as ambiguously defined *networks*.[58] One of the few at least somewhat specific definitions of a jihadist network is given by the Dutch intelligence service AIVD, who describe it

---

57 Crenshaw, *Explaining Terrorism*, 69.
58 Sageman, *Leaderless Jihad*, 140-43.

as a 'fluid, dynamic, vaguely delineated structure comprising a number of interrelated persons (radical Muslims) who are linked both individually and on an aggregate level (cells/groups). They have at least a temporary common interest, i.e. the pursuit of a jihadism-related goal (including terrorism)'.[59] Finally, Ligon et al. describe *groups* as social arrangements that lack shared efforts directed at attaining a commonly held goal.[60]

4.4.1 The Hofstadgroup's organizational structure

Evidence for a defined organizational structure is almost entirely absent in the case of the Hofstadgroup until its second incarnation in early 2005. To begin with, many participants have categorically denied the existence of any kind of formal group or organization.[61] Furthermore, no 'official' list of participants was ever encountered and there does not appear to have been an initiation process for aspirants nor any other sort of (semi-)formal mechanism for distinguishing between those within the group and those outside of it.[62] Instead, the Hofstadgroup resembled an amorphous community of like-minded individuals spread over several nearby cities.[63] It was not truly one group but a collection of smaller subgroups, revolving around a nucleus in The Hague and one in Amsterdam.[64] As a result of this lack of centralization, not all participants knew each other.[65] The spread-out nature of the group further underlines the ambiguity of its organizational structure.

There is even considerable confusion over whether a commonly accepted name for the group existed. Some publications, videos, and websites related to the Hofstadgroup began to feature a logo bearing the titles 'Lions of Tawheed' and 'Polder Mujahideen'[66] from early 2004 onward. Yet there are contradictory accounts regarding the degree to which these monikers

---

59 General Intelligence and Security Service, 'Violent Jihad in the Netherlands', 14.
60 Ligon et al., 'Putting the "O" in VEOs', 120.
61 Dienst Nationale Recherche, 'RL8026', VERD: 19476-77, 19866, 19918, 20005, 20017, 20080, 20228, 20363; GET: 18415; 01/17: 4099-4100; Former Hofstadgroup Participant 3, 'Personal Interview 1', 3-4; Former Hofstadgroup Participant 1, 'Personal Interview 2', 14-15.
62 Although one participant did drink the breast milk of the Syrian preacher's wife, this seemingly ritualistic act of bonding was not performed by others within the group and appears to have affirmed a private bond of friendship bordering on kinship rather than a pledge of allegiance. Dienst Nationale Recherche, 'RL8026', VERD: 19744-45; Nesser, *Jihad in Europe*, 345.
63 Former Hofstadgroup Participant 3, 'Personal Interview 1', 3-4; Van der Hulst, 'Terroristische Netwerken', 8-27.
64 Former Hofstadgroup Participant 4, 'Personal Interview 2', 1.
65 Vermaat, *Nederlandse Jihad*, 164; Former Hofstadgroup Participant 4, 'Personal Interview 1', 1.
66 A 'polder' is a characteristic feature of the Dutch landscape.

were used by the wider group.[67] While one witness recalled hearing one or two individuals referring to themselves as 'Lions of Tawheed', an interviewee mentioned that this term was used largely in jest.[68] Another former participant did identify himself as a 'Lion of Tawheed' but implied that it was not so much a specific group name as a broader term used to express one's adherence to this core tenet of Salafist Islam.[69] The name 'Lions of Tawheed' seemed to play a more prominent role during 2005's Hofstadgroup resurgence, where it turns up in association with numerous publications and videos produced and promulgated by one of the core participants.[70] It remains unclear, however, whether the other participants in the Piranha group designated themselves as such.

In the wake of Van Gogh's murder, two individuals within the extremist inner circle were overheard identifying themselves with the murderer and using the name the 'Brigades of the Islamic Jihad'.[71] Like the 'Lions of Tawheed' designation, it remains unclear whether this truly reflected a commonly used group name or merely individual braggadocio. Based on the currently available data, it seems likely that these examples reflect the shared kinship of the group's extremist inner circle and indicate some early ad hoc attempts at forging a stronger collective identity among them. It is unlikely, however, that these designations reflected the existence of a tangible group structure or that they encompassed the wider Hofstadgroup.

The Hofstadgroup lacked true leadership or even a rudimentary hierarchical structure for the better part of its existence.[72] But it did have individuals who stood higher on the social pecking order through, for example, their greater command of Arabic. Van Gogh's murderer was esteemed for his knowledge of Islam, yet he does not appear to have occupied a leadership position and is frequently referred to as a rather quiet and withdrawn individual.[73] The person who most closely resembled the group's leader was Abu Khaled, the middle-aged Syrian

---

67 The logo may not even have been made by a participant: Former Hofstadgroup Participant 4, 'Personal Interview 2', 1.
68 Dienst Nationale Recherche, 'RL8026', 01/17: 4099; Former Hofstadgroup Participant 3, 'Personal Interview 1', 5.
69 Former Hofstadgroup Participant 1, 'Personal Interview 2', 17.
70 Meijer, 'Inhoud Van De Religieuze', 29-30.
71 Dienst Nationale Recherche, 'RL8026', AHA07/24: 3082; Nesser, *Jihad in Europe*, 353-54.
72 Public Prosecutor 1, 'Personal Interview 1', 51; Former Hofstadgroup Participant 3, 'Personal Interview 1', 4; Former Hofstadgroup Participant 1, 'Personal Interview 2', 31-32; Dienst Nationale Recherche, 'RL8026', VERD: 19479, 19876.
73 Former Hofstadgroup Participant 3, 'Personal Interview 1', 4; Former Hofstadgroup Participant 1, 'Personal Interview 2', 13; NCTV Employee 1, 'Personal Interview 2', 2; Dienst Nationale

man mentioned earlier. His role as a religious instructor gave him a prominent and well-respected position within the group and a good deal of authority.[74] At the same time, there is little to suggest his influence extended beyond providing religious instruction; there are no concrete signs that he took a leadership position in the sense of shaping the Hofstadgroup organizationally or setting out operational goals.[75] Two former participants labeled the Syrian as an important source of religious knowledge and a good teacher, but not a leader or even a particularly inspiring individual.[76]

The conclusion that the Hofstadgroup lacked clear leadership needs to be qualified somewhat when looking at 2005's Piranha case. This 'second wave' of the group brought with it tentative signs of a burgeoning hierarchy. Most notably, two individuals who had belonged to the 'original' Hofstadgroup's inner circle began to direct the activities of some other group participants, for instance by instructing them to rent an apartment in Brussels that was used to hold meetings.[77] Additionally, there were signs that these two ringleaders provided direction to group participants on matters related to the planning of as many as three tentative terrorist plots.[78] The Piranha group never developed a formal hierarchy, but these developments indicate it might have been headed in that direction had arrests in June and October 2005 not put an end to the group.

Two other attributes of terrorist *organizations*, a systematic decision-making process and the distribution of clearly defined organizational roles and tasks, were also largely absent. For the most part, the group did little beyond holding frequent meetings where they discussed their extremist religious views or simply chatted and relaxed.[79] Whatever activities were undertaken were initiated on an ad hoc basis by individuals or by small groups of two or three, such as the attempts to reach foreign conflict zones during 2003.[80] There is little to indicate that these attempts were the result of a collectively made decision. Perhaps the strongest reference

Recherche, 'RL8026', VERD: 19868, 20212, 20227; Vidino, 'The Hofstad Group', 586-87; Public Prosecutor 2, 'Personal Interview 1', 4.
74   Dienst Nationale Recherche, 'RL8026', VERD: 19480, 19705-706, 19747; 01/17: 4095.
75   NCTV Employee 1, 'Personal Interview 1', 2; Public Prosecutor 1, 'Personal Interview 1', 8.
76   Former Hofstadgroup Participant 1, 'Personal Interview 2', 33; Former Hofstadgroup Participant 3, 'Personal Interview 1', 4.
77   Dienst Nationale Recherche, 'Piranha', 63, 187, 11782-85.
78   Ibid., 34-35, 8357-59, 8382-83, 8388, 8390-91; Vidino, 'The Hofstad Group', 584.
79   Former Hofstadgroup Participant 3, 'Personal Interview 1', 5; Former Hofstadgroup Participant 1, 'Personal Interview 3', 2.
80   Dienst Nationale Recherche, 'RL8026', 01/13: 140-43; Erkel, *Samir*, 194-97.

to a decision-making process stems from one of the letters left by Van Gogh's murderer, in which he advises the group to discuss whether or not to publish a pamphlet in which he threatens the Dutch people.[81] Examples of a distribution of tasks and roles are similarly weak and limited to the joint administration of at least one website and one participant's avowedly self-appointed task of publishing online anything written by Van Gogh's assassin-to-be.[82]

No data was encountered to suggest that participants in the 2005 Piranha case had developed a systematic decision-making process. There were, however, some indications that tasks relevant to the preparation of the three terrorist plots under consideration were distributed among participants. For instance, one participant was used as a courier, fetching a package containing information on potential targets for an attack from one of the group's ringleaders and bringing it to the other.[83] Likewise, the Islamic wife of one of these main protagonists actively tried to gather information on the addresses of several Dutch politicians.[84] Once again it should be stressed that these signs of a division of tasks were distinctly tentative. Even so, they do mark a change from the 'first wave' Hofstadgroup that again underscores the Piranha group's development towards a slightly more organizationally defined entity.

To summarize, until the Hofstadgroup's resurgence during 2005's Piranha case, it appears to have lacked virtually all of the characteristics of a terrorist organization as defined by Crenshaw. Its boundaries were vague and ambiguous and there was no hierarchy to speak of. Neither does the available data allow for the existence of a decision-making process or anything but the most basic division of tasks. While some of these organizational aspects became noticeably more pronounced in 2005, this development fell well short of qualifying the Hofstadgroup as an actual organization. The very absence of clear organizational aspects points instead towards the greater applicability of viewing the Hofstadgroup as a jihadist network. But the accuracy of this qualification revolves around the existence of one crucial element from the AIVD's definition of a jihadist network that has not yet been discussed in detail; namely, a common effort directed towards preparing an act of terrorism.

---

81 Dienst Nationale Recherche, 'RL8026', AHB03/27: 4043.
82 Ibid., AHA04/21: 1324-43; Former Hofstadgroup Participant 1, 'Personal Interview 2', 32.
83 Dienst Nationale Recherche, 'Piranha', 61.
84 Ibid., 36, 40-64, 156-62.

4.5 Group involvement in terrorism?

The available evidence suggests that, between the fall of 2003 and the final wave of arrests in October 2005, several participants considered committing acts of terrorism in the Netherlands. One of them carried out his intentions and murdered Van Gogh, whereas the other alleged plots did not advance beyond rudimentary planning stages. For the 'network' label to be applicable to the Hofstadgroup, these plots and the murder of Van Gogh need to have represented a communal effort. The crux of the matter is, however, that the only actual terrorist attack that took place appears to have been the work of an individual and that the majority of all the other potential or alleged attempts to plan an attack were likewise projects initiated by individuals or small sub-groups. Clear *group* involvement in terrorism was almost entirely absent until 2005's Piranha case.

House searches conducted by the Dutch police in October 2003 and June 2004 uncovered materials indicative of an interest in constructing an explosive device, but on both occasions those items belonged to one individual.[85] Although two other participants had made inquiries about fertilizer in a garden store in June 2004 as well, it is unclear whether this was a related development.[86] In any case, the police did not uncover evidence to substantiate a suspicion that the wider group was involved with the arrested individual's attempts at constructing a bomb. This was the same person who, also by himself, carried out the potential reconnaissance of the AIVD headquarters in June 2004.[87] Similarly, as chapter 3's chronological overview of events described in more detail, the police investigation failed to uncover any *concrete* evidence to support a conclusion other than that the murder of Van Gogh was planned, prepared, and executed by a single person.[88]

The hand grenade thrown at police officers in November 2004 was a premeditated act of violence. The two Hofstadgroup participants who occupied the apartment that was stormed by the police had discussed beforehand that they would use the weapon to resist arrest.[89] But as an essentially defensive measure, the intended effect of the violent act was limited to keeping the police at bay. It was not meant as a means of communicating with audiences beyond the direct targets of that violence and can therefore

---

85   Dienst Nationale Recherche, 'RL8026', 01/01: 38-45.
86   Ibid., 01/01: 40; 01/13: 175.
87   Ibid., 01/01: 38-45.
88   Van Straelen, 'Requisitoir in De Strafzaak Tegen Mohammed B.', 6-7.
89   Dienst Nationale Recherche, 'RL8026', AHA07/24: 3034, 3047.

not be classified as an act of terrorism. As such, this incident is given no further attention in this discussion of whether or not the Hofstadgroup was communally involved in (preparing) acts of terrorism.

In April 2005, the individual who had been found in possession of materials indicating an interest in constructing an explosive device was released from custody. Together with another extremist participant of the Hofstadgroup who had evaded capture following Van Gogh's murder, he tried to breathe new life into what was left of the Hofstadgroup. With the assistance of several other individuals who had been on the fringes of the Hofstadgroup during 2004, as many as three rudimentary plots appear to have been considered. The first, which came to the police's attention in June, revolved around attacking specific Dutch politicians. The second potential plot came to the fore in August and centered on shooting down an El-Al plane at Amsterdam's Schiphol Airport. In October 2005, the police received information indicating the possible existence of a third plot aimed at striking the AIVD headquarters. It was the brainchild of the remaining key player within the group, the same individual who was suspected of plotting a terrorist attack in October 2003 and June 2004.[90]

None of these plots appear to have developed beyond basic planning and preparatory stages and the alleged plan to attack an El-Al plane using an RPG comes across as distinctly fanciful. Given the controversial use of intelligence information as the evidentiary basis for these terrorist conspiracies, care must be taken not to accept their existence as simple facts.[91] Nevertheless, while the plots apparently developed during 2003 and 2004, as well as the attack on Van Gogh, were predominantly the work of individuals, the revitalization of the Hofstadgroup during 2005's Piranha case produced the first tentative signs that terrorist aims were being developed communally. This designates 2005 as the first time that the Hofstadgroup clearly *began* to resemble a jihadist terrorist network.

Given the necessary time and freedom of operation, it is likely that the Hofstadgroup would have developed into a more clearly defined terrorist network. One former participant opined that there was within the group a clear trend towards the communal use of violence.[92] However, there is a risk in attaching too much importance to such statements and succumbing to 'what if' history. Given the tentative nature of the signs toward communal

---

90 Dienst Nationale Recherche, 'Piranha', 40-41, 44, 49, 51-53, 60, 158, 1056, 6386, 7273, 7278, 8326, 11404.
91 Eijkman and Van Ginkel, 'Compatible or Incompatible; 'Hoge Raad Vernietigt Veroordeling'.
92 Former Hofstadgroup Participant 4, 'Personal Interview 2', 4-5.

involvement in terrorism, and the fact that they did not manifest themselves until late in the group's lifespan, the Hofstadgroup's organizational nature is best captured by Ligon et al.'s use of the term 'group', which expressly omits the communal focus on the achievement of a shared goal.[93] For the largest part of its existence, the Hofstadgroup was closer to what Sageman has called a 'bunch of guys', rather than a terrorist organization or network.[94] Consequently, the Hofstadgroup is deliberately labeled as a group throughout this book.

4.6 Conclusion

This chapter examined to what degree the 'homegrown', 'jihadist', 'network', and 'terrorist' descriptors commonly ascribed to the Hofstadgroup were accurate reflections of its nature. The results suggest the need for a nuanced perspective on all of these elements, problematizing previous claims that the group was a 'quintessential' example of this typology of terrorism.[95] Instead, it was in many ways an ambiguous entity; not entirely homegrown, not exclusively Salafi-Jihadist in ideological orientation, neither clearly a network nor an organization but more accurately described as a 'group', and largely lacking signs of communal involvement in terrorism until its 2005 'Piranha' resurgence.

Nevertheless, some contours can be drawn. Throughout its existence, the group resembled a set of concentric circles. At its core was a relatively small number of participants who married Salafi-Jihadist beliefs to the conviction that jihad was a personal duty. Surrounding them was a larger group of individuals who shared an interpretation of Islam largely in line with Salafi-Jihadist beliefs but who showed no real interest (yet) in becoming involved in acts of violence. A much smaller third group of participants adhered to Salafist principles but did not see the use of violence as legitimate. Finally, at the very edges of the group, there was a very small minority of individuals who appear to have had very little interest in fundamentalist, radical, or extremist interpretations of Islam altogether.

A second important conclusion is that the Hofstadgroup was never static but undergoing a continuous process of ideological and organizational development. Although the group had very few identifiable organizational

---

93 Ligon et al., 'Putting the "O" in VEOs', 120.
94 Sageman, *Leaderless Jihad*, 69.
95 Vidino, 'Radicalization, Linkage, and Diversity', 4.

characteristics between 2002 and 2004, it began to develop a rudimentary hierarchy and division of tasks in 2005. Crucially, the Hofstadgroup was in an ideological sense not always and never entirely a terrorist group. In 2003, its most militant participants wanted to become foreign fighters, not terrorists conducting attacks in the Netherlands. That changed from late 2003 onward, as several of them began to show a clear interest in carrying out acts of violence at home.

Although the group showed clearer signs of communal involvement in terrorism from 2005 onward, it always contained participants who did not fully, or even not at all, share the inner-circle's beliefs in the legitimacy and *personal necessity* of engaging in this form of political violence. These nuances make it difficult to close this chapter with a single, clear response to the question of what the Hofstadgroup was. On the one hand its extremist and militant inner circle made it a terrorist network under construction. On the other, for most of its participants the Hofstadgroup was a venue to meet like-minded individuals and a place where both world affairs and religion were discussed from a point of view that was always fundamentalist, often radical but not necessarily violent.

5 Structural-level factors: Facilitating and motivating involvement[1]

Following the multilevel analytical framework set out in Chapter 2, this second part of the book begins by looking at the influence of structural-level factors. Terrorist groups are shaped by the social, political, and economic environment in which they find themselves. How did such factors influence involvement processes in the Hofstadgroup? This chapter is organized using Crenshaw's division of structural-level factors into those that enable and those that motivate involvement in terrorism. Consequently, the analysis begins with a discussion of facilitating conditions such as popular support for terrorism and potential counterterrorism shortcomings. It then turns to motivational ones such as relative deprivation and political grievances before concluding with a brief look at the structural-level precipitant that most likely triggered the murder of Theo van Gogh.

5.1 Structural-level factors influencing involvement in terrorism

The structural level provides an 'ecological' understanding of involvement in terrorism based on the relationship between terrorists and their surroundings.[2] There is no simple causal relationship between structural-level factors, such as illiteracy or political grievances, and terrorism.[3] After all, of the millions of people exposed to such factors, only a handful become involved in terrorism. That is why referring to such structural factors as 'root causes' of terrorism, as especially politicians are sometimes apt to do, is misleading.[4] Structural conditions are not a 'special' category of explanatory variables. They must be complemented with insights from the group and individual levels of analysis to provide a holistic understanding of involvement in terrorism. Their contribution to this understanding, however, is an important one. Structural-level factors influence the *opportunities* and

---

1 This chapter has been published in amended form as: Schuurman, Bakker, and Eijkman, 'Structural Influences on Involvement'.
2 Lia and Skjølberg, 'Causes of Terrorism', 40.
3 Horgan, *The Psychology of Terrorism*, 85-86.
4 Forest, 'Exploring Root Causes', 1-2; Bakker, 'Zin En Onzin', 542-47.

motives for involvement in terrorism as well as potentially *precipitating* an actual attack.

This tripartite distinction is based on Crenshaw's classic work on the causes of terrorism. It distinguishes between '*preconditions*, factors that set the stage for terrorism over the long run, and *precipitants*, specific events that immediately precede the occurrence of terrorism'.[5] Crenshaw further distinguishes between preconditions that 'provide opportunities for terrorism to happen', and those that 'directly inspire and motivate terrorist campaigns'.[6] This distinction usefully emphasizes that structural factors can provide *opportunities* and *motives* for involvement in terrorism, as well as *triggers* for an actual attack. Indicative of the staying power of Crenshaw's subdivision of terrorism's structural factors, is that it has been maintained in more recent publications.[7] Consequently, it is used here to organize the discussion of the various structural-level hypotheses.

A review of the literature reveals a large number of potential structural-level factors relevant to understanding involvement in terrorism (Table 6). After undertaking an initial assessment of their applicability to the Hofstadgroup case study, it became apparent that several of them could be excluded as potential explanations at the outset. These omissions were based on one of two considerations: either the explanation was of limited applicability to the Netherlands as a country, or the available data simply did not support seeing a particular variable as relevant to the Hofstadgroup and its participants. Examples of the former include absolute poverty, sudden and marked population growth, and state collapse; conditions that have not existed in the Netherlands for decades. Neither was the country undergoing a process of urbanization or modernization, beset by war or violent social unrest, or suddenly exposed to the vagaries of a globalized economy.

With regard to the Hofstadgroup, it rapidly became apparent that its participants did not attempt to manipulate the mass media for their own ends and there was no evidence that an overlap between criminal and terrorist networks exerted an influence on the group's development. Furthermore, despite the Dutch involvement in the Iraq and Afghanistan interventions, the Hofstadgroup cannot be seen as 'spillover' from those conflicts as the group was predominantly Dutch, not Afghan or Iraqi in origin. Rather than introduce and discuss all of the structural-level factors listed in Table 6 in detail only to conclude their irrelevance, the discussion limits itself to those

---

5   Crenshaw, 'The Causes of Terrorism', 381. Emphases in original.
6   Ibid.
7   Bjørgo, 'Conclusions', 258; Newman, 'Exploring the "Root Causes"', 751.

that are in theory applicable to the Netherlands as a country and for which there is at least some empirical support in the data. Those excluded from analysis have been struck through.

Table 6   Structural-level explanations for involvement in terrorism

Preconditions: Opportunities	Preconditions: Motives	Precipitants
The Internet	(Relative) Deprivation	~~Government's excessive use of force~~
Popular support for terrorism	Intergroup inequality	~~Government attempts reforms~~
External assistance	Political grievances	
Social/ cultural facilitation of violence	Clash of value systems	
Ineffective counterterrorism	~~Economic globalization~~	
Political opportunity structure	~~Cultural globalization~~	
~~Modernization~~	~~Urbanization~~	
~~Population growth/ youth bulge~~	~~Modernization~~	
~~Shifts ethnic/ religious balance society~~	~~Spillover from other conflicts~~	
~~Urbanization~~	~~State sponsorship of terrorism~~	
~~Mass media~~	~~Power structure international system~~	
~~Organized crime – terrorism nexus~~	~~Failed/ failing states~~	
	~~Armed conflict~~	

5.2   Preconditions: Providing opportunities for terrorism

The preconditions discussed in this section primarily influence the opportunities for engaging in terrorist activities. The qualification is important, as several of the factors discussed in this section not only enabled involvement in the Hofstadgroup, but, as will be seen, also exerted an (indirect) motivational influence.

5.2.1   The Internet

The Internet can provide opportunities for involvement in terrorism in several ways. In a practical sense, it can be used to gain knowledge about the construction and use of explosives. The Internet can also bring together like-minded individuals regardless of their physical distance from one another and it can link local militants to broader global movements, all of this while providing at least a degree of anonymity.[8] The web can also function as an easy-to-use propaganda platform, making a terrorist group's message instantly available to a potential audience of millions. By projecting images of war and injustice across the globe, the Internet invites some of its users to suffer vicariously.[9] As such, the Internet can have a crucial influence on what Egerton calls the construction of a 'political imaginary' in which young Muslims from Western countries establish a common cause with 'brothers and sisters' they will most likely never meet.[10]

All of these functions of the Internet facilitated the Hofstadgroup's growth. By providing easy access to large amounts of information on Islam, jihadist groups, and geopolitical affairs, the Internet first of all became a key enabler of participants' adoption of radical and extremist views.[11] Data suggests that for some, the Internet became a source of answers to questions that parents and imams were unwilling or unable to discuss.[12] Questions such as: Does Islam condone terrorism? What is the cause of the Palestinians' plight? Why did the United States and its allies intervene in Afghanistan and Iraq? Secondly, the World Wide Web made available information of a more practical sort. One participant was found in possession of photographs and maps of Dutch government buildings and critical infrastructure that he had downloaded from the Internet, possibly as part of a reconnaissance of potential targets.[13] Several others had downloaded bomb-making manuals.[14]

A number of participants met each other online before developing 'real-world' connections.[15] In the fall of 2003, two participants used the web to reach out to other young Muslims in order to entice them to travel to

---

8 Sageman, 'The Turn to Political Violence', 122-23; Stenersen, 'The Internet', 216-31.
9 Oleson and Khosrokhavar, *Islamism as Social Movement*, 28.
10 Egerton, *Jihad in the West*, 92, 94-96; Egerton, 'The Internet and Militant Jihadism', 116, 124-25.
11 Former Hofstadgroup Participant 1, 'Personal Interview 2', 12; 'Personal Interview 3', 1; A[.], 'Deurwaarders', 3-9; Former Hofstadgroup Participant 3, 'Personal Interview 1', 1; Groen and Kranenberg, *Women Warriors*, 21; Benschop, 'A Political Murder Foretold'.
12 A[.], 'Deurwaarders', 3-4, 10; Former Hofstadgroup Participant 1, "Personal Interview 3', 1; Former Hofstadgroup Participant 3, 'Personal Interview 1', 7-9; Former Hofstadgroup Participant 1, 'Personal Interview 2', 11-12.
13 Dienst Nationale Recherche, 'RL8026', 01/01: 40, 42.
14 Ibid., 01/01: 42, 144, 160-61, 171; 01/13: 102-04; Dienst Nationale Recherche, 'Piranha', 163-66; Groen and Kranenberg, *Women Warriors*, 43-44.
15 Dienst Nationale Recherche, 'RL8026', 01/01: 33; 01/17: 4002, 4084, 4114; Former Hofstadgroup Participant 3, 'Personal Interview 1', 7; Groen and Kranenberg, *Women Warriors*, 22.

Pakistan or Afghanistan.[16] From the summer of 2004 until early 2005, one member of the group's inner circle in particular utilized online communication tools to instill the 'right' interpretation of tawhid and the necessity of takfir in aspirants.[17] Thus, the Internet also provided opportunities for the group's organizational and ideological development and enabled its activities. Finally, the Internet served as a propaganda tool.[18] Hofstadgroup participants made and administered simple websites that expounded radical and extremist interpretations of Islam, advocated the rejection of democracy, and glorified terrorism. Such sites also offered practical advice on preparing for jihad, advertised materials published by participants, in particular Van Gogh's murderer-to-be, and threatened the group's enemies in texts and videos.[19]

The Internet was thus an essential enabling factor for the Hofstadgroup's emergence. It provided an easy way for (future) participants to meet each other, propagate their views, and gain access to ideological and practical information that fueled their increasing radicalism. That is not to say the group was entirely dependent on this medium. For instance, as later chapters will show, preexisting ties of friendship, introductions, and chance encounters were also crucial group-formation mechanisms. Nonetheless, it is hard to imagine that the group's participants would have experienced the same degree of exposure to extremist's ideologies, terrorist propaganda, and vicarious experiences of injustice had they not had access to the Internet.

5.2.2   Popular support for terrorism

The importance of popular support for groups who violently challenge a state's power has long been recognized in the context of guerrilla warfare and counterinsurgency operations.[20] Popular support can be seen as a vital resource for terrorist and insurgent groups, as it enables their access to the weapons, finances, recruits, and intelligence information necessary

---

16   Dienst Nationale Recherche, 'RL8026', 01/01: 123-26; 01/13: 134-36.
17   Ibid., 01/17: 4002-03, 4026-27, 4048-53, 4084-87.
18   Ibid., AHD08/37: 8771-72; Former Hofstadgroup Participant 1, 'Personal Interview 1', 5; 'Personal Interview 2', 18-19, 30.
19   Dienst Nationale Recherche, 'RL8026', 01/01: 163, 200-03; 01/13: 165-67; AHA04/21: 1326-27, 1423-443; AHA05/22: 2021; AHA06/23: 339; AHD03/32: 6440-42; Former Hofstadgroup Participant 1, 'Personal Interview 2', 18-19, 32; Benschop, 'A Political Murder Foretold'.
20   Tse-Tung, *On Guerrilla Warfare*; Petraeus and Amos, 'FM 3-24: Counterinsurgency'.

to carry out a prolonged campaign of violence.[21] Conversely, when such non-state actors lose the support of the people they claim to represent, they are frequently unable to persevere against the materially stronger government forces that hunt them.[22]

Leiken has claimed that the Hofstadgroup enjoyed far more popular support than 'marginal' terrorist groups such as the Italian Red Brigades or the German Red Army Faction.[23] However, the truth is that both these groups could count on substantial support, especially among students, while there simply is no evidence that the Hofstadgroup was receiving similar support from the Muslim community in the Netherlands.[24] Unlike the BR and RAF, the Hofstadgroup did not inspire imitation; no follow-up generations of terrorists materialized after the October 2005 arrests.[25] The group's extremist stance on what constituted 'true' Islam and the (implied) allegations of apostasy that it leveled against the majority of (Dutch) Muslims, effectively ruled out the possibility of it acquiring broad support among Dutch Muslims.[26] The Hofstadgroup was not a popularly supported vanguard movement but a fringe group that intimidated its potential supporters almost as much as it threatened declared enemies.[27] Concrete popular support was therefore not a factor that meaningfully enabled participants' involvement processes.

5.2.3   External assistance

Similar to broad-based popular support, specific sources of external assistance, whether other terrorist groups, state sponsors, or transnational private support networks, can significantly increase opportunities for engaging in terrorism.[28] These parties can make available funding, weapons, and access to paramilitary training camps. They can also provide guidance or even outright operational leadership that can facilitate preparations for

---

21 Ross, 'Structural Causes', 324; Duyvesteyn and Schuurman, '(Counter) Terrorism and Public Support'.
22 Schuurman, 'Defeated by Popular Demand', 152-75.
23 Leiken, 'Europe's Angry Muslims', 126.
24 Hewwitt, 'Terrorism and Public Opinion', 145-70.
25 Merkle, 'West German Left-Wing Terrorism', 173-90; Weinberg, 'The Red Brigades', 32-37.
26 Former Hofstadgroup Participant 3, 'Personal Interview 1', 2-3.
27 Peters, 'De Ideologische En Religieuze Ontwikkeling', appendix: Overzicht teksten geschreven of vertaald door Mohammed B., 7-8, 10-11, 15, 21-24, 29-30, 42-53; NOVA, 'Videotestament Samir A.'.
28 Lia and Skjølberg, 'Causes of Terrorism', 18-21, 53-56; Ross, 'Structural Causes', 324; Pearce, 'Religious Sources of Violence', 121.

a terrorist attack.[29] Although the Hofstadgroup was not a widely-support group, it may still have benefited from more tightly demarcated external help. The next two sections assess whether the Hofstadgroup was subject to external guidance and whether external sources of support provided practical benefits conducive to involvement in terrorism.

The police files make numerous suggestions that the Hofstadgroup was under some form of external guidance. At one point the Dutch intelligence service AIVD claimed that the group's religious instructor belonged to a group that 'could be seen as a successor or branch of the Bin Laden organization'.[30] The files contain no information of any kind to support this claim, however. Another intelligence report held that a second participant had links to unspecified foreign terrorist organizations.[31] Although this individual did have an uncle who was detained in Guantanamo Bay, there is nothing to suggest that this had any bearing on the events surrounding the Hofstadgroup.[32] The absence of factual evidence to corroborate claims such as these suggests that they should be treated as highly speculative.

The Hofstadgroup was also acquainted with three middle-aged Syrian men who like its religious instructor, held fundamentalist views. At least one of them had been involved with the Muslim Brotherhood before he fled Syria in the 1990s.[33] Yet, once again, there is nothing to actually suggest that these men provided leadership or that there was a connection between the Hofstadgroup and the Muslim Brotherhood. Then there is the Chechen man whose fingerprints were found on the farewell letter of Van Gogh's killer and whose uncle the FBI suspected of being an illegal arms dealer involved with Chechen terrorist groups.[34] This individual was arrested in early 2005, not long after the arrest of a fellow countryman whose fingerprints had also been found on the murderer's belongings. Both were quickly released for lack of evidence of involvement in the Van Gogh murder. While it has remained a mystery how the fingerprints got on the letter, the absence

29 General Intelligence and Security Service, 'Violent Jihad in the Netherlands', 22-23.
30 'een organisatie die gezien kan worden als opvolger of tak van de Bin Laden-organisatie': Dienst Nationale Recherche, 'RL8026', AHA01/18: 82.
31 Ibid., AHA01/18: 106.
32 A[.], 'Deurwaarders Van Allah', 51; AIVD Employee 1, 'Personal Interview 1', 1.
33 Dienst Nationale Recherche, 'RL8026', 01/01: 32, 37; VERD: 19669, 19675, 19684, 19693, 19703, 19708, 19703-704, 19740-741, 19754, 19820; GET: 8349; Commissie van Toezicht betreffende de Inlichtingen- en Veiligheidsdiensten, 'Toezichtsrapport Met Betrekking Tot Mohammed B.', 11.
34 Dienst Nationale Recherche, 'RL8026', 01/01: 93-96; NCTV Employee 1, 'Personal Interview 1', 6; Derix, 'Hoe Kwam Toch'.

of evidence to suggest they had a role in the murder is another argument against the notion that the Hofstadgroup was under external guidance.³⁵

Of all the possible ties between the Hofstadgroup and foreign extremists or even terrorist organizations, the most plausible are those that came to light in October 2003. Intelligence information and the behavior of the participants concerned bore out that there were contacts between the travelers to Pakistan or Afghanistan and an unnamed 'emir', as well as with a Moroccan man in Spain who was suspected of involvement in the 2003 Casablanca bombings.³⁶ Yet there is no concrete evidence to suggest that these ties amounted to outside operational guidance. The 'emir' most likely tasked the Hofstadgroup participants in question with convincing other Dutch Muslims to travel to Pakistan or Afghanistan and the Moroccan man appears to have solicited the group's help in order to remain at large.³⁷ Beyond speculation, there is little to suggest these men were instructing the Hofstadgroup to carry out acts of terrorism.

There are also numerous pieces of information in the police files which suggest that external parties provided the Hofstadgroup with practical benefits conducive to carrying out acts of terrorism. Several intelligence reports raise the possibility that the group received funding. Possible donors were Saudi-Arabians, Dutch Muslim extremists who wanted Hirsi Ali and Van Gogh killed and a leading participant's criminal associates.³⁸ Given the absence of any supporting evidence, these claims should once again be treated as distinctly speculative. Investigations also failed to support the idea that the group's weapons were externally supplied.³⁹ A Hofstadgroup participant did claim that the hand grenades were provided by an AIVD informant. These accusations led to the alleged informant's arrest in late 2005, but charges were dropped in March 2006 due to lack of evidence.⁴⁰

Another instance of possible external support stems from September 2005. At that time, the Piranha group's main protagonist met a Belgian

35 Derix, 'Hoe Kwam Toch'.
36 Dienst Nationale Recherche, 'RL8026', 01/01: 23-25; AHA01/18: 80-81; RHV01/66: 18846.
37 Ibid., 01/01:23-27; 01/13: 134-36, 140-46; RHV01/66:18791-879; Police Investigator 1, 'Personal Interview 3', 1.
38 Dienst Nationale Recherche, 'RL8026', AHA01/18: 82; AHA03/20: 1188-89; Dienst Nationale Recherche, 'Piranha', REL00: 40-42.
39 Dienst Nationale Recherche, 'RL8026', 01/01: 38, 89-90; 01/13: 95-98; Dienst Nationale Recherche, 'Piranha', 62, 13157; Police Investigator 2, 'Personal Interview 1', 3; Public Prosecutor 1, 'Personal Interview 1', 18.
40 Groen, 'Saleh B. Blijft Leveren Granaat Ontkennen'; 'Saleh B. Niet Meer Verdacht Van Terroristische Daden'.

national at a train station in The Hague. Accounts of what transpired differ. The Dutch police believe that the Belgian man asked his Dutch counterpart to participate in a suicide operation while investigative journalists claim that the Belgian offered three female suicide terrorists to the Hofstadgroup participant but was turned down.[41] As neither of these scenarios materialized, there is little basis to assume this meeting had any actual influence on the Piranha group's possibilities for engaging in terrorism.

The most plausible claim of external assistance concerns the possibility that two participants underwent paramilitary training during their 2003 trip to Pakistan or Afghanistan. A trip that may have been facilitated by an individual who some participants later claimed had been working on behalf of the AIVD.[42] Although the paramilitary training hypothesis is similarly based on intelligence information, it is corroborated by at least some circumstantial evidence; a participant's statement that he heard one of the travelers claim as much and this same traveler's repeated online bragging about his proficiency with weapons.[43] In November 2004, the latter also threw a hand grenade at the police officers that came to arrest him and used a mirror to peek at them while remaining behind cover.[44] Both of these actions may be further hints that he had received at least some basic training.

In short, the Hofstadgroup's emergence does not appear to have been meaningfully enabled by either external guidance or support. The one possible exception being that the two participants who traveled to Pakistan or Afghanistan may have undergone some basic paramilitary training. Several participants clearly had the desire to travel to foreign jihadist battle zones and they would probably have reveled in the chance to receive guidance from actual jihadist militants or ideologues. Why such connections did not materialize remains grounds for speculation; perhaps the trips to Pakistan or Afghanistan were simply too short to make meaningful connections, perhaps their youth and lack of experience with militancy made the Hofstadgroup's travelers unappealing to potential foreign handlers. Whatever the case, the inapplicability of external support underlines the group's homegrown status.

---

41 Dienst Nationale Recherche, 'Piranha', 151-52, 191-92; Groen and Kranenberg, *Women Warriors*, 144-46.
42 Erkel, *Samir*, 195; Vermaat, *Nederlandse Jihad*, 33.
43 Dienst Nationale Recherche, 'RL8026', 01/01: 123-26; 01/13: 140-45; AHD08/37: 8595, 8774-775; 8880, 8919, 8928-929.
44 Ibid., AGV01/62: 17978; Public Prosecutor 1, 'Personal Interview 1', 37-38.

5.2.4 Social or cultural facilitation of violence

Individuals exposed to cultural or social values that convey a negative attitude towards out-groups or glorify violence may be more likely to see the use of terrorism as justifiable.[45] Several empirical studies indicate that Muslims *in general* are not more likely than non-Muslims to commit or suffer from political violence.[46] At the same time, research also suggests that *fundamentalist* and *militant interpretations* of Islam can inculcate intolerance, hatred, and a positive disposition towards the use of force as a means of dealing with perceived enemies.[47]

A 2015 study by Koopmans indicates that fundamentalist views are widespread among Sunni Muslims in a variety of European countries, including the Netherlands, and that these views correspond with hostility toward out-groups.[48] For instance, more than 50% of Muslims polled believed that the West was out to destroy Islam, a figure that rose to more than 70% among 'very religious fundamentalist Muslims'.[49] The data for this particular study were collected in 2008 and it presents an aggregate of several countries, meaning that the findings are not directly applicable to the situation in the Netherlands as encountered by the Hofstadgroup's participants. However, it seems reasonable to assume that these views did not suddenly develop and thus that many participants grew up in a social environment in which similar views were prevalent. All the more so since numerous participants attended mosques in which the fundamentalist Salafist brand of Islam was preached.[50]

Koopman's study is not the only one that provides insights into the attitudes and beliefs of Dutch Muslims. A 2004 report commissioned by the Netherlands Institute for Social Research (SCP) concluded that there was a trend towards secularization among Dutch Muslims of Moroccan and Turkish origin.[51] This finding seems to contradict Koopman's work, however the SCP report also noted that close to 100% of respondents indicated that Islam was

---

45 Crenshaw, *Explaining Terrorism*, 94-96; Milla, Faturochman, and Ancok, 'The Impact of Leader-Follower Interactions', 93-95; Schwartz, Dunkel, and Waterman, 'Terrorism', 540-42.
46 Conrad and Milton, 'Unpacking the Connection', 316, 331; Fish, Jensenius, and Michel, 'Islam and Large-Scale Political-Violence', 1328, 1342.
47 Loza, 'The Psychology of Extremism and Terrorism', 144, 149.
48 Koopmans, 'Religious Fundamentalism and Hostility', 33-57.
49 Ibid., 43, 45.
50 A[.], 'Deurwaarders'; Former Hofstadgroup Participant 1, 'Personal Interview 2', 14; Dienst Nationale Recherche, 'RL8026', AHA03/20: 860; 01/17: 4019, 4084, 4159; VERD: 19652, 19853, 20004, 20114, 20234; Former Hofstadgroup Participant 3, 'Personal Interview 1', 8; Groen and Kranenberg, *Women Warriors*, 239.
51 Phalet, Ter Wal, and Van Praag, 'Moslim in Nederland', 11, 13, 17.

very important to them, 57% of respondents with a Moroccan background felt individuals should follow Islamic rules and 30% of this same group thought Islam and 'modern life' were incompatible.[52] Additionally, a majority of Dutch-Moroccans adhered to an orthodox interpretation of their faith.[53]

Interestingly, a 2012 follow-up study by the SCP criticized the 'secularization' thesis, finding instead that mosque attendance was no longer declining and that there were relatively few differences in the strictness of religious attitudes between first- and second-generation Muslim immigrants.[54] Neither the 2004 nor the 2012 SCP report directly supports Koopmans's conclusions. However, by providing indications of the (growing) prevalence of orthodoxy among Dutch Moroccan Muslims and the great importance this group attached to its Islamic identity, they do lend further credibility to the findings presented by Koopmans.

The above discussion leads to the tentative conclusion that, by instilling a sense of hostility towards the Western world, social facilitation of fundamentalism likely lowered Hofstadgroup participants' threshold to seeing the use of violence as legitimate. This is anecdotally supported by the finding that family members of the murderer who resided in Morocco, together with some of the other residents of their village, showed support for the murder.[55]

However, it would go too far to argue, on what is circumstantial evidence, that exposure to fundamentalist Islam facilitated the *use* of violence. After all, with so many Dutch Muslims exposed to similar attitudes, how can it be explained that only the Hofstadgroup displayed such outspokenly militant views and behavior? Furthermore, the fundamentalist Salafist variety of Islam to which the Hofstadgroup by and large subscribed, comes in at least three varieties of which only the Salafi-Jihadist one openly advocates the use of force.[56] Explaining some participants' (intended) acts of violence therefore necessitates broadening the analysis beyond structural-level factors to incorporate social dynamics and personal backgrounds, as the next chapters will do.

5.2.5   Ineffective counterterrorism

According to Crenshaw, one of the most important permissive causes of terrorism is a government's 'inability or unwillingness' to prevent it.[57] The

---

52   Ibid., 18.
53   Ibid., 19.
54   Maliepaard and Gijsberts, 'Moslim in Nederland 2012', 12, 16.
55   Chorus and Olgun, *Broeders*, 33-35.
56   Wiktorowicz, 'Anatomy of the Salafi Movement', 208.
57   Crenshaw, 'The Causes of Terrorism', 382.

various police investigations into the Hofstadgroup's activities and the AIVD's monitoring of the group indicate the Dutch authorities were certainly not unwilling to address the threat posed by this group. But can hindsight indicate areas where the response was ineffective or counterproductive?

After Van Gogh's death, the Dutch Review Committee on the Intelligence and Security Services (CTIVD) concluded that the AIVD had incorrectly dismissed the filmmaker's murderer as a peripheral member of the Hofstadgroup.[58] A conclusion shared by the Service's acting director at the time.[59] Although the AIVD had possessed information that the killer-to-be fulfilled a central role in the Hofstadgroup, had a history of violent outbursts, and was writing increasingly extremist tracts, this data had not been analyzed in its totality before the murder.[60] The CTIVD was careful to stress that the AIVD did not possess information indicating that Van Gogh's murderer was planning to commit an attack.[61] Whether extra attention from the AIVD would have prevented Van Gogh's killer from striking therefore remains highly speculative. But at the very least, the AIVD's misdiagnosis benefited the killer by allowing him to carry out his preparations largely unnoticed.

What clearly did enable Van Gogh's killer to strike was the fact that his target's accessibility. As a public figure, Van Gogh was easily recognized and because he cycled to his work in Amsterdam he was also easy to find. Crucially, he had steadfastly refused the Dutch authorities' offer of increased personal protection in the wake of the negative fallout produced by the airing of *Submission, part 1* in August 2004. By contrast, the film's co-author Hirsi Ali had been under round-the-clock protection since November 2002.[62] This difference probably explains why the killer chose Van Gogh over Hirsi Ali, whose status as an apostate would otherwise have made her the more attractive target.[63] Arguably, Van Gogh's decision not to accept personal protection provided a larger opportunity for his killer to strike than the AIVD's misdiagnosis. The attack on the filmmaker can in any case not simply be put down to 'counterterrorism failure'.

58 Commissie van Toezicht betreffende de Inlichtingen- en Veiligheidsdiensten, 'Toezichtsrapport Met Betrekking Tot Mohammed B.', 21-22.
59 'AIVD Geeft Verkeerd'. Is this citation complete?
60 Commissie van Toezicht betreffende de Inlichtingen- en Veiligheidsdiensten, 'Toezichtsrapport Met Betrekking Tot Mohammed B.', 27-28.
61 Ibid., 14.
62 Chorus and Olgun, *In Godsnaam*, 123-24, 171-76; Van Straelen, 'Requisitoir in De Strafzaak Tegen Mohammed B.', 9.
63 Chorus and Olgun, *Broeders*, 20.

On 10 November 2004, five police officers were wounded when a Hofstadgroup participant threw a hand grenade at them during an arrest attempt. The AIVD had wired the apartment sometime prior to the raid and, read with the benefit of hindsight, one of the recorded conversations strongly hints that the occupants possessed grenades and planned to use them against the police; 'you wait until they enter and then you throw one, yes?'[64] Having gotten hold of this text during the spring of 2005, the Dutch television program *Netwerk* reported that the AIVD could have known grenades were present in the apartment, implying that the service had failed to properly alert the police.[65] In October 2005, the Hofstadgroup participant who threw the grenade told *Netwerk* that he had gotten the weapon through an acquaintance who, he claimed, worked for the AIVD. His lawyer and those of other Hofstadgroup participants shared these suspicions, leading to the alleged AIVD agent being heard in court as a witness.[66]

As previously mentioned, charges against the alleged informant were dropped in early 2006. There was no forensic evidence tying him to the hand grenades. Neither could it be proven that he had been the elusive second perpetrator of the supermarket robbery conducted by a Hofstadgroup participant in early 2004; one Hofstadgroup defendant claimed the individual in question only 'got away' because he was already working for the AIVD.[67] Other than the testimony of an individual with a stake in alleging that the AIVD had enticed his use of violence by supplying him with grenades through an informant, and a wiretapped conversation that makes an implicit reference to the weapons, there is no concrete evidence to support the notion that the AIVD could have forewarned their police partners. On the whole, ineffective counterterrorism does not appear to have been a major enabler of the Hofstadgroup's activities. However, had the Service not misdiagnosed Van Gogh's killer, it might arguably have made it more difficult for the latter to plan and prepare his attack.

5.2.6 Political opportunity structure

The 'political opportunity structure' concept essentially bridges the gap between preconditions that provide opportunities and those that supply

---

64 'jij wacht totdat zij binnenkomen en dan doe jij eentje gooien, ja?': Dienst Nationale Recherche, 'RL8026', AHA07/24: 3047.
65 Remkes, 'Kamerstukken 2, 2004-2005, 29754, Nr. 22', 1-3.
66 Vermaat, *Nederlandse Jihad*, 61; 'Saleh B. Niet Meer Verdacht Van Terroristische Daden'.
67 Groen, 'Saleh B. Blijft Leveren Granaat Ontkennen', 62-63; 'Saleh B. Niet Meer Verdacht Van Terroristische Daden'; Vermaat, *Nederlandse Jihad*, 63.

motives for involvement in terrorism.[68] Adherents of the 'strategic school' posit that the openness of democratic societies can enable violent acts of resistance.[69] Institutions such as a free press and an independent judiciary limit the power of the government over its citizens; basic rights such as freedom of assembly and the largely unrestricted movement of people and goods make it easier to prepare acts of violence.[70] By contrast, because autocratic regimes lack such freedoms and suffer no restraints on their executive power, the opportunities for engaging in terrorism are fewer.[71]

With regard to motive, the 'political access school' argues that democracies discourage terrorism because they provide avenues for the non-violent resolution of conflicts and afford citizens influence in the political process.[72] Here it is the autocratic regimes that are at a disadvantage, as their lack of freedoms, frequent human-rights abuses, and the absence of opportunities for peaceful political participation make violent opposition the only option for people wishing for change.[73] While this seems to put democracies ahead on paper, there is considerable empirical evidence that democratic states are no less vulnerable to terrorism.[74] This may at least in part stem from the fact that, while democratic states are less likely to experience domestic terrorism, their frequently assertive foreign policies increases their exposure to international or transnational terrorism.[75]

The Hofstadgroup clearly benefited from the democratic freedoms available to it. Arguably, it would have been far more difficult in an authoritarian regime to hold frequent private meetings, use the Internet to espouse extremist views and attract like-minded individuals, and to travel abroad to Belgium, Spain, and even Pakistan or Afghanistan. At the same time, the Dutch authorities did not stand idly by. Tempering the opportunities provided by the Dutch political system was the fact that group participants were effectively under AIVD surveillance from mid-2002 onwards. Combined with numerous rounds of arrests between 2003 and 2005, this

---

68 Oleson and Khosrokhavar, *Islamism as Social Movement*, 21-22; Collier and Hoeffler, 'Greed and Grievance', 587-88.
69 Eyerman, 'Terrorism and Democratic States', 151-52.
70 McAllister and Schmid, 'Theories of Terrorism', 251-52.
71 Eubank and Weinberg, 'Terrorism and Democracy', 156; Piazza, 'Draining the Swamp', 522-23.
72 Eyerman, 'Terrorism and Democratic States', 152.
73 Li, 'Does Democracy?', 278; Piazza, 'Draining the Swamp', 523.
74 Piazza, 'Democracy and Free Markets', 83-84; Eubank and Weinberg, 'Terrorism and Democracy', 160; Robison, Crenshaw, and Jenkins, 'The Social Origins', 2019.
75 Savun and Phillips, 'Democracy, Foreign Policy', 879, 886, 893-94; Lia and Skjølberg, 'Causes of Terrorism', 35-36.

proved a considerable impediment to its ability to operate.[76] One former participant described the October 2003 arrests as having a paralyzing effect on the group, leading to such a preoccupation with personal safety that group meetings became less frequent and attempts to reach foreign conflict zones ceased altogether.[77]

The second conclusion is that access to the political system had little dampening effect on the Hofstadgroup's more committed participants' motivation to use violence. Initially, some participants appeared to have a modicum of faith in democratic forms of protest. Two attended rallies; one in support of Palestine in 2002, and one against the Iraq war in 2003.[78] One of these individuals was also temporarily a member of the Arab European League (AEL) in 2003, but quickly disowned it because '[they] want everything via democracy'.[79] Other participants never even considered such avenues. One interviewee argued vehemently that the AEL had never held any appeal for himself or the others because its leader was a Shiite, a denomination they considered heretical and worse than unbelievers.[80] More generally, data suggests that the group saw democratic means for voicing dissent or achieving change as ineffective and even illegitimate as it meant working with and within a man-made democratic system rather than a divinely inspired one.[81]

Civil liberties and constraints on the Dutch government's powers enabled the Hofstadgroup's emergence, yet not to the degree that the authorities were impotent. As the multiple arrests and prison sentences indicate, the state was still able to mount an assertive response. Despite access to the political system, the country's political opportunity structure also motivated involvement in militancy because democratic laws and institutions were seen as unpalatable and illegitimate. The net effect of these various influences cannot be quantified, yet it seems clear that the Netherlands' political

---

76 Commissie van Toezicht betreffende de Inlichtingen- en Veiligheidsdiensten, 'Toezichtsrapport Met Betrekking Tot Mohammed B.', 8; Former Hofstadgroup Participant 3, 'Personal Interview 1', 5-6.
77 Former Hofstadgroup Participant 1, 'Personal Interview 1', 4-5.
78 A[.], 'Deurwaarders', 10; Community Policing Officer 1, 'Personal Interview 1', 4-5; Erkel, *Samir*, 119-20.
79 'ze willen alles via de democratie': Dienst Nationale Recherche, 'RL8026', AHD09/38: 9201. See also: A[.], 'Deurwaarders Van Allah', 31.
80 Former Hofstadgroup Participant 1, 'Personal Interview 2', 29; 'Personal Interview 1', 2.
81 Former Hofstadgroup Participant 1, 'Personal Interview 2', 28-30; Dienst Nationale Recherche, 'RL8026', AHB02/26: 3776-77; AHD02/31: 5611; De Koning, '"We Reject You"', 98-99; Peters, 'De Ideologische En Religieuze Ontwikkeling', 4.

opportunity structure both enabled involvement in the Hofstadgroup and helped bring about the adoption of radical and extremist views.

5.3 Preconditions: Providing motives for terrorism

Opportunities alone are unlikely to lead to terrorism unless groups or individuals with the *motive* to carry out acts of violence make use of them. It is to this second category of structural-level preconditions that the discussion now turns.

5.3.1 (Relative) deprivation and intergroup inequality

A common-sense assumption frequently voiced by politicians is that poverty and lack of education are causes of terrorism.[82] Scholarship on the issue provides a more nuanced picture. Some studies lend support to this view, finding that countries experience less terrorism as they become economically more developed[83] and that increased personal wealth is linked to decreased support for political violence.[84] For instance, in research based on opinion polling, Fair and Shepherd found that the moderately poor were more likely to support terrorism.[85] Looking specifically at European homegrown jihadism, Bakker's study shows that most individuals in his sample came from a relatively low socioeconomic background.[86]

Conversely, Piazza finds no significant relationship between low economic development and terrorism.[87] Various scholars posit that terrorists are actually less likely to come from impoverished backgrounds than their peers.[88] In contrast to the Bakker study, the jihadists in Sageman's sample mostly enjoyed a relatively well-off middle-class existence.[89] Although Sageman looked at internationally operating jihadists and Bakker focused on European jihadists, the differences are still striking. A similar dichotomy

---

82 See the examples in: Piazza, 'Rooted in Poverty', 159-60.
83 Li and Schaub, 'Economic Globalization and Transnational Terrorism', 254; Barros, Faria, and Gil-Alana, 'Terrorism against American Citizens', 56, 66; Feridun and Sezgin, 'Regional Underdevelopment and Terrorism', 229.
84 MacCulloch, 'The Impact of Income', 843; Schbley, 'Torn between God, Family, and Money', 182.
85 Fair and Shepherd, 'Who Supports Terrorism?', 52, 71.
86 Bakker, 'Characteristics of Jihadi Terrorists', 140.
87 Piazza, 'Rooted in Poverty', 170-71.
88 Berrebi, 'Evidence About the Link between Education', 17-18; Krueger and Malečková, 'Education, Poverty and Terrorism', 131, 135; Pape, *Dying to Win*, 215.
89 Sageman, *Understanding Terror Networks*, 73-74.

emerges with regard to the relationship between education and terrorism. Some studies encourage the idea that terrorism attracts the uneducated.[90] Others fail to support such hypotheses or reach diametrically opposed conclusions.[91] Given these conflicting findings, it is unclear whether poverty and lack of education *as such* can function as motives for terrorism.

Research suggests that deprivation's ability to contribute to the onset of political violence is particularly pronounced when it is experienced *relative* to other individuals or groups. Gurr defines relative deprivation as the perceived discrepancy between the 'values' people expect to achieve, such as political influence or material well-being, and their actual capacity for doing so.[92] When groups perceive that they are unfairly economically disadvantaged or politically disenfranchised vis-à-vis another class, religious group, or ethnic minority, relative deprivation can become a powerful motivation for political action and, potentially, violence.[93] Poverty or socioeconomic disadvantages become markedly more potent motivational preconditions for terrorism when they overlap with intergroup inequality.[94]

A 2005 report on the integration of minorities in the Netherlands indicated that non-Western immigrants and their children were socioeconomically disadvantaged compared to the indigenous population. For instance, they had lower educational qualifications, were more likely to be unemployed, earned less income, underperformed at school, and were disproportionally represented in statistics on crime.[95] Another report showed that Dutch Muslims also faced discrimination on the labor market.[96] Given the predominance of Dutch Moroccans in the Hofstadgroup, it is interesting to note that the Moroccan community is frequently cited as the one most strongly affected by these problems.[97] Researchers have also argued that

---

90   Bravo and Dias, 'An Empirical Analysis of Terrorism', 337; Post, 'The Socio-Cultural Underpinnings', 64; Von Hippel, 'The Roots of Terrorism', 28-30.
91   Krueger and Malečková, 'Education, Poverty and Terrorism', 125-26,131-32, 135; Bakker, 'Characteristics of Jihadi Terrorists', 140; Berrebi, 'Evidence About the Link between Education', 17; Pape, *Dying to Win*, 214; Sageman, *Understanding Terror Networks*, 74-77; Testas, 'Determinants of Terrorism', 262-63.
92   Gurr, *Why Men Rebel*, 13, 25-26.
93   Gurr, 'Why Minorities Rebel', 166-67, 188-89; Gurr, *Why Men Rebel*, 9, 13, 33-34, 37; Stewart, 'Crisis Prevention', 252-53.
94   Piazza, 'Poverty, Minority Economic Discrimination', 348-50; Murshed and Gates, 'Spatial-Horizontal Inequality', 132-33.
95   *Jaarrapport Integratie 2005*, 45, 50-51, 75-76, 83, 85-86, 89, 90-91, 98, 100-01, 132-44, 148-62.
96   Andriessen et al., *Liever Mark Dan Mohammed?*, 11-22.
97   General Intelligence and Security Service, 'Violent Jihad in the Netherlands', 35-36; *Jaarrapport Integratie 2005*, 45, 83, 148-62.

the increasingly vituperative debate on Islam and multiculturalism in the Netherlands has engendered feelings of alienation among (young) Dutch Muslims.[98] Was such relative deprivation also a factor underlying involvement in the Hofstadgroup?

Perhaps surprisingly, there are virtually no indications that income inequality, lack of access to educational opportunities, political representation, or other examples of intergroup inequality played a role in the adoption of radical or extremist views or motivated involvement in the Hofstadgroup. Admittedly, one individual's involvement began when he failed to obtain an internship through what he believed was discrimination because of his Moroccan heritage.[99] However, this person was quick to emphasize that this experience did not *motivate* his involvement but indirectly *facilitated* it. Without an internship to go to he simply had more time to spend on other pursuits, one of which turned out to be a growing interest in radical Islam that in time would lead him towards the group.[100]

There are, however, several indications that participants experienced a sense of being second-rate citizens because of their faith. It is here that emphasis must be placed on the polarizing influence of the debate on Islam and the integration of (Muslim) minorities that had been waged in Dutch society since the late 1990s. Politicians such as Pim Fortuyn, Rita Verdonk, and Geert Wilders led a debate that was increasingly critical of Islam and immigration. Moreover, it was often voiced in crude or harsh tones; Van Gogh's writings being a case in point. These developments not only had a polarizing influence on Dutch society by seemingly setting Muslim immigrants and their children against the 'autochthonous' population, but also strengthened feelings of exclusion amongst young Muslim citizens in particular.[101] Keeping this sociopolitical context in mind, several findings stand out.

Particularly telling is the reaction of one Hofstadgroup participant to news that a Dutch prisoner who murdered an Iraqi man was released from jail; 'your blood is blood, but our blood is water'.[102] Several encountered (verbal) aggression aimed at their religious convictions or Moroccan heritage.[103]

---

98   Bakker, 'Islamism, Radicalisation and Jihadism in the Netherlands', 169-70; De Koning and Meijer, 'Going All the Way', 223-24.
99   Former Hofstadgroup Participant 1, 'Personal Interview 2', 3.
100 Former Hofstadgroup Participant 1, 'Personal Interview 3', 1.
101 De Koning and Meijer, 'Going All the Way', 223-24.
102 'jullie bloed is bloed, maar ons bloed is water': Dienst Nationale Recherche, 'RL8026', AHA05/22: 1876.
103 Ibid., 01/17: 4145, 4198; AHD08/37: 8569-70, 8574; Groot Koerkamp and Veerman, *Het Slapende Leger*, 24; Former Hofstadgroup Participant 5, 'Personal Interview 1', 4.

During police questioning, one suspect lamented that the murder of Van Gogh would only increase the gulf between Muslims and non-Muslims.[104] Another told officers that Dutch society had become more intolerant and callous towards Muslims after 9/11.[105] Others spoke out angrily against what they saw as the media's unfavorable portrayal of Islam, its perceived tendency to under-report Muslim suffering around the globe and its vilification of men like Bin Laden as terrorists.[106] In some of his writings, Van Gogh's murderer-to-be criticized the Dutch government's integration policies, which he saw as thinly veiled attempts to encourage Muslims to abandon their faith.[107]

Such experiences with discrimination strengthened participants' convictions and fed their hatred for unbelievers. But, one potential exception notwithstanding,[108] there is little to suggest that these experiences triggered or motivated involvement, or that they were central to planned and perpetrated acts of terrorism. In fact, various findings *disavow* this line of reasoning. Several participants spoke positively about their experiences as Muslims in the Netherlands, praising the country's religious freedom.[109] More importantly, the Hofstadgroup's extremist elements advocated violence not because they felt alienated or discriminated, but as punishment for those who insulted Islam.[110] Although the Dutch 'debate on Islam' had been gaining momentum since the 1990s, it did not really become a topic of conversation within the group until the release of the Islam-critical film *Submission* in August 2004.[111] As one former participant put it, the debate on Islam was 'secondary'; while Hirsi Ali and Van Gogh deserved to be killed, this individual was primarily focused on supporting Islamist insurgents in places such as Afghanistan.[112]

---

104 Dienst Nationale Recherche, 'RL8026', VERD: 20105.
105 Ibid., VERD: 20456.
106 A[.], 'Deurwaarders', 3, 9-10; Dienst Nationale Recherche, 'RL8026', AHA05/22: 1876; AHB02/26: 3776-77; AHD08/37: 8614-17, 8733-734; Erkel, *Samir*, 215; Peters, 'De Ideologische En Religieuze Ontwikkeling', appendix: Overzicht teksten geschreven of vertaald door Mohammed B., 18-19, 22; Former Hofstadgroup Participant 5, 'Personal Interview 1', 4.
107 Peters, 'De Ideologische En Religieuze Ontwikkeling', appendix: Overzicht teksten geschreven of vertaald door Mohammed B., 15, 22, 48.
108 A[.], 'Deurwaarders', 3.
109 Groen and Kranenberg, *Women Warriors*, 68, 94-95, 195; Dienst Nationale Recherche, 'RL8026', AHA04/21: 1633; VERD: 20229; 01/17: 4004.
110 Dienst Nationale Recherche, 'RL8026', 01/17: 4131.
111 Former Hofstadgroup Participant 1, 'Personal Interview 2', 23-24.
112 Former Hofstadgroup Participant 4, 'Personal Interview 2', 5.

As the example given above illustrates, Van Gogh and Hirsi Ali became hated public figures because of how they spoke about Islam and its prophet, not because they engendered or exacerbated feelings of exclusion from Dutch society.[113] Which is not to say that experiences of exclusion, or feelings of being second-rate citizens did not exert an influence on the group's development. They contributed to the drawing of sharper boundaries between Muslim and non-Muslim citizens in the Netherlands and increased participants' antagonistic views of the latter. The available data on the Hofstadgroup, however, does not allow relative deprivation to be ascribed more than such a supportive role when explaining how its participants became involved. Although the Dutch debate on Islam certainly had its influence on the Hofstadgroup, and despite the emphasis frequently placed upon it when explaining involvement in homegrown jihadism, it does not appear to have been a particularly salient explanatory variable.

5.3.2   Political grievances

The perception that governments or their policies are unjust and lack legitimacy can provide a powerful impetus for participation in political violence.[114] From this perspective, people turn to terrorism because they see it as a tool they can use to redress such grievances and exert political influence through violence.

The data reveals that numerous participants reacted strongly to armed conflicts involving Muslims. News about the suffering of co-religionists in places like Palestine or about terrorist attacks carried out by Muslims had a range of effects. As vicarious experiences of injustice and shock, they helped bring about an interest in Islam and geopolitics, triggering searches for information that contributed to the adoption of radical and extremist interpretations of Islam.[115] As an interviewee recalled his reaction to the 9/11 attacks: 'At first you think like "terrible, what happened there [...] No religion can justify that". So, you investigate. [...] And then I found a fatwa by [Hamoud al-Aqla al-Shuebi] [...] in which he approved of [the attacks]

---

113   Former Hofstadgroup Participant 1, 'Personal Interview 1', 1; 'Personal Interview 2', 23-24.
114   LaFree and Ackerman, 'The Empirical Study of Terrorism', 360-62; Crenshaw, 'The Causes of Terrorism', 383-84; Sprinzak, 'The Process of Delegitimation', 50-68.
115   A[.], 'Deurwaarders', 3, 5-9; Erkel, *Samir*, 48-49, 69; Groen and Kranenberg, *Women Warriors*, 19, 79; Former Hofstadgroup Participant 1, 'Personal Interview 2', 10-11; De Graaf, *Gevaarlijke Vrouwen*, 249-50; Former Hofstadgroup Participant 5, 'Personal Interview 1', 1; Vermaat, *Nederlandse Jihad*, 163.

[...] and I thought it was nice to see how he explained all that and actually also presented evidence [of its permissibility]'.[116]

These geopolitical events also helped shape a Manichean outlook in which 'true' Muslims were assaulted by both external and internal enemies; principally, the United States, its Western-European allies, Israel, and what participants considered apostate or heretical Muslim regimes.[117] Particularly influential in this regard was the U.S.-led 'War on Terror', which many participants saw as a war against Islam.[118] As one wrote, 'I gained feelings of hate towards anyone who supported Bush in his crusade, not just the Netherlands, but also Arabic apostate leaders'.[119] Another important effect of these geopolitical grievances was their ability to justify violence by portraying it as a defensive and righteous response to Muslim suffering.[120] One of the travelers to Pakistan or Afghanistan wrote his mother explaining that he had left because the ummah was under attack; he had gone to help expel the unbelievers from the land of jihad.[121]

In early 2003, the desire to help Muslims in conflict zones led one of the group's most committed extremists to attempt to reach Islamist insurgents in Chechnya.[122] Later that year, three others traveled to Pakistan or Afghanistan, likely with a similar purpose in mind. By late 2003, however, the focus of the Hofstadgroup's militant core began to shift towards possible actions within the Netherlands. This transition was partly practical; by

---

116 'In eerste instantie denk je van "verschrikkelijk, wat daar gebeurt [...] Dat kan toch geen enkele religie goedkeuren". Dus dan ga je onderzoeken. [...] En dan kwam ik een keer een fatwa tegen van Hammoud bin Aqla [...] waarin hij [de aanslagen] goedkeurt. [...] En ik vond het wel mooi om te zien hoe hij dat allemaal uiteenzette en eigenlijk ook met bewijzen kwam': Former Hofstadgroup Participant 1, 'Personal Interview 2', 11.

117 A[.], 'Deurwaarders', 4-5, 7, 9; Dienst Nationale Recherche, 'RL8026', 01/13: 163; Former Hofstadgroup Participant 3, 'Personal Interview 1', 6-7; Peters, 'De Ideologische En Religieuze Ontwikkeling', appendix: Overzicht teksten geschreven of vertaald door Mohammed B., 33.

118 A[.], 'Deurwaarders', 4, 7, 9; Dienst Nationale Recherche, 'RL8026', 01/13: 173; GET: 4127-28; Erkel, *Samir*, 74-75; Former Hofstadgroup Participant 3, 'Personal Interview 1', 6-7; Former Hofstadgroup Participant 4, 'Personal Interview 2', 5; Groen and Kranenberg, *Women Warriors*, 19; Peters, 'De Ideologische En Religieuze Ontwikkeling', appendix: Overzicht teksten geschreven of vertaald door Mohammed B., 33.

119 'ik kreeg haatgevoelens jegens iedereen die achter Bush stond in zijn kruistocht, niet alleen Nederland, maar ook de Arabische afvallige leiders': A[.], 'Deurwaarders', 9.

120 Ibid., 3, 5-8; Dienst Nationale Recherche, 'RL8026', 01/01: 131; AHA04/21: 1666; 01/13: 163; AHB01/25: 3166-68; GET: 4128, 18116; Former Hofstadgroup Participant 1, 'Personal Interview 1', 6; Erkel, *Samir*, 65-67; Groen and Kranenberg, *Women Warriors*, 68-70, 169-70; Peters, 'De Ideologische En Religieuze Ontwikkeling', appendix: Overzicht teksten geschreven of vertaald door Mohammed B., 33.

121 Dienst Nationale Recherche, 'RL8026', 01/13: 163.

122 A[.], 'Deurwaarders', 10.

this time the group had clearly attracted the attention of the police and AIVD, making foreign travel much more difficult. It was also influenced by political grievances; as a loyal ally of the United States and Israel, and as a contributor to the interventions in Afghanistan and Iraq, the Dutch government was increasingly seen as sharing responsibility for the harm that had befallen Muslims. In the eyes of some participants it had become a legitimate target.[123]

Geopolitically inspired grievances formed key explanatory factors. They were crucial to understanding how and why many participants came into contact with radical and extremist interpretations of Islam. The vicarious sense of outrage and injustice that images of their co-religionists' suffering induced were key to the establishment of a common cause between the Hofstadgroup's (future) participants and the global ummah. For some, these grievances motivated and justified a desire to strike back, to avenge perceived injustices against fellow Muslims. Indeed, the Dutch role in the interventions in Afghanistan and Iraq motivated some participants to pursue plans for terrorism in the Netherlands. In the absence of geopolitical events involving the perceived victimization of Muslim populations, the Hofstadgroup would arguably not have existed or developed in the way it did.

5.3.3   A clash of value systems?

Several authors have argued that European homegrown jihadism arose out of a fundamental incompatibility between radical Islam and liberal democracy.[124] It is a line of reasoning that resembles Huntington's thesis that the dominant source of post-Cold War conflict would be '[t]he fault lines between civilizations'.[125] The broader literature on political violence is, however, equivocal on the matter. For instance, while Senechal de la Roche argues that greater 'cultural distance' is positively associated with a higher probability of collective violence,[126] Fearon and Laitin find no clear

---

123   Ibid., 4-5, 9; Former Hofstadgroup Participant 1, 'Personal Interview 1', 6; De Graaf, *Gevaarlijke Vrouwen*, 256-57; Dienst Nationale Recherche, 'RL8026', 01/01: 131; 01/13: 61; 01/17: 4069; AHA01/18: 100; AHA05/22: 2228; Erkel, *Samir*, 74-75, 118-19; Groen and Kranenberg, *Women Warriors*, 20-21; NOVA, 'Videotestament Samir A.'; Peters, 'De Ideologische En Religieuze Ontwikkeling', appendix: Overzicht teksten geschreven of vertaald door Mohammed B., 32-34; Van San, Sieckelinck, and De Winter, *Idealen Op Drift*, 47-48.
124   Spruyt, 'Liberalism and the Challenge of Islam', 318-24; Cliteur, 'De Lankmoedige Elite', 232-34; Leiken, 'Europe's Angry Muslims', 121-22; Leiken, 'Europe's Mujahideen', 3.
125   Huntington, 'The Clash of Civilizations?', 22.
126   Senechal de la Roche, 'Collective Violence', 108-09.

link between ethnic or religious diversity and the outbreak of civil wars and insurgencies.[127]

At first glance, the Hofstadgroup's radical and extremist views and its participants' rejection of democratic laws, values, and institutions certainly made them incompatible with Dutch liberal democracy. Furthering this divide, many participants did not see themselves as Dutch.[128] A crucial point to make, however, is that these attitudes do not appear to have *motivated* involvement in the Hofstadgroup but rather to have *stemmed* from it. Prior to their involvement in the group, most participants led apparently well-integrated lives; attending school, holding (part-time) work, and enjoying recreational activities like other Dutch citizens their age. Several individuals did not become practicing Muslims until contact with Hofstadgroup participants led to a reorientation on their faith.[129] Others were converts to Islam.[130]

Even among those who had had a religious upbringing, clear signs of outright hostility towards Western culture and politics did not manifest themselves *until after* they had adopted radical or extremist interpretations of Islam.[131] As previously discussed, many did grow up in a social environment in which negative out-group stereotypes were prevalent, arguably lowering barriers to seeing violence against these perceived enemies as justified. This social facilitation potentially made it *easier* for Hofstadgroup participants to come to see terrorist violence as necessary and legitimate. However, most did not appear to have started their participation in the group with pro-violence convictions already firmly in place.

These findings underline the importance of distinguishing between Islam and radical or extremist interpretations of the religion such as Salafi-Jihadism. The available data provide little to suggest that the Hofstadgroup was a manifestation of an inherent incompatibility between Islam and Western democracy. They do, however, show that such an adversarial relationship developed once radical and extremist views were adopted. This speaks to the power of the Salafi-Jihadist ideological narrative to instill or sharpen preexisting in-group/out-group distinctions and thus lay the basis for intergroup hostility and violence.

---

127 Fearon and Laitin, 'Ethnicity, Insurgency, and Civil War', 75-76, 78, 83-84.
128 Former Hofstadgroup Participant 2, 'Personal Interview 1', 2.
129 Dienst Nationale Recherche, 'RL8026', 01/17: 4002, 4047, 4051, 4061; GET: 18157, 18215; VERD: 9917, 9935, 20012, 20225, 20131; Former Hofstadgroup Participant 2, 'Personal Interview 1', 7.
130 Dienst Nationale Recherche, 'RL8026', 01/17: 4084, 4145, 4177; VERD: 20461, 20518.
131 Chorus and Olgun, *In Godsnaam*, 44-53; A[.], 'Deurwaarders', 1-3.

5.4 Structural-level precipitants: Submission, part 1

Precipitants are 'specific events that immediately precede the occurrence of terrorism'.[132] Given that Van Gogh's murder was the only terrorist attack to actually be carried out by a Hofstadgroup participant, can a precipitant event be identified in the time period leading up to it? It seems highly likely that the killer was triggered by the broadcast of the short film *Submission, part 1* on 29 August 2004 on Dutch national television.[133] Although Van Gogh's assailant never explicitly referred to the film in his writings or in court, he chose to murder its director and he left a note on his body threatening Hirsi Ali, who came up with the idea for the film in the first place.

Additional, albeit circumstantial, corroboration for the conclusion that *Submission* triggered the murder of Van Gogh is that other Hofstadgroup participants also reacted strongly, if only in words, to the film. Death threats were posted on Hofstadgroup-administered forums,[134] at least one individual told another participant that he wanted to see Hirsi Ali and Van Gogh killed because of *Submission*[135] and several, while disagreeing with the murder, believed Van Gogh had 'asked for it'.[136] One interviewee claimed that the film helped swing the group's focus towards waging jihad in the Netherlands.[137] Despite the shared antagonism, however, it was only Van Gogh's killer who acted.

5.5 Conclusion

This chapter focused on structural-level factors relevant to understanding how and why involvement in the Hofstadgroup materialized. It did so by utilizing Crenshaw's distinction between 'preconditions' that enable or motivate involvement in terrorism and 'precipitants' that spark an actual attack.[138] Structural factors not only provided *opportunities* for the Hofstadgroup's emergence, but also formed parts of some of its participants' motivation to engage in violence, and contributed to a change in those

---

132 Crenshaw, 'The Causes of Terrorism', 381.
133 Public Prosecutor 1, 'Personal Interview 1', 28; Public Prosecutor 2, 'Personal Interview 1', 4; NCTV Employee 1, 'Personal Interview 1', 4.
134 Dienst Nationale Recherche, 'RL8026', 01/13: 165-66.
135 Ibid., 01/13: 74.
136 Ibid., 01/17: 4231; VERD: 20226-28, 20231, 20319, 20462.
137 Former Hofstadgroup Participant 1, 'Personal Interview 2', 23-24.
138 Crenshaw, 'The Causes of Terrorism'.

motives from becoming a foreign fighter to waging violent jihad in the Netherlands. Structural factors also played a key role in triggering the terrorist attack on Van Gogh.

With regard to facilitation, the role of the Internet was especially important. It exposed Hofstadgroup participants to geopolitical developments, militant interpretations of Islam, practical knowledge on the use of weapons and explosives and formed an easy-to-use communications tool and propaganda platform. Another facilitating factor was the openness of Dutch society, which afforded the group considerable freedom to organize, travel, and propagate their views. Thirdly, it is likely that growing up in a social environment in which Islamic fundamentalist views were prevalent lowered at least some participants' threshold to seeing the use of violence as legitimate by instilling a sense of out-group hostility directed at the Western world. Finally, the AIVD's misdiagnosis of Van Gogh's killer as a peripheral group participant and, in particular, Van Gogh's refusal to accept police protection, increased the attacker's opportunities to strike.

Looking at motivational preconditions, geopolitical grievances stand out. Conflicts involving Muslims populations, the U.S.-led 'War on Terror', and terrorist attacks such as those orchestrated on 9/11 had several influences. They triggered searches for answers that contributed to group participants' eventual adoption of radical and extremist views, instilled the conviction that a war against Islam was being waged, and made retaliatory violence seem both justified and necessary. Political grievances also motivated some participants to start thinking about conducting a terrorist attack in the Netherlands, as opposed to joining Islamist insurgents overseas.

Perhaps surprisingly, there are no clear indications that socioeconomic inequality, the harsh tone of the Dutch integration debate, or lack of access to the democratic political system directly motivated involvement in the Hofstadgroup. Experiences with discrimination did, however, strengthen participants' convictions and feed their hatred of unbelievers. Finally, the precipitant event that likely triggered the murder of Van Gogh was the broadcast of *Submission*, a short Islam-critical film that he had directed and which caused considerable offense among Hofstadgroup participants.

Structural-level factors were crucial to understanding how and why involvement in the Hofstadgroup's emerged. Yet the present analysis falls short in that the factors described are experienced by many more people than those that actually become involved in the Hofstadgroup. Why, with so many other Dutch Muslims exposed to images of war and conflict involving their co-religionists, and with similar opportunities for engaging in violence, did only the Hofstadgroup's participants react by embracing radicalism and militancy? The inability of the structural level of analysis to account for the variable influence of factors such as political grievances or relative deprivation points to the need to utilize other analytical perspectives. This chapter has hinted at the importance of group dynamics on numerous occasions. It is to this topic that the discussion now turns.

6 Group dynamics I: Initiating and sustaining involvement

Terrorism is predominantly a group phenomenon.¹ This draws attention to the second part of the multilevel analytical framework outlined in Chapter 2; namely, the role of group dynamics. How do terrorist groups influence the worldview and behavior of their participants? In this first of two chapters on group dynamics and involvement in terrorism, the focus is on the group processes that draw and bind people to terrorist groups. Seven group-level hypotheses are analyzed and applied to the data on the Hofstadgroup to understand the role of group dynamics in bringing about participation and how they subsequently influenced participants' adoption of radical and extremist beliefs. The analysis of the role of group dynamics is completed in the next chapter, which discusses their influence on the commission of actual terrorist attacks.

6.1 Group dynamics and involvement in terrorism

Group dynamics have attracted considerable attention from terrorism researchers.² In recent years, this level of analysis has been described as of above-average explanatory potential when it comes to understanding involvement. Kleinmann, for instance, found that '[g]roup-level processes are the most significant mechanism for radicalization of both convert and non-convert homegrown Sunni militants in the United States'.³ In *Leaderless Jihad*, Marc Sageman argues that both micro and macro perspectives on terrorism are limited in their ability to offer an understanding of terrorism and that a middle-ground analysis is needed, one in which ample attention is paid to the *relationships between terrorists*, such as leader-follower interactions.⁴ A first step towards assessing whether group dynamics can also offer useful insights into how involvement in the Hofstadgroup came about, is inventorying relevant explanations at this level of analysis.

---

1   Nesser, 'Toward an Increasingly Heterogeneous Threat', 440, 450; Spaaij, 'The Engima of Lone Wolf Terrorism', 859.
2   Della Porta, 'Recruitment Processes', 307-16; McCauley and Segal, 'Social Psychology of Terrorist Groups', 331-46.
3   Kleinmann, 'Radicalization of Homegrown Sunni Militants', 288.
4   Sageman, *Leaderless Jihad*, 23-24.

Several authors have conducted literature reviews of group-level factors relevant to terrorism.[5] These provide useful overviews of the most prevalent hypotheses, but generally do not organize them according to a particular logic. There is no equivalent to Crenshaw's division of the structural-level causes of terrorism into preconditions and precipitants that can be used to organize the discussion of the group level of analysis.[6] A solution is provided by Taylor and Horgan, who distinguish *involvement decisions* from *event decisions*, essentially arguing that the processes by which people become involved in terrorist groups are distinct from those that lead some group members to participate in actual attacks.[7] Joining a terrorist group does not mean that the participant will also become involved in actual violence.

Following Taylor and Horgan's argument, the group level of analysis has been divided into two. The first part deals with group processes that influence how and why people join and stay in extremist or terrorist groups. The second focuses on group dynamics that influence the commission of terrorist attacks. Because the literature on both of these subjects is extensive, each is discussed in a separate chapter. The current one focuses on the contribution made by group-level factors to bringing about and sustaining involvement in terrorism. A review of the literature on terrorism revealed eight group-level explanations other researchers have thought relevant to this discussion (Table 7). Only one hypothesis could be dismissed out of hand. The literature indicates broad consensus that 'brainwashing', the idea that people can be coerced to adopt ideas, does not constitute a credible, empirically substantiated hypothesis.[8] Despite being an explanation encountered with some frequency in journalistic accounts of involvement in terrorism, it is not given further consideration here.[9]

---

5 Borum, 'Radicalization into Violent Extremism I', 7-36; LaFree and Ackerman, 'The Empirical Study of Terrorism', 355-60; Veldhuis and Staun, *Islamist Radicalisation*, 39-51.
6 Crenshaw, 'The Causes of Terrorism', 381.
7 Taylor and Horgan, 'A Conceptual Framework', 592; Horgan, *Walking Away from Terrorism*, 13, 142-46; Taylor, 'Is Terrorism a Group Phenomenon?', 125-26.
8 Dawson, 'The Study of New Religious Movements', 3; Hofmann and Dawson, 'The Neglected Role', 351, 60; Sageman, *Understanding Terror Networks*, 124-25.
9 Derix, 'Volgelingen Syriër "Opgefokt En Gehersenspoeld"'; Van der Veen, 'Kijken: 10 Jaar Na De Aanslagen'.

Table 7 Initiating and sustaining involvement in terrorist groups

Terrorist group formation
Social identity and the benefits of group membership
Socialization into a worldview conducive to terrorism
The underground life
Social learning theory
The influence of leaders
Peer pressures
~~Brainwashing~~

6.2 Terrorist group formation

Terrorist group formation is generally seen as either a top-down or a bottom-up process. The first revolves around premeditated attempts by recruiters to encourage or coax others into joining an established terrorist organization.[10] Blazak, for instance, has found that such activities are prevalent among American Nazi skinheads.[11] Bottom-up group formation is a much more autonomous process, whereby like-minded individuals come together without the intervention of recruiters linked to established terrorist organizations.[12] Autonomous group formation is not random, however. Research shows that participation in radical or extremist groups is often guided by preexisting social ties.[13] People become involved in groups, terrorist or otherwise, to a large extent because family members, friends, or acquaintances are already participating who thus provide exposure and easy access to said groups.[14]

The lack of recruiters does not mean that bottom-up processes are necessarily completely volitional. In the context of Italian left-wing extremism, Della Porta found that the desire to obtain the approval of companions already part of clandestine organizations influenced the involvement process of new members.[15] This desire not to be seen remaining on the sidelines exerted a form of peer pressure that propelled non-committed friends towards participation. Similar sentiments, albeit much more

---

10 Kruglanski and Fishman, 'Psychological Factors', 13.
11 Blazak, 'White Boys to Terrorist Men', 990-94.
12 Veldhuis and Staun, *Islamist Radicalisation*, 48-49.
13 Della Porta, 'Recruitment Processes', 309-10; Lofland and Stark, 'Becoming a World-Saver', 862-75.
14 Munson, *The Making Of*, 48-54, 187-89; McCauley and Segal, 'Social Psychology of Terrorist Groups', 338.
15 Della Porta, 'Recruitment Processes', 310.

strongly expressed, were found among members of Palestinian terrorist groups. As a participant of one such group stated, '[a]nyone who didn't enlist during that period (*intifada*) would have been ostracized'.[16] Even in the absence of conscious efforts at recruitment, terrorist groups can still exert a powerful pull on potential members.

Various studies indicate that the formation of homegrown jihadist groups, particularly in the first decade of the 21st century, is largely a bottom-up process.[17] Most homegrown jihadists are 'connected by blood, marriage, and close friendships'.[18] Yet autonomous group formation should not be taken as an essential characteristic of European homegrown jihadism. Nesser's research on jihadist groups active in Europe between 1995 and 2010 shows a mixture of top-down and autonomous patterns of group formation.[19] The rise of autonomously formed groups in the Hofstadgroup time period appears strongly related to intensified domestic and international counterterrorism efforts that seriously hampered the ability of groups like al-Qaeda to operate internationally and made it more difficult for Western citizens to travel to Afghanistan and Iraq.[20] The homegrown nature of entities like the Hofstadgroup may reflect geopolitical realities rather than a consciously chosen organizational format.

The Hofstadgroup was no exception to the autonomous group formation trend. One interviewee described it as a 'circle of acquaintances'.[21] Many participants had been long-time friends, had grown up together in the same neighborhood, attended the same schools, or visited the same mosques. Others met each other in asylum seekers' centers, were colleagues, or became acquainted through an Internet café they frequented.[22] Those who did not have preexisting ties to other participants got to know them through

---

16 Post, Sprinzak, and Denny, 'The Terrorists in Their Own Words', 178.
17 Bakker, 'Characteristics of Jihadi Terrorists', 142; Bartolo, 'Decentralised Leadership in Contemporary Jihadism', 52-54; Roy, 'Al-Qaeda', 22-23; Sageman, *Understanding Terror Networks*, 107-20; Sageman, *Leaderless Jihad*, 66, 109; Vidino, 'Radicalization, Linkage, and Diversity', ix, 3-4.
18 Harris-Hogan, 'Australian Neo-Jihadist Terrorism', 311.
19 Nesser, *Jihad in Europe*, 523-25.
20 Sageman, 'Confronting Al-Qaeda', 22-24.
21 'een vriendenkring': Former Hofstadgroup Participant 3, 'Personal Interview 1', 4.
22 Dienst Nationale Recherche, 'RL8026', VERD: 19444, 19459, 19675, 19717, 19858-860, 19877, 19916, 19980, 19994, 20079, 20112, 20115, 20174; GET: 18215, 18312-313, 18374-375, 18414, 20348; 01/17: 4176; AHA03/20: 1227; Dienst Nationale Recherche, 'Piranha', 11520; Van der Hulst, 'Terroristische Netwerken', 15; Former Hofstadgroup Participant 4, 'Personal Interview 2', 3; Erkel, *Samir*, 78-79; Chorus and Olgun, *Broeders*, 7, 17-18, 83; Vermaat, *Nederlandse Jihad*, 109-10, 119, 193.

introductions by mutual acquaintances,[23] online discussion forums,[24] or by being brought along to a group meeting.[25] As far as can be gleaned from the available data, peer pressure does not appear to have propelled involvement. Instead, group formation throughout the Hofstadgroup's existence was driven almost entirely by individuals who came together, volitionally and by chance, through preexisting social networks.

The Hofstadgroup's largely autonomous formation begs the question whether recruitment played any role at all. The October 2003 attempts by two participants to entice other young Muslims to travel to Pakistan or Afghanistan do not count, as this recruitment effort was not geared towards enlarging the Hofstadgroup itself or forming a separate terrorist cell in the Netherlands. Several group participants did, however, use the Internet to spread their views and engaged in online chat conversations with people in the hope of converting them to their point of view.[26] On the whole, however, the evidence suggests that these online outreach activities were principally focused on conveying the 'right' religious views rather than deliberate attempts to form or enlarge an extremist organization. As such, they seem better described as a form of outreach or missionary zeal.

An anecdote that more clearly raises the possibility of recruitment involved one of the middle-aged Syrian men, detailed in Chapter 3 and Chapter 5, who appeared on the group's fringes. An interviewee recalled speaking with this individual at a mosque several times. During those talks, the Syrian man explained that the interviewee's failure to get an internship was due to the 'unbelievers' not granting Muslims anything. Recognizing that he had struck a chord, the Syrian man later suggested that the interviewee meet with someone to discuss this topic further and gave him the phone number of a Hofstadgroup participant. Following this introduction, the interviewee soon found himself in the house of Van Gogh's

---

23   Dienst Nationale Recherche, 'RL8026', 01/17: 4001, 4004, 4086-87; AHA05/22: 2566; Dienst Nationale Recherche, 'Piranha', 313-17, 3756; Former Hofstadgroup Participant 4, 'Personal Interview 2', 3; Erkel, *Samir*, 186, 257, 61; Groen and Kranenberg, *Women Warriors*, 24-25, 123; De Koning, 'Changing Worldviews and Friendship', 385-86.
24   Former Hofstadgroup Participant 3, 'Personal Interview 1', 7; Dienst Nationale Recherche, 'RL8026', VERD: 18410; 01/17: 4001-4003, 4084, 4124; Groen and Kranenberg, *Women Warriors*, 22.
25   Former Hofstadgroup Participant 1, 'Personal Interview 2', 7-8; Dienst Nationale Recherche, 'RL8026', VERD: 19459, 19465, 19475, 20217; 01/17: 4087, 4124, 4178-4179; Erkel, *Samir*, 37-38, 78-79, 186.
26   Dienst Nationale Recherche, 'RL8026', 01/17: 4002-03, 4020, 4026-31, 4047-51, 4084-85, 4128; GET: 18410; Former Hofstadgroup Participant 1, 'Personal Interview 2', 18-19, 32; Former Hofstadgroup Participant 5, 'Personal Interview 1', 1-3.

future killer and attending lectures given by Abu Khaled, an acquaintance, moreover, of the Syrian man who suggested the interviewee make contact with the group.[27]

While this series of events is suggestive of recruitment, two factors advocate caution in using this description. First of all, there is no evidence that the first of the two Syrian men mentioned above had a hand in referring other individuals towards the group. This raises the possibility that it was a chance encounter that provided the Syrian man with the opportunity to put like-minded individuals in touch with one another. Moreover, there is nothing to suggest that the Hofstadgroup's religious instructor was himself making deliberate efforts to enlarge the group through recruitment. His role appears to have been limited to conveying a fundamentalist interpretation of Islam.[28] It is unlikely, therefore, that the two Syrian men were working together as part of a deliberate effort to enlarge the Hofstadgroup.

Recruitment may have played a role in 2005's Piranha case. Two participants claimed in court that they were coerced into providing assistance.[29] However, the truthfulness of these assertions is questionable. Other participants have claimed that the couple, who became key witnesses for the prosecution, presented themselves as helpless victims only to avoid being sentenced.[30] A judge labeled the couple's testimony as 'untrustworthy' for similar reasons.[31] In lieu of more convincing or concrete evidence to the contrary, the conclusion remains that the Hofstadgroup's formation was an overwhelmingly autonomous process. Its participants were not vulnerable youngsters who were sought out by recruiters with the specific aim of turning them into Islamist extremists. Instead, group formation depended predominantly on preexisting social ties, with a lesser role for introductions through friends or acquaintances and the transmutation of virtual connections into 'real-life' ones.

27 Former Hofstadgroup Participant 1, 'Personal Interview 2', 2-5.
28 A[.], 'Deurwaarders', 24; Former Hofstadgroup Participant 1, 'Personal Interview 1', 2-3; 'Personal Interview 2', 8-9; Dienst Nationale Recherche, 'RL8026', 01/13: 136-40; 01/17: 4002, 4026, 4048-50, 4090-91, 4096, 4098, 4129, 4179, 4146, 4201; AHB02/26: 3796-803; Erkel, *Samir*.
29 Dienst Nationale Recherche, 'Piranha', 209-14, 218-27.
30 'Getuige Piranha-Zaak Zelf Radicaal'; Kranenberg and Groen, 'Kroongetuigen Vallen in Eigen Kuil'.
31 Kranenberg and Groen, 'Kroongetuigen Vallen in Eigen Kuil'.

6.3   Social identity and the benefits of group membership

People have a universal desire to attain a satisfactory self-image, and an important part of that image is shaped by the 'social identity' derived from group membership.[32] Through a process of 'social categorization', individuals impose order on a complex social environment by subjectively dividing it into a multitude of groups. These groups are not necessarily formal organizations but may also include 'cognitive entities' based, for example, on social class, ethnicity, or religion.[33] People tend to identify themselves with numerous groups simultaneously, with contextual factors influencing when a certain group-based identity is activated. For instance, someone's social identity as a supporter of a soccer team will be more prominent during match attendance than in a work environment. But some social identities can become so important that they are 'chronically salient', influencing all aspects of life.[34]

Terrorist groups provide chronically salient social identities through the demands placed on members. Participants are not only required to risk life and liberty but to reimagine themselves according to the group's particular reality, be that as holy warriors, a revolutionary vanguard, or nationalist freedom fighters.[35] But with social categorization providing individuals with a veritable marketplace of groups to choose from in their pursuit of self-fulfillment, why would someone be drawn to those involved in political violence in the first place?[36] As Dalgaard-Nielsen writes, the success of a movement depends on its ability to promote a worldview that resonates with potential recruits.[37] What benefits can terrorist groups offer their members that outweigh the very real risks of imprisonment and death?

People may join a terrorist group because they value the cause it strives for, essentially engaging in terrorism for strategic reasons.[38] The strategic rationale of terrorism is explored in more detail in Chapter 7. For now, it is sufficient to note that a considerable body of research indicates that such instrumental motives are certainly not the only, and perhaps

---

32   Tajfel, 'Social Identity', 68-69.
33   Tajfel and Turner, 'An Integrative Theory', 40.
34   Ellemers, Spears, and Doosje, 'Self and Social Identity', 164, 166.
35   Kruglanski, Chen, and Golec, 'Individual Motivations', 70-84; Hemmingsen, 'The Attractions of Jihadism'.
36   Tajfel, 'Social Identity', 69.
37   Dalgaard-Nielsen, 'Violent Radicalization in Europe', 802.
38   Crenshaw, 'Theories of Terrorism', 14-15.

not even the most important, benefits of membership. Participation in terrorism can also provide *emotional* satisfaction, such as the ability to violently avenge perceived wrongs, *cognitive* benefits, such as the idea that one is fighting for a worthy cause, *social* assets like increased status and comradeship and, finally, opportunities for *personal gain* simply by taking under threat of violence what would otherwise have remained beyond reach.[39]

These rewards of group membership can explain not only why people *become* involved in terrorism but also why they *remain* involved. The benefits outlined in the previous paragraph can become so important to participants that they perpetuate their involvement, make disengagement more difficult, and stifle criticism of group norms or behavior.[40] In extreme cases, individuals' social identity can have such a powerful influence on their worldview and behavior that they subjugate themselves entirely to the aims and well-being of the group, even willingly sacrificing their own lives.[41] Can social identity and the benefits of group membership explain the attraction of the Hofstadgroup?

Part of the Hofstadgroup's appeal was that participants could imagine themselves as one of the few righteous Muslims in a country filled with unbelievers, sinners, and apostates. For many participants, the group was an alternative to a Dutch Islamic community 'tainted' by imams who refused to discuss jihad in order to appease the Dutch government and by fellow believers who failed to live and worship as 'true' Muslims.[42] The group's religious nature was not just some superficial gloss but its central appeal.[43] This is aptly illustrated by an interviewee who adamantly dispelled the idea, put forward in Dutch media, that the group practiced a 'cut-and-paste Islam'[44], insisting that religious beliefs were not only taken extremely seriously but rigorously studied during gatherings.[45] Such statements suggest that by enabling self-perception as a 'true' Muslim,

---

39 McCauley and Segal, 'Social Psychology of Terrorist Groups', 336; Victoroff, 'The Mind of the Terrorist', 30; Crenshaw, *Explaining Terrorism*, 75-82; Al Raffie, 'Social Identity Theory', 67-68.
40 Pynchon and Borum, 'Assessing Threats', 349.
41 Ellemers, Spears, and Doosje, 'Self and Social Identity', 163.
42 Dienst Nationale Recherche, 'RL8026', 01/17: 4016, 4030, 4048-51, 4085-86, 4090-93, 4127, 4131; Former Hofstadgroup Participant 3, 'Personal Interview 1', 1-2, 5, 9; Former Hofstadgroup Participant 1, 'Personal Interview 2', 11-12, 18-21, 27; Groen and Kranenberg, *Women Warriors*, 215.
43 Former Hofstadgroup Participant 1, 'Personal Interview 1', 1; Former Hofstadgroup Participant 4, 'Personal Interview 2', 3; Former Hofstadgroup Participant 5, 'Personal Interview 1', 1-2.
44 Oostveen, 'De Knip- En-Plak-Islam'.
45 Former Hofstadgroup Participant 1, 'Personal Interview 2', 12-13.

the cognitive benefits of participation were an important part of the group's appeal.

Participation in the Hofstadgroup also provided social and emotional benefits. Many participants valued simply being among friends; chatting, playing some soccer, or sharing a meal.[46] One interviewee recalled feeling a strong sense of belonging and friendship during his very first encounter with other participants, which motivated him to keep going back.[47] Another participant, an illegal immigrant, supposedly said that he greatly missed his family in Morocco, but that his 'brothers' had become his new family and that he loved them very much.[48] In jail after the murder of Van Gogh, one participant bragged about his Hofstadgroup 'membership', indicating participation could also bring the benefits of status.[49] An emotional benefit for participants was their ability to enter into short-term 'marriages', officiated by the groups' religious authority figures, which enabled them to have sex without breaking Islamic injunctions against casual relationships.[50]

An important finding is thus that the cognitive, social, and emotional benefits *sustained* participation. However, there are no indications that they also *initiated* involvement. No one seems to have consciously sought out the Hofstadgroup because they wanted so share in the self-perception of being a 'true believer' or because they were looking for comradeship. Partly this can be explained by the group's lack of a clear organizational structure and the fact that it was largely anonymous and unknown until Van Gogh's murder; few people were aware of its existence and outsiders had no clear point of contact to facilitate entry. Although the group became a household name after November 2004, it also became much more secretive during 2005's Piranha case, again precluding easy access by potential newcomers. Instead, preexisting social networks brought like-minded individuals together, after which group-identity-related processes bound them together and worked to prolong their involvement.

---

46   Dienst Nationale Recherche, 'RL8026', 01/17: 4158; VERD: 19475, 19477, 19479-80, 19866, 19935, 19980, 20012, 20131, 20213, 20228, 20313, 20363, 20468, 20484; Former Hofstadgroup Participant 1, 'Personal Interview 1', 2; 'Personal Interview 2', 13; 'Personal Interview 3', 3; Former Hofstadgroup Participant 3, 'Personal Interview 1', 1, 9; Vermaat, *Nederlandse Jihad*, 112, 17.
47   Former Hofstadgroup Participant 1, 'Personal Interview 2', 6-9.
48   Dienst Nationale Recherche, 'RL8026', 01/17: 4049.
49   Vermaat, *Nederlandse Jihad*, 105.
50   Dienst Nationale Recherche, 'RL8026', 01/17: 4003, 4053, 4086-87, 4101, 4110-111, 4114-115, 4145-147, 154; Groen and Kranenberg, *Women Warriors*, 30-33; Chorus and Olgun, 'Op De Thee', 7.

6.4 Socialization into a worldview conducive to terrorism

As Della Porta argues, 'conversion to violence requires a specific redefinition of reality'.[51] In other words, an individual's willingness to commit acts of terrorism is a process that is generally not completed by the mere act of *joining* a terrorist group. An important next step is formed by members' internalization of worldviews and group norms conducive to the use of violence.[52] Before the next paragraphs discuss the group-based mechanisms that led the Hofstadgroup's participants to adopt such views, it is instructive to briefly revisit what those views were. How were they conducive to seeing terrorism as a legitimate form of behavior?

Chapter 3 concluded that it is problematic to speak of a single or commonly held 'Hofstadgroup ideology'. Yet broadly shared ideological themes existed which could provide justifications and even imperatives for the use of violence. The most important of these were a sense of crisis which mandated participation in violent jihad and a dichotomous worldview that made clear distinctions between a small rightly guided in-group and a much larger and threatening out-group. For instance, Van Gogh's killer believed the Islamic world was beset by both external enemies (American imperialism, Western materialism, corrupt Middle-Eastern regimes) and foes within (apostates, Shiite heretics, 'Westernized' Muslims). Only an 'awakening' to these realities and a willingness to fight and sacrifice in defense of 'true' Islam could stave off the religion's imminent demise and the persecution of its adherents.[53]

Participants also placed considerable emphasis on their beliefs' normative aspects. Only polities structured and run in accordance with a strict and dogmatic interpretation of Islamic law ('Sharia') were seen to suffice.[54] The group could also be very inward-looking. De Koning aptly described participants as engaged in a 'competition of piety'.[55] Not only did they harshly judge Muslims outside of the group's boundaries, their critical eye did not spare compatriots who failed to adhere to group norms, such as growing a beard, or who were deemed to have committed transgressions such as accepting the aid of a lawyer, thereby undermining Allah's status

---

51 Della Porta, *Social Movements*, 136.
52 Egerton, *Jihad in the West*, 151; Silke, 'Holy Warriors', 111.
53 Peters, 'Dutch Extremist Islamism', 145-59.
54 Dienst Nationale Recherche, 'RL8026', 01/13: 63-64, 124-25, 127-31, 137, 140, 151, 163; AHA03/20: 1171; AHA06/23: 2555; AHA07/24: 3226; 01/17: 4049-50, 4052, 4131; Peters, 'De Ideologische En Religieuze Ontwikkeling', 2-12.
55 De Koning, 'Changing Worldviews and Friendship', 387.

as the sole source of legal authority.[56] Some went so far as to refuse to participate in a game of soccer as doing so would implicitly mean accepting the man-made and therefore tawhid-undermining rules of the Dutch soccer association.[57]

The normative aspects of the Hofstadgroup's ideology also fed participants' adversarial relationship with out-groups. Most notably in the case of takfir, as excommunication carries with it the justification to murder the apostate.[58] Extremist elements within the group also took their understanding of tawhid to mean that non-Islamic laws could and should be flaunted and that unbelievers' property and, in some cases, even their lives were free for the taking.[59] In short, while the Hofstadgroup lacked a clearly defined and commonly held ideology, the group's more extremist participants in particular held to and conveyed beliefs that could provide motivations and justifications for the use of violence. These beliefs also provided normative standards by which Muslims both in and outside of the group were judged, creating behavioral and ideological rules to which participants were expected to adhere. The next sections discuss how these views were spread and upheld.

6.5   The underground life

A group's 'social reality value' is its ability to define moral standards for its members and enforce their compliance.[60] For example, groups with high social reality value are better able to influence their members' thinking on such matters as what constitutes 'good' and who or what is 'evil'.[61] An important variable that determines a group's social reality value is the degree of 'competition' it faces from other groups. As section 6.3 explained, people tend to have numerous social identities whose salience is often context dependent; a person's professional attitudes and behavior will

---

56   Dienst Nationale Recherche, 'RL8026', VERD: 19475; De Koning, 'Changing Worldviews and Friendship', 387-88; Groen and Kranenberg, *Women Warriors*, 181; Former Hofstadgroup Participant 3, 'Personal Interview 1', 2-3; Chorus and Olgun, *Broeders*, 16-17; Former Hofstadgroup Participant 4, 'Personal Interview 2', 3.
57   Former Hofstadgroup Participant 1, 'Personal Interview 3', 2.
58   Brooke, 'Jihadist Strategic Debates', 202; Dienst Nationale Recherche, 'RL8026', 01/17: 4052.
59   'RL8026', 01/13: 161-62; AHD08/37: 8713-14, 8765-66; AHD09/38: sessie 13; VERD: 19745; GET: 4086, 4094.
60   McCauley and Moskalenko, 'Mechanisms of Political Radicalization', 423-24.
61   Ibid., 423.

tend to dominate in a work setting, affiliation with a certain sports team during matches, etcetera. When numerous group memberships 'compete' for influence on a person's values and behavior, it is unlikely that any one in particular will become predominant. However, when all but one group identity remains, its ability to exert such control increases markedly.[62]

The criminal nature of terrorism forces those who engage in it to lead a covert existence. As authorities deploy more means to apprehend or kill terrorists, the latter's need for secrecy increases. The necessity of maintaining operational security can force terrorist groups to 'go underground', that is to lead an entirely secret and withdrawn existence. Once underground, their members have only each other to rely on, leading to increased interdependence, the strengthening of interpersonal bonds, and a heightened desire to protect comrades and the larger group.[63] 'Having entered a world of conspiracy and danger, the [terrorists] are bound together before a common threat of exposure, imprisonment or death'.[64] In such a setting, the group's social reality value increases dramatically, as does its ability to influence members' worldviews and behavior. Isolation can thus increase a terrorist group's ability to fashion the worldviews of its adherents, facilitating their acceptance of political violence as necessary and legitimate.[65]

The Hofstadgroup's participants gradually withdrew from society. Mosque attendance was largely supplanted by privately held discussions and prayers.[66] The group became the focal point of social interactions, in some cases entirely supplanting old friends and family.[67] A number of participants saw each other on an almost daily basis and several of them even lived together for varying periods of time.[68] One of the travelers to Pakistan or Afghanistan quit a part-time job because he felt it clashed with his religious convictions. Some others abandoned school or jobs for similar

---

62   Ibid.
63   Ibid.; Pynchon and Borum, 'Assessing Threats', 350; Della Porta, *Social Movements*, 133-35, 180; Egerton, *Jihad in the West*, 156-57; Veldhuis and Bakker, 'Causale Factoren Van Radicalisering', 458-59.
64   Crenshaw, *Explaining Terrorism*, 107.
65   Egerton, *Jihad in the West*, 155.
66   Dienst Nationale Recherche, 'RL8026', 01/17: 4002, 4004, 4016, 4049, 4054, 4092, 4177-179, 4199; Former Hofstadgroup Participant 1, 'Personal Interview 2', 11-12, 20; Former Hofstadgroup Participant 3, 'Personal Interview 1', 8-9.
67   Dienst Nationale Recherche, 'RL8026', 01/17: 4049.
68   Former Hofstadgroup Participant 1, 'Personal Interview 3', 2; Dienst Nationale Recherche, 'RL8026', 01/13: 23-24, 92; AHA03/20: 860; VERD: 20212; Dienst Nationale Recherche, 'Piranha', REL00: 51-53.

reasons or were encouraged to do so.[69] The numerous arrests, the knowledge that the group had attracted the AIVD's attention, and the inability or unwillingness of imams to discuss jihad-related topics formed external pressures towards isolation.[70] In the words of an interviewee: '[y]ou were at home or at [Van Gogh's future killer's] home. That was it really'.[71] The latter even described a diminishing social circle as the abandonment of an old life filled with unbelief and therefore as signifying a true believer.[72]

Yet the Hofstadgroup's withdrawal from society fell short of what could be considered 'going underground'. Many participants, including members of the extremist inner circle, continued to hold (part-time) jobs or attend school.[73] Their participation in online discussion forums and their attempts at convincing other young Muslims of the validity of their views occasionally exposed them to dissenting opinions.[74] Although the authorities' interest in them sparked a degree of watchfulness bordering on the paranoid, with participants removing the batteries from cell phones during meetings, none of them went 'off the grid' until 2005's Piranha case.[75] Even then, only two individuals did so; the person who evaded arrest in November 2004 and his Islamic wife.[76] By contrast, the other ringleader of the Piranha case continued to live at home with his family until his apprehension in October 2005.

Because the Hofstadgroup as a whole never went underground, the degree to which isolation influenced its internal cohesion and social reality value was limited. Nevertheless, the trend towards increasing isolation, one that was particularly noticeable among the more extremist participants, had two important consequences. First of all, it made participants relatively more exposed to people with radical and extremist ideas while lessening their

---

69   Dienst Nationale Recherche, 'RL8026', AHA03/20: 1299; VERD: 20114; De Koning and Meijer, 'Going All the Way', 231.
70   Former Hofstadgroup Participant 1, 'Personal Interview 2', 11; Dienst Nationale Recherche, 'RL8026', 01/13: 104; AHA05/22: 1811-13, 1837; Former Hofstadgroup Participant 3, 'Personal Interview 1', 5-6, 8-9.
71   'Je was thuis of bij Mohammed B. thuis. Dat was het eigenlijk': Former Hofstadgroup Participant 1, 'Personal Interview 2', 20.
72   Dienst Nationale Recherche, 'RL8026', AHD02/31: 5793.
73   Ibid., AHA03/20: 860; AHA04/21: 1664; AHD04/33: 6716-19; AHF01/39: 9279, 9349, 9462, 9535, 9620; AHF02/40: 10000, 10032; AHF03/41: 311; VERD: 9443, 9852, 9915, 9981, 20111, 20217, 20463-464, 20518-519; Dienst Nationale Recherche, 'Piranha', 38.
74   Dienst Nationale Recherche, 'RL8026', AHD07/36: 8400-01, 8409-12; AHD09/38: 9173-75, 9179-81, 9184-95, 9216-220; Former Hofstadgroup Participant 1, 'Personal Interview 2', 18-19, 30-31.
75   Former Hofstadgroup Participant 3, 'Personal Interview 1', 5-6; Former Hofstadgroup Participant 1, 'Personal Interview 2', 25-26; Former Hofstadgroup Participant 4, 'Personal Interview 1', 1.
76   Dienst Nationale Recherche, 'RL8026', 01/17: 4062.

contacts with individuals who could have challenged their increasing extremism. Secondly, by cutting ties to former friends, the Hofstadgroup rose in importance as the center of participants' social life. Isolation therefore sustained involvement by increasing the group's importance as participants' foremost sources of social ties. It also catalyzed participants' adoption of views that saw the use of violence as justified and necessary.

6.6   Social learning theory

The application of social learning theory to the study of delinquency essentially teaches that 'criminal behavior is learned through interactions with others, especially in intimate, primary groups'.[77] While specific attention is given to the role of primary groups such as family and close friends as the setting in which the mechanisms that constitute social learning theory are at their most influential, this form of learning is not exclusively reliant on face-to-face interactions. It can also take place through exposure to extremist materials encountered on social media or the emulation of attitudes or behavior seen on television.[78] Social learning theory can be used to explain pro-social as well as criminal attitudes and actions.[79] Whether social learning leads to one or the other depends on a range of factors.

Several circumstances make it is more likely that social learning will contribute to violent behavior. The first is 'differential association' or relatively greater exposure to individuals or groups who commit violence or justify its use. When others are seen to engage in criminal or violent activities without suffering negative consequences, or even benefiting from it, the observer's previously acquired inhibitions to delinquent behavior may be lowered. Second, violence is more likely when the 'social learner' is exposed to individuals who hold beliefs that portray such behavior in neutral or positive terms. Third, violence is more likely when its perceived benefits outweigh perceived costs, a calculation that can be influenced, for instance, through religious beliefs or political convictions that portray violence as necessary for the attainment or defense of a greater good. Finally, violent

---

77   Sellers, Cochran, and Winfree, 'Social Learning Theory', 109.
78   Bandura, *Social Learning Theory*, 2-13; Pauwels and Schils, 'Differential Online Exposure', 1-29.
79   Pauwels and Schils, 'Differential Online Exposure', 3.

behavior becomes more likely when individuals have violent 'role models' they can observe directly or indirectly, such as through the Internet.[80]

The Hofstadgroup was a prime setting in which social learning could exert its influence for two reasons. First of all, the group was increasingly the main or even exclusive source of social contacts for many participants. Secondly, social gatherings were the group's most frequent communal activity. Socializing with friends was an important aspect of these meetings, but they were also used for lectures and discussions on fundamentalist, radical, and extremist interpretations of Islam.[81] These gatherings were not formal seminars dedicated to religious indoctrination, however. They appear to have been organized largely on an ad hoc basis, without mandatory attendance and with little in the way of a syllabus to structure the discussions and lectures.[82] While some participants showed up several times a week or even every day, others attended only once or twice a month.[83]

Social learning exerted a notable influence on Hofstadgroup participants in several ways. First of all, through direct association with individuals who supported the use of violence in principle and practice.[84] Several witnesses and an interviewee mentioned or implied that the intensive contacts they had with other Hofstadgroup participants led them to adopt their points of view, even if only for a time.[85] For instance, one witness explained that she may have become willing to use violence had the group's influence not been restrained by the contacts she still maintained with ideologically non-radical individuals.[86] Likewise, a former participant explained that his ultimate disavowal of extremist Islam only came about after he had physically distanced himself from the Hofstadgroup and was thus no longer

---

80 Akers and Silverman, 'Toward a Social Learning Model', 20-24.
81 Dienst Nationale Recherche, 'RL8026', 01/13: 115; AHA02/19: 86-87, 100; AHA06/23: 2585-86, 2600, 2693; AHA09/26: 3799-803; AHD01/30: 5499-503; 01/17: 4090-99, 4201; Former Hofstadgroup Participant 1, 'Personal Interview 1', 2-3; 'Personal Interview 2', 12-13; Former Hofstadgroup Participant 3, 'Personal Interview 1', 2, 4-5, 9.
82 Former Hofstadgroup Participant 1, 'Personal Interview 3', 3; 'Personal Interview 2', 14-15; Dienst Nationale Recherche, 'RL8026', VERD: 19476-77, 19479, 19918-919, 19944, 20080, 20228, 20363, 20486; 01/17: 4099-4100; Former Hofstadgroup Participant 4, 'Personal Interview 2', 3; Former Hofstadgroup Participant 3, 'Personal Interview 1', 5; Former Hofstadgroup Participant 5, 'Personal Interview 1', 2.
83 Dienst Nationale Recherche, 'RL8026', VERD: 19476, 19866, 19980, 20313, 20484.
84 For instance: Vermaat, *Nederlandse Jihad*, 14.
85 Dienst Nationale Recherche, 'RL8026', 01/13: 133-34; 01/17: 4030-32, 4084-86, 4127-128; Former Hofstadgroup Participant 3, 'Personal Interview 1', 10; Former Hofstadgroup Participant 5, 'Personal Interview 1', 1-2, 5.
86 Dienst Nationale Recherche, 'RL8026', 01/17: 4028-32, 4050-51.

exposed to the ideas and norms propagated by his erstwhile peers.[87] Two interviewees' recollection of the Van Gogh murder is especially striking. One admitted initially feeling a sense of awe for the murderer, while another explained that he was inspired to plan an attack of his own.[88]

Social learning also influenced Hofstadgroup participants by exposing them *indirectly* to 'role models' of violent behavior and radical or extremist interpretations of Islam. Police investigators found that participants shared (parts of) a large digital 'library' containing books and treatises by Salafist thinkers and theologians who justified violence, such as Muhammad ibn Abd al-Wahhab and Sayyid Qutb.[89] Furthermore, participants exchanged various digital media that included video and audio files in which jihadist militants or ideologues practiced and preached religiously justified violence. These included grisly videos of war crimes perpetrated by Chechen jihadists that were occasionally watched during group gatherings.[90] Finally, there was the Internet which facilitated access to numerous jihadist role models; most notably men like Osama bin Laden, the 9/11 hijackers and Abu Musab al-Zarqawi, leader of al-Qaeda in Iraq until his death in 2006.[91]

Social learning also made a contribution to the adoption of militant beliefs and some participants' willingness to use terrorism by helping instill the notion that the use of violence would be met with reward. The clearest example of this concerns the 2004 Madrid bombings. To the group's more militant elements, the attack demonstrated that terrorism in Europe was feasible, legitimate, and effective, as the withdrawal of Spanish troops from Iraq was seen as a direct consequence of the attack.[92] The attack helped shift the motivation of some of the most militant participants from joining jihadist insurgents overseas to conducting terrorism in the Netherlands. Social learning again played a role in instilling the view that death in the service of Islam would be rewarded with martyrdom. This occurred partly through exposure to ideological materials and role models mentioned in previous

---

87   Former Hofstadgroup Participant 3, 'Personal Interview 1', 11.
88   Former Hofstadgroup Participant 1, 'Personal Interview 1', 6; 'Personal Interview 2', 27-28; Former Hofstadgroup Participant 3, 'Personal Interview 1', 10.
89   Dienst Nationale Recherche, 'RL8026', 01/13: 47; NCTV Employee 1, 'Personal Interview 2', 2; Vermaat, *Nederlandse Jihad*, 164.
90   Dienst Nationale Recherche, 'RL8026', 01/13: 47, 138-40; AHA07/24: 2865-66; GET: 4128, 4179, 18231, 18410, 18452; VERD: 9477-9478, 20014, 20113; Groen and Kranenberg, *Women Warriors*, 43-44; Vermaat, *Nederlandse Jihad*, 13, 54, 82, 110-11, 126, 139, 154, 169, 176, 181, 196.
91   A[.], 'Deurwaarders Van Allah', 14; Former Hofstadgroup Participant 3, 'Personal Interview 1', 9.
92   Former Hofstadgroup Participant 1, 'Personal Interview 2', 22-23; De Koning and Meijer, 'Going All the Way', 232; Former Hofstadgroup Participant 4, 'Personal Interview 2', 5.

paragraphs, and partly in a far more direct fashion.[93] One female participant was promised a 'beautiful martyr's death' by a male group member who suggested they drive a car filled with explosives into a shopping center.[94]

Social learning forms a key explanatory factor for how participants adopted extremist views and, in some cases, planned or perpetrated acts of terrorism. It shows that extremist views and behavior were in large part *taught* and *copied*. Direct interactions with individuals who justified terrorism, including some who tried to join Islamist insurgents overseas and one who committed an actual terrorist attack, were key to the conveyance of attitudes favorable to the use of violence and provided role models of militancy to be emulated. Indirect exposure to jihadist role models, terrorist attacks, and extremist materials, principally via the Internet, further taught participants to see terrorism as justified, necessary, and effective. Through the notion of martyrdom, they were brought to believe that death in the service of Islam held distinct *personal* advantages that outweighed the costs of forfeiting life on earth. In short, social learning constituted a particularly important explanatory variable at the group-level of analysis.

6.7 The influence of leaders

Leaders are individuals with the ability to harness their followers' energy 'in a concerted coordinated effort to achieve the organizational mission and objectives'.[95] Within the specific context of terrorist groups, leaders' influence allows them to do more than exert operational control and guidance. They can also play an important role in safeguarding the group's cohesion and in socializing its members into an extremist worldview.[96] Leaders' ability to function as such depends on their credibility and authority, which can stem from several sources, such as ideological knowledge, operational expertise, or personal charisma.[97] Keeping to the division of the group-level

---

93 Dienst Nationale Recherche, 'RL8026', 01/01: 25-26, 28; 01/13: 81, 130-31, 134, 151, 163; AHB03/27: 4040-41; AHD07/36: 8411, AHD08/37: 573-574, 594, 773-775; Peters, 'De Ideologische En Religieuze Ontwikkeling', 14, appendix: Overzicht teksten geschreven of vertaald door Mohammed B., 38; NOVA, 'Videotestament Samir A.'.
94 Groen and Kranenberg, *Women Warriors*, 82.
95 Winston and Patterson, 'An Integrative Definition', 7.
96 Crenshaw, 'The Causes of Terrorism', 389; 'The Psychology of Political Terrorism', 390; Mandel, 'The Role of Instigators', 6; Milla, Faturochman, and Ancok, 'The Impact of Leader-Follower Interactions', 96-97.
97 Crenshaw, *Explaining Terrorism*, 93; Hofmann and Dawson, 'The Neglected Role', 349; Milla, Faturochman, and Ancok, 'The Impact of Leader-Follower Interactions', 92.

analysis over two chapters, the following paragraphs deal with leaders' ability to shape terrorist groups organizationally and ideologically. The next chapter looks at their ability to instigate terrorist attacks.

Abu Khaled, the middle-aged Syrian man who provided religious instruction until he fled the country on the day of Van Gogh's murder was the group's most important ideological authority.[98] There are, however, no indications that this man actively sought to create a common group ideology or harness its participants' energy for particular ends, as the above-mentioned definition of leadership requires.[99] This may not have been possible even if he had wanted to; participants appear to have seen him as a good teacher, but not as a leader, as someone who had to be obeyed, or even as a particularly inspiring individual.[100] His role is best described as an 'epistemic authority'; an individual whose perceived knowledge enabled him to provide an authoritative interpretation of religious and political matters to the other participants.[101]

Van Gogh's future murderer certainly gained the respect of other participants for his knowledge of Islam.[102] His writings and his teachings at group gatherings began to include clear incitement to violence from March 2004 onward.[103] But like Abu Khaled, Van Gogh's murderer does not seem to have actively tried to force the group into a certain ideological mold or to shape it organizationally. Descriptions paint him as quiet, withdrawn, and as someone who was neither seen as a leader nor assumed such a role.[104] Essentially the same conclusion is reached with regard to other individuals whom the group held in high esteem, some of whom acquired status through their greater knowledge of Arabic or their outspoken militancy. While their higher status meant that they were relatively influential in the conveyance

---

98 Chorus and Olgun, *Broeders*, 19; Former Hofstadgroup Participant 4, 'Personal Interview 2', 4.
99 NCTV Employee 1, 'Personal Interview 1', 2; Public Prosecutor 1, 'Personal Interview 1', 8.
100 Former Hofstadgroup Participant 1, 'Personal Interview 2', 4; Former Hofstadgroup Participant 3, 'Personal Interview 1', 33; Chorus and Olgun, *Broeders*, 48; Vermaat, *Nederlandse Jihad*, 33, 83, 87, 112; Former Hofstadgroup Participant 5, 'Personal Interview 1', 3.
101 Kruglanski, Chen, and Golec, 'Individual Motivations'.
102 Dienst Nationale Recherche, 'RL8026', VERD: 19918, 19935, 20004-05, 20012-13, 20079, 20227, 20236; Former Hofstadgroup Participant 1, 'Personal Interview 1', 3; Former Hofstadgroup Participant 3, 'Personal Interview 1', 4.
103 Peters, 'Dutch Extremist Islamism', 150-59; Groen and Kranenberg, *Women Warriors*, 81; Vermaat, *Nederlandse Jihad*, 19.
104 Former Hofstadgroup Participant 3, 'Personal Interview 1', 3-4; Former Hofstadgroup Participant 1, 'Personal Interview 2', 13; Dienst Nationale Recherche, 'RL8026', VERD: 19478, 19868, 19868, 20212, 20227; Public Prosecutor 2, 'Personal Interview 1', 4; Former Hofstadgroup Participant 4, 'Personal Interview 1', 2.

of fundamentalist, radical, or extremist interpretations of Islam, none appear to have had the ability or inclination to consciously shape the group, whether ideologically or organizationally.[105]

At least as far as the ideological and organizational development of the group was concerned, the Hofstadgroup lacked clear leaders. While its social pecking order included individuals with more influence over matters of ideology than others, these persons are more accurately described as *authority figures* than as leaders. It could be argued that participants saw men like Bin Laden or al-Zarqawi as their leaders, but this does not change the group's essentially leaderless nature. While such jihadist role models certainly had a major influence, it was indirectly and unconsciously exercised. There is no reason to believe that foreign jihadists knew of the Hofstadgroup's existence, let alone tried to exercise control over its activities to accomplish a joint goal.

6.8 Peer pressure

Peer pressure plays an important role in upholding and inculcating group norms,[106] which Pynchon and Borum define as the 'implicit and explicit expectations for the conduct and opinions of individual members'.[107] In Crenshaw's words, 'peer pressure can induce people to perform acts that they would ordinarily be prevented from doing by moral restraints'.[108] Peer pressure is of course not a mechanism unique to terrorist groups, but its influence in that particular setting is notable. For groups involved in illegal or violent activities, internal dissent can be dangerous, making them especially susceptible to producing strong internal pressures towards conformity.[109] The following paragraphs discuss four forms of peer pressure found in the literature and assess whether they played a role in the Hofstadgroup's development.

---

105 Former Hofstadgroup Participant 3, 'Personal Interview 1', 4; NCTV Employee 1, 'Personal Interview 1', 3; Former Hofstadgroup Participant 2, 'Personal Interview 1', 4; Former Hofstadgroup Participant 1, 'Personal Interview 1', 3; 'Personal Interview 2', 13-14; Dienst Nationale Recherche, 'RL8026', AHA05/22: 2174-75; Former Hofstadgroup Participant 5, 'Personal Interview 1', 3.
106 Bartlett and Miller, 'The Edge of Violence', 16.
107 Pynchon and Borum, 'Assessing Threats', 350.
108 Crenshaw, 'The Psychology of Political Terrorism', 397.
109 Crenshaw, *Explaining Terrorism*, 106; Horgan, *The Psychology of Terrorism*, 125; McCauley and Segal, 'Social Psychology of Terrorist Groups', 335.

Extremity shift (also known as 'risky shift'[110] or 'group polarization'[111]) is a process whereby a group's 'average' opinion becomes increasingly extreme over time. The first reason for this is what McCauley and Segal label 'variance decrease'; the tendency of groups to become more homogeneous as individuals with deviating views leave or are expelled.[112] Secondly, 'social comparison' plays a role. Individuals may vie for their peers' approval or pursue status by championing the group's values. In the process, they create an incentive for their compatriots to do the same, as no one wants to be seen to be lagging behind in enthusiasm. This creates a process whereby individuals trigger each other to voice ever more extremist positions in order to stand out positively, thus steadily moving the group as a whole to more militant points of views. Finally, there is the 'relevant arguments' mechanism, whereby group discussions will be biased in favor of views that support group norms, thereby contributing to their acceptance.[113]

Another way in which peer pressure can exert its influence is through the 'majority effect'. Over the course of several experiments, Asch found that many individuals will adjust their opinions to correspond to the majority view expressed by the group in which they are participating, even if that view is clearly wrong.[114] During one such experiment a research subject was asked to compare a line with several other lines of varying length and to judge which of those matched the first. When the other study participants, who were actually working together with the researcher, suddenly and unanimously started giving wrong answers to this simple task, more than a third of the research subjects felt compelled to go along with the majority. Those who did stick to their opinion experienced self-doubt, felt uneasy about their conspicuous deviance, and feared the group's disapproval.[115] Asch's research is a testament to both the power of the group in shaping the views of individuals and the difficulties of maintaining a contrary opinion.

Two forms of peer pressure specific to terrorist groups are public commitments to violence and what Crenshaw calls the 'blood price' of involvement.[116] Some terrorist organizations make their members publicly commit to carrying out an act of violence. Videotapes of would-be suicide bombers announcing their intentions and bidding farewell to friends and families

---

110   Silke, 'Holy Warriors', 111.
111   Pynchon and Borum, 'Assessing Threats', 344.
112   McCauley and Segal, 'Social Psychology of Terrorist Groups', 340-42.
113   Ibid., 341-42; Pynchon and Borum, 'Assessing Threats', 344.
114   Asch, 'Studies of Independence and Conformity', 1-70.
115   Asch, 'Opinions and Social Pressure', 31-35.
116   Crenshaw, 'The Psychology of Political Terrorism', 396.

are an especially strong example of this practice.[117] Although ostensibly framed as an inspirational message, the public distribution of such videos creates strong pressures on the would-be terrorist to follow through. Once such a statement of intention has been recorded and publicized, there can be no going back without considerable loss of face. Finally, there is the 'blood price' to be reckoned with; the death or capture of comrades may prompt remaining group members to strengthen their adherence to the norms the fallen represented as a coping mechanism for dealing with their loss.[118]

Peer pressure had a notable influence on Hofstadgroup participants' adoption of fundamentalist, radical, and extremist views although not all participants were equally exposed to it.[119] However, of the mechanisms identified above only evidence of the extremity shift and, to a smaller degree, the majority effect was found in the data. While one of the Piranha ringleaders did record a video that, in tone and content, strongly resembled a statement of intent to commit violence, there are no indications that he was pressured in any way to do so. Similarly, witnessing the arrest of group participants does not seem to have noticeably led the remainder to strengthen their ideological convictions. It could be argued that these arrests did contribute to group solidarity, however, as they prompted several instances of participants collectively donating money to their arrested friends' wives.[120]

Variance decrease was the most notable aspect of extremity shift within the Hofstadgroup. Newcomers were questioned about their interpretation of tawhid to assess whether it corresponded with the group norm of denouncing democracy and its supporters.[121] This provided a basic degree of homogeneity by keeping out individuals with markedly different opinions on the matter. For instance, an old friend of Van Gogh's killer-to-be stopped visiting him because he did not agree with the increasingly extremist views being espoused at his friend's house.[122] It seems that extremity shift was also taking place via the relevant arguments mechanism. Hofstadgroup participants fanned each other's radicalism by constantly talking about fundamentalist Islam and jihad and because there were few divergent opinions on these topics.[123]

---

117 Merari, 'Social, Organizational, and Psychological Factors', 79-80; Kruglanski and Fishman, 'Psychological Factors', 23.
118 Crenshaw, 'The Psychology of Political Terrorism', 396.
119 Former Hofstadgroup Participant 4, 'Personal Interview 2', 3.
120 Dienst Nationale Recherche, 'RL8026', 01/13: 89-92.
121 Former Hofstadgroup Participant 3, 'Personal Interview 1', 2-3.
122 Dienst Nationale Recherche, 'RL8026', 01/13: 132; GET: 18414-22.
123 Former Hofstadgroup Participant 3, 'Personal Interview 1', 10.

Such like-mindedness was further established by the importance attached to takfir. According to one interviewee, it was an almost daily practice for participants to ask each other whether they were willing to excommunicate a wide range of Muslims who failed to live up to the group's extreme views.[124] Given that acceptance of takfir was the majority opinion, this practice is reminiscent of the majority effect described above. As the 'correct' answer was clearly to support a very broad application of takfir, holding on to divergent opinions became more difficult. This emphasis on an unbridled interpretation of takfir also contributed to further variance decrease; in late 2004, several participants broke with the Hofstadgroup because they felt the use of takfir had gone too far.[125]

On several occasions, pressure was deliberately exerted to engender acceptance of group norms and to maintain the group's organizational integrity. A female participant was repeatedly shown videos of suicide bombers and told that she would one day commit a similar attack. She was also given a knife to hold and made to watch footage of people having their throats cut, while another participant told her she would learn how to slaughter too.[126] In another example, a participant who questioned the group's use of takfir was met with verbal aggression; some of the other participants present went so far as to demand this individual retake the confession of faith.[127]

There were also less sinister but still notable instances of peer pressure. One male participant was questioned about his lackluster participation in prayer sessions and repeatedly lectured about his refusal to grow a long beard to the point that he no longer felt welcome.[128] Another was told he was not allowed to talk with girls.[129] Although attendance of Hofstadgroup gatherings was not mandatory, anyone who showed up infrequently was liable to get a call from other participants asking them to explain their absence. Those who persisted risked becoming the subject of malicious rumors that he or she had become an apostate.[130] Several women, who disengaged from the group because they felt the use of takfir went too far,

---

124 Ibid., 2-3.
125 Dienst Nationale Recherche, 'RL8026', 01/17: 4002-03, 4018-20, 4030, 4048-58, 4085-86, 4092, 4100, 4125-127, 4129, 4204; Groen and Kranenberg, *Women Warriors*, 37, 93.
126 Dienst Nationale Recherche, 'RL8026', 01/13: 35, 134, 162; Groen and Kranenberg, *Women Warriors*, 81-82.
127 Former Hofstadgroup Participant 5, 'Personal Interview 1', 2-3.
128 Dienst Nationale Recherche, 'RL8026', VERD: 19475.
129 Chorus and Olgun, *Broeders*, 83.
130 Former Hofstadgroup Participant 3, 'Personal Interview 1', 5.

expressed fear of reprisals.[131] Two of them were threatened for cooperating with the police.[132]

These examples show that peer pressure influenced the Hofstadgroup's development in two ways. First, it played an important role in propagating and maintaining adherence to fundamentalist and extremist group norms (growing a beard, readiness to use takfir, etc.). Second, peer pressure made it harder for individuals to cease participation by making such a decision costly in terms of reputation damage and personal threats. Like the trend towards isolation, peer pressure contributed to the Hofstadgroup's cohesion and facilitated the spread of radical and extremist views.

6.9 Conclusion

This chapter has highlighted that the Hofstadgroup's formation was heavily reliant on preexisting ties of friendship, rather than conscious attempts at recruitment. Once initial participation had come about through these social networks, various group processes began to bind participants together, giving the Hofstadgroup a degree of organizational substance. The application of social identity theory revealed the key role that the social, cognitive, and emotional benefits of participation had in sustaining involvement. By and large, participants did not seek out the Hofstadgroup because they wanted to become extremists or terrorists. Instead, it appears that they found their way into this group and were then motivated to stay for reasons such as friendship and the sense of being among 'true' Muslims.

Social learning theory provided a key explanation for how fundamentalist and extremist ideas and models of behavior were transmitted among members of the group. This occurred both directly (e.g. during lectures) and indirectly (e.g. by watching jihadist videos that glorified violence) through exposure to justifications for violence and to violent role models like Bin Laden and al-Zarqawi. Another important dynamic was the group's voluntary isolation from Dutch society which increasingly cut its participants off from opinions and norms contrary to their own. Over time, this increased the Hofstadgroup's social reality value, or the degree to which participants were influenced by commonly held views and norms, and strengthened its

---

131 Dienst Nationale Recherche, 'RL8026', 01/17: 4018-20, 4029, 4052, 4092; Groen and Kranenberg, *Women Warriors*, 91, 101.
132 Dienst Nationale Recherche, 'RL8026', 01/17: 4122, 13; Groen and Kranenberg, *Women Warriors*, 98-102.

cohesion as participants' social circle gradually excluded anyone outside of the group's boundaries.

Some group-level factors influenced the Hofstadgroup through their *absence*. The Hofstadgroup lacked clear leaders who could or tried to shape the group ideologically or organizationally. While several authority figures existed whose lectures and writings were important to the group's adoption of fundamentalist, radical and extremist views, none appear to have had the ability or desire to purposefully mold the group. Ideological conformity and a degree of organizational integrity were safeguarded largely autonomously through various forms of peer pressure. Group extremity shift and the majority effect induced some individuals with contrary views to leave the group. The considerable importance placed on the themes of tawhid and takfir compelled participants to adopt these views as their own. Peer pressure also threw up barriers to disengagement from the group and was on occasion exerted on specific individuals to gain their compliance with group norms.

These conclusions underwrite the importance of the group-level of analysis for achieving an understanding of how involvement in terrorist groups is initiated and sustained. What the preceding analysis has left unanswered, however, is whether group processes can shed light on the Hofstadgroup's actual and intended use of violence. That discussion is the subject of the next chapter.

7 Group dynamics II: Involvement in acts of terrorist violence[1]

An individual's participation in a terrorist group, the mere act of 'joining', does not necessarily lead to their involvement in terrorist attacks.[2] As Taylor and Horgan argue, 'involvement decisions' are distinct from 'event decisions'.[3] As such, any attempt to understand the commission of terrorist acts must go beyond explanations for why people join and remain in terrorist groups to look specifically at how the decision to use violence came about. The previous chapter discussed the group-level factors that initiated and sustained involvement in the Hofstadgroup. The following pages complete the group-level analysis by analyzing whether it offers answers to why some participants became involved in actual terrorist violence or intended to do so.

7.1 Group-level explanations for terrorist violence

The literature reveals several group-level explanations for the use of terrorist violence, all of which will be discussed in the following paragraphs (Table 8). The most common assumption is that terrorism is *strategic*; a consciously chosen means to achieve certain (political) ends.[4] A second and perhaps less widely acknowledged perspective states that terrorism can stem from *organizational* motives for violence such as the desire to avenge killed or captured comrades.[5] The literature also reveals two other subjects relevant to a group's ability and inclination to use such violence. The first is the relationship between a terrorist group's organizational structure and its lethality.[6] The second consists of various social-psychological factors that can lower individuals' inhibitions towards harming or killing others. These are the diffusion of responsibility that can take place in group settings, the

---

[1] This chapter has been published in amended form as: Schuurman and Horgan, 'Rationales for Terrorist Violence in Homegrown Jihadist Groups'.
[2] Taylor and Horgan, 'A Conceptual Framework', 592; Horgan, *Walking Away from Terrorism*, 142-43.
[3] Taylor, 'Is Terrorism a Group Phenomenon?', 125-26.
[4] Crenshaw, 'The Logic of Terrorism', 371-82.
[5] Crenshaw, 'Theories of Terrorism', 13-31.
[6] Asal and Rethemeyer, 'The Nature of the Beast', 437-49.

closely related phenomenon of deindividuation, and the role of authority figures in ordering or legitimizing violence.[7]

Table 8 Committing acts of terrorism

Organizational lethality	Overcoming barriers to violence	Rationales for terrorism
Organizational lethality	Diffusion of responsibility Deindividuation Authorization of violence	Strategic Organizational

7.2 Organizational structure and lethality

Research has found several organizational characteristics that increase a terrorist group's lethality.[8] The first is rallying around a religious or ethno-nationalist ideology, which is seen as leading to stronger 'othering' of out-groups perceived to be inferior. The second characteristic is a positive correlation between group size and lethality, possibly due to larger groups having access to more human capital in the form of people with the skills required for organizing and executing terrorist attacks. Ties to other terrorist organizations and control of territory make up characteristics three and four, which are respectively explained as providing increased access to relevant information, means and expertise, and as conveying resources and shelter conducive to organizational growth and longevity.[9] Later research by Asal et al. also underscored terrorists' technical expertise as a lethality-increasing factor.[10]

The Hofstadgroup could count on few of the above characteristics. It had no territorial control whatsoever. It did have international links to several individuals who may have been involved in terrorism. But as Chapter 5 argued, these ties did not provide the Hofstadgroup with significant benefits in terms of increasing its ability to plan and execute a terrorist attack, beyond the *possibility* that two participants had undergone basic paramilitary training overseas. Neither did the Hofstadgroup's fairly large size of approximately forty participants provide it with much in the way of terrorism-relevant human capital. None of the group's participants were

---

7   Borum, *Psychology of Terrorism*, 48-49.
8   Asal and Rethemeyer, 'The Nature of the Beast', 437-49.
9   Ibid., 437-41, 443-44, 446.
10 Asal et al., 'Killing Range', 401-27.

experienced militants and the largely unsuccessful trips abroad did little to alter this fact. Neither did the group contain people knowledgeable about such terrorist essentials as the construction of explosives.

The one organizational characteristic conducive to increased lethality that the Hofstadgroup had, was a religious ideology based on an extremist interpretation of Islam. This allowed a dichotomous 'us versus them' worldview to take hold, especially among the more militant participants. This sharp distinction between a small in-group of the righteous and various out-group enemies, ranging from apostate Muslims to Western states engaged in a perceived 'war against Islam', lowered the threshold to seeing the use of violence as acceptable. On the whole, however, the Hofstadgroup's organizational characteristics conferred upon it a relatively low level of inherent lethality. This is a potential explanation for why so few participants actually became involved in (preparations for) terrorism and why Van Gogh's murder was the only attack to go beyond planning and preparatory stages.

7.3 Group influences that lower barriers to violent behavior

In his review of the relevant literature, Borum identifies four group effects that can lower individuals' thresholds to using violence.[11] One of these, group norms that legitimize the use of violence, will not be repeated here as both the previous paragraph and the last chapter have affirmed that such norms existed within the Hofstadgroup. Instead, the next paragraphs focus on the diffusion of individual responsibility, the related concept of deindividuation and, thirdly, obedience to authority.

7.3.1 Diffusion of responsibility and deindividuation

Soccer hooliganism and mass looting show that, under particular circumstances, crowds can bring out antisocial behavior in the individuals that constitute them.[12] Given the propensity for large groups to behave violently, early social scientists described such collective behavior in terms of irrationality and anarchy.[13] While recent research has shown such qualifications

---

11 Borum, *Psychology of Terrorism*, 48-49.
12 Russell, 'Sport Riots', 367-68.
13 Reicher, 'Psychology of Crowd Dynamics', 185-86.

to be inaccurate,[14] group participation can affect individuals' behavior by 'diffusing' their personal sense of responsibility to the collective.[15] When everyone is responsible for what happens, no one person can be held accountable.[16] In such a setting, individuals' internal barriers to otherwise prohibited behavior, including involvement in acts of violence, are lowered.[17]

The lowering of inhibitions to deviant behavior can also result from 'deindividuation'. Postmes and Spears define it as a 'psychological state of decreased self-evaluation and decreased evaluation apprehension causing antinormative and disinhibitive behavior'.[18] Put another way, people are more likely to act in otherwise prohibited ways when they lose the sense that they will or can be held accountable for their actions. Silke has argued that anonymity-induced deindividuation is particularly likely to lead to an increased likeliness of violent behavior.[19] His research on interpersonal assaults in Northern Ireland shows that masked attackers were significantly more likely to display higher levels of aggression and punitive treatment of their victims than those whose identities were not similarly concealed.[20]

Hofstadgroup participants were involved in two acts of violence; the murder of Van Gogh and the throwing of a hand grenade at police officers. As neither of the two perpetrators was disguised or in any other sense unrecognizable, anonymity-induced deindividuation is ruled out as an explanatory variable. Likewise, there is currently no data to suggest that either of these individuals experienced a diffusion of responsibility based on their participation in a larger group. Van Gogh's killer acted alone and while the hand grenade thrower was accompanied by another Hofstadgroup participant at the time of the incident, there is no data to suggest the other person's presence induced a diffusion of personal responsibility. A 'group' of two seems simply too small for its participants to experience such an effect.

7.3.2   Authorization of violence

Milgram's famous 1963 study dramatically highlighted some humans' willingness to use violence when ordered to do so.[21] In the experiment, test

---

14   Ibid., 182-208.
15   Borum, *Psychology of Terrorism*, 49.
16   Garnett, 'The Causes of War', 81.
17   Pynchon and Borum, 'Assessing Threats', 345-46.
18   Postmes and Spears, 'Deindividuation', 238.
19   Silke, 'The Internet & Terrorist Radicalisation', 33.
20   Silke, 'Deindividuation, Anonymity, and Violence', 493-94, 496.
21   Milgram, 'Behavorial Study of Obedience',", 371-78.

subjects administered what they thought were increasingly strong electric shocks to other people on the instigation of a scientific authority figure, despite being able to hear the screams and pleas of the 'victim' (who in actuality was an accomplice of the experimenter).[22] The test subjects clearly believed that their actions were causing pain to another human being and displayed high levels of stress while following the instructions given to them. Nevertheless, a majority of test subjects continued to perform as ordered. Milgram's study highlights a mechanism known as 'displacement of authority'.[23] Most test subjects continued to give 'electric shocks' because in their perception it was ultimately not they who were responsible, but the experimenter issuing commands. Can obedience to authority explain why some Hofstadgroup participants planned or executed acts of terrorism?

The most notable authority figures were the middle-aged Syrian religious instructor Abu Khaled and Van Gogh's future murderer. As the previous chapter noted, the Syrian was crucial to the conveyance of fundamentalist and radical convictions that contributed to the delegitimization of Dutch society and politics. It is certainly *plausible* that he was in some way involved with the murder of Van Gogh, especially as he left for Syria on the very day of the attack. Yet despite considerable speculation to this end,[24] there is currently no concrete data to suggest that Abu Khaled *directly* legitimized or encouraged the use of violence.[25] It could well be that future research will convincingly show this individual *did* have a role in the murder of Van Gogh or the other planned attacks. For now, however, there is no concrete empirical evidence to support this line of reasoning.

The writings of Van Gogh's future murderer show that he began to develop extremist views from approximately March 2004 onward.[26] One participant recalled that he preached that the 'blood and money' of unbelievers was fair game.[27] As such Van Gogh's future assailant certainly provided justifications for the use of violence, but he too never appears to have directly instigated other participants to commit such acts. Both Abu Khaled and Van Gogh's assailant conferred ideas that, to different degrees, provided participants

22   Ibid.
23   Borum, *Psychology of Terrorism*, 49-50.
24   Former Hofstadgroup Participant 4, 'Personal Interview 2', 4.
25   Dienst Nationale Recherche, 'RL8026', 01/13: 136-40; AHA04/21: 1632-35, 1646; 01/17: 4002, 4026, 4048-4050, 4090-4091, 4096, 4098, 4129, 4179, 4146, 4201; AHB11/26: 3796-803; VERD: 19480, 20131, 20213, 20363; Former Hofstadgroup Participant 1, 'Personal Interview 1', 2-3; 'Personal Interview 2', 8-9; A[.], 'Deurwaarders', 24; Erkel, *Samir*, 190-92.
26   Peters, 'Dutch Extremist Islamism', 150-59.
27   Groen and Kranenberg, *Women Warriors*, 81.

with legitimizations for the use of violence. However, they did not explicitly order its use.

In November 2004, just after Van Gogh's murder, a listening device recorded one participant telling another to use a hand grenade should the police come to arrest them. 'Because there will be a ring at the door before their arrival, what do you do? You make... you wait until they enter and then you throw one, yes?'[28] In an earlier conversation, however, the 'instructor' uses 'we' to refer to how they would react to a police raid.[29] Likewise, during the 'siege' of their apartment on 10 November, this individual spoke with 'we' when phoning several friends to tell them they had thrown a grenade at the police.[30] On that day he was also heard saying '[y]ou just need to get that thing and throw it outside' to his compatriot.[31] But none of the remaining three hand grenades were used. These conversations suggest that this individual either was not trying to or lacked the authority to command the use of violence, making it unlikely the authorization of violence was a factor in the use of the grenade.

Based on the above examples and the remainder of the empirical data, there is little to suggest that among the group's participants were those with the authority, ability, and desire to order the execution of terrorist attacks.[32] But what about those authority figures outside its borders? It has been noted several times that there is no concrete evidence that the Moroccan jihadist residing in Spain and the unnamed Afghan or Pakistani 'emir' authorized or instigated the use of violence by those participants they were in contact with.[33] But they were not the only external authority figures.

In chat conversations dated to September 2003, two participants describe their separate encounters with a Dutch convert to Islam who became a radical preacher. In these chats, both participants claim to have received confirmation from this preacher that it was religiously justified to steal from or kill representatives of the Dutch government.[34] The preacher in question has denied any involvement with the two Hofstadgroup participants

---

28 'Want er wordt straks vóór hun aankomst gebeld, wat doe je? Jij maakt... jij wacht totdat zij binnenkomen en dan doe jij eentje gooien, ja?':Dienst Nationale Recherche, 'RL8026', AHA07/24: 3047.
29 Ibid., AHA07/24: 3034.
30 Ibid., AHA07/24: 3091.
31 'Je moet dat ding gewoon pakken en naar buiten gooien': Ibid., AHA07/24: 3119; Vermaat, *Nederlandse Jihad*, 49.
32 Dienst Nationale Recherche, 'RL8026', VERD: 19479, 19876; Former Hofstadgroup Participant 1, 'Personal Interview 2', 14-15; Vidino, 'The Hofstad Group', 586-87.
33 Dienst Nationale Recherche, 'RL8026', 01/01: 23-25.
34 Ibid., AHD08/37: 8713-14, 8765-66; NOVA, 'Chatgesprekken Jason W.'

and claims to have barely met them.³⁵ While the Hofstadgroup men may have given a more militant interpretation to his words than the preacher intended, the latter's radical convictions seem in little doubt. During a November 2004 television appearance, he said that he was pleased to hear of Van Gogh's death and would not feel sorry if right-wing politician Geert Wilders contracted a deadly disease.³⁶ These remarks lend credibility to the idea that the Hofstadgroup participants were able to construe from the preacher's words a legitimization for violence, although it is unlikely he ever issued any kind of direct 'order' to that extent.

One of the imams of the Salafist as-Soennah mosque in The Hague gained notoriety for a sermon he delivered shortly before the murder of Van Gogh. The imam provided various examples of the punishment reserved for those who mock the Prophet Muhammad and beseeched his god to give Van Gogh and Hirsi Ali deadly, incurable diseases. He was, however, careful to not openly incite to violence.³⁷ Although Van Gogh's killer does not appear to have attended this particular sermon, he and other participants in the Hofstadgroup were known to have frequented the imam's mosque.³⁸ The imam has claimed that his sermon was intended to channel his listeners' anger and frustration over the activities of Van Gogh and Hirsi Ali as a means of creating a buffer against violence.³⁹ Even if this surprising interpretation of his words is true, the incident suggests that participants had access to authority figures whose words could easily be *interpreted* as justifications for violence.

Extremist imams, ideologues, and militants that influenced the Hofstadgroup through books, television, and the Internet, provided the clearest justifications for and calls to violence. Yet their influence was indirect. Men like Osama bin Laden or Abu Musab al-Zarqawi never specifically instructed or authorized the Hofstadgroup to carry out an attack. Van Gogh's killer found a particularly compelling justification to murder blasphemers in the work of the fourteenth-century Salafist scholar Ahmad ibn Taymiyya. Crucially, however, interpreting this work as a personal duty for the individual believer to act as judge, jury, and executioner was something that the killer *had to do himself.*⁴⁰

35 Alberts and Derix, 'Balkenende in 2003'.
36 '"U Wilt Misschien"'.
37 Groen and Kranenberg, *Women Warriors*, 233-40.
38 Dienst Nationale Recherche, 'RL8026', VERD: 19562, 19853, 20004, 20114-115; Groen and Kranenberg, *Women Warriors*.
39 Groen and Kranenberg, *Women Warriors*, 236-45.
40 Peters, 'Dutch Extremist Islamism', 156.

To the previous chapter's conclusion that the Hofstadgroup lacked leaders who shaped the group ideologically or organizationally, this section adds the finding that it also lacked what could be termed *operational* leaders.[41] Authority figures both in and outside of the group, as well as jihadist 'role models' provided plentiful (implied) justifications for the use of terrorism. But none actively moved participants from the conviction that violence was permissible to actual participation in violent behavior. The lack of direct personal contacts with people authorizing or ordering the use of terrorism was significant. It meant that the degree to which Hofstadgroup participants could displace responsibility for any harm they inflicted on others was limited, leaving a significant obstacle to the use of violence intact. It also supports a previous finding that the impetus for acts of terrorism was left to the initiative of individual participants. Planning or perpetrating acts of terrorism remained a predominantly *personal* rather than *group-based* undertaking.

7.4 The rationality of terrorism

The remainder of this chapter addresses whether strategic or organizational rationales for terrorism can explain the Hofstadgroup's planned and perpetrated attacks. This discussion, however, builds on the assumption that terrorism can be seen as the end-result of an essentially rational decision-making process. In other words, that terrorism is not (solely) the domain of the irrational fanatic or the mentally disturbed psychopath. The following paragraphs briefly outline this argument in order to support the analysis of the strategic and organizational rationales that follows.

All rationality is 'bounded' in the sense that people seldom have perfect information on which to base their decisions or may simply not be able to accurately foresee all possible consequences of the courses of action available to them.[42] Thus, the decision to engage in high-risk behavior such as terrorism does not necessarily imply irrationality; it may simply have seemed the best option available at the time. Secondly, although rational choice theory has at times advocated that decision making is motivated solely by the maximization of narrowly defined self-interest,[43] in reality

---

41 Dienst Nationale Recherche, 'RL8026', VERD: 19479, 19876; Former Hofstadgroup Participant 1, 'Personal Interview 2', 14-15; Vidino, 'The Hofstad Group', 586-87.
42 Simon, 'Rationality in Political Behavior', 46-47.
43 Caplan, 'Terrorism', 94-95.

many people engage in collective action at considerable personal risk, such as strikes or rebellions.[44] This indicates that self-interest can extend to the pursuit of altruistic or collectively held goals.[45] Even suicide terrorism, seemingly the ultimate negation of self-interest, can be construed as rational behavior provided that the perpetrator believes death in pursuit of his or her cause will guarantee the bestowment of status, benefits to family, or rewards in an afterlife that warrant the loss of life.[46]

A substantial body of empirical research lends further credence to the notion of that terrorists are essentially rational actors. Terrorists have been shown to adapt their behavior in response to the obstacles and opportunities provided by prevailing physical, social, and political circumstances.[47] For instance by adjusting operational methods or switching to different targets in response to heightened security measures,[48] reserving suicide attacks for targets against which 'conventional' modes of attack are less likely to be successful,[49] and considering beforehand how the use of suicide attacks will affect their popular standing.[50] Terrorist organizations have also been found to time their attacks in an attempt to maximize both their long-term and immediate effects.[51]

It has been noted that terrorism is seldom effective in the long run,[52] and that the stated goals of contemporary religious terrorists are so utopian as to defy rational expectations of achievability.[53] However, there *are* examples of terrorism proving strategically effective,[54] and its short-term benefits, such as limited concessions or simple recognition, may obscure its poor long-term chances of success.[55] The literature also cautions against taking

---

44 Scott, 'Rational Choice Theory', 132-33.
45 Shughart, 'Terrorism in Rational Choice Perspective', 126.
46 Hafez, 'Rationality, Culture, and Structure', 180-81; Kacou, 'Five Arguments', 539-47; Tosini, 'Calculated, Passionate, Pious Extremism', 394-415.
47 Shapiro, 'Terrorist Decision Making', 9-13.
48 Berrebi, 'Evidence About the Link between Education', 172-73; Clauset et al., 'The Strategic Calculus of Terrorism', 6-33; Dugan, LaFree, and Piquero, 'Testing a Rational Choice Model of Airline Hijackings', 356-57; Sandler and Enders, 'An Economic Perspective', 311-13.
49 Berman and Laitin, 'Hard Targets', 30-31.
50 Bloom, *Dying to Kill*, 78.
51 Kliot and Charney, ' Geography of Suicide Terrorism', 353.
52 Abrahms, 'The Political Effectiveness of Terrorism', 366-93; Cronin, *How Terrorism Ends*, 211-12, 215-17.
53 Nalbandov, 'Irrational Rationality', 92-96, 102.
54 Hoffman, 'The Rationality of Terrorism', 258-72; Kydd and Walter, 'The Strategies of Terrorism', 49.
55 Gould and Klor, 'Does Terrorism Work?', 1459-510; Krause, 'The Political Effectiveness of Non-State Violence', 259-94; Marsden, 'Succesful Terrorism', 134-50.

terrorists' utopian rhetoric at face value. While terrorist groups may claim to be driven by religious motives and otherworldly rewards, their behavior often belies realism and a focus on the here and now. For instance, the fact that Hamas videotapes would-be suicide bombers' last wills to reinforce their resolve, indicates that even these ideological extremists realize that when put to the test, their operatives may not hold to professed beliefs as closely as they claimed.[56] In short, existing research makes a strong case for analyzing terrorism as a rational form of behavior.

7.5 Terrorism as the result of strategic considerations

The academic literature widely considers terrorism to be a strategy; a means consciously chosen to achieve certain (political) ends.[57] Despite projecting an image of irrational fanaticism, suicide terrorism is no exception in this regard, especially when viewed from the perspective of the *organizations* deploying such attacks.[58] As Pape states, it is not simple fanaticism that explains organizations' use of suicide terrorism, but a belief in the efficacy of this mode of attack.[59] From the strategic perspective, terrorism is just one particular form of political violence whose adoption is dictated by circumstances.[60] The strategic rationale brings to light that terrorism is a form of behavior rather than an inherent quality of certain types of people; it is something individuals can opt to *do*, not an expression of what they *are*.

Any group may opt to utilize terrorist violence as a strategy for a variety of reasons.[61] Some employ it as a form of psychological warfare, extracting concessions from opponents through the (threatened) use of indiscriminate violence.[62] Groups might also utilize terrorist violence to demonstrate a government's impotence,[63] to advertise their goals and grievances to a (global) audience, to establish revolutionary conditions, or to entice government

---

56 Miller, 'Terrorist Decision Making,' 138.
57 Crenshaw, 'The Logic of Terrorism', 371-82; LaFree et al., 'Spatial and Temporal Patterns', 7-29; Lake, 'Rational Extremism', 15-29; Neumann and Smith, *The Strategy of Terrorism*; Shapiro, 'Terrorist Decision Making', 5-20.
58 Hoffman and McCormick, 'Terrorism, Signaling', 243-81; Pape, 'The Strategic Logic', 1-19; Pape, *Dying to Win*; Pedahzur, *Suicide Terrorism*.
59 Pape, 'The Strategic Logic', 1-19.
60 Merari, 'Terrorism as a Strategy', 213-51.
61 Jackson, 'Organizational Decisionmaking', 221-28; Kydd and Walter, 'The Strategies of Terrorism', 59.
62 Schmid, 'Terrorism as Psychological Warfare', 137-46.
63 Neumann and Smith, 'Strategic Terrorism', 571-95.

over-reaction as a means of delegitimizing the authorities.⁶⁴ Furthermore, terrorist attacks can be intended to alter the behavior of the groups with which the perpetrators identify, for instance by gaining popular support or new recruits, or by convincing their supporters that armed resistance is feasible.⁶⁵

Scenarios in which a cost-benefit analysis could swing in favor of terrorism include the exhaustion of non-violent options or seeing other groups successfully utilize this form of political violence. Alternatively, the narrow popular appeal of extremist groups' goals or strong government repression may rule out political attempts at achieving change, making terrorism more attractive from the outset. There may also be a sudden opportunity that makes terrorism seem an appealing option, such as repressive government measures that (temporarily) provide popular legitimacy for striking at the authorities. Finally, terrorism can become attractive when a group is forced onto the defensive, turning it into a means of showing continued strength and ability to act despite state success or increased repression.⁶⁶

Van Gogh's attacker left behind numerous writings that provide an interesting perspective on his views. In some of these texts, he threatened perceived enemies or called upon Muslims to rise up and fight in defense of their faith.⁶⁷ But to what end? Beyond advocacy of religious dogmatism and general calls to militancy and resistance, concrete strategic goals are absent. While Van Gogh's murderer does at one point declare that it is 'but a matter of time' before the Dutch government will fall to Islamist forces, there is no indication that he worked to hasten this ultimate victory or had any practical ideas on how to bring it about.⁶⁸

The *lack* of strategic motives is also apparent in the final statement that Van Gogh's murderer gave in court on 9 August 2005. 'I acted out of faith. And I have even declared that had it been my father or my brother, I would have done exactly the same'.⁶⁹ Neither is there a clear indication that he killed for political motives in any of the seven 'open letters' he wrote prior to carrying out his attack. The letters threaten the Dutch people as a whole with further acts of terrorism and single out several politicians known for

---

64   Crenshaw, 'The Logic of Terrorism', 371, 377-79.
65   Lustick, 'Terrorism in the Arab-Israeli Conflict', 514-52.
66   Crenshaw, 'The Logic of Terrorism', 373-76.
67   Peters, 'De Ideologische En Religieuze Ontwikkeling', appendix: Overzicht teksten geschreven of vertaald door Mohammed B., 12-56.
68   Peters, 'Dutch Extremist Islamism', 158-59.
69   'Ik heb gehandeld uit geloof. En ik heb zelfs aangegeven dat als het mijn vader was geweest of broertje had ik precies hetzelfde gedaan': NOS, 'Verklaring Mohammed B. In Tekst', 2.

their critical stance on Islam. The letters also admonish the (global) Muslim community for standing by in the face of oppression and encourage young Dutch Muslims to follow the 'true' path of (extremist) Islam.[70] They suggest that the murderer was motivated by a strongly held belief that it was his personal duty to kill blasphemers, as well as a desire to avenge perceived injustices, rather than an ambition to attain political goals more specific than rallying potential supporters to his worldview.

In 2005, another member of the group's extremist inner circle made a videotape in which he threatens the Dutch government and its citizens for their participation in the Iraq war. He also calls upon his fellow believers to 'attack or be attacked' in defense of oppressed Muslims worldwide.[71] But other than a call for the Dutch to 'keep your hands off of the Muslims everywhere in the world', he does not formulate clear political goals.[72] A concrete strategic rationale was also absent from this individual's 2003 attempt to reach Chechnya and, prior to that, his ambition to go to the Palestinian territories. Instead, both the videotaped message and his unfinished autobiography reveal an idealistic desire to help oppressed Muslims, the need to find a release for feelings of anger and revenge, a sense of personal religious duty, and the emulation of jihadist role models. In a telling reference to his desire to go to the Palestinian territories, he writes 'I did not think at all, about where I would go, what I would do, about nothing'.[73] The need to 'do something' was all-important.

The motives of other Hofstadgroup participants with violent intentions follow a similar pattern. The letter a third inner-circle member left his mother before embarking for Pakistan or Afghanistan makes clear that he left to 'drive out the unbelievers' and 'establish the Islamic state'.[74] Although these are clear goals on paper they hardly appear outside of this one letter. When he mentions his travels in chat conversations during the fall of 2003, the emphasis is always on the action itself, rather than its significance as a means towards certain ends. Rather than stressing the need for an Islamic state in Afghanistan, for instance, this individual seemed almost singularly interested in discussing the specific weapons he used, the training

---

70 Peters, 'Dutch Extremist Islamism', 156-57.
71 NOVA, 'Videotestament Samir A.'.
72 'Houden jullie handen af van de moslims overal in de wereld': Ibid.
73 'Ik dacht helemaal niet na, over waar ik daar naar toe zou gaan, wat ik daar zou kunnen doen, over niets': A[.], 'Deurwaarders', 4.
74 'om er de ongelovigen te verdrijven, en te helpen om de Islamitische staat op te richten': Dienst Nationale Recherche, 'RL8026', 01/13: 163.

he allegedly underwent, the hardships he faced, and the people he met.[75] Adventure and action trumped strategic considerations.

Political-strategic considerations were not entirely absent from the motives of those Hofstadgroup participants who actually carried out or planned to carry out a terrorist attack. There are also some indications that the group's most militant participants discussed – and disagreed – about how the use of violence could best suit their aims; some wanted to focus on attacks in the Netherlands while others wished to join Islamist insurgents overseas.[76] But as the various examples given above have shown, strategic rationales were never clearly expressed. Instead, such ambitions to commit acts of terrorism as emerged from the group hinted at strongly held convictions and violent emotions as motivational forces. The next section considers whether organizational rationales for violence can shed light on their origins.

7.6 Terrorism as the result of organizational dynamics

Semi-clandestine and ideologically oriented organizations such as terrorist groups face considerable constraints on decision-making processes. Their social isolation or, in some cases, even completely underground existence makes them inherently inward-looking. Among the effects of such an existence are increased cohesion among militants and a heightened desire to strike out at those who threaten the group.[77] But studies reveal that by making the group the sole source and filter for information about the outside world, increased solidarity can also skew the analysis of the likely consequences of attacks as well as the cost benefit calculation that led to the adoption of terrorism in the first place.[78]

Furthermore, highly cohesive in-groups that need to make decisions in times of crisis and in conditions of considerable stress are vulnerable to 'groupthink'. This refers to a setting in which loyalty to group norms and social pressures towards conformity override critical thinking and the voicing of doubts.[79] Groupthink further deteriorates the ability of (terrorist)

---

75   Ibid., 01/01: 123-26; AHA05/22: 2176; AHD07/36: 8401-02; AHD08/37: 569-571, 595-597, 618-619, 635-637, 715-717, 767-769, 773-775, 880, 919-931; AHD09/38: 9049, 9054-56.
76   Former Hofstadgroup Participant 4, 'Personal Interview 2', 3-4.
77   McCauley and Moskalenko, 'Mechanisms of Political Radicalization', 421-24.
78   Della Porta, 'Recruitment Processes', 310; Crenshaw, 'The Logic of Terrorism', 372; Della Porta, *Social Movements*, 114, 186, 204.
79   Janis, 'Groupthink', 84-85.

groups to objectively interpret reality, can lead them to overestimate their own capabilities, to dismiss information or criticisms that do not fit their preconceptions, and to hold stereotypical views of the enemy that prohibit a realistic assessment of their opponents' capabilities and likely responses.[80]

The effects of group psychology surpass merely placing constraints on the rationality of decision-making processes. Some authors propose that group dynamics override strategic considerations in contributing to the decision to use terrorist violence.[81] Although terrorist groups often present themselves as ideologically driven organizations that use violence to achieve political aims, such strategic rationales are not necessarily the primary incentive guiding members' participation. Instead, personnel may be drawn by a host of non-political considerations such as social solidarity, status, or the personal gratification found in adherence to the group's worldview.[82] Through its ability to deliver these benefits, the group's importance can become so great that its wellbeing becomes its members' greatest priority.[83] Over time, 'proximate' objectives such as group survival can supersede 'ultimate' political purpose, leading terrorist groups to persevere even in the face of outright failure and making terrorism a goal in itself.[84]

The literature review revealed six group-based motives for terrorist violence. The first is the incentive of redemption, whereby membership of violent groups that adhere to strict moral or religious codes offers individual participants a road to salvation.[85] In such a setting, the 'motivation for terrorism may be to transcend reality as much as to transform it'.[86] The second is the action imperative. Impatient for results and disillusioned with or otherwise dismissive of the path of non-violence, terrorist groups frequently develop strong internal pressures towards carrying out a violent act. Such a need to 'do something' is not necessarily tied to instrumental reasoning.[87] Thirdly, there is the emulation of other terrorists held in high esteem by the group. Their modus operandi, their justifications for violence,

---

80 Ibid., 85-88; McCormick, 'Terrorist Decision Making', 488-89; Crenshaw, *Explaining Terrorism*, 107.
81 Ozer, 'The Impact of Group Dynamics', 63-75.
82 Abrahms, 'What Terrorists Really Want', 101-03.
83 Della Porta, *Social Movements*, 134, 177-78, 183.
84 Crenshaw, 'Theories of Terrorism', 19-22; McCauley and Segal, 'Social Psychology of Terrorist Groups', 336-37; McCormick, 'Terrorist Decision Making', 489-90; McAllister and Schmid, 'Theories of Terrorism', 227; Post, 'Terrorist Psycho-Logic', 38.
85 Crenshaw, 'Theories of Terrorism', 20.
86 Ibid.
87 McCormick, 'Terrorist Decision Making', 487; Crenshaw, 'Theories of Terrorism', 20; Sageman, 'The Next Generation of Terror', 40-41.

and even the manner in which these role models issue communiqués can become templates and incentives for admirers' own actions.[88]

The fourth group-driven motivation for terrorism found in the literature sees such violence occur as a response to counterterrorism measures taken by the authorities.[89] Attacking the state is of course most readily associated with strategic rationales for terrorism. But as the state reacts to terrorist attacks and terrorist groups lose comrades to firefights or arrests, what began as a politically strategic use of force has a tendency to devolve into a highly personal struggle in which the desire for vengeance can override strategic considerations and instigate further violence.[90] Such a spiral of revenge is documented, for instance, by Della Porta in her research on the Italian and German left-wing terrorist groups that were active between 1960 and 1990.[91]

The fifth and sixth organizational rationales for terrorism are competition with other extremist groups and intragroup conflict. When different terrorist groups emerge that share the same goals, appeal to the same ideology, and (claim to) represent the same segment of a population, the likeliness of competition increases. In the struggle for such resources as media attention, recruits, and popular legitimacy, terrorist groups may begin to use violence against their competitors as well as their primary out-group enemy.[92] Intragroup conflicts and disagreements, finally, have been hypothesized to lead to violence when they become so extreme that the projection of this disaffection onto external enemies is the only way of keeping the terrorist group from falling apart.[93]

The empirical data on the Hofstadgroup appears to match four of the six organizational rationales for violence outlined above. These are the 'redemption', 'emulation', 'reactions to state countermeasures', and 'competition with other extremist groups' hypotheses.

7.6.1 The group as a vehicle for redemptive violence

Van Gogh's murderer was clearly motivated by the incentive of religious salvation. His declaration in court and the farewell letter he left his family

---

88   McCormick, 'Terrorist Decision Making', 488; Crone, 'Religion and Violence', 291-307.
89   Lia and Skjølberg, 'Causes of Terrorism', 17.
90   McCauley and Moskalenko, 'Mechanisms of Political Radicalization', 425.
91   Della Porta, *Social Movements*, 155, 183.
92   Bloom, *Dying to Kill*, 78-79, 94-97; Crenshaw, 'Theories of Terrorism', 24; McCauley and Moskalenko, 'Mechanisms of Political Radicalization', 424; McCauley and Segal, 'Social Psychology of Terrorist Groups', 335; Ross, 'Structural Causes', 323; Tilly, *The Politics of Collective Violence*, 76.
93   McCauley and Segal, 'Social Psychology of Terrorist Groups', 335.

revealed a man driven by the desire to act in accordance with his religious convictions and the hope that he would gain a favored place in an afterlife.[94] Although these themes are less prominent in the case of the individual who videotaped a threat to the Dutch public, his message similarly stresses that waging defensive jihad is a religious duty. He also told his parents that he acted out of fear for disobeying his god's commandments and his message appears to glorify self-sacrifice in name of Islam.[95] A desire for martyrdom and its associated awards is also a commonly recurring theme in a third participant's chat conversations about his motives for traveling to Pakistan or Afghanistan.[96]

It is clear that group processes contributed to the adoption of such radical and extremist convictions. However, there is little to indicate that the aforementioned individuals' desire to engage in religiously inspired violence resulted directly from their participation in the Hofstadgroup. Neither is there cause to assume that they sought out the Hofstadgroup because they hoped it would enable them to engage in such violence. Instead, as the next chapter will detail, the available evidence points to the influential role of largely idiosyncratic personal factors. In the case of Van Gogh's murderer these were the loss of his mother and his discovery of religious texts mandating the murder of blasphemers.[97] For the videotaped individual, a desire to assist oppressed Muslims worldwide mixed with personal animosity towards the Dutch state. These findings hint at motives for terrorism that were primarily personal rather than group-based.

7.6.2 The influence of role models on the use of violence

Emulation of role models certainly formed an incentive for violence among some Hofstadgroup participants. Van Gogh's murderer followed precepts mandating the murder of blasphemers set out in a centuries-old work by a leading Salafist scholar.[98] The videotaped message discussed earlier bore a close stylistic resemblance to similar communiqués published by jihadists like Osama Bin Laden; studded with Quranic recitation and a firearm clearly displayed.[99] However, in both examples the sources being emulated lay

---

94 Dienst Nationale Recherche, 'RL8026', AHB03/27: 4033-41; NOS, 'Verklaring Mohammed B. In Tekst'.
95 NOVA, "Videotestament Samir A.".
96 Dienst Nationale Recherche, 'RL8026', AHD08/37: 8573-74, 8594, 8773.
97 Peters, 'Dutch Extremist Islamism', 145-59.
98 Ibid., 155-56.
99 NOVA, 'Videotestament Samir A.'.

outside of the Hofstadgroup itself, meaning they cannot be earmarked as reflecting organizational rationales for violence.

There is only one notable example where emulation of a Hofstadgroup participant contributed to another's motivation for violence. One interviewee explained that he and his comrades saw the murder of Van Gogh as setting an example that they too needed to follow.[100] Thus, Van Gogh's murder inspired the interviewee to start considering an attack of his own. Fortunately, the individual in question was arrested before he was able to act on his intentions. Although only one example, it points to the potentially significant influence of copycat behavior in bringing about further acts of terrorism.

7.6.3 Interaction with the Dutch authorities

The organizational dynamic that most clearly contributed to some participants' desire to use violence was the Hofstadgroup's increasing antagonism towards the Dutch state. First of all, the experience of being arrested and imprisoned clearly increased the hatred felt by some of those in and around the group towards the state and its representatives.[101] For instance, one participant claimed that his arrest following an altercation with a police officer in 2002 strengthened his conviction that Muslims were being persecuted by unbelievers.[102] The female participants interviewed by Groen and Kranenberg were furious about the rough manner in which they had been apprehended and the authors noted the radicalizing effects of these experiences.[103] Similarly, one interviewee mentioned that, initially, his incarceration only strengthened his convictions and his hatred.[104]

Most importantly, the counterterrorism activities of the Dutch state seem to have engendered within some participants a desire to strike back. In chat messages dated to October 2003 an inner-circle member expressed anger at the drafting of new laws which, he claimed, would land him and his compatriots in jail.[105] Although he does not specify them, he was probably referring to the legislative proposals that would result in the 2004 Crimes of

---

100   Former Hofstadgroup Participant 1, 'Personal Interview 2', 27.
101   Former Hofstadgroup Participant 3, 'Personal Interview 1', 5-6; Vermaat, *Nederlandse Jihad*, 215.
102   Erkel, *Samir*, 35-40.
103   Groen and Kranenberg, *Women Warriors*, 147, 183.
104   Former Hofstadgroup Participant 1, 'Personal Interview 1', 4.
105   Dienst Nationale Recherche, 'RL8026', AHD08/37: 8600.

Terrorism Act.¹⁰⁶ The sources also make clear that this person felt a strong antipathy towards the AIVD.¹⁰⁷ Furthermore, in a letter likely written by this same individual, he responds to the then Deputy Prime Minister's 'declaration of war' against terrorism that was issued in the wake of Van Gogh's murder. With those words, the letter warns, the 'gates of hell' have been opened and a total war begun that can only end in the victory of either the forces of unbelief or those of Islam.¹⁰⁸

No one was more strongly affected by the Hofstadgroup's increasingly antagonistic relations with the Dutch state than the participant who in 2005 would record a threatening video message. This person appears to have developed a particular hatred for the Dutch justice system and the AIVD.¹⁰⁹ After his release from custody in early 2005, police intelligence revealed that he was driven to rectify the '1-0' the Dutch state had scored against him, indicating that he was at least partly motivated by a desire for revenge.¹¹⁰ While the participants' antagonistic interactions with the Dutch authorities were arguably the single most important organizational rationale for violence, the examples given in this paragraph once again hint that this rationale may have been as much *personal* as it was *group*-based in origin.

7.6.4 Competition with other extremist groups

Rivalry with other extremist groups did not occur because of an absence of potential competitors with whom to vie for recruits, resources, or standing. The Hofstadgroup was not one of many similar entities but, at the time, a relatively unique phenomenon in the Netherlands. However, if this line of reasoning is broadened slightly to encompass disagreements between an extremist group and the wider (non-violent) social movement to which it relates, then a new perspective comes to the fore centered on the Hofstadgroup's discontent with the wider Dutch Salafist community and moderate Muslims in general.

---

106 Van der Woude, *Wetgeving in Een Veiligheidscultuur*, 206-07; Van der Laan, 'Donners Rigoureuze Maatregelen'.
107 Dienst Nationale Recherche, 'RL8026', AHA05/22: 2169; AHD08/37: 8552, 8607-608.
108 'de poorten van de hel opengezet': Ibid., 01/13: 151; 'Kabinet Bindt Strijd Aan Met Moslimterreur'.
109 Erkel, *Samir*, 35-40, 199-200, 206-08, 218-19, 227-28, 240-41; Calis, 'Iedereen Wil Martelaar Zijn', 3; Dienst Nationale Recherche, 'RL8026', AHD08/37: 8552.
110 Dienst Nationale Recherche, 'Piranha', 151, INL05: 8327.

De Koning and Meijer attribute particular importance to this relationship. They argue that the progressively harsher tone of the public debate on Islam in the Netherlands, coupled with the increased public scrutiny of Salafist mosques after two young Dutch Salafists were killed in Kashmir in 2002, pressured representatives of mainstream Salafism to become more moderate. This accommodating attitude left the Hofstadgroup's young radicals disappointed with mainstream Salafism, which contributed both to the group's formation as well as to the conviction of its more extremist participants that jihad was the only legitimate way forward.[111]

The available empirical data partly supports this line of reasoning. Various sources reveal that Dutch Salafist imams' unwillingness or inability to discuss jihad-related topics led to considerable frustration and resentment among the Hofstadgroup's participants. This was exacerbated by the 2003 decision of influential Saudi-Arabian Salafist religious authorities to follow their government's line in condemning jihadists such as Bin Laden and Abu Musab al-Zarqawi. To at least several members of the Hofstadgroup, the Dutch Salafist mosques' decision to adopt a similar stance epitomized their betrayal of 'true Islam' and its champions. Both of these developments led to a reorientation on other, more extremist, sources of information and to a stronger focus on the group as a venue for discussing and learning about Islam rather than the mosque, leading to the elimination of the latter's potentially moderating influence.[112]

However, this falling out with the Salafist movement does not appear to have formed a direct motive for violence. While the group felt a strong disdain for Salafists, moderate Muslims and organizations claiming to represent the interests of Muslims in the Netherlands, clear indications that this sparked a strong desire to use violence against them are lacking. With the exception of an October 2003 chat message in which one participant expressed his desire to slaughter 'fake Muslims', and which reads more like bragging than an actual intention to use violence, the sources predominantly convey a sense of disappointment and disgust. For instance, one of the letters left behind by Van Gogh's murderer shows his disappointment with Muslim scholars and religious leaders for concealing the 'truth' of their

---

111 De Koning and Meijer, 'Going All the Way', 225, 231, 233-34, 236.
112 Former Hofstadgroup Participant 3, 'Personal Interview 1', 7-8; Former Hofstadgroup Participant 1, 'Personal Interview 1', 7; 'Personal Interview 2', 16; A[.], 'Deurwaarders', 3-5; Peters, 'De Ideologische En Religieuze Ontwikkeling', appendix: Overzicht teksten geschreven of vertaald door Mohammed B., 42-45; Dienst Nationale Recherche, 'RL8026', AHD02/31: 5791; AHB01/25: 3303; AHA05/22: 2168, 2172, 2179; AHD07/36: 8412; AHD08/37: 614, 638-642; De Koning, 'Changing Worldviews and Friendship', 374, 385-88.

religion from their followers. By contrast, the message to Dutch citizens and politicians is not one of disappointment, but of death threats.[113]

In conclusion, the empirical data reveals several motives for terrorism that resemble a number of the organizational rationales for terrorism identified in the literature. However, the most important conclusion to be drawn here is that the extent to which these motives truly had their basis in group dynamics is in most cases limited. Mirroring the conclusion reached with regard to strategic rationales, it seems that the motives for violence found among Hofstadgroup participants are more accurately explained as the result of factors at the individual level of analysis.

7.7 Conclusion

This chapter assessed whether group-level explanations for terrorist violence could account for the Hofstadgroup's planned and perpetrated attacks. The discussion began with an examination of the ways in which a terrorist group's organizational structure can influence its lethality. Except for adherence to an extremist interpretation of Islam that portrayed violence as necessary and justified, the Hofstadgroup lacked the characteristics thought to correspond with a higher degree of deadliness, such as skilled operatives.

Next, the analysis turned to group effects that can lower individual participants' thresholds to engaging in violent behavior; diffusion of responsibility, deindividuation, and displacement or responsibility to authority figures. Only the last of these factors was found to have exerted an influence, albeit in a very limited capacity. While the group had access to authority figures ranging from its Syrian religious instructor Abu Khaled to jihadist role models like Bin Laden who provided (implicit) justifications for the use of violence, none directly authorized or ordered the use of terrorism. This meant that participants were limited in the degree to which they could displace responsibility for harming and killing others, leaving a significant obstacle to the use of violence in place and making the development of terrorist plots dependent on their own initiative.

The remainder of the chapter dealt with strategic and organizational rationales for terrorism. On the whole, neither rationale could provide a convincing explanation for the terrorist acts planned or perpetrated by Hofstadgroup participants. There is little to indicate that the group's most

---

113   Peters, 'De Ideologische En Religieuze Ontwikkeling', appendix: Overzicht teksten geschreven of vertaald door Mohammed B., 32-56.

militant participants did more than pay lip service to strategic motives such as establishing theocratic rule in the Netherlands or inspiring potential followers to copy their violent examples. Organizational dynamics had a more noticeable, if still minor, influence. The most salient being the Hofstadgroup's increasingly antagonistic relationship with the Dutch state, which may have engendered the desire to commit attacks as a form of revenge within at least one participant and the 'example' set by the murder of Van Gogh, which inspired at least one other participant to plan an attack of his own.

In a sense, this chapter's most important contribution to understanding the factors that governed processes of involvement in the Hofstadgroup has been to highlight where group-level accounts for terrorism fall short. The Hofstadgroup's planned and executed terrorist attacks cannot convincingly be explained as the result of either strategic or organizational rationales. Instead, they appear to have originated from these individuals' personal backgrounds, experiences and convictions. Gaining a clearer understanding of why some participants (planned to) engage in terrorism therefore requires turning to that level of analysis next.

8 Individual-level analysis I: Cognitive explanations

In this first of two chapters on the individual level of analysis, the emphasis is on cognitive explanations for participation in terrorism. How can ways of thinking, a person's idiosyncratic perception of events and people, contribute to their becoming involved in an extremist or terrorist group? After a brief explication of the individual level of analysis, the chapter opens by discussing 'radicalization', the most influential cognitive explanation for terrorism to have emerged since the 9/11 attacks. It then moves on to the related concept of fanaticism before turning to how 'cognitive openings' can trigger processes leading to involvement in terrorism. The chapter closes with an appraisal of the roles that cognitive dissonance and moral disengagement can play in bringing about participation. The next chapter completes the individual-level analysis by utilizing various explanations centered on the idea of distinct psychological traits as contributing to the likeliness of involvement in terrorism.

8.1 Structuring the individual-level of analysis

As Crenshaw commented in 1998, 'terrorism is not the direct result of social conditions but of individual perceptions of those conditions'.[1] Similarly, Borum emphasizes that most violence is intentional; a wide variety of factors play a role in bringing it about, but at the end of the day it is still about individuals consciously engaging in this form of behavior.[2] The structural and group-level factors discussed in previous chapters form an integral part of the puzzle of how and why people become involved in homegrown jihadist entities like the Hofstadgroup. But any assessment of this question that does not take the individual-level perspective into account, will remain incomplete.

There is a large body of work that studies terrorism from the perspective of the individual perpetrator.[3] This book utilizes two broad lines of inquiry

---

1 Crenshaw, 'Questions to Be Answered', 250.
2 Borum, *Psychology of Terrorism*, 11.
3 Ibid.; Borum, 'Radicalization into Violent Extremism II', 37-62; Victoroff, 'The Mind of the Terrorist', 3-42.

found in this literature to structure the individual-level discussion. Whereas the next chapter utilizes approaches that see terrorists as psychologically distinctive, for instance in terms of higher incidences of mental illness, the present one focuses on cognitive explanations.

The study of cognition is 'concerned with the internal processes involved in making sense of the environment and deciding what action might be appropriate'.[4] Victoroff highlights the distinction between cognitive capacity and cognitive style. The first 'refers to mental functions, such as memory, attention, concentration, language, and the so-called "executive" functions, including the capacity to learn and follow rules, to anticipate outcomes, to make sensible inferences, and to perform accurate risk-benefit calculations'.[5] Cognitive style 'refers to ways of thinking – that is, biases, prejudices, or tendencies to over- or underemphasize factors in decision making'.[6] Reflecting the literature on terrorism's focus on this latter aspect of cognitive psychology, this chapter assesses how ways of thinking can contribute to involvement in terrorism (Table 9).

A qualification that needs to be made before proceeding to the analysis proper, is that it is not possible to provide a detailed look at every single Hofstadgroup participant. The sources currently available are simply not expansive enough to allow an in-depth reconstruction of the life history, motivations for involvement, psychological state, and other relevant personal factors for each and every participant. The available information is also skewed in that relatively more is known about the group's most extremist participants due to the police's greater interest in those individuals. While the two chapters that form the individual-level of analysis draw upon as much data as is available in an attempt to provide insights relevant to the group as a whole, these limitations cannot be entirely overcome.

Table 9   Individual-level analysis I: Cognitive explanations

Radicalization
Fanaticism
Cognitive openings and 'unfreezing'
Cognitive dissonance and moral disengagement

---

4   Eysenck and Keane, *Cognitive Psychology*, 1.
5   Victoroff, 'The Mind of the Terrorist', 26.
6   Ibid.

8.2 Radicalization

For well over a decade, academics, policy makers, journalists and the general public have been debating involvement in terrorism as a process characterized by 'radicalization'.[7] The concept's obverse, 'deradicalization', has similarly become central to more recent questions about if and how former terrorists can be re-integrated into society.[8] But despite its ubiquitous use, radicalization has also attracted considerable criticism.[9]

A first issue is the lack of consensus on what radicalization encompasses. Some scholars[10] and government agencies[11] use it in a rather broad sense to designate the processes leading up to involvement in terrorism. For Horgan, 'violent radicalisation [...] encompasses the phases of a) becoming involved with a terrorist group and b) remaining involved and engaging in terrorist activity'.[12] Similarly, Kruglanski and colleagues see radicalization as 'a movement in the direction of *supporting* or *enacting* radical behavior'.[13] McCauley and Moskalenko view it as 'increased preparation for and commitment to intergroup conflict'.[14] Several relatively complex models for involvement in terrorism, such as Moghaddam's 'staircase' and McCauley and Moskalenko's 'pyramid' models can also be subsumed under this behaviorally-oriented approach to radicalization.[15]

A second perspective sees radicalization as a process of *cognitive* change which results in the internalization of radical or extremist beliefs.[16] Neumann, for instance, argues that 'at the most basic level, radicalization can be defined as the process whereby people become extremists'.[17] Similarly, Slootman and Tillie, as well as Buijs and Demant, see radicalization as a

---

7 Crone, 'Radicalization Revisited', 587.
8 Koehler, *Understanding Deradicalization*.
9 Horgan, 'Psychology of Terrorism', 200.
10 Davis and Cragin, *Social Science for Counterterrorism*, xxiv; Dawson, 'The Study of New Religious Movements', 4; Della Porta and LaFree, 'Guest Editorial', 5; King and Taylor, 'The Radicalization of Homegrown Jihadists', 603.
11 See Danish, Dutch, and Swedish government definitions in: Schmid, 'Radicalisation, De-Radicalisation', 12.
12 Horgan, *Walking Away from Terrorism*, 152.
13 Kruglanski et al., 'The Psychology of Radicalization and Deradicalization', 70.
14 McCauley and Moskalenko, 'Mechanisms of Political Radicalization', 416.
15 Borum, 'Radicalization into Violent Extremism II', 38-43; King and Taylor, 'The Radicalization of Homegrown Jihadists', 605; McCauley and Moskalenko, 'Mechanisms of Political Radicalization', 416-28; Moghaddam, 'The Staircase to Terrorism', 161-69.
16 Borum, 'Understanding the Terrorist Mindset', 7-10; Hannah, Clutterbuck, and Rubin, 'Radicalization or Rehabilitation', 2.
17 Neumann, 'The Trouble with Radicalization', 874.

process centered on the 'delegitimization' of the established societal and political order, leading to a desire for radical change that in its most extreme form could include the use of violence.[18] Horgan contrasts 'violent radicalization' with 'radicalization', the latter signifying the 'social and psychological process of incrementally experienced commitment to extremist political or religious ideology'.[19]

A third set of definitions of radicalization explicitly link beliefs to behavior.[20] Silber and Bhatt have argued that radicalization is the 'progression of searching, finding, adopting, nurturing, and developing [an] extreme belief system to the point where it acts as a catalyst for a terrorist act'.[21] Dalgaard-Nielsen sees 'violent radicalization' as a 'process in which radical ideas are accompanied by the development of a willingness to directly support or engage in violent acts'.[22] Neumann writes of 'the process (or processes) whereby individuals or groups come to approve of and (ultimately) participate in the use of violence for political aims'.[23] Other authors make a more implicit connection between extremist beliefs and involvement in terrorism.[24] The key point is that radicalization is frequently interpreted as a process in which the adoption of radical ideas precedes or even leads to involvement in radical behavior. This implied or explicitly stated connection is radicalization's biggest flaw.

To be clear, none of the authors mentioned in the previous paragraph argue that beliefs alone are sufficient to explain involvement in terrorism. Yet the centrality of this link, explicitly stated or not, in many 'radicalization'-based explanations is difficult to overlook. Indeed, the very term 'radicalization' implies that radical (or as is more often the case 'extremist') ideas are key to understanding terrorism. It is clear the beliefs can play a crucial role in motivating and legitimizing terrorism.[25] Yet by raising beliefs as the key element to understanding terrorism, 'radicalization' often

---

18   Slootman and Tillie, 'Processen Van Radicalisering', 24; Buijs and Demant, 'Extremisme En Radicalisering', 173; Demant et al., 'Decline and Disengagement', 12-13.
19   Horgan, *Walking Away from Terrorism*, 152.
20   See also: Genkin and Gutfraind, 'How Do Terrorist Cells Self-Assemble', 2; Vidino and Brandon, 'Countering Radicalization', 9.
21   Silber and Bhatt, "Radicalization in the West," 16.
22   Dalgaard-Nielsen, 'Violent Radicalization in Europe', 798.
23   Neumann, 'Prisons and Terrorism', 12.
24   For instance: Gielen, *Radicalisering En Identiteit*, 14; Ongering, 'Home-Grown Terrorism and Radicalisation in the Netherlands', 3; Porter and Kebbell, 'Radicalization in Australia', 213; Tsintsadze-Maass and Maass, 'Groupthink and Terrorist Radicalization', 736.
25   Borum, *Psychology of Terrorism*, 45-47; Kruglanski, 'Inside the Terrorist Mind', 274-75; Kruglanski et al., 'The Psychology of Radicalization and Deradicalization', 76-78.

overstates the explanatory potential of this variable while leaving others underemphasized.[26]

As Kundnani aptly summarizes the problem, 'the radicalization literature fails to offer a convincing demonstration of any causal relationship between theology and violence'.[27] Essentially, the vast majority of people with extremist beliefs never act on them.[28] Strikingly, research has also shown that not all those who *do* become terrorists are (primarily) motivated by extremist ideologies.[29] For instance, a study on American Muslims found radical Islamic beliefs to be unrelated to support for terrorism or the conviction that the U.S. was waging a war on Islam.[30] Even Palestinian suicide terrorists appear to be motivated by more than just extremist beliefs.[31] In short, most radicals do not become terrorists and not all terrorists are (primarily) ideologically driven. Another reason for skepticism about the degree to which beliefs motivate behavior is that terrorists' may have *learned* to describe their motivations in ideological terms during their socialization into the group.[32] Such justifications may obscure other motivating factors of equal or greater significance.

The overstated link between beliefs and behavior still found in a significant portion of the literature on radicalization is the concept's primary shortcoming. Yet there are more reasons why radicalization is a problematic framework through which to study involvement in terrorism. Some of the more detailed models of involvement in terrorism tend to be quite linear; suggesting a sequential progression through distinct stages that seems an overly neat categorization of a complex reality.[33] As scholars and practitioners have remarked, it is inaccurate to view radicalization as 'a "conveyor belt" that starts with grievances and ends with violence, with

---

26   Aly and Striegher, 'Examining the Role of Religion', 850, 860; Bartlett and Miller, 'The Edge of Violence', 2; Knefel, 'Everything You've Been Told About Radicalization Is Wrong'; Kühle and Lindekilde, *Radicalization among Young Muslims in Aarhus*, 134-35. See also comments by Horgan in: Neumann, 'The Trouble with Radicalization', 878.

27   Kundnani, 'Radicalisation', 21.

28   Borum, 'Rethinking Radicalization', 1-2; 'Radicalization into Violent Extremism I', 8; Khalil, 'Radical Beliefs and Violent Actions', 198-211; McCauley and Moskalenko, *Friction*, 219-21; Taylor, 'Conflict Resolution', 1.

29   Abrahms, 'What Terrorists Really Want', 98-99; Taylor and Quayle, *Terrorist Lives*, 37-38.

30   McCauley, 'Testing Theories of Radicalization', 309. For a critique of this very point, see: Mullins, 'Radical Attitudes and Jihad', 313-14.

31   Merari, 'Psychological Aspects of Suicide Terrorism', 106; Merari et al., 'Making Palestinian "Martyrdom Operations"', 109-10.

32   Horgan, 'From Profiles to Pathways', 81, 86-87.

33   King and Taylor, 'The Radicalization of Homegrown Jihadists', 605.

easily discernible signposts along the way'.³⁴ Moreover, empirical data to support these models is still frequently lacking.³⁵ Finally, the utility of radicalization as a concept is hampered by the inherently subjective nature of how to define what views and behaviors are 'radical'.³⁶

For all of these reasons, this book has neither adopted radicalization as an overarching explanatory framework, nor as shorthand for the process leading up to terrorism. Still, its centrality in the debate on terrorism means that it cannot be sidestepped entirely. Previous chapters discussed the contents of Hofstadgroup participants' ideological convictions and the manner in which group processes contributed to the adoption of these views. Shared ideological convictions were the group's most important defining characteristic and formed an important part of the 'glue' that held its participants together. What needs to be elucidated here is whether radicalization can explain involvement in the group and, most importantly, why some individuals planned and perpetrated acts of terrorism.

Cognitive-leading-to-behavioral radicalization appears well suited to explaining the behavior of Van Gogh's murderer-to-be. This individual was set on a quest for answers by the death of his mother in 2001 and quickly came to adopt a fundamentalist interpretation of Islam.³⁷ Contacts with like-minded individuals and the middle-aged Syrian religious instructor Abu Khaled strengthened his new identity as a 'true' Muslim and catalyzed a process whereby he adopted ever more radical views.³⁸ Van Gogh's future assailant kept on radicalizing until he embraced clearly extremist convictions and concluded that violence against those who insulted Islam and its prophet was not only justified, but a personal duty.³⁹ By actually murdering Van Gogh for blasphemy, the attacker represents a clear case of someone whose extremist convictions both motivated and justified his use of violence.⁴⁰

At first glance, the same appears to hold true for the individual who recorded a threatening video message in 2005. He too adopted extremist views after a negative experience, namely his perception that Muslims were

---

34 Patel, "Rethinking Radicalization," 9; McCauley and Moskalenko, *Friction*, 218-19.
35 King and Taylor, 'The Radicalization of Homegrown Jihadists', 615-16; Borum, 'Radicalization into Violent Extremism I', 15.
36 Neumann, 'The Trouble with Radicalization', 876-77.
37 Dienst Nationale Recherche, 'RL8026', AHB03/27: 4040.
38 Ibid., AHA03/20: 861; Peters, 'De Ideologische En Religieuze Ontwikkeling', 8.
39 Peters, 'Dutch Extremist Islamism', 145-59; Peters, 'De Ideologische En Religieuze Ontwikkeling', 1-87.
40 NOS, 'Verklaring Mohammed B. In Tekst'; Peters, 'Dutch Extremist Islamism', 155-56.

persecuted the world over, and his growing extremism was also mediated by his involvement with like-minded individuals and authority figures like the Hofstadgroup's Syrian religious instructor Abu Khaled.[41] But in contrast to the experience of Van Gogh's murderer, this individual's internalization of an extremist worldview and his involvement in the Hofstadgroup did not immediately lead to the intention to commit acts of terrorism. Instead, he initially wanted to join Islamist insurgencies in Palestine or Chechnya.[42] Only after attempts to reach those regions had failed did this person begin to show an interest in what appear to have been plans to commit terrorist attacks in the Netherlands.[43]

A more important difference is that, while Van Gogh's killer appeared to be strongly and singularly motivated by his convictions, this second individual's desire to commit acts of terrorism was at least party driven by a personal desire for revenge. What is known of this person indicates that he felt a very strong antipathy towards the Dutch justice system and the secret service AIVD.[44] In early 2005, just after his release from custody, police intelligence information indicated he wanted to rectify the '1-0' that the authorities had scored against him.[45] Undoubtedly, extremist convictions played a role in this individual's violent intentions. But the strong hints of a more personal motive already diminish the degree to which 'radicalization' can provide a full explanation for his (intended) behavior. His is a case where it is difficult to assess the degree which extremist religious views *motivated* his intended violence vis-à-vis *justified* acts he felt compelled to undertake on more personal grounds.

Studying the wider group's involvement through the 'radicalization' lens underlines the problematic link between beliefs and behavior. Despite the fact that most Hofstadgroup participants held a Salafi-Jihadist worldview, the overwhelming majority of them never committed an act of terrorism, nor were they involved in preparations for one. As one of the group's extremist participants recalled, most of his erstwhile compatriots turned out to be 'wannabes'.[46] The single attack to materialize was the murder of Van Gogh and, as previous chapters have detailed, even the *intention* to commit violence was limited to a handful of the group's almost forty participants.

41   A[.], 'Deurwaarders', 3-10; 'Deurwaarders Van Allah', 32.
42   A[.], 'Deurwaarders', 10-11; De Graaf, *Gevaarlijke Vrouwen*, 258-59.
43   Dienst Nationale Recherche, 'RL8026', 01/01: 25-26.
44   Erkel, *Samir*, 35-40, 199-200, 206-08, 218-19, 227-28, 240-41; Calis, 'Iedereen Wil Martelaar Zijn', 3; Dienst Nationale Recherche, 'RL8026', AHD08/37: 8552.
45   Dienst Nationale Recherche, 'Piranha', 151, INL05: 8327.
46   'wannabes': Former Hofstadgroup Participant 4, 'Personal Interview 1', 2.

Among this minority was one of the interviewees, who recounted that he only began to develop an interest in actually 'doing something' after the murder of Van Gogh made him and his friends feel it was now their turn to prove themselves.[47] While Van Gogh's murderer was guided largely by his extremist convictions, other participants' motives for violence included a significant amount of non-ideological factors as well.

What about the notion, implied within various interpretations of radicalization, that the adoption of radical beliefs precedes involvement in radical or extremist groups? This sequence of events did hold true for a number of individuals, including Van Gogh's murderer and the person who in 2003 tried to reach Chechnya.[48] But in a significant number of cases, increased interest in radical and extremist Islam *followed from* involvement.[49] The experiences of one interviewee were exemplary in this regard, as his initial attraction to the group was not the worldview he encountered there or his own ideological preoccupations, but rather the simple fact that he enjoyed the others' company and friendship. Only gradually did he begin to adopt the worldview espoused by people like Van Gogh's future assailant.[50]

Finally, what of some radicalization theories' implied determinism, whereby those who radicalize will adopt ever more extremist convictions over time? Again, it appears only partly applicable to the Hofstadgroup. Some participants 'stopped' at a certain level of 'radicalness', for instance by adopting a Salafist interpretation of Islam that did not see the use of violence as legitimate.[51] Three participants appeared to have little or no interest in radical or fundamentalist beliefs altogether.[52] A small number of people also disengaged from the group because they came to disagree with the emphasis on takfir, even though they had previously supported it.[53] For the

47   'iets doen': Former Hofstadgroup Participant 1, 'Personal Interview 2', 27.
48   A[.], 'Deurwaarders', 3-11; 'Deurwaarders Van Allah', 30-32; Alberts et al., De Wereld Van Mohammed B.'; Dienst Nationale Recherche, 'RL8026', 01/17: 4002; Groen and Kranenberg, *Women Warriors*, 20-25; Peters, 'Dutch Extremist Islamism', 150-51; Former Hofstadgroup Participant 3, 'Personal Interview 1', 7-9; Former Hofstadgroup Participant 4, 'Personal Interview 2', 1-3.
49   Vermaat, *Nederlandse Jihad*, 169, 81; Dienst Nationale Recherche, 'RL8026', GET: 18125, 18157; VERD: 9917, 9935, 20012, 20131, 20225.
50   Former Hofstadgroup Participant 1, 'Personal Interview 2', 5-7.
51   Dienst Nationale Recherche, 'RL8026', GET: 4018-20, 4129, 4132, 4146, 4148, 4159; VERD: 20083, 20567; Groen and Kranenberg, *Women Warriors*, 98-99.
52   Dienst Nationale Recherche, 'RL8026', VERD: 19477-78, 19480, 19597, 19654, 20522, 20535, 20566.
53   Ibid., 01/17: 4002-03, 4018-20, 4030, 4062, 4048-58, 4085-86, 4092, 4100, 4125-127, 4129, 4204; Groen and Kranenberg, *Women Warriors*, 36-37, 93.

Hofstadgroup's participants, 'radicalization' was neither predetermined to end at the adoption of extremist views or participation in acts of terrorism, nor an irreversible process.

In short, radicalization is of limited value when it comes to understanding involvement in the Hofstadgroup. Contrary to this concept's central assumption, the vast majority of participants did not act upon the views they held. Conversely, at least two individuals with apparent intentions to commit acts of terrorism were motivated by more than ideology alone. Secondly, the idea that an initial adoption of radical convictions precedes involvement in an extremist group does not match the experiences of all Hofstadgroup participants. Finally, the deterministic nature of some radicalization approaches cannot account for the minority of participants who retained 'merely' radical or fundamentalist worldviews, or even abandoned previously held extremist beliefs. Radicalization's biggest contribution as an analytical lens is that it underscores the heterogeneous and non-deterministic nature of involvement in the Hofstadgroup.

8.3 Fanaticism

Although radicalization is a problematic explanation for involvement in terrorism for a variety of reasons, this does not mean that the role that beliefs play in these processes should be dismissed. What is needed is an explanation that allows for a more nuanced understanding of the role between beliefs and behavior. An explanation that meets this criterion is Taylor's concept of fanaticism, which the British psychologist developed in the early 1990s.

Taylor is careful to stress that fanaticism and 'normal' behavior are different points on the same continuum; the fanatic is not intrinsically different.[54] Neither is fanaticism as static state; no one is born into fanaticism, it is a state of mind that can be adopted and abandoned over time. Fanaticism is understood as behavior that displays 'excessive enthusiasm' for certain religious or political beliefs.[55] According to Taylor, ideologies can influence behavior because they essentially prescribe a variety of rules that link an individual's current action to distant outcomes.[56] For instance, religious belief can motivate specific behavior by connecting distant outcomes, such

---

54 Taylor, *The Fanatics*, 14.
55 Ibid., 34.
56 Ibid., 112-13, 269; Taylor and Horgan, 'The Psychological and Behavioural Bases', 53-56, 58.

as salvation in an afterlife, to daily behavior such as prayer. For the vast majority of people, religious or political beliefs are not the only influence on their behavior. But for the fanatic, 'the influence of ideology is such that it excludes or attenuates other social, political or personal forces that might be expected to control and influence behaviour'.[57]

Taylor stipulates ten qualities of fanaticism that can be useful in gauging the degree to which radical or extremist beliefs can influence behavior. These are 1) an excessive focusing on issues of concern to the fanatic; 2) a world view that is solely based on ideological convictions; 3) an insensitivity to others and to 'normal' social pressures; 4) a loss of critical judgment in that the fanatic is apt to pursue ends and utilize means that seem to run contrary to his or her personal interest; and 5) a surprising tolerance for inconsistency and incompatibility in the beliefs held. In addition, Taylor describes fanatical behavior as apt to display: 6) great certainty in the appropriateness of the actions taken; 7) a simplified view of the world; 8) high resistance to facts or interpretations that undermine the convictions held; 9) disdain for the victims of the fanatic's behavior; and 10) the construction of a social environment that makes it easier to sustain fanatical views.[58]

In addition, Taylor stresses three contextual elements that make it more likely that fanatically held ideological beliefs will lead to violence.[59] The first is millenarianism, or the belief that the world is facing an impending and apocalyptic disaster or change. The very imminence of millenarian beliefs can strengthen their ideological control over individual behavior, as the consequences of the believer's actions are no longer relegated to a distant future. Additionally, some ideologies advocate violent action as a way of hastening the advent of a new world order.[60] The second factor is the totality of ideological control; when there is little to no 'public space' in which the ideology and its alternatives can be freely debated, the ideology's influence over every aspect of its adherents' lives will increase.[61] The third factor is the militancy of the ideological belief itself.[62]

Fanaticism stresses that there is a *conditional* link between extremist beliefs and extremist behavior. Moreover, the concept goes at least some way towards illuminating the circumstances under which the likeliness of such a relationship occurring may increase. It does so by highlighting the

57 Taylor, *The Fanatics*, 33.
58 Ibid., 38-55.
59 Ibid., 114, 181.
60 Ibid., 121-58.
61 Ibid., 160-78.
62 Ibid., 114.

contextual factors that can enable beliefs to exert stronger control over behavior, as well as the ten aspects of fanaticism itself that, when present, may further increase the likeliness of radical and extremist views actually influencing someone's actions. For these reasons, fanaticism should be considered as an alternative, or perhaps an addition, to current radicalization-based concepts that by and large lack precisely this conditional element.

Taylor's concept of fanaticism is intended as an explanation for individual engagement in political violence. It therefore makes sense to limit this analysis to those persons in the Hofstadgroup who committed, or most clearly intended to do so, an act of terrorism.

Van Gogh's murderer harnessed at least eight of the ten 'qualities of the fanatic' that Taylor describes.[63] From 2003 onward, his life began to revolve entirely around his Salafi-Jihadist based convictions, which became the sole filter through which he interpreted the world. A world that he viewed in dichotomous terms; consisting of 'true' Muslims and their enemies.[64] His abandonment of work and education imply an insensitivity to 'normal' societal pressures and his decision to murder Van Gogh and then claim complete responsibility for it in court appear contrary to his own best interests.[65] The fashion in which he murdered Van Gogh and his statement in court that he would have done the same had family members been the blasphemers, indicate both a high degree of certainty in the justness of his actions and a dismissive attitude towards his victims.[66] Finally, by limiting his social circle to like-minded individuals, Van Gogh's assailant constructed a 'fanatical world' that reinforced and sustained his views.[67]

The individual who, among other things, tried to reach Chechnya and played a central role in 2005's Piranha case, also displayed signs of fanaticism. These included black-or-white reasoning, a preoccupation with ideological concerns and a worldview shaped by his Salafi-Jihadist beliefs.[68] Given these similarities, why did only Van Gogh's assailant act on his convictions? Perhaps this second person was simply apprehended before he could strike. However, the available evidence suggests a different explanation. First of all, this person appears to have been less fanatical in

---

63 Ibid., 38-55.
64 Peters, 'Dutch Extremist Islamism', 145-59; Buijs, Demant, and Hamdy, *Strijders Van Eigen Bodem*, 43-49.
65 'Laatste Woord Mohammed B.'
66 Ibid.
67 Alberts et al., 'De Wereld Van Mohammed B.', 6.
68 A[.], 'Deurwaarders', 3-11; NOVA, 'Videotestament Samir A.'; Van San, Sieckelinck, and De Winter, *Idealen Op Drift*, 46-47.

the sense that his beliefs were not the alpha and omega of his existence. Instead, he was primarily motivated by a desire to aid and avenge what he saw as the Muslim victims of Western aggression. His beliefs certainly played a role in that quest, but as mentioned in a previous paragraph, their role may have been to *justify* violence as much as *motivate* it.

Two other explanations for this difference can be gained by considering the three factors that Taylor identifies as making it more likely that fanatically held beliefs will actually lead to violent behavior.[69] As the Salafi-Jihadist views that both men held were clearly militant in content, this factor offers few answers.[70] It is with regard to millenarianism that an important first distinction presents itself. Both men believed a global war against Islam was taking place.[71] Yet it is only in the writings of Van Gogh's killer that this struggle takes on an apocalyptic flavor and is presented as the violent apogee of an age-old struggle between the forces of Satan and those of Truth that demands immediate action on the part of 'true believers'.[72] By contrast, in the videotaped threat to the Dutch government and people, arguably the most militant expression of the other individual's views, millenarian motifs are absent.[73]

Taylor's third factor that can lead fanatics to violence centers on the totality of ideological control, which is more likely in societies with limited 'public space'.[74] As Chapter 6 noted, most participants, including extremists like the Piranha group's ringleader discussed here, retained at least some connections to the world outside the group through old friends, school, work, or the simple fact that they lived with their parents. Not so in the case of Van Gogh's murderer-to-be. He had lived on his own since 2000, quit his part-time job and his studies following the death of his mother in December 2001, and stopped his volunteer work for an Amsterdam community center in July 2003.[75] Gradually, he cut off contacts with his old friends and limited his social circle to fellow Hofstadgroup participants.[76] He was 'always at home reading and translating'.[77] Within these self-imposed confines, the

69 Taylor, *The Fanatics*, 113-14.
70 Wiktorowicz, 'Anatomy of the Salafi Movement', 207-39.
71 NOVA, 'Videotestament Samir A.'; Van San, Sieckelinck, and De Winter, *Idealen Op Drift*, 48; Peters, 'Dutch Extremist Islamism', 145, 152-54.
72 Peters, 'De Ideologische En Religieuze Ontwikkeling', 3-6; Peters, 'Dutch Extremist Islamism', 146-48.
73 NOVA, 'Videotestament Samir A.'.
74 Taylor, *The Fanatics*, 114, 160-67.
75 Alberts et al., 'De Wereld Van Mohammed B.', 1; Chorus and Olgun, *In Godsnaam*, 53-58.
76 Alberts et al., 'De Wereld Van Mohammed B.', 6.
77 Groen and Kranenberg, *Women Warriors*, 9.

convictions of Van Gogh's future assailant could become all-encompassing and ever-present, exerting behavioral control to a degree not found among his compatriots.

Fanaticism makes an important contribution to the present analysis by explaining, at least partially, why of the numerous ideological extremists in the Hofstadgroup's inner circle, only Van Gogh's killer turned convictions into violent action. Van Gogh's killer acted on his beliefs because he was the most fanatical of the group's participants, because his views had a notable apocalyptical edge and, most saliently, because they were adopted and nurtured in a social setting characterized by a lack of countervailing opinions not experienced to the same degree by his compatriots. Fanaticism therefore affords an understanding of how beliefs can lead to violence that is instrumental to explaining the murder of Van Gogh.

8.4   Cognitive openings and unfreezing

Wiktorowicz describes a 'cognitive opening' as a questioning of previously held beliefs, brought on by a sudden sense of crisis that can be economic, social, political, or personal in nature.[78] Cognitive openings, or 'trigger events' more broadly, are seen by several authors as factors that can kickstart the process by which people come to adopt extremist beliefs and participate in political violence.[79] Once open to new ideas, an individual can become attracted to radical or extremist groups provided there is a sense of 'frame alignment', in which the group's representation of reality matches the individual's experience and preconceptions.[80] The crises which can produce cognitive openings need not be personally experienced. People may empathize with the suffering of others, for instance through televised reporting on war and conflict, and experience 'vicarious deprivation' that can prompt them to reevaluate their convictions or take action.[81]

In a similar argument, McCauley and Moskalenko posit that there is a higher chance that people will become involved in terrorism when they are

---

78   Wiktorowicz, 'Joining the Cause: Al-Muhajiroun and Radical Islam', 1, 7-8.
79   Ellis et al., 'Trauma and Openness', 857-83; Ilardi, 'Interviews with Canadian Radicals', 726-27; Porter and Kebbell, 'Radicalization in Australia', 227; Wiktorowicz, 'Joining the Cause: Al-Muhajiroun and Radical Islam', 1; Wilner and Dubouloz, 'Transformative Radicalization', 423.
80   Wiktorowicz, 'Joining the Cause: Al-Muhajiroun and Radical Islam', 5.
81   Schmid, 'Radicalisation, De-Radicalisation', 26; Silke, *Terrorism*, 66-67; Sageman, *Leaderless Jihad*, 72-75; Sageman, 'The Next Generation of Terror', 40-41.

suddenly detached from their everyday commitments and acquaintances. Individuals undergoing such 'unfreezing' become more open to meeting new people and entertaining new ideas. For instance, moving to a new city may prompt people to make new friends or, more dramatically, government collapse might necessitate looking for other means or organizations to ensure personal safety.[82] The unfreezing hypothesis is, in turn, reminiscent of what Munson refers to as 'biographical availability'; his study indicated that a majority of people who became involved in pro-life activism were in a period of personal transition at the moment of contact with the pro-life movement, whereas those who remained uncommitted had stable life situations.[83] Cognitive openings, unfreezing, and biographical availability all suggest that a sudden change or a period of personal transition can make individuals more amenable to becoming involved in activism, radical or extremist groups, and even terrorism.

Cognitive openings and the trigger events that led to them played an important role in bringing about participation in the Hofstadgroup. For several individuals, these trigger events were political in nature. As a teenager, the individual who tried to reach Chechnya in 2003 was gripped by news footage of the Israeli-Palestinian conflict and the Balkan war. The start of the Second Intifada (2000) led to a burgeoning perception that Muslims were being specifically persecuted the world over.[84] Then he saw the dramatic footage of the Palestinian boy Muhammad al-Durrah and his father being killed after getting caught in a cross fire between Israeli and Palestinian forces.[85] This particular incident triggered a belief that 'Muslims were being wronged' and led him to question whether he should go and help the Palestinian people, 'if necessary by fighting'.[86]

The most influential trigger events of all were undoubtedly the 11 September 2001 terrorist attacks on the United States. They prompted a number of future participants to search for answers about the attackers' motives and Islam's stance on such violence, searches that brought them into contact with political Islam and Salafi-Jihadist justifications for violence.[87] As one future participant described this period; 'I was on the Internet so often

---

82   McCauley and Moskalenko, *Friction*, 75-88.
83   Munson, *The Making Of*, 37.
84   A[.], 'Deurwaarders', 4.
85   Ibid., 4-6.
86   'dat de moslims onrecht word aangedaan', 'desnoods met vechten': Ibid., 4.
87   Groen and Kranenberg, *Women Warriors*, 18-19; Former Hofstadgroup Participant 1, 'Personal Interview 2', 10-11; De Graaf, *Gevaarlijke Vrouwen*, 249.

and so long that I began to lose weight'.[88] In addition, the attacks and the U.S.-led military response they evoked brought about a burgeoning political consciousness. One female participant described being shocked by what she saw as U.S. president George W. Bush's declaration of war against Muslims. This compelled her to choose sides for 'the Muslims' and fueled her interest in Islam.[89]

Trigger events could also be distinctly personal. Van Gogh's murderer's adoption of a fundamentalist and extremist interpretation of Islam was initiated by two events. The first was his imprisonment from July to August 2001 for assaulting two police officers with a knife. It seems that his imprisonment engendered a desire to make a fresh start and it was in prison that he began studying the Quran in earnest.[90] The more important trigger event was the death of his mother in December 2001. Van Gogh's future assailant would later write about the influence her death had on him in a farewell letter he left his family: '[i]t has not eluded you that I have changed since the death of my mother. In the wake of her death I have undertaken a search to uncover the truth'.[91] These triggers awakened the 'need for a new spiritual orientation', setting him on a significance quest that, through the mediation of group influences such as the teachings of Abu Khaled, would lead him to religious fanaticism and terrorist violence.[92]

Other future participants were also set on a path towards involvement by similarly eye-opening personal experiences. One man told police that he reoriented himself on his faith two years earlier after coming to believe he was fatally ill.[93] A female participant who was raised a Muslim realized she knew very little about her faith after meeting a Dutch convert. 'The convert laughed in my face, but then invited me to join her to go to the mosque one time. It took a while before I went, but that woman got stuck in my head: *she is Dutch and knows everything about Islam, while I am Muslim and know nothing*. From then on, I went every Friday. I would put on a headscarf and it felt great! I was so proud!'[94] This young woman's renewed interest in her

---

88 'Ik zat zo vaak en zo lang achter het Internet dat ik begon af te vallen': A[.], 'Deurwaarders', 9.
89 Groen and Kranenberg, *Women Warriors*, 19.
90 Chorus and Olgun, *In Godsnaam*, 51-53.
91 'Het is jullie niet ontgaan dat ik sinds het overlijden van mijn moeder veranderd ben. Ik heb sinds het overlijden van mijn moeder een zoektocht ondernomen om de waarheid te achterhalen': Dienst Nationale Recherche, 'RL8026', AHB03/27: 4040-41; Alberts et al., 'De Wereld Van Mohammed B.'
92 Peters, 'Dutch Extremist Islamism'.
93 Dienst Nationale Recherche, 'RL8026', VERD: 20242.
94 Groen and Kranenberg, *Women Warriors*, 24 (Italics added).

faith led her to make the acquaintance of Hofstadgroup participants and from there to become involved in the group herself.⁹⁵

Asked why he considered using violence, an interviewee listed several factors. One of them was his experience of watching a propaganda video:

> And what really actually triggered me, was when I saw a Palestinian woman be mistreated by Israeli soldiers. So that was for me something, and and, and when you also heard that, you know with Islamic songs in the background, and and, and yes, that was very emotional. Because I, I saw actually my mother there in front of me. [...] Yes, that was... Look, when you a, a Palestinian woman, with headscarf, you know, then you see, then she is already something recognizable you know and then you saw her fall on the ground and when she wanted to get up she got a... [...] So that you can, you can see again in the film. And that was emotional. And, and uhh, that was then something that made me think 'Fucking Jews', you know.⁹⁶

With regard to 'unfreezing', there were at least two participants who experienced a marked change in their everyday life prior to becoming involved or turning to (fundamentalist) Islam. One was a young man who could not find the internship he needed to finish his education and suddenly had a lot of time on his hands, some of which he spent at a mosque. There he met a Syrian man who told him that his failure to get an internship was due to unbelievers' hatred for Muslims. This conversation was the starting point of his search for information about (extremist) Islam and led to him being introduced to the Hofstadgroup by the same Syrian man.⁹⁷ The second individual was an illegal immigrant from Morocco; it appears that the group took the place of the friends and family he dearly missed.⁹⁸

Cognitive openings and unfreezing constitute essential pieces of the Hofstadgroup puzzle as they can explain how the initial steps towards

---

95 Ibid., 24-25.
96 'En wat mij eigenlijk vooral de trigger was, was toen ik een Palestijnse vrouw zag mishandeld worden door Israëlische militairen. Dus dat was voor mij iets, en en, en als je ook dat hoorde, weet je met Islamitische liederen op de achtergrond, en en, en ja, dat was heel emotioneel. Omdat ik, ik zag eigenlijk mijn moeder daar voor me. [...] Ja, dat was... Kijk, als jij een, een Palestijnse vrouw, met hoofddoek, weet je, dan zie je, dan is ze al iets herkenbaars weet je en die zag je dan op de grond laten vallen en als ze wilde opstaan dan krijgt ze een...[...] Dus dat kun je, kun je terugzien in de film. En dat was emotioneel. En, enne, dat was toch wel iets waarvan ik dacht van "Kutjoden"weet je.': Former Hofstadgroup Participant 1, 'Personal Interview 2', 10.
97 Ibid., 2-6.
98 Dienst Nationale Recherche, 'RL8026', 01/17: 4049; Chorus and Olgun, *Broeders*, 36-37.

involvement came about. For a significant number of individuals, participation resulted from a sudden period of uncertainty in which they were prompted to question their own beliefs and understanding of the world. A process that made them open to making new friends and interested in exploring new ideas. Furthermore, the examples of unfreezing illuminate the role that chance plays in bringing about involvement. Had the individual who could not find an internship been successful in his search, it is quite possible that he would never have become involved in the Hofstadgroup. Similarly, would the Moroccan illegal immigrant have become involved in the Hofstadgroup if he had made friends with people who were not interested in radical and extremist interpretations of Islam? Chance may not be a particularly satisfying explanatory variable, but these examples suggest it cannot be overlooked.

8.5 Cognitive dissonance and moral disengagement

People's opinions are continuously challenged by new information or contrarian views. For instance, a creationist who learns of the theory of evolution may be shocked to see his or her idea that the world was created in a number of days challenged by a completely different explanation. Such experiences can lead to 'cognitive dissonance'; a psychological tension between beliefs and information or views that challenge them. Cognitive dissonance can also result from a disparity between beliefs and behavior; someone who smokes while knowing it poses a health risk or, closer to the topic at hand, willfully harming or killing others while being aware of the legal and moral prohibitions against such behavior.[99]

The unpleasant psychological tension gets stronger as dissonance increases.[100] People who engage in terrorism and other forms of violent behavior are therefore especially likely to suffer its effects. Without ways in which to rationalize or ameliorate the tension that follows from the breach of legal and moral codes that the commission of terrorist acts entails, such behavior could well remain taboo or unsustainable for any prolonged period of time. As Maikovich argues, it might be the ability to overcome such cognitive dissonance that separates those who do become involved in terrorism from those who remain militant in thoughts only.[101] The following

---

99 Festinger, *A Theory of Cognitive Dissonance*, 1-31.
100 Ibid., 16.
101 Maikovich, 'A New Understanding of Terrorism', 377.

paragraphs look at several strategies for coping with cognitive dissonance and pay particular attention to the mechanism of moral disengagement.

One way of dealing with the cognitive dissonance that may result from participation in terrorism is to justify present actions based on past behavior. If it was right to do something the first time, it cannot be wrong to do it again. If it was justifiable to lend logistical support to a terrorist attack in the past, why should it be wrong to become more closely involved in the execution of the next one? Isn't the person supplying the bomb just as responsible as the one pressing the button? As past actions form the foundations for subsequent ones, this mechanism of dealing with cognitive dissonance through self-justification sets people on a 'slippery slope' that leads to ever greater involvement in terrorist activities. Self-justificatory arguments can also form an obstacle to disengagement, as ceasing this involvement means questioning the moral permissibility of past behavior.[102]

Involvement in terrorism comes at a significant price. Terrorists must deal with the death or capture of their comrades, abandon alternate career paths, and live under the continuous threat of being arrested or killed. Over time, the price of involvement can add up to form a 'sunk cost' that is so high that continued participation is the only way to justify it. As long as the struggle is not abandoned, past sacrifices can still be justified as having been necessary contributions to the achievement of future goals worthy of the sacrifice. Abandoning the cause or group before those goals have been realized would mean accepting that such costs have been incurred for nothing.[103] Thus, when faced with failure or the realization that past sacrifices have been futile, renewed commitment to the terrorist group and its cause can be a (temporarily) effective way of avoiding this very unpleasant form of cognitive dissonance.

A particularly powerful way of rationalizing the use of violence and overcoming the inhibitions to harming and killing others found in the vast majority of people, is through moral disengagement. Bandura posits moral disengagement as a way of bypassing or selectively deactivating internally held moral standards that prevent inhumane behavior, thereby avoiding the self-condemnation that would otherwise follow when those standards of behavior are breached.[104] Moral disengagement is itself made possible

---

102 Crenshaw, *Explaining Terrorism*, 129; McCauley and Segal, 'Social Psychology of Terrorist Groups', 342-43; McCauley and Moskalenko, 'Mechanisms of Political Radicalization', 419-21; Schmid, 'Radicalisation, De-Radicalisation', 22.
103 Della Porta, *Social Movements*, 181; Taylor, *The Fanatics*, 75-77; Crenshaw, *Explaining Terrorism*, 127.
104 Bandura, 'Mechanisms', 161-65.

by several factors highlighted in Bandura's work as well as the broader literature on terrorism. These include the availability of moral justifications for violence, the displacement or diffusion of personal responsibility, disregarding or distorting the consequences of violence, blaming the victims, and dehumanizing opponents.[105]

Several factors affecting moral disengagement have already been discussed in previous chapters and will not be dealt with in detail here. For instance, it was established that the Salafi-Jihadism-based worldview to which the Hofstadgroup's extremist participants adhered, allowed them to see violence as morally justified and necessary. Chapter seven noted that the group had recourse to authority figures that provided them with (implicit) justifications for violence, but none that allowed for a displacement of personal responsibility to occur by ordering attacks to be carried out. Those participants who carried out acts of violence were therefore hard put to obscure their personal agency as a means of overcoming moral obstacles to the use of violence. What remains to be assessed is whether disregard for the consequences of violence, blaming the victims, and dehumanization had a hand in bringing about participants' (intended) acts of terrorism.

Disregard for the consequences of violence is a way of avoiding or minimizing personal responsibility for the harm inflicted on others by ignoring or downplaying the damage wrought. It is easier to use violence, for instance, when the results are not directly witnessed such as through the use of remote-controlled weapons or when a chain of command distances the individual who orders an attack from those actually carrying it out.[106] By portraying their violence as defensive, in response to provocation, or as rightful retribution, terrorists legitimize their acts by *blaming their victims*; essentially arguing that they brought it on themselves.[107] With regard to *dehumanization*, Bandura argues that when a deliberate effort is made to present the other as something reprehensible, dangerous, and less than human, natural feelings of empathy wane and personal inhibitions against using violence are more easily overcome.[108]

McCauley and Moskalenko view dehumanization as the result of 'essentialist thinking' which often takes hold among groups or individuals that are in conflict with one another. The first indicator of this way of

---

105 Ibid., 161.
106 Ibid., 177-78.
107 Ibid., 184-85; Borum, *Psychology of Terrorism*, 51.
108 Bandura, 'Mechanisms', 180-82. For an example of how dehumanization can contribute to violence, see: Lankford, 'Promoting Aggression and Violence', 394.

thinking is over-generalization; for instance, by seeing the violent behavior of individuals as reflecting the 'evil nature' of the entire group, nation or culture they represent. The second telltale sign is fear that the in-group will somehow be contaminated by contact with out-group members. Third is the use of derogatory designations for out-group members that essentializes them as inherently evil and frequently denies them even their humanity; for example, by referring to enemies as 'roaches' or 'pigs'.[109] By contrast, when terrorists refer to themselves they tend to use words that convey legitimacy and heroism, such as 'soldier', 'revolutionary', or 'mujahid' (warrior for the faith).[110]

For most of the Hofstadgroup's participants, 'involvement' was limited to attending group gatherings, discussing radical and extremist interpretations of Islam, and perhaps spreading such views online. In lieu of involvement in clearly illegal or morally questionable behavior, such as preparations for an actual attack, the likeliness that these participants suffered significant cognitive dissonance was small. Their limited degree of involvement also came at relatively low personal cost; commitments outside of the group, such as study or work, did not necessarily have to be abandoned. Although many participants ultimately paid for their involvement with arrest and imprisonment, these costs were arguably not apparent *during* their involvement and thus did not trigger self-justificatory mechanisms that could lead to prolonged or intensified commitment to the group.

Those participants most likely to experience major cognitive dissonance were those who actually planned or perpetrated acts of terrorism. Most notably, Van Gogh's assailant and the individual who tried to reach Chechnya in 2003 and who appeared interested in committing a terrorist attack in the Netherlands in 2004 and 2005. Both men rapidly embraced ever-more extremist views and eventually became involved in (plans for) acts of terrorism. They also incurred costs for their involvement in militancy; Van Gogh's murderer gave up work, study, and old friends to focus entirely on his religious convictions and his new-found circle of acquaintances. The second individual was arrested multiple times in the period from 2003 to 2005 and spent time in prison. Yet despite these outward signs reminiscent of the slippery-slope and sunk-cost mechanisms, there were no indications that either of them utilized such rationalizations. What they did do, was rely on various forms of moral disengagement.

---

109 McCauley and Moskalenko, *Friction*, 161-67.
110 Bandura, 'Mechanisms', 170; Crenshaw, 'The Psychology of Political Terrorism', 398; Loza, 'The Psychology of Extremism and Terrorism', 149; Della Porta, *Social Movements*, 174-76.

Both of these participants availed themselves of ideological justifications for violence. For instance, both referred to Quranic verses extolling the necessity and justness of violent jihad.[111] They also displaced their individual responsibility for violence by portraying their (intended) actions as religiously mandated.[112] Van Gogh's murderer explained his decision to his family by writing that he had 'chosen to fulfill [his] duty towards Allah'.[113] Likewise, the second individual addressed the following words to his family:

> know that this is the right path and know that I commit this deed out of fear for the punishment of Allah, the almighty, for he says [...] 'If you do not sally forth, He shall punish you with a painful punishment', and out of obedience to Allah, who says: 'For you it is mandated to fight, irrespective of how much you dislike it.'[114]

In other words, there was no place for *personal* feelings about the use of violence; it simply had to be done.

Neither of these individuals appears to have disregarded the (potential) consequences of their actions. They did, however, consistently blame their victims. Consider this phrase from the videotaped warning message one of them recorded in 2005:

> Sheikh Osama bin Laden [...] sheikh Ayman al-Zawahiri [...] [a]nd our beloved sheikh Abu Musab al-Zarqawi [...] have warned you. But you have only committed more injustices, you crusaders. You supported Bush when he uttered his famous word: 'Let the crusades begin.' I tell you that between us and you only the language of the sword shall apply until you leave the Muslims alone and choose the path of peace.[115]

---

111 Peters, 'De Ideologische En Religieuze Ontwikkeling', appendix: Overzicht teksten geschreven of vertaald door Mohammed B., 27-28, 32-45, 50-56; NOVA, 'Videotestament Samir A.'.
112 Dienst Nationale Recherche, 'RL8026', AHB03/27: 4040-41; NOVA, 'Videotestament Samir A.'; Peters, 'De Ideologische En Religieuze Ontwikkeling', appendix: Overzicht teksten geschreven of vertaald door Mohammed B., 18, 27-28, 32-33; A[.], 'Deurwaarders', 9.
113 'Ik heb ervoor gekozen om mijn plicht tegenover Allah te vervullen': Alberts and Derix, 'Mohammed B. Schreef'.
114 'weet dat dit het juiste pad is en weet dat ik deze daad verricht uit vrees voor de straf van Allah, de Verhevene, omdat Hij zegt: [...] "Als jullie niet uitrukken, zal Hij jullie straffen met een pijnlijke bestraffing", en uit gehoorzaamheid aan Allah, die zegt: "Aan jullie is voorgeschreven te strijden, hoezeer het jullie ook tegenstaat"': NOVA, 'Videotestament Samir A.'.
115 'Sheikh Osama bin Laden [...] sjeikh Ayman al-Zawahiri [...] [e]n onze geliefde sheikh Abou Moesaab Al-Zarqawi [...] heeft jullie wel eens gewaarschuwd. Maar jullie hebben alleen maar meer onrecht gepleegd, jullie kruisvaarders. Jullie steunden Bush toen hij zijn bekende woord

Van Gogh's assailant uses the same reasoning in his 'Open Letter to the Dutch People':

> Millions and millions of Muslims have been raped and slaughtered like animals and there seems to be no end in sight. You, as unbelieving Dutch citizens, must know that your government is partly to blame for this. [...] Because the policy of your government is supported by your ballot and they govern on your behalf, your blood and possessions have become halal [permitted] for the Islamic Ummah.[116]

Both men dehumanized their opponents through the persistent use of derogatory religious signifiers. Consider what Van Gogh's murderer told Van Gogh's mother in court: 'I don't feel your pain. [...] Partly because I can't sympathize with you because you are an unbeliever'.[117] Such dehumanization was widespread within the group. Non-Muslims were called 'kuffar' or simply 'unbelievers', underscoring their fundamental otherness.[118] The words 'zindiq'[119] or 'mortad'[120] (both mean apostate), 'munafiq'[121] (hypocrite/Muslim without true faith), and 'mushrik'[122] (polytheist/one who recognizes other authorities than god alone, e.g. democratic governance) were similarly

---

heeft uitgesproken: "Laat de kruistochten beginnen." Ik zeg jullie dat er tussen ons en jullie alleen de taal van het zwaard zal gelden tot jullie de moslims met rust laten en de weg van de vrede kiezen': Ibid.

116 'Miljoenen en miljoenen Moslims zijn als beesten verkracht en afgeslacht en hier lijkt geen einde aan te komen. U, als ongelovige Nederlander, moet weten dat uw regering hier mede aan schuldig is. [...] Omdat het beleid van uw regering door uw stembiljet wordt ondersteund en zij namens u regeren is uw bloed en bezittingen voor de Islamitische Ummah halaal geworden': Peters, 'De Ideologische En Religieuze Ontwikkeling', appendix: Overzicht teksten geschreven of vertaald door Mohammed B., 33.

117 'Ik voel uw pijn niet. [...] Deels kan ik niet met u meevoelen omdat u een ongelovige bent': 'Laatste Woord Mohammed B.'

118 Dienst Nationale Recherche, 'RL8026', 01/01: 123; GET: 4048, 4052, 4092; AHA03/20: 1171, 1176-77, 1179; AHB03/27: 4035-36, 4041; Peters, 'De Ideologische En Religieuze Ontwikkeling', appendix: Overzicht teksten geschreven of vertaald door Mohammed B., 27-28, 40, 50; NOVA, 'Chatgesprekken Jason W.'; Groen and Kranenberg, *Women Warriors*, 38.

119 Peters, 'De Ideologische En Religieuze Ontwikkeling', 16, appendix: Overzicht teksten geschreven of vertaald door Mohammed B., 40.

120 Dienst Nationale Recherche, 'RL8026', AHA04/21: 1324-25.

121 Ibid., GET: 4052, 4085; Peters, 'De Ideologische En Religieuze Ontwikkeling', 27, appendix: Overzicht teksten geschreven of vertaald door Mohammed B., 22, 40, 50; Groen and Kranenberg, *Women Warriors*, 37.

122 Dienst Nationale Recherche, 'RL8026', GET: 4048; Peters, 'De Ideologische En Religieuze Ontwikkeling', 31, appendix: Overzicht teksten geschreven of vertaald door Mohammed B., 18, 22-23; Groen and Kranenberg, *Women Warriors*, 66; NOVA, 'Videotestament Samir A.'.

used against 'false' and 'deviant' Muslims.[123] Given that the group saw death as the penalty for apostasy, many of these terms carried a very clear connotation; these people deserve to be killed.[124] Another important example of derogatory language is the recurring use of 'taghut' (idolater/idolatry) to refer to leaders, political systems, or state institutions that claim authority based on anything other than Sharia law, as an attempt to paint their claims to power as illegitimate.[125]

All of these mechanisms worked to lower psychological inhibitions to the use of violence and were especially important for the group's most militant participants. The available evidence illustrates that moral disengagement was a key individual-level enabler of terrorist violence. It forms an important factor in the explanation for the group's planned and perpetrated acts of violence by making it easier to consider the use of violence without seeing it as morally reprehensible.

8.6 Conclusion

Although radicalization has become the predominant explanation for involvement in terrorism in the post-9/11 period, this chapter's findings problematize its explanatory potential in several ways. Certainly, Van Gogh's murderer appeared to be a text-book case of radicalization as he was ultimately motivated by his convictions to commit a terrorist attack. The problem is that radicalization cannot explain why the vast majority of the other participants who also held extremist views did *not* act on them. Moreover, some participants only adopted radical views *after* becoming involved; disabusing the notion that radicalization precedes such participation. Finally, the findings belied the idea that radicalization is linear or deterministic; some participants held radical views but never developed extremist ones and a small number even turned away from previously held extremist points of view. Radicalization, in short, could not convincingly explain involvement in the Hofstadgroup.

---

123 Former Hofstadgroup Participant 1, 'Personal Interview 1', 2.
124 Peters, 'De Ideologische En Religieuze Ontwikkeling', 16; Wiktorowicz, 'Anatomy of the Salafi Movement', 228.
125 Dienst Nationale Recherche, 'RL8026', AHA03/20: 1171, 1177; AHA09/26: 3801-02; GET: 4002, 4026, 4128; Peters, 'De Ideologische En Religieuze Ontwikkeling', 28-29, appendix: Overzicht teksten geschreven of vertaald door Mohammed B., 10-11, 23-24, 34, 40; NOVA, 'Videotestament Samir A.'.

Fanaticism provided a more nuanced understanding of the link between beliefs and actions. Unlike radicalization, it is specific enough to explain why not all of those who hold radical or extremist beliefs will act on them by making violent behavior contingent on several contextual factors. Although the Hofstadgroup's extremists shared a militant belief system, only Van Gogh's murderer infused them with a millenarian flavor that mandated action on the part of 'true believers' to stave off a disastrous and final defeat. More importantly, Van Gogh's killer led the relatively most isolated existence of the Hofstadgroup's participants. Virtually unchallenged by different opinions encountered at work, school, or in family life, the future murderer's beliefs could exert a markedly greater influence on his behavior. It was this context that allowed his fanatical convictions to lead to fanatical behavior.

This chapter also discussed the important role that 'cognitive openings' and the related concept of 'unfreezing' played in bringing about involvement in the Hofstadgroup. Triggered by events ranging from the 9/11 attacks to personal loss, many future participants went through a period in which they questioned previously held beliefs, or were suddenly open to new ideas and acquaintances. These experiences were critical in making them interested in radical and extremist interpretations of Islam and the company of like-minded individuals and thus formed a key element in the Hofstadgroup's formation. Unfreezing also drew attention to the role of chance in bringing about involvement in extremist or terrorist groups. Had some of the Hofstadgroup's participants not run into individuals interested in extremist interpretations of Islam, it is quite possible they would never have become involved in the group.

A discussion of cognitive dissonance and the various ways in which it can be managed, rounded off this first part of the individual-level analysis. Through such mechanisms as attributing the blame for their own violent intentions to the actions of their victims, emphasizing religious precepts that mandated the use of violence, and the dehumanization of opponents, the Hofstadgroup's most militant participants were able to prevent debilitating psychological discomfort that could otherwise result from the use of violence. Moral disengagement therefore played an important role in making possible the acts of terrorism planned and perpetrated by some of the group's participants.

These findings have made an important contribution towards understanding involvement in the Hofstadgroup from an individual-level perspective. But they represent only a part of the various explanations that this level of analysis has to offer. The next chapter completes the individual-level analysis by addressing whether explanations based on mental illness, psychoanalysis, personality characteristics, and emotional states can yield explanations for involvement in homegrown jihadist groups.

9 Individual-level analysis II: Terrorists as psychologically distinctive

This chapter completes the two-part examination of the individual-level of analysis. The explanations discussed in the following pages share a focus on explaining involvement in terrorism as resulting from the distinct psychological features of individual perpetrators. The first three paragraphs in particular embody the assumption that terrorists are somehow different from 'normal' individuals. They assess mental illness, psychological trauma, and personality characteristics as factors that can increase the likeliness of involvement in terrorism. The chapter's second half departs from the focus on psychological abnormality to look at the role of emotions in bringing about involvement in terrorist groups and terrorist attacks. In particular, frustration-induced anger and fear of death are discussed as potentially relevant explanatory variables.

Two recurrent trends in research on terrorism have been the search for a distinctive terrorist personality or profile and the idea that terrorism can be explained as the result of mental illness or psychological damage incurred during childhood. In particular, the argument that terrorists are psychopaths has attracted considerable attention and criticism. Numerous authors have lamented the empirically poorly substantiated nature of such claims.[1] The difficulty of accessing terrorists for research purposes, let alone carrying out clinical studies on them, means that explanations which hold that involvement in terrorism stems from distinct psychological qualities must be treated with care.[2] On the basis of a literature review, the author identified five themes in this literature that form the main points of discussion (Table 10).

Table 10   Individual-level analysis II: Terrorists as psychologically distinctive

Psychopathology
Psychoanalysis, significance loss and identity-related alienation
Terrorist personality or profile
Anger and frustration
Mortality salience

---

1   Horgan, *The Psychology of Terrorism*, 3; Victoroff, 'The Mind of the Terrorist', 31; Silke, 'Cheshire-Cat Logic', 52-53.
2   Horgan, *The Psychology of Terrorism*, 3-4.

9.1 Terrorists as psychopaths

Perhaps because it is comforting to see terrorist violence as the work of mentally disturbed individuals, terrorists are frequently seen as psychopathic individuals, particularly in the popular perception.[3] Research on the subject has reached far more cautious conclusions, however. Numerous scholars have cautioned that there is insufficient empirical evidence to support the notion that terrorists are psychopaths.[4] Psychopaths would also make highly unreliable and dangerous operatives, making it likely that they would be shunned by terrorist groups.[5] Neither is it convincing to argue that terrorism's severe 'occupational hazards' would only be acceptable to the mentally unstable. There is a wide range of people who hold dangerous jobs, such as police officers and soldiers, who are not considered mentally disturbed.[6] For these reasons, psychopathy ranks among the most criticized explanations for involvement in terrorism.

Psychopathy, however, is a specific personality disorder. While it is no longer seen as a viable explanation for involvement in terrorism by most scholars, research on the broader spectrum of mental health problems paints a far more nuanced picture. For instance, a study by Kleinmann cites evidence that terrorists are more likely to suffer from mental health issues such as schizophrenia than the general population.[7] Lankford addresses this topic in greater detail and reports that a significant percentage of suicide attackers suffered from depression, post-traumatic stress disorder, and 'other mental health problems'.[8] In an explorative study based on access to police files, Weenink writes that just under 50% of his sample of Dutch jihadists displayed 'problem behavior' and that 6% had diagnosed mental health problems.[9]

---

3   Borum, *Psychology of Terrorism*, 31; Silke, 'Cheshire-Cat Logic', 56-57.
4   Corrado, 'A Critique of the Mental Disorder Perspective', 295-304; Crenshaw, 'The Psychology of Political Terrorism', 385; Hudson, 'The Sociology and Psychology of Terrorism', 60; Kruglanski and Fishman, 'What Makes Terrorism Tick?', 140-41; McCauley, 'Psychological Issues in Understanding Terrorism', 5-6; McCauley and Segal, 'Social Psychology of Terrorist Groups', 333; Merari, 'Psychological Aspects of Suicide Terrorism', 107; Ruby, 'Are Terrorists Mentally Deranged?', 22; Silke, 'Cheshire-Cat Logic', 53, 60-62; Victoroff, 'The Mind of the Terrorist', 12-14.
5   Alderdice, 'The Individual, the Group', 201; Beck, 'Prisoners of Hate', 210; Borum, *Psychology of Terrorism*, 32; Frost, 'Terrorist Psychology', 42-43; Schmid, 'Radicalisation, De-Radicalisation', 21.
6   Ruby, 'Are Terrorists Mentally Deranged?', 21.
7   Kleinmann, 'Radicalization of Homegrown Sunni Militants', 287-88.
8   Lankford, 'Précis of the Myth of Martyrdom', 354-55.
9   Weenink, 'Behavioral Problems', 24-27.

Corner and Gill found that some 42% of lone actors experienced mental health problems, compared with some 28% for the general population and approximately 3% for group-based terrorists.[10] When accounting for the potential influence of mental health problems, it is therefore important to distinguish between various forms of terrorism. It is also crucial to not blindly equate the diagnosis of a mental health issue with an explanation for how that person became involved in terrorism. Mental health problems encompass a broad spectrum of ailments, including many relatively benign ones. With the exception of serious disorders such as psychopathy, which can be directly linked to lowered barriers towards the use of violence, it is often not immediately clear if and how a particular mental health disorder contributed to the involvement process. For example, many people will suffer some form of depression during their lives yet the vast majority of these individuals will not become involved in any kind of violent behavior.

Studies like Weenink's and Corner and Gill's lend considerable credibility to the notion that behavioral issues and mental health problems other than psychopathology can play a role in bringing about involvement in terrorism. They also illustrate that the mental health question cannot be seen dichotomously. Terrorists are not either psychopathic or mentally healthy individuals, but, like the population in general, may suffer from a range of issues whose potential to influence their behavior is often far from immediately clear.[11] Given the history of poorly supported claims of terrorists' abnormality, caution remains in order when looking at terrorism from this perspective. Perhaps the most significant issue here has been the ongoing difficulty of carrying out clinical diagnoses on actual terrorists.[12] Hopefully, future studies will be able to gather more evidence and further advance a debate that has been at the core of the study of terrorism for decades.

The only two participants subjected to extensive psychological and psychiatric assessments were Van Gogh's killer and the individual who videotaped threats to the Dutch public in 2005.[13] Van Gogh's assailant steadfastly refused to cooperate with specialists at the psychiatric observation clinic Pieter Baan Center (PBC) in Utrecht. Nevertheless, in the report presented during his trial, PBC experts concluded that there was no indication that he had refused cooperation on pathological grounds and that the little data they had gathered was insufficient to warrant the view

10 Corner, Gill, and Mason, 'Mental Health Disorders', 562.
11 Gill and Corner, 'There and Back Again', 239.
12 Merari, 'Psychological Aspects of Suicide Terrorism', 104.
13 Former Hofstadgroup Participant 1, 'Personal Interview 2', 3-4.

that Van Gogh's killer suffered from some kind of disorder.[14] Initially, the participant who videotaped threats also refused to cooperate.[15] But by early 2005, a psychological report was submitted to the court that concluded he too did not suffer from a personality disorder.[16]

Within the broader Hofstadgroup, reliable indications of mental illness are virtually absent. The one clear case concerns a young man on the fringes of 2005's Piranha group. In October 2007, he escaped from a psychiatric hospital and stabbed two police officers, one of whom then shot the assailant dead.[17] While this individual clearly suffered from mental health problems, at present there are simply no indications that these issues contributed to his (peripheral) participation in the group. There is therefore little cause to amend the overall conclusion that mental health problems do not offer an explanation for involvement in the Hofstadgroup.

9.2   Psychoanalysis

Psychoanalysis was pioneered by Sigmund Freud in the late nineteenth century. In explaining human behavior, it affords a key role to the influence of repressed or unconsciously held desires.[18] The origins of these desires are attributed to various phases of childhood mental development, with particular emphasis on 'unresolved intrapsychic conflict' that occurred during this period.[19] In the second half of the twentieth century, psychoanalytical approaches began to be used to explain involvement in terrorism. Narcissism-aggression theory, for instance, holds that ego-damage suffered during childhood or adolescence can lead individuals to terrorism as a way of projecting inner pain on external targets.[20] Another approach posits that the inability to live up to societal expectations and norms can prompt the adoption of 'negative identities', whereby the damaged individual embraces precisely those values that society abhors and becomes somebody by embodying the 'nobody'.[21]

---

14   Amsterdam District Court, 'LJN AU0025', 8-9.
15   'Psychisch Onderzoek Naar Samir A. Levert Niets Op'.
16   'Rechter Wil Meer Getuigen'.
17   Groen, Kranenberg, and Schenk, 'Bilal B. Was Bekende Van Hofstadgroep'.
18   Arena and Arrigo, *The Terrorist Identity*, 3-4; Horgan, *The Psychology of Terrorism*, 57.
19   Victoroff, 'The Mind of the Terrorist', 22.
20   Post, 'Terrorist Psycho-Logic', 27; Ross, 'A Model of the Psychological Causes', 134; Victoroff, 'The Mind of the Terrorist', 23-24.
21   Hudson, 'The Sociology and Psychology of Terrorism', 20; Crenshaw, 'The Psychology of Political Terrorism', 393.

Psychoanalytical approaches have lost ground in contemporary psychological and psychiatric research.[22] One problematic aspect of these theories is their lack of strong empirical support.[23] Another issue is their embodiment of the 'fundamental attribution error'. That is the human tendency to ascribe the behavior of others to innate qualities and to downplay the role of circumstances. Essentially, psychoanalytical approaches 'overestimate the internal causes of terrorist behavior'.[24] Finally, psychoanalytical explanations are hard to falsify; how can the assertion of an *unconsciously held* desire be refuted?[25]

While Post acknowledges the absence of 'major psychopathology', he holds to the psychoanalytical approach essentially as a way of continuing the argument that terrorists are intrinsically different.[26] Likewise, Merari and colleagues assert in one publication that the suicide terrorists they studied showed no evidence of psychopathic tendencies, but argue in another that 40% of the same sample did display subclinical (i.e. not definitely observed) suicidal tendencies that, moreover, the subjects themselves may have held without being aware of them.[27] As Silke and Horgan point out, psychoanalytical approaches essentially provide a way of promulgating the questionable argument that terrorism results from some form of mental illness.[28]

Given their empirical and theoretical deficiencies, 'classic' psychoanalytical approaches such as narcissism-aggression theory will not be used to study involvement in the Hofstadgroup. Instead, the discussion continues with two more recently coined explanations that depart from the psychoanalytical tradition of subconsciously held desires and psychological damage incurred during childhood and adolescence, yet also resemble it in their emphasis on (perceived) shortcomings in an individual's sense of self as motivating behavior. These lines of inquiry focus on 'significance quests' and identity-related alienation.

---

22   Horgan, *The Psychology of Terrorism*, 57; Victoroff, 'The Mind of the Terrorist', 26.
23   Arena and Arrigo, *The Terrorist Identity*, 24-25; Borum, *Psychology of Terrorism*, 11; Corrado, 'A Critique of the Mental Disorder Perspective', 298-304; Horgan, *The Psychology of Terrorism*, 57; Rogers, 'Psychology of Violent Radicalization', 36; Silke, 'Cheshire-Cat Logic', 52-67; Victoroff, 'The Mind of the Terrorist', 22.
24   Arena and Arrigo, *The Terrorist Identity*, 4.
25   Victoroff, 'The Mind of the Terrorist', 26.
26   Post, 'Terrorist Psycho-Logic', 25-27.
27   Merari et al., 'Personality Characteristics', 95-96; Merari et al., 'Making Palestinian "Martyrdom Operations"', 118.
28   Horgan, *The Psychology of Terrorism*, 61; Silke, 'Cheshire-Cat Logic', 64-67.

9.3 Significance quests and identity-related alienation

Psychological research has identified the wish to attain and maintain a sense of personal significance as a key human need.[29] Kruglanski et al. present this 'fundamental desire to matter, to be someone, to have respect' as terrorists' overarching motivation.[30] Such a yearning may be triggered by real, perceived, or potential significance loss, which itself may be brought about by, for instance, existential anxiety, social isolation, (group-based) humiliation, or deprivation.[31] Significance quests are not envisioned as purely defensive reactions to (potential) significance loss, however. Involvement in terrorism may also come about as the result of an opportunity for marked 'significance gain', such as the chance to acquire social standing by committing a 'martyrdom' (suicide) attack.[32]

Research has provided empirical support for the notion that the desire to (re)gain a sense of personal significance can contribute to processes of involvement in terrorism.[33] However, it should be noted that a desire for significance is of course not unique to terrorists. The likeliness that such quests will increase the probability of involvement in terrorism appears dependent on contextual factors. These are the perception of *unjust* personal or group-based deprivation, the ability to point to a hostile responsible party and the availability of justifications for violence.[34]

Identity-related alienation essentially holds that children of Muslim immigrants to Western countries can come to feel that they neither belong to the country and culture of their parents, nor to the country and culture of their birth. Too modern to fit into the first and too different in appearance and upbringing to fit seamlessly into the latter, these second- and third-generation immigrants may come to lack a clear sense of identity. Experiences with discrimination or exclusion can exacerbate this feeling of alienation and add a keen sense of frustration and anger towards their fellow citizens. In such a setting, radical and extremist interpretations of Islam can become especially attractive through their ability to offer straightforward explanations ('you didn't get the job because unbelievers hate Muslims'),

---

29 Kruglanski and Orehek, 'The Role of the Quest', 154.
30 Kruglanski et al., 'The Psychology of Radicalization and Deradicalization', 73.
31 Kruglanski and Fishman, 'What Makes Terrorism Tick?', 142-45; Kruglanski et al., 'The Psychology of Radicalization and Deradicalization', 74-76; Kruglanski et al., 'Fully Committed', 331-57.
32 Kruglanski et al., 'The Psychology of Radicalization and Deradicalization', 75-76.
33 Ilardi, 'Interviews with Canadian Radicals', 717-18.
34 Kruglanski and Orehek, 'The Role of the Quest', 163.

provide a clear sense of identity ('you're not Dutch or Moroccan, but a Muslim') and a militant purpose ('you must defend your religion').[35]

The clearest and most consequential significance quest among Hofstadgroup participants was the one that Van Gogh's future murderer underwent. The killer himself made this very clear in a farewell letter he wrote to his family: 'It has not eluded you that I have changed since the death of my mother. In the wake of her death I have undertaken a search to uncover the truth. [...] I have chosen to fulfill my duty to Allah and to trade my soul for paradise'.[36] The death of his mother triggered a cognitive opening that set Van Gogh's killer on a quest for answers that led him, in rapid succession, to embrace fundamentalist, radical, and extremist interpretations of Islam.[37] Ultimately, his desire to be a 'true' Muslim resulted in the belief that blasphemers should be killed and that it was his personal duty to carry out the punishment, thus restoring some of the significance lost by the Prophet Muhammad at the hands of Van Gogh and Hirsi Ali.

The partial autobiography written by the individual who tried to reach Chechnya in 2003 and who videotaped a threat to the Dutch public in 2005 reveals that he too experienced a significance quest. In a revealing passage, he states:

> [o]n the Internet, I went looking for answers about Islam, I looked at websites belonging to Hamas and later I discovered al-Qaeda. I no longer watched gruesome images [of Muslim suffering], I had seen enough. Now I went looking for answers; 'how should a Muslim react to all this injustice?'[38]

---

35   Cottee, 'Jihadism as a Subcultural Response', 731, 738; Dalgaard-Nielsen, 'Violent Radicalization in Europe', 800; Loza, 'The Psychology of Extremism and Terrorism', 150; McCauley and Moskalenko, *Friction*, 85-88; Mullins, 'Iraq Versus Lack of Integration', 119; Roy, 'Euro-Islam', 28-30, 36-38.

36   'Het is jullie niet ontgaan dat ik sinds het overlijden van mijn moeder veranderd ben. Ik heb sinds haar overlijden een zoektocht ondernomen om de waarheid te achterhalen. [...] Ik heb ervoor gekozen om mijn plicht tegenover Allah te vervullen en mijn ziel in te ruilen voor het Paradijs.': Dienst Nationale Recherche, 'RL8026', AHB03/27: 4040-41; Alberts et al., 'De Wereld Van Mohammed B.'

37   Peters, 'Dutch Extremist Islamism', 145-59.

38   'Op het Internet, ging ik op zoek naar antwoorden over de Islam, ik keek op websites van Hamas en later ontdekte ik die van Al-Qaida. Ik keek niet meer naar gruwelijke beelden, ik had genoeg gezien. Nu ging ik op zoek naar antwoorden; "hoe dient een moslim te reageren op al deze onrechtvaardigheid?"': A[.], 'Deurwaarders Van Allah', 11.

The desire for vengeance, according to Kruglanski et al., focuses on restoring an individual or group's loss of significance.[39] The quest to restore significance to Muslims affected by armed conflict, and to attain status as a 'true' Muslim in the process, would play a key role in this individual's behavior throughout the 2002-2005 existence of the group.

With regard to the broader group, significance quests drew participants to the group and motivated their continued presence. Numerous individuals were searching for the 'true' or 'right' interpretation of Islam and were able to address such questions within the group.[40] Groen and Kranenberg's interviews with female Hofstadgroup participants show that at least some of these young women were drawn to radical Islam by a search for identity and that, more generally, they were exploring what roles women were allowed or expected to fulfill in jihad.[41] Lastly, the various recent converts in the group's ranks are also considered to have undergone significance quests around the time of their involvement, as conversion to a religion suggests a search for meaning and answers to the larger questions of life and death.[42] Indeed, one convert described how the desire to become a 'perfect Muslim' brought about the adoption of jihadist beliefs, which this individual saw as representing 'true' Islam.[43]

Many Hofstadgroup participants wanted to deepen their understanding of their faith and to ascertain what it meant to be a Muslim in a time when across the globe large numbers of co-religionists were affected by armed conflict. The sense of injustice, the perception that Western nations and 'apostate' Muslims were responsible for this state of affairs, and the availability of ideological justifications for violence, both online and within the group, created a context in which significance quests led to an increased likeliness of involvement in extremism and even terrorism. For the group's most militant participants, the significance quest concept suggests that the (intended) use of terrorism stemmed in part from their desire to become 'true' Muslims and to restore some of the significance they perceived their co-religionists and the faith as a whole had lost at the hands of Western military interventions in Muslim countries and the actions of blasphemers like Van Gogh.

---

39   Kruglanski et al., 'The Psychology of Radicalization and Deradicalization', 73-74.
40   Dienst Nationale Recherche, 'RL8026', AHA04/21: 1593-94, 1604-605, 1612-613; VERD: 19849, 19917-918, 19935, 19945, 20004, 20012-13, 20225, 20242; Vermaat, *Nederlandse Jihad*, 208; Former Hofstadgroup Participant 5, 'Personal Interview 1', 1.
41   Groen and Kranenberg, *Women Warriors*, 18, 65.
42   Dienst Nationale Recherche, 'RL8026', GET: 4084, 4145, 177; VERD: 20461, 20518-519.
43   'perfecte moslim': Former Hofstadgroup Participant 4, 'Personal Interview 1', 2.

These findings complement the conclusion of Chapter 7 that strategic and organizational rationales for the group's planned and perpetrated acts of terrorism were largely absent. The significance quest concept suggests that these acts are better understood as distinctly personal in origin. They resembled what McCormick labels the 'expressionist' tradition of terrorism; rooted in a nineteenth-century philosophy of revolutionary violence, it sees the use of violence as a means of *personal expression* and redemption, rather than as a means for achieving political objectives.[44] The Hofstadgroup's most militant participants were looking to restore significance lost by themselves and their co-religionists, and in the process solidify their own sense of identity and purpose, rather than aiming to achieve strategic goals.[45]

Several publications on the Hofstadgroup raise identity-related alienation as a possible explanation for the adoption of radical and extremist views by the group's participants.[46] It also features prominently in the autobiography of a young Dutch Muslim who was arrested on terrorism-related charges in September 2004.[47] Although not part of the Hofstadgroup, his background and convictions were similar to those who were, suggesting that identity-related alienation could have played a role in the Hofstadgroup. The available empirical evidence, however, paints a different picture. It is clear that some participants strongly identified with an imagined worldwide community of believers, an association that superseded their national identities.[48] But there is simply insufficient evidence to suppose that this self-perception as a member of the global ummah stemmed from identity-related issues.

Only one explicit reference to identity-related alienation was encountered. It stems from a chat session in which one of the men who traveled to Pakistan or Afghanistan in 2003 reprimanded a chat-partner for indicating she struggled with reconciling her Moroccan heritage and her Dutch upbringing. Such problems were irrelevant, according to the traveler, as she should not see herself as Moroccan or Dutch but as Muslim.[49] While it may be argued that his reply signified his own struggles with a lack of

---

44 McCormick, 'Terrorist Decision Making', 477.
45 Former Hofstadgroup Participant 5, 'Personal Interview 1', 4.
46 Buijs, Demant, and Hamdy, *Strijders Van Eigen Bodem*, 61-62, 218-28, 247; Buruma, *Murder in Amsterdam*, 121-22; Spruyt, 'Liberalism and the Challenge of Islam', 320-21; Transnational Terrorism Security & the Rule of Law Project, 'The "Hofstadgroep"', 12.
47 Kaddouri, *Lach Met De Duivel*, 24, 28, 35.
48 Dienst Nationale Recherche, 'RL8026', 01/13: 99, 163; 01/17: 4128, 18410; AHA05/22: 2228; Van San, Sieckelinck, and De Winter, *Idealen Op Drift*, 46-48; Erkel, *Samir*, 48; Peters, 'De Ideologische En Religieuze Ontwikkeling', 4, 6, 16.
49 Dienst Nationale Recherche, 'RL8026', AHD08/37: 8519.

belonging, there is no actual evidence to support this possibility. In lieu of clear evidence to the contrary, identity-related alienation does not appear to offer an explanation for involvement in the Hofstadgroup.

9.4 The terrorist personality or profile

Another line of inquiry at the individual-level of analysis questions whether there is a particular 'terrorist personality'. This immediately raises objections on a conceptual level, as 'terrorist' is not a singular or clearly defined typology. Terrorists fulfill a variety of roles, adhere to different ideological convictions, and come together in numerous organizational structures, ranging from strict hierarchies to loosely constituted networks.[50] It is therefore likely that, as Victoroff writes, 'any effort to uncover the "terrorist mind" will more likely result in uncovering a spectrum of terrorist minds'.[51] In light of these considerations it comes as little surprise that attempts to compose a distinct terrorist personality profile have floundered.[52] Personality factors alone simply do not offer a credible explanation for why some people become involved in terrorist groups and political violence.

Neither does an examination of terrorists' backgrounds reveal a distinctive profile; socioeconomic, demographic, or otherwise.[53] Writing of terrorists in the 1980s, McCauley and Segal characterized them as mostly male, mostly young, predominantly from middle-class families, and usually in possession of at least some university education.[54] These characteristics are too generic to offer explanations for involvement in terrorism. Similar research on 21st-century jihadists has likewise failed to produce a profile specific enough to have much explanatory value.[55] In his study of 336 European jihadists, Bakker concludes that 'there is

---

50 Borum, *Psychology of Terrorism*, 35-36; Horgan, 'From Profiles to Pathways', 84, 86; Horgan, 'Understanding Terrorist Motivation', 110; Ligon et al., 'Putting the "O" in VEOs', 110-17; Victoroff, 'The Mind of the Terrorist', 5-7.
51 Victoroff, 'The Mind of the Terrorist', 7.
52 Borum, *Psychology of Terrorism*, 35-36; Horgan, 'Understanding Terrorist Motivation', 110; Horgan, *Divided We Stand*, 79; Hudson, 'The Sociology and Psychology of Terrorism', 9, 60; Merari et al., 'Personality Characteristics', 96-97.
53 Nevertheless, the appeal of profiles is such that their use in a law enforcement setting has continued. See, for instance: Eijkman, 'Has the Genie Been Let out of the Bottle?', 1-21.
54 McCauley and Segal, 'Social Psychology of Terrorist Groups', 332.
55 Silber and Bhatt, 'Radicalization in the West', 23, 57; Porter and Kebbell, 'Radicalization in Australia', 226-27; Merari et al., 'Personality Characteristics', 90-91.

no standard jihadi terrorist'.[56] The individuals in his sample were mostly single males who were not particularly young, often hailed from the lower socioeconomic strata, and often had a criminal record.[57] In similar work, Sageman found that the jihadists he studied mostly led middle-class existences, a contrast with Bakker's work that adds further diversity to the profile of the 'average' jihadist.[58]

Recognizing the heterogeneity of terrorists' backgrounds, several efforts have been made to differentiate between 'typical' members of jihadist groups based on their motivations for involvement instead.[59] Nesser distinguishes between idealistic and militant 'entrepreneurs', their equally ideologically motivated and loyal 'protégés' who occupy junior leadership positions, the 'misfits' who are motivated more by personal problems than ideological commitment, and 'drifters' who become involved more or less through chance.[60] More recent empirical work on the Provisional IRA has disaggregated data on terrorists' backgrounds based on the roles or functions they performed within that organization.[61] One such study found that younger members were more likely to be involved in violent front-line activities.[62] While these important efforts draw attention to the various roles that exist within terrorist organizations, they are not specific enough to provide an explanation for involvement based on particular personality characteristics.

Some researchers have looked at personality characteristics as predisposing risk factors for involvement in terrorism.[63] Aggressiveness, for instance, has been linked to an increased likelihood of involvement in criminal violence.[64] Della Porta found prior experience with using violence for political means to be one of the most important factors in the backgrounds of Italian terrorists of the 1970s and 1980s.[65] Several authors argue that terrorism

---

56 Bakker, 'Characteristics of Jihadi Terrorists', 143.
57 Ibid., 140-42.
58 Sageman, *Understanding Terror Networks*, 73-74.
59 Nesser, 'Joining Jihadi Terrorist Cells in Europe', 87-114; Venhaus, 'Why Youth Join Al-Qaeda', 8-11.
60 Nesser, 'Joining Jihadi Terrorist Cells in Europe', 92-94.
61 Bloom, Gill, and Horgan, 'Tiocfaid Ár Mná', 67-70; Gill and Horgan, 'Who Were the Volunteers?', 451-53.
62 Gill and Horgan, 'Who Were the Volunteers?', 451-52.
63 Borum, *Psychology of Terrorism*, 15-16, 36; Crenshaw, *Explaining Terrorism*, 100; Horgan, 'From Profiles to Pathways', 84-85; Hudson, 'The Sociology and Psychology of Terrorism', 60; Post, 'Terrorist Psycho-Logic', 27.
64 Silke, *Terrorism*, 67-68; Taylor, 'Is Terrorism a Group Phenomenon?', 125.
65 Della Porta, 'Recruitment Processes', 313.

might be especially attractive to highly authoritarian individuals.[66] People for whom honor is an important value are more likely to favor an aggressive response to perceived external threats.[67] Alternatively, individuals with a higher preference for social inequality (social-dominance orientation) and hierarchical social relations are more likely to hold negative attitudes towards out-groups which, in turn, might signify a lower threshold to using violence or seeing its use as legitimate.[68]

Other characteristics that could potentially heighten the likeliness of involvement in terrorism are prejudice,[69] youth and immaturity,[70] a desire for action, glory, adventure or the thrill of war and violence,[71] the lack of a clear sense of purpose,[72] impatience with words or a dissatisfaction with the efficacy of political activities,[73] and a desire for status.[74] Horgan also notes anger or alienation, identification with victims of injustice, and the belief that violence is not inherently immoral.[75] Doosje et al. add that personal uncertainty with regard to self and worldviews, and perceived intergroup threat can contribute to support for a radical belief system.[76] Some scholars argue that altruism should also be counted among these characteristics, as terrorists are liable to view their own actions as the selfless promotion of a common good.[77] Finally, Pedahzur et al. find that suicide terrorism is partly motivated by fatalism.[78]

The literature indicates that there is no such thing as a terrorist personality or profile. These findings once again underline the fallacy of seeing

---

66 Taylor, *The Fanatics*, 70-71; Schwartz, Dunkel, and Waterman, 'Terrorism', 544; McCauley and Segal, 'Social Psychology of Terrorist Groups', 333.
67 Barnes et al., 'My Country, My Self', 2-4, 19.
68 Levin et al., 'Social Dominance and Social Identity in Lebanon', 253-55; Pratto et al., 'Social Dominance Orientation', 741-58.
69 Taylor, *The Fanatics*, 68-69.
70 Crenshaw, *Explaining Terrorism*, 100-01; Locicero and Sinclair, 'Terrorism and Terrorist Leaders', 236, 242.
71 Bartlett and Miller, 'The Edge of Violence', 14-15; Cottee and Hayward, 'Terrorist (E)Motives', 966-69; Crenshaw, 'The Psychology of Political Terrorism', 385-88; Ilardi, 'Interviews with Canadian Radicals', 719-20; Post, 'Terrorist Psycho-Logic', 27.
72 Schwartz, Dunkel, and Waterman, 'Terrorism', 544-45.
73 Horgan, 'From Profiles to Pathways', 85; McCauley and Segal, 'Social Psychology of Terrorist Groups', 333.
74 Bartlett and Miller, 'The Edge of Violence', 15; McCauley and Moskalenko, *Friction*, 62-64.
75 Horgan, 'From Profiles to Pathways', 84-85.
76 Doosje, Loseman, and Van den Bos, 'Determinants of Radicalization of Islamic Youth', 587, 589-91.
77 Silke, *Terrorism*, 68-70; Pedahzur, Perliger, and Weinberg, 'Altruism and Fatalism', 408-09.
78 Pedahzur, Perliger, and Weinberg, 'Altruism and Fatalism', 409.

terrorists as people who are somehow distinct in terms of psychology, mental illness, or character. However, the potential relevance of personality characteristics for understanding involvement in terrorism should not be ruled out altogether. There may be predisposing risk factors that increase the likeliness, however slightly, of certain individuals becoming involved in terrorism.

Several findings stand out which suggest that personality characteristics had a role to play in influencing the behavior of several leading Hofstadgroup participants. The clearest and most important of these is Van Gogh's murderer's history of violent behavior. In June 2000, this individual was detained after having been involved in a bar fight. A year later, he displayed threatening behavior to officers who visited his parental home on a matter related to his sister. In July 2001, he stabbed a policeman in an Amsterdam park and then threw the knife at another officer. These offenses resulted in a sentence of twelve weeks' imprisonment. In May 2004, another incident involving Van Gogh's future assailant was registered; this time he had threatened to kill a social services employee. Finally, on 24 September of the same year, he was arrested for aggressive behavior towards police officers after having been caught using public transport without a valid ticket.[79]

None of these observations form a clinical diagnosis of an aggressive predisposition. Yet it is striking that this person is the only Hofstadgroup participant who had such an extensive history of violent behavior and the only one to have committed an act of premeditated aggression.[80] Although it is hard to evaluate their accuracy, there are also several descriptions of Van Gogh's murderer by former colleagues, friends, and other group participants that paint him as someone who could be short-tempered and who was prone to (verbally) aggressive outbursts.[81] Furthermore, the professionals who sought to examine him at the PBC *speculated* that he may have suffered from an aggression disorder.[82] At the very least, his history of violent behavior showed him to be an individual who could match the

---

79 Commissie van Toezicht betreffende de Inlichtingen- en Veiligheidsdiensten, 'Toezichtsrapport Met Betrekking Tot Mohammed B.', 12-14; Alberts et al., 'De Wereld Van Mohammed B.'
80 Although he was not the *only* participant to have previously engaged in violent behavior: Vermaat, *Nederlandse Jihad*, 109.
81 Alberts et al., 'De Wereld Van Mohammed B.'; Dienst Nationale Recherche, 'RL8026', GET: 18415-16; Former Hofstadgroup Participant 2, 'Personal Interview 1', 2; Chorus and Olgun, *Broeders*, 19-20; Vermaat, *Nederlandse Jihad*, 141; Former Hofstadgroup Participant 5, 'Personal Interview 1', 5.
82 'Mohammed Bleef Gesloten Boek in Observatiekliniek'.

intention to use violence with a proven capability to do so. It is likely that this disposition contributed to his ability to commit murder.

One of the men who traveled to Pakistan or Afghanistan was clearly influenced by a longing for adventure, excitement, and a boyish fascination with weapons. The descriptions of his experiences that he gave to others frequently revolved around his self-described expertise with various weapons, the interesting people he met, and the hardships he had to endure; from vigorous physical training to diets that allegedly included eating tree bark.[83] Based on the degree of self-aggrandizement in his chat conversations with others, it also seems clear that this person sought and enjoyed the status of being (seen as) a warrior for his faith.[84] Likewise, an interviewee described a longing for adventure and romantic notions of what it meant to participate in jihad as partly motivating his attraction to Salafi-Jihadism and his involvement in the group. He also reflected that he had been driven by 'youthful naiveté'.[85]

While not so much a personality characteristic as an element of someone's personal background, data suggests that being a recent convert made at least some participants more susceptible to adopting extremist views. As newcomers to Islam, converts' lack of knowledge about their religion appears to have made them more likely to see the group's 'born Muslims' as sources of religious authority, especially when they had (some) command of Arabic.[86] Two final 'predisposing risk factors' found among a larger number of Hofstadgroup participants, were identification with the victims of perceived injustice, and the belief that violence is not inherently immoral.[87]

None of the personality characteristics described in the previous paragraphs preordained these individuals' future participation in the Hofstadgroup. Still, personality characteristics appear to have played a secondary, supportive role in bringing about involvement. That contribution was to make those who had these characteristics more likely to become

---

83 Dienst Nationale Recherche, 'RL8026', AHA05/22: 2166, 2175-76; AHD08/37: 8595-97, 8618-619, 8635-636, 8768-769, 8774-775, 8880, 8919, 8929-931; AHD09/38: 9056.
84 Ibid., AHA05/22: 2166; AHD08/37: 8571, 8593-95, 8635, 8716, 8767-768, 8773, 8880, 8919, 8928; AHD09/38: 9048-49, 9054-56.
85 'jeugdige naïviteit': Former Hofstadgroup Participant 3, 'Personal Interview 1', 9-10.
86 Former Hofstadgroup Participant 5, 'Personal Interview 1', 2-3.
87 A[.], 'Deurwaarders', 3, 5-8; Former Hofstadgroup Participant 1, 'Personal Interview 1', 6; De Graaf, *Gevaarlijke Vrouwen*, 258; Dienst Nationale Recherche, 'RL8026', 01/01: 131; AHA04/21: 1666; 01/13: 163; AHB01/25: 3166-68; GET: 4128, 18116; De Koning, 'Changing Worldviews and Friendship', 385; Erkel, *Samir*, 65-67; Groen and Kranenberg, *Women Warriors*, 18-21, 68-70, 169-70; Peters, 'De Ideologische En Religieuze Ontwikkeling', appendix: Overzicht teksten geschreven of vertaald door Mohammed B., 33; Vermaat, *Nederlandse Jihad*, 216, 227.

interested in radical or extremist interpretations of Islam, the company of like-minded individuals and, in some cases, involvement in acts of terrorism.

9.5 The role of emotions: anger

Emotions, in particular anger, have played a background role in many of the explanations discussed over the past several chapters. The final two sections of this chapter delve deeper into how they can influence involvement in terrorism. It does so by highlighting two emotional states that the literature earmarks as being especially relevant; frustration-induced anger and fear of death.

Aggressive behavior can be instrumental or emotional. In the first case, aggression is consciously chosen as the means to achieve certain ends; in the latter, aggression is brought on by anger which in turn is a response to insult, physical pain, or frustration.[88] Anger is frequently encountered as a (contributing) factor in explanations for involvement in terrorism, particularly in the shape of a personal grievance and a desire for revenge.[89] Of the triggers of anger, it is the link between frustration and aggression in particular that has become a frequently encountered explanation for terrorism and political violence. In its original incarnation, frustration-aggression theory held that frustration occurs when an individual's expectancy of reward is thwarted, prompting aggression towards the source of that thwarting. However, if, for instance, fear of punishment makes such a course of action ill-advised, the intended aggression may also be displaced onto substitutes.[90]

Frustration-aggression theory has found its way into numerous explanations for political violence, such as Gurr's thesis that deprivation can lead to rebellion through the activation of the frustration-aggression mechanism.[91] Despite its popularity, the theory has also attracted considerable criticism, most notably based on the straightforward observation that virtually everyone experience frustrations but only very few people engage in violence because of it.[92] This has led Berkowitz to propose a modification of the

---

88 McCauley, 'Psychological Issues in Understanding Terrorism', 7-8, 16; Taylor, *The Fanatics*, 4-6.
89 McCauley and Moskalenko, *Friction*, 13-18; Merari, 'Psychological Aspects of Suicide Terrorism', 107.
90 Berkowitz, 'Frustration-Aggression Hypothesis', 60-61.
91 Gurr, *Why Men Rebel*, 9.
92 Victoroff, 'The Mind of the Terrorist', 19; Horgan, *The Psychology of Terrorism*, 54-56.

original theory which stresses the importance of situational and personal factors in bringing about an actual aggressive response to frustration, notably the degree to which the frustrating event is perceived as unpleasant, deliberate, and personal.[93] As it is largely *subjective* whether frustration leads to aggression, the presence of relative deprivation as an explanatory variable can be difficult to ascertain objectively.

Anger forms a key explanatory variable when accounting for the behavior of the group's most militant participants. Consider the vicariously experienced insult and pain in one future participant's reaction to what he saw as the injustices being perpetrated against Muslims in places like Chechnya and Palestine:

> [W]hy is a Muslim casualty worth less than a non-Muslim casualty? [...] Why do [the U.S. and Europe] only attack the Muslim world? [...] [E]ach time on television when they called the perpetrators of the attacks of 11 September terrorists, I always shouted at the television: 'You are the terrorists!' [...] [T]he oppression, that gripped me, many videos were available, from babies with a hole of 10 cm in their stomach because a bullet came out there, to children who were taken from under the rubble, horrible things that were done with women, it was never warriors that I saw, the innocent were the target, they were hit.[94]

The desire to address these injustices by meting out vengeance to those he held responsible remained this person's predominant motivation throughout his involvement with the Hofstadgroup.[95] But his aggression was also fed by what appears to have been a personal vendetta against the state institutions that had monitored, arrested, and imprisoned him, frequently in what he experienced as a hard-handed and humiliating fashion.[96] This may explain why this individual appeared to be conducting reconnaissance

---

93 Berkowitz, 'Frustration-Aggression Hypothesis', 60, 62, 71.
94 'waarom is een moslim dode minder waard dan een niet-moslim dode?', 'waarom vallen ze alleen de islamitische wereld aan?', 'elke keer als ze op de televisie de plegers van de aanslagen van 11 september terroristen noemde, schreeuwde ik altijd naar de televisie: "Jullie zijn terroristen" [...] de onderdrukking, dat greep mij aan, veel video's waren er te zien, van baby's die een gat van 10 cm in hun buik hebben omdat daar een kogel uit is gekomen, kinderen die vanonder de puin werden gehaald, verschrikkelijke dingen die met vrouwen werden gedaan, het waren nooit strijders die ik zag, de onschuldige waren het doelwit, zij werden getroffen': A[.], 'Deurwaarders', 4-5, 8-9.
95 Ibid., 11-12; Erkel, *Samir*, 227; NOVA, 'Videotestament Samir A.'.
96 Dienst Nationale Recherche, 'Piranha', REL00: 29; NOVA, 'Informatie AIVD En Politie Uit Strafdossier'; Erkel, *Samir*, 199-200, 206-08, 218-19, 227-28, 240-41.

of the AIVD headquarters in 2004 and why he appeared interested in planning attacks against the same organization in 2005.[97] It also fits with a police intelligence report earmarked as 'reliable' which indicated that upon his release in early 2005 this participant was driven to rectify the '1-0' in the unbelievers favor.[98] Essentially, his aggression appears to have been motivated by a desire to avenge both the injustices suffered by Muslims worldwide and the affronts he had suffered personally.

Aggression brought on by insult-induced anger appears the most likely explanation for what triggered the murder of Van Gogh. The assailant's discovery of religious injunctions that mandated him to kill blasphemers occurred in the summer of 2004.[99] The Van Gogh production of Hirsi Ali's movie *Submission, part 1* aired on 29 August and was met with revulsion and anger by people in and around the Hofstadgroup, precisely because it was considered blasphemous.[100] As one participant reflected on the murder during questioning; 'I think that [...] Van Gogh apparently hurt [the killer] so much that this happened. This speaks of revenge'.[101] It seems likely that Van Gogh was killed not just because he had violated the murderer's religious beliefs, but deeply insulted him in the process.

Within the broader Hofstadgroup there were a number of people for whom anger factored into bringing about their initial involvement. For some, this anger was a response to the perceived persecution of Muslims similar to the example given above, triggering a search for answers which ultimately led to the adoption of extremist ideas and to making the acquaintance of like-minded individuals.[102] Others were angered by Dutch imams' unwillingness to address questions related to the legitimacy of violent jihad or to discuss the wars taking place in Muslim countries. Frustrated by what they saw as cowardice, these individuals looked for alternative sources of religious authority, finding it online and within the Hofstadgroup.[103] Anger also contributed to sharper in-group/out-group

---

97 Dienst Nationale Recherche, 'RL8026', 01/01: 43-45; Dienst Nationale Recherche, 'Piranha', REL00: 46-56; NOVA, 'Informatie AIVD En Politie Uit Strafdossier'.
98 Dienst Nationale Recherche, 'Piranha', REL00: 29.
99 Peters, 'Dutch Extremist Islamism', 155-56.
100 Former Hofstadgroup Participant 1, 'Personal Interview 2', 23-24; Dienst Nationale Recherche, 'RL8026', 01/13: 74, 161; AHA04/21: 1324-30; Erkel, *Samir*, 223.
101 'Ik denk dat [...] van Gogh hem blijkbaar zoveel pijn heeft gedaan dat dit is gebeurd. Hier spreekt wraak uit.': Dienst Nationale Recherche, 'RL8026', VERD: 20231.
102 Vermaat, *Nederlandse Jihad*, 163.
103 De Koning, 'Changing Worldviews and Friendship', 385, 387; Former Hofstadgroup Participant 3, 'Personal Interview 1', 7-9; A[.], 'Deurwaarders', 4-6; Former Hofstadgroup Participant 1, 'Personal Interview 2', 11-12; Dienst Nationale Recherche, 'RL8026', GET: 4018.

distinctions; the aforementioned individuals came to feel a strong disdain for 'mainstream' Salafism and several individuals came to hate the Dutch authorities after being arrested and imprisoned.[104]

Anger played an important role in bringing about involvement in the Hofstadgroup and contributed to (planned) acts of terrorism. As an explanatory factor, anger also underlines the need to qualify the role that beliefs play in these processes. The individual who wanted to go to Chechnya was guided by a sense of idealism; a desire to help what he saw as the victims of oppression. Although his adoption of Salafi-Jihadist beliefs gave him a religious vocabulary in which to express and justify that desire, it was his anger at perceived mistreatment that initially sparked his interest in militancy and it remained a factor of influence throughout his involvement in the group. While data pertaining to the role of anger is limited to a relatively small number of participants, its influence among those individuals was considerable.

9.6 Mortality salience

Terror Management Theory holds that thinking about the finality of life ('mortality salience') can give rise to considerable existential anxiety ('terror'), and motivate people to look for ways of relieving these fears by imbuing their existence with meaning.[105] Religion and its promise of life-after-death is one way in which people can alleviate such stress. But worldly ideologies or straightforward membership of a group can also fulfill this function by making individuals part of something larger than themselves or by providing them with an opportunity to obtain a degree of immortality by contributing to something that will outlast their death. Terrorist groups' trumpeting of clear ideological goals and a righteous cause, as well as their ability to offer members a chance to live on in communal memory as martyrs and the promise of a place in heaven, can make them powerful beacons to those looking for existential meaning.[106]

---

104 Vermaat, *Nederlandse Jihad*, 215; Groen and Kranenberg, *Women Warriors*, 147, 183; Former Hofstadgroup Participant 1, 'Personal Interview 1', 4.
105 Dechesne et al., 'Literal and Symbolic Immortality', 722-34; Pyszczynski, Motyl, and Abdollahi, 'Righteous Violence', 14.
106 McBride, 'The Logic of Terrorism', 561-65; Cottee and Hayward, 'Terrorist (E)Motives', 965-66, 973-74; Kruglanski and Fishman, 'What Makes Terrorism Tick?', 143-44.

Mortality salience has been shown to lead to heightened esteem for an individual's own group, culture, and ideology.[107] This is directly related to such groups' ability to lower the fear of death by providing their members with meaning and significance. Conversely, mortality salience can lead to heightened hostility towards out-groups and alternative ideologies, as their existence competes with, and thus undermines, the ability to the in-group or a particular ideology to alleviate the fear of death.[108] Mortality salience may increase support for violent measures against out-groups perceived to be threatening.[109] An interesting aspect of mortality salience in the context of involvement in terrorism is that it can establish a feedback loop that traps members in loyalty to both the cause and the group. As participation in acts of terrorism increases the chance of death, existential anxiety is renewed, leading to a stronger focusing on the group and its ideology to alleviate this stress, thereby prolonging involvement in terrorism and prompting the next round of existential anxiety.[110]

Several participants feared punishments in an afterlife.[111] Those who experienced such anxieties appear to have become more closely tied to the beliefs they thought would save them from the tortures of hell. In a telling example, one female participant told police officers that during her involvement in the group she experienced a period of great anxiety concerning the right interpretation of Islam. She was shocked by the extremist interpretation promulgated within the group, especially as it meant denouncing her own family as apostates. At the same time, she worried that it might actually represent 'true' Islam and that her failure to uphold such views would lead to terrible punishments in the afterlife.[112] Although she eventually disengaged from the group, these existential fears initially tied her more closely to the group and its extremist views.[113]

It was not simply a fear of what an afterlife might hold that influenced the behavior of some Hofstadgroup participants. The obverse also applied. In at least one case, a participant was motivated to become a 'true' Muslim not just to avoid eternal punishment, but to garner eternal reward. In

---

107 Kruglanski and Fishman, 'Psychological Factors', 11.
108 Pyszczynski, Motyl, and Abdollahi, 'Righteous Violence', 14-15.
109 Mandel, 'The Role of Instigators', 6; Silke, *Terrorism*, 71-72.
110 McBride, 'The Logic of Terrorism', 567-68.
111 A[.], 'Deurwaarders Van Allah', 7; Dienst Nationale Recherche, 'RL8026', AHB03/27: 4041; Groen and Kranenberg, *Women Warriors*, 39-40; Former Hofstadgroup Participant 4, 'Personal Interview 2', 2; NOVA, 'Videotestament Samir A.'.
112 Dienst Nationale Recherche, 'RL8026', GET: 4020, 4028, 4030, 4050-51.
113 Ibid., 4028-32, 4051.

addition to fear of hell there was the desire to gain a place in paradise.[114] This desire for personal salvation was also a factor in the acts of terrorism planned and perpetrated by the group's militant inner circle. Van Gogh's assailant and the individual who recorded a threatening video message in 2005 both stated that their actions were driven by the desire to avoid god's displeasure and to attain a place in paradise.[115] Fear of death and a longing for paradise were powerful and distinctly personal existential motives underlying several participants' involvement process and, in some cases, the planning or perpetration of acts of terrorism.

9.7 Conclusion

A first clear conclusion to emerge from this chapter is that there is no current empirical basis to assume that major psychopathology or mental health issues more generally offer a viable explanation for Hofstadgroup participants' behavior. Neither was there data to suggest that identity-related alienation formed an explanation for involvement. Quests to gain or restore both personal and communal significance, on the other hand, appear to have been a crucial element driving participation at the individual level of analysis. They led to political and religious awakenings, the desire to become a 'true' Muslim and, in some cases, the wish to avenge personal or communally experienced 'significance loss' through violence. This concept suggests that the group's planned and perpetrated acts of terrorism were a form of personal expression rather than grounded in strategic or organizational rationales.

The discussion then turned to the role of personality characteristics. It is questionable whether there is such a thing as a 'terrorist profile'. However, research does indicate that certain predisposing risk factors may increase the likeliness of involvement in terrorism. Applied to the Hofstadgroup, this analytical perspective highlighted a keenness for adventure, identification with victims of perceived injustice, and, in the case of Van Gogh's future assailant, a history of violent behavior. Predisposing risk factors that played a supportive role in explaining what made at least some of the Hofstadgroup's participants more susceptible to adopt extremist views and to plan or perpetrate acts of terrorism.

---

114 Former Hofstadgroup Participant 4, 'Personal Interview 2', 2.
115 Dienst Nationale Recherche, 'RL8026', AHB03/27: 4041; NOVA, 'Videotestament Samir A.'; Alberts and Derix, 'Mohammed B. Schreef'.

For some participants, frustration-induced anger influenced their initial involvement process. Unable to get satisfactory answers to their questions about jihad-related topics at their mosques, some of these young men and women became dissatisfied with 'mainstream' Islam and were drawn towards venues where they *could* discuss the themes they were interested in, such as Hofstadgroup gatherings. Anger also features prominently in the acts of violence that were plotted or undertaken by the group's most extremist participants. The individual who tried to reach Chechnya in 2003 was angered by the perceived injustices suffered by his co-religionists around the world, as well as his increasingly antagonistic relationship with the Dutch authorities. Likewise, it appears that the immediate trigger for the attack on Van Gogh was the anger and hurt that *Submission*'s release provoked in the filmmaker's assailant.

One final factor that appears to have influenced at least several Hofstadgroup participants was a fear of death and of ending up in hell in particular. This formed a powerful existential motive that kept at least several participants closely wedded to their extremist beliefs, albeit in at least one case for only a brief period of time, as these beliefs were thought to offer the best way of avoiding punishments in the afterlife. Fear of displeasing their god and, conversely, a desire to attain paradise was also a factor in the planned and perpetrated acts of terrorism committed by the group's militant inner-circle. This factor once again underlined the distinctly personal, as opposed to strategic or organizational, rationales for the use of terrorism found among the Hofstadgroup's participants.

10   Conclusion

Following the 9/11 attacks, research on terrorism benefited from an influx of new researchers and funding. However, almost fifteen years and an untold number of publications later, many aspects of terrorism are still poorly understood. That also applies to the focus of this book; namely, how and why people become involved in European homegrown jihadism. Chief among the various reasons for this state of affairs has been the long-standing scarcity of primary-sources-based research. The difficulties involved in accessing (former) terrorists for interviews or using data gathered by government agencies, has made researchers overly reliant on media reporting. A secondary source of information that is frequently very succinct, potentially biased, and too often inaccurate; in other words, incapable of serving as the main, let alone the *only*, foundation for academic research.

There are dozens of potential explanations for involvement in terrorism. Yet the scarcity of primary sources means that most of these have been insufficiently empirically assessed, raising concerns about their validity. These issues shaped this book's methodological approach in two ways. First, collecting primary-sources-based data was seen as a prerequisite. Second, because no single theoretical perspective on involvement in terrorism could count on strong empirical support, a multi-theoretical analytical framework was adopted. This second decision also followed from the widely-held view that involvement in terrorism is the result of a complex process in which a multitude of factors, spread over multiple levels of analysis, play a role. Consequently, this book chose to study involvement by combining the breadth of existing insights, divided over the structural, group, and individual levels of analysis, with extensive primary-sources-based data.

Terrorism, the deliberate use of indiscriminate violence against civilians for propagandistic purposes and psychological effects, comes in many forms. This study focused specifically on the 'homegrown jihadist' typology as it manifested itself in Europe from 2004 onward, most notably with the attacks in Madrid that year and London in July 2005. The attacks in Paris and Brussels in 2015 and 2016, as well as the large number of Europeans who have joined terrorist groups in Syria and Iraq since 2014, have demonstrated that this form of terrorism continues to be a pan-European security threat. Research on European homegrown jihadism is therefore of ongoing relevance for policy makers, counterterrorism practitioners, and journalists as well as academics. From the European homegrown jihadist typology, one case was selected for in-depth analysis; the Dutch 'Hofstadgroup' that existed between 2002 and 2005.

Case selection was partly practical; the author was able to gain access to the Dutch police files on the group and managed to interview several former participants, thus addressing the scarcity of primary sources noted above. No less important, there are sufficient similarities between the Hofstadgroup and the broader European homegrown jihadist trend, as well as the European 'foreign fighters' who have left for Syria and Iraq over the past few years, to allow the case to inform the wider debate on this typology of terrorism. Finally, existing research on the Hofstadgroup reflects the issues present in the literature on terrorism remarked on above in that it is predominantly based on secondary sources. Work on the Hofstadgroup has also been largely descriptive, emphasizing that there is room for research on how and why participants became involved that is both empirically grounded and theoretically informed in its analysis.

Guiding the research was the following overarching question: What factors governed the involvement processes of participants in the Hofstadgroup during its 2002-2005 existence? The main research question was addressed through three subsidiary ones. The analysis turned first to structural, then group-level, and finally individual-level explanations for involvement in the Hofstadgroup. For each of these levels of analysis, literature reviews identified existing explanations for involvement in terrorism which were then utilized as 'lenses' through which to study the empirical data, thus allowing relevant explanatory factors and processes to be identified. This concluding chapter draws together the various analytical strands. It then presents academic and policy-relevant implications that are relevant to homegrown jihadism more broadly and rounds off the discussion with a brief examination of the present study's limitations and fruitful avenues for future research.

10.1 Key findings

Analyzing involvement in the Hofstadgroup using three levels of analysis allowed a multifaceted perspective on the participation process to emerge. Each level of analysis contained numerous relevant factors and found that they fulfilled different roles. Some contributed to the motive for involvement in the group or the use of violence, others enabled this process. Yet others were triggers; setting individuals on a path toward participation in the group and, in some cases, the planning or perpetration of specific acts of terrorism. Furthermore, there was no single, commonly experienced process of involvement in the Hofstadgroup. Participants found and remained in the group for a variety of reasons. Additionally, the findings show that 'involvement' took on numerous forms, the majority of which were not directly related to the commission of acts of terrorist violence. Crucially, the factors governing the involvement processes were heterogeneous in nature. Even so, some generalizations can be made.

The structural level of analysis looked at the broader social and political context in which involvement in the Hofstadgroup came about. It revealed the crucial role of geopolitical events such as the 9/11 attacks and the U.S.-led 'War on Terror' that followed. In many future Hofstadgroup participants, these events triggered 'cognitive openings' that led them to study the motives of the terrorists and to scrutinize Western states' foreign policies. These geopolitical events led many participants to become acquainted with radical and extremist interpretations of Islam, and contributed to a political awakening that, rightly or wrongly, produced a sense of Muslim victimization across the globe at the hands of Western imperialists and corrupt Middle-Eastern regimes. A sense of vicarious victimization and the desire to help and avenge co-religionists in places like Palestine and Afghanistan became key motives for some of the group's most militant participants, their desire to travel abroad as foreign fighters and, later, to plan acts of terrorism in the Netherlands.

Structural-level factors were also important as enablers of involvement processes and as the likely trigger for the murder of filmmaker Theo van Gogh by a Hofstadgroup participant. The Internet and its easy access to extremist ideology and jihadist 'role models' facilitated the adoption of radical and pro-violence worldviews. The freedoms offered by the Dutch liberal democratic political system made it easy to hold private meetings, to access and disseminate radical and extremist views, and to travel abroad. Widespread conservative views within the Dutch Muslim community 'socially facilitated' participants' adoption of fundamentalist and radical convictions. Lack of police protection for Van Gogh made him an easy target. Finally, the airing of the controversial Islam-critical film *Submission, part 1* that Van Gogh directed, was in all likeliness the structural-level factor that triggered the murderer to plan, prepare, and execute his attack.

Contrary to the assumption frequently made by politicians and the media, there were no clear indications that socioeconomic inequality played a role in motivating involvement in the Hofstadgroup or bringing about its adoption of extremist views. Neither did the harsh tone of the Dutch debate on integration and Islam feature as an important factor in motivating involvement or sparking a desire to utilize terrorist violence. Participants did indeed face discrimination, and even physical violence, based on their religious convictions, but these experiences were principally important in sustaining rather than motivating their involvement in the group. That the Hofstadgroup was not a response to grievances shared by the broader Dutch Muslim community was also apparent by its lack of popular support. This was not a vanguard movement, but an extremist cell that was as critical of its potential supporters as it was of non-Muslim 'unbelievers'.

The group level of analysis focused specifically on intra-group dynamics. It was able to account for how the Hofstadgroup formed, what kept it together, and how radical and extremist views were adopted and maintained. Preexisting social ties brought like-minded individuals together who were then bound by friendship and a shared sense of identity that revolved around their interpretation of Islam. Within this setting, social learning increased participants' exposure to views legitimizing and justifying the use of violence, strengthening their division of the world into a small group of the righteous threatened by a large and hostile out-group of unbelievers and apostates. Lectures, interaction with other participants, and exposure to jihadist 'role models' in and outside of the group were crucial to the exploration and adoption of new identities as 'true' Muslims. The group's isolationist tendencies increased its cognitive and behavioral influence over participants. Peer pressures toward ideological conformity served a similar purpose by engendering a degree of ideological homogeneity among participants.

A key finding was that the group-level of analysis was unable to fully account for the acts of terrorism that some participants planned or perpetrated. The motives for these attacks were distinctly personal in origin, rather than the result of communal deliberations. This stemmed from the peculiar organizational characteristics of the Hofstadgroup and its lack of clear leaders in particular. There were numerous authority figures, but none of them tried to be, or were seen as, leaders who could mold the group ideologically, organizationally, or operationally. The absence of leaders also meant that participants could not in any significant sense displace their personal responsibility for violence to leaders who had ordered or organized attacks. Any impetus for committing an act of violence depended predominantly on the initiative and ability of individual participants.

The individual level of analysis studied participants' biographical backgrounds and personal characteristics. It helped explain what triggered involvement processes, what led some participants to consider or use terrorism, how those individuals were able to overcome inhibitions to the use of force, and it shed light on what it was that made these particular individuals more likely to participate in violence than others. A small number of individuals became involved in the Hofstadgroup as a result of 'unfreezing'; the dissolution of everyday commitments or old social networks that made them more amenable to making new acquaintances or considering new ideas. The majority, however, experienced cognitive openings that prompted a reexamination of previously held beliefs or a search for answers to the bigger questions of life, death, and religious identity. Trigger events for these cognitive openings were a mix of the geopolitical and the personal, but in many cases, they resulted in 'significance quests'; attempts to find personal meaning in a reorientation on radical or extremist Islam.

A key explanatory factor was found in the concept of fanaticism. Fanaticism not only accounted for the central motive in Van Gogh's murder but was specific enough to explain why out of a group of several religious extremists, only one acted on those beliefs. The key to this distinction was the personal context in which extremist beliefs were adopted. The murderer stood out because 1) his life revolved around his beliefs to a degree not seen among his compatriots; 2) he infused those beliefs with a distinct apocalyptical edge; and 3) he was the most socially isolated of all participants, minimizing the influence of countervailing opinions. These findings do not imply that extremist beliefs were absent from the acts of terrorism planned by other participants. But they do suggest that in those cases beliefs were less central to the motive to commit acts of terrorism.

The inability of beliefs alone to explain either involvement in the Hofstadgroup or the planning or perpetration of acts of terrorism by its militant inner circle, was a recurring and distinctly important finding. Even Van Gogh's murderer's violent actions cannot be *entirely* explained by his fanatical beliefs. The individual level of analysis also revealed the important role of cognitive mechanisms in overcoming psychological boundaries to the use of violence; namely, dehumanization, the attribution of blame to the victims of (intended) violence and the relegation of personal responsibility to the highest religious authority. It further pointed to the role of powerful emotions in contributing to the motive for violence; anger brought about by perceived injustice, disappointment in 'mainstream' Islam, the deep hurt caused by blasphemy against a beloved religious figure, and fear of God's displeasure in an afterlife.

This latter point is particularly important in understanding why people became involved in the Hofstadgroup, why they adopted and held to extremist convictions, and why some of them felt that violence was not only justified by a personal duty. Fear of ending up in the torments of hell for failure to be a 'true' Muslim and its obverse, a desire for the rewards of paradise, formed an existential motive that appears to have been at the core of at least several participants' involvement experiences. This existential anxiety led to a quest for answers about what it meant to be a 'true' Muslim and, especially among the group's more militant participants, fed the conviction that jihad was a religious duty that could not be forfeited.

The individual-level analysis also uncovered several factors whose relevance lay in their inability to explain involvement processes, in particular the concept of radicalization. Its principal shortcoming was the finding that the majority of participants with radical or extremist views did not act on them. Similarly, Hofstadgroup participants were not psychopaths and there were no diagnosed signs of what could be termed more minor mental health problems. Neither did identity-related alienation offer a convincing explanation for involvement. The one personality-related factor of relevance was the discovery of several predisposing risk factors that appeared to make involvement in the group's extremist inner circle more likely. These were adventure seeking, identification with victims of perceived injustice, and a history of violent behavior.

The findings outlined in the previous paragraphs address the main research question by highlighting those factors that were most important to understanding the involvement processes of Hofstadgroup participants. But for a fuller understanding of the how and why of involvement in the Hofstadgroup, and to appreciate the relevance of these findings to the broader typology of European homegrown jihadism, it is necessary to look beyond the findings themselves to their broader implications. How can this study contribute to an understanding involvement in European homegrown jihadism?

10.2 Implications for research on European homegrown jihadism

To reiterate a general but important finding, it is striking that even in this one group, involvement processes took on a variety of shapes and that involvement was not a singular 'end state' but meant different things to different participants. This heterogeneity underlines the difficulty of generalizing about the factors governing involvement in extremism and terrorism.[1] Secondly, the findings emphasize that gaining a comprehensive

---

1 For a similar conclusion, see: Geelhoed, *Purification and Resistance*, 211-12.

or holistic understanding of involvement in homegrown jihadism requires a broad analytical perspective that utilizes multiple levels of analysis. No single explanation or level of analysis offered a sufficient account for involvement in the Hofstadgroup. From this follows the first of seven key implications; namely, that the relative importance of particular factors to the involvement process is liable to change over time.

10.2.1   The 'driving force' of involvement processes is liable to change

The findings illustrated that the factors which *led* to involvement in the Hofstadgroup were frequently different from those that *sustained* it, which in turn differed from those that triggered some participants to plan or actually carry out a terrorist attack. Van Gogh's murderer, for instance, reoriented himself on his beliefs after time spent in prison and the death of his mother. His involvement process was sustained and catalyzed by the like-minded individuals he met, principally Abu Khaled, whose teachings influenced his burgeoning radicalism. The murder itself draws attention to yet another set of influential factors; including the killer's violence-prone personality, his belief that murder in the name of his religion was justified and mandated, and a deep-seated desire to avoid his god's displeasure and achieve a favorable place in the afterlife.

Another participant's involvement process began after experiencing job-market discrimination. Without an internship to complete his studies, he had large amounts of time on his hands, some of which he spent at his local mosque, talking with people he may otherwise have neglected. Through one of those people he was introduced to the Hofstadgroup. Once there, it was not the radical or extremist ideas being discussed that bound him to the group, but the sense of friendship he experienced. Only after becoming involved did he begin to internalize the extremist beliefs that his newfound friends propagated. His intention to plan an actual attack was predicated on different factors still. One of these was a propaganda video in which a Muslim woman who resembled his mother was mistreated by Israeli soldiers. Another was the murder of Van Gogh, which this participant saw as highly inspirational because it was perpetrated by a close friend. It also made him feel it was now his turn to demonstrate commitment to shared values and carry out an attack of his own.

Numerous other examples could be given that would illustrate a similar process. What they underline is that what could be termed the 'driving force' behind an individual's participation process is likely to shift over time. For instance, in the second example structural factors (discrimination against people of Moroccan descent) precipitated the involvement process, group-level factors sustained it (the social benefits of group membership), and a mix of individual and group-level factors (vicarious injustice and emulation of role models) contributed to this individual's desire to plan a terrorist attack.

In her research on Italian and German left-wing terrorism, Della Porta found that different stages of the involvement process are governed by different levels of analysis.[2] The present study reiterates this conclusion for the European homegrown jihadist typology of terrorism. It adds two further points. First, a multicausal, multilevel, and dynamic perspective on involvement processes in extremist and terrorist groups is a prerequisite for an accurate analysis of how and why participation comes about and is sustained. Secondly, even within a single extremist or terrorist group, the 'driving force' of involvement processes can differ markedly between participants. For instance, whereas one individual may be drawn towards extremism by geopolitical events, another's entry in such a milieu may be primarily motivated by a personal crisis or preexisting friendships.

10.2.2 Involvement in extremist and terrorist groups takes various forms

Not only are involvement processes in general characterized by a continuously shifting emphasis on particular explanatory variables, but the shape of these processes is likely to have distinct characteristics that vary between individual participants. Research is beginning to place considerable emphasis on the variety of roles and positions that members of extremist and terrorist groups may occupy.[3] Not all participants in such groups are directly involved in acts of terrorist violence; in fact, most will be preoccupied with questions of logistics, propaganda, or recruitment. Appreciating the variety and fluidity of involvement processes even within one particular extremist or terrorist group is key to beginning to understand how roles within such organizations are allocated.

Indeed, one question raised in the introduction and returned to throughout the manuscript, was what differentiated those Hofstadgroup participants who used terrorist violence or planned to do so from those that did not. Although no conclusive or broadly generalizable answer to

---

2   Della Porta, *Social Movements*, 10.
3   Nesser, 'Joining Jihadi Terrorist Cells in Europe', 87-114; Bloom, Gill, and Horgan, 'Tiocfaid Ár Mná', 67-70; Gill and Horgan, 'Who Were the Volunteers?', 451-53.

this question was found, the use of a multicausal and multilevel analytical framework did reveal several noteworthy partial explanations. These included the fact that only Van Gogh's murderer had a history of violent behavior, giving him a proven ability to match words with deeds, and that he adhered his extremist beliefs more fanatically than his compatriots. Particularly strong identification with Muslim victims of war across the globe and a personal hatred toward elements of the Dutch state were key elements setting apart a second individual in the group's extremist inner circle from the majority of participants who (apparently) did not plan to use actual violence.

Additionally, this research has highlighted that involvement in extremist and terrorist groups should not be seen as having a singular end state or form. Not all of those who became involved in the Hofstadgroup actually remained a part of it; some chose distance themselves from the group for a variety of reasons. Furthermore, those who did remain a part of the group displayed varying degrees of commitment to the religious convictions and political goals that formed the group's shared interests and worldview. It would be very interesting for future research to look more closely at the differences between those participants in extremist groups who do use terrorist violence and those who do not.

10.2.3 The nature of the group shapes the involvement experience

A third key implication is that the nature of the group itself directly influences the involvement experience. Most important in this regard were the Hofstadgroup's lack of ideological and operational leaders, and the virtual absence of communal efforts to achieve terrorism-related goals until the very end of its existence. There was never a particularly clear or singular 'Hofstadgroup ideology' to which participants were socialized, creating a relative tolerance for divergent views. In addition to the Salafi-Jihadist majority, the group also contained ideological extremists who gave it sect-like qualities and, on the opposite end of the spectrum, a small number of participants without clearly radical or extremist religious views or a complete lack of interest in religion altogether. Crucially, the absence of operational leaders meant that the development of terrorism-related plans was ad hoc and highly dependent on the initiative of individual participants.

These characteristics hampered the Hofstadgroup's development into a more ideologically homogeneous and action-oriented entity. It never became a structured organization and only began to resemble a loosely constituted network by the end of its existence. For the largest part of its

2002-2005 existence, it remained a loosely bound group of friends and acquaintances, a 'Bunch of Guys' in Sageman's words, spread over several cities.[4] As a result of this organizational ambiguity, Hofstadgroup participants were left with a degree of ideological and operational freedom that placed a premium on their own initiative. Had participants found themselves in an actual organization or network with clear leaders, one that tolerated no dissent from a particular worldview, and that communally planned and executed terrorist attacks, their involvement experience would have been quite different. This finding suggests that in order to account for how and why participation in European homegrown jihadism comes about, the characteristics of the group in question form a set of contextual factors that cannot be overlooked.

10.2.4 Fanaticism rather than radicalization

This study found that 'radicalization' and its frequently implied link between radical beliefs and radical behavior was unable to provide a satisfactory account for participation in the Hofstadgroup. Primarily, it could not explain why of the numerous Salafi-Jihadist extremists, only a very small minority acted or planned to act on those beliefs. Secondly, the findings problematized the linear and deterministic notions found in some older radicalization-based thinking. Some participants became involved in the group before adopting radical or extremist views, a number of them never went beyond 'merely' radical views, and several participants disengaged even though they had previously held extremist views.

None of which is to say that beliefs are not important to understanding involvement in homegrown jihadism. A shared set of core beliefs was the basis for the Hofstadgroup's formation and allowed a dichotomous and militant view of the world to take hold. Furthermore, beliefs were crucial motivational components of the planned and perpetrated acts of terrorism. Just as important was their ability to justify the use of violence. But fundamental as beliefs are to understanding involvement in European homegrown jihadism, they are clearly incapable of accounting for participation in and of themselves. Radicalization has been the preeminent explanation for involvement in terrorism for more than a decade. This makes its overemphasis on the degree to which radical beliefs can motivate violent behavior all the more problematic.

---

4 Sageman, *Leaderless Jihad*, 69.

For a more accurate understanding of involvement in terrorism to emerge, the concept of radicalization needs to be reexamined. An alternative way of studying the role that extremist beliefs can play in motivating terrorist violence was found in Taylor's concept of fanaticism.[5] A crucial difference between the concepts of radicalization and fanaticism is that the latter is specific enough to explain why merely holding extremist beliefs is insufficient to explain the turn to violence. Fanaticism emphasizes the role of contextual factors, such as the degree to which extremist beliefs are challenged by contradictory points of view, in increasing the likeliness that the internalization of such beliefs will result in violent behavior. This makes it a theoretically and empirically robust alternative, or addition, to 'radicalization'.

10.2.5 Involvement as personal expression rather than strategic calculation

Although terrorism is frequently understood as a form of violence that is utilized to achieve specific (political) aims, such instrumental or strategic considerations were virtually absent among Hofstadgroup participants. Instead, the motives underlying the planned and perpetrated acts of terrorism had a distinct personal edge; affirming the perpetrator's identity as a 'true' Muslim, avenging the Muslim community, claiming retribution for insults and pain suffered personally, and avoiding god's displeasure through a commitment to violent jihad. This latter point in particular was found to have exerted a strong influence on several participants; fear of hell and a desire for paradise sustained both involvement in the group and adherence to extremist views. These powerful emotions also appeared to factor into several inner-circle extremists' decisions to use terrorist violence. Although it arose in part as a response to worldly issues, such as the 9/11 attacks and the War on Terror, participation in the Hofstadgroup was primarily a vehicle for finding, embracing, and expressing a newfound identity as 'true' Muslims.

As such, understanding why people become involved in European homegrown jihadism, and in preparations for actual attacks, may be less about asking what they are hoping to achieve than it is about who or what they are hoping to be. This is not to argue that participants such as those found in the Hofstadgroup's militant core never considered strategic issues, because they did. The point is that their desire to 'do something' in

---

5 Taylor, *The Fanatics*.

response to what they perceived to be Western aggression against Muslims or the insidious machinations of apostate regimes, was more about taking action than about whether or not those actions stood a chance of actually achieving something. Provided this finding can be replicated, it argues for a subtle reconsideration of the motives driving participation in European homegrown jihadism.

10.2.6 Neither victims nor psychopaths

Terrorists are frequently portrayed as psychopaths or as people who embrace violence after becoming victimized, for instance by political oppression, socioeconomic inequality, or discrimination. With the exception of discrimination, which played a supportive role in sustaining some participants' involvement in the group and which strengthened their dichotomous worldview, none of these factors were found to have influenced involvement in the Hofstadgroup. Perhaps most surprising given its prominence in the literature, the research found little support for the hypothesis that identity-related alienation played a significant role in motivating or sustaining involvement in the Hofstadgroup. Neither did socioeconomic deprivation offer a convincing explanation for involvement; the group's participants came from a variety of backgrounds. Only a very small minority could be objectively labeled as unemployed or (relatively) uneducated.

Just as it can make intuitive sense to see homegrown jihadists as people who have in some way been victimized, it can be comforting to think of people who embrace extremist ideas or even participate in terrorist violence as psychopaths. Yet the lack of empirical support for such positions found in this research, and echoed in the broader literature, should function as a caution against this line of reasoning. More generally speaking, these results against intuitively convincing but empirically poorly supported explanations. Extremism and terrorism are subjects far too complex to be adequately explained by the 'crazy or victimized' dichotomy. Only through nuanced analysis and empirical validation of assumptions can our understanding of involvement in this form of political violence be significantly advanced.

10.2.7 The often-overlooked role of chance

A final research-relevant implication centers on the role of chance. In the study of war, chance and luck are understood to be factors that can exert a tremendous influence on the development and outcome of conflicts.[6] Within the context of terrorism studies, however, these elements are seldom mentioned. This is surprising, as research on the backgrounds of terrorists has indicated that happenstance can play an important role in bringing about involvement. This study finds support for this point of view. The vast majority of participants did not make a conscious decision to become involved in the Hofstadgroup. More often than not their participation came about through people they happened to know or meet. The role of such chance encounters should also serve to demystify the involvement process. Participation in the Hofstadgroup was not a conscious decision made by Islamist radicals and extremists with a view toward organizing for violence, but frequently a much more unintentional process based on happenstance and a tenuous shared commitment to Salafi-Jihadist views.

10.3   Policy-relevant implications

With regard to policy-relevant implications, the study supports the notion that seeing involvement in terrorism as the result of underlying 'root causes' such as poverty, discrimination, or radicalization is a dead end. No single factor has such explanatory potential. By acknowledging the multifaceted nature of the involvement process, more options for prevention, or for the reintegration of convicted offenders, can be identified. By focusing on more than radical and extremist beliefs, practitioners can develop interventions aimed at other aspects of the involvement process. For instance, the role played by the various attractions of group membership suggests not only the potential value of taking people from this social environment but also the need to provide them with alternatives that similarly offer benefits such as camaraderie and a positive self-image.

Another potential avenue for preventing involvement or recidivism is taking seriously the perceived injustice and the sense of altruism that drives some of these individuals. As factually incorrect or uncomfortable as we may find the idea that Western intervention in Muslim countries equates with a war against Islam that justifies retaliatory violence, such ideas have considerable potential to motivate involvement and for that reason alone should be taken seriously. Because of the popularity of the radicalization concept, homegrown jihadist groups are frequently understood purely in terms of their religious convictions. What the results presented here have

---

6   Von Clausewitz, *On War*, 101, 138-40.

suggested, is that the motives both for involvement in these groups and the commission of acts of terrorism can be distinctly worldly. Real or vicariously experienced political grievances tied to events in the Muslim world are a key explanatory factor. Interventions, when undertaken early enough, could focus on channeling the altruistic desire to help others that sometimes lies at heart of these perceptions into non-violent avenues.

Another policy-relevant aspect of this work lies in its use of police files as primary sources. These files contained large amounts of relevant information that had not yet been used in prior research on the Hofstadgroup. Although using police files for research purposes presents its own set of challenges, being able to access this material was a prerequisite for coming to a more empirically robust understanding of participants' involvement processes. They were thus indispensable to moving beyond the overreliance on secondary sources noted earlier as a long-standing issue in research on terrorism. It is to be hoped that authorities within and beyond the Netherlands will recognize the potential for mutual benefits when researchers are allowed access to such material.

10.4 Limitations and future research

In closing, it is valuable to acknowledge this study's limitations and the various avenues for future research. One particular limitation is that this book focused almost exclusively on proximate factors; those directly influencing involvement in the Hofstadgroup. It has largely remained unclear, for instance, what underlying factors made this group's participants more likely than other young Dutch Muslims to experience cognitive openings that in many cases led to their involvement. Why were others not similarly affected by the 9/11 attacks or images of Muslim suffering? Secondly, the study focused primarily on the Hofstadgroup itself rather than the broader social, cultural, and political environment from which it emerged. There is considerable room for research on the role of underlying factors in bringing about involvement, as well as the relationship between the Hofstadgroup and the broader environment from which it emerged.

The single case-study research design remains this study's foremost limitation. A comparative approach was not taken because the emphasis placed on gathering and utilizing primary sources, and the in-depth qualitative nature of the analysis, would then simply not have been feasible within any reasonable amount of time. Nevertheless, it is argued that the findings presented in these pages are relevant not just for the Hofstadgroup itself but for the broader typology of European homegrown jihadism it represents for several reasons. First of all, the Hofstadgroup was one of several similar groups that arose in other European countries from the early 2000s onward. Secondly, single case-study research designs are useful for empirically assessing the validity of explanations held to be of general applicability, such as 'radicalization'. By critically and empirically examining numerous commonly found explanations for involvement in terrorism, the analysis was able to make a contribution to the larger debate about how to understand and study involvement in extremist and terrorist groups.

That being said, a fruitful avenue for future research would be to apply the multilevel analysis for understanding involvement to a wider selection of cases. Comparative research would be useful for distinguishing between factors of general relevance to the (European) homegrown jihadist typology and those unique to particular cases. As previously noted, such research could also usefully focus on what distinguishes those participants of extremist groups that do use (or plan to use) terrorist violence from those that do not. Can differences in their backgrounds, personality characteristics, or involvement processes be identified that can explain how and why some take up violent roles in such groups while others do not?

Another methodological limitation lies in the utilization of multiple theories spread over three levels of analysis. While the choice for breadth over depth provided a valuable appreciation of the multifaceted nature of involvement processes, it arguably did a disservice to the individual explanations. After all, many of them are sufficiently nuanced and well developed to warrant chapters or even entire studies of their own. Future research could turn this emphasis on its head and study particular hypotheses in more depth.

The primary sources utilized here form both a unique strong point and a weakness. The police files and interviews with former participants in particular offered a wealth of detailed information, much of it never before utilized in research on the Hofstadgroup. While such primary sources are important for reaching an empirically better-supported understanding of involvement processes, they also pose several issues. The police files in particular focused primarily on the participants deemed the most violent, leaving many others relatively understudied. Similarly, interviews could only be held with the relatively small number of former participants willing to talk. The end result of both these issues is that a lot is known about some key participants while others remain relatively poorly understood.

A more fundamental issue is that these sources are not freely available, hampering the transparency of the claims presented here. Although this issue could not be fully resolved, several measures were taken to minimize its impact. First of all, references to the police files and interviews were complemented with publicly available sources wherever possible. Secondly, links to those parts of the police files that had been leaked to the press and subsequently published online were provided wherever relevant. Finally, readers were asked to keep in mind that the use of restricted information is quite common in the social sciences. Interview transcripts, for instance, are rarely made freely available for reasons of privacy. The primary sources used in this study are thus less of an exception with regard to transparency than might first be apparent.

10.5 Toward a more empirical study of terrorism

Improving our understanding of how and why people become involved in European homegrown jihadism and indeed in terrorism more broadly, requires three things. The first is an analytical approach that recognizes involvement as a process in which numerous and interrelated factors, spread over multiple levels of analysis, play a role. Moreover, the 'driving force' of said process is likely to change over time, demanding analytical flexibility in order to account for why people join, why they stay, and why some of them perpetrate acts of terrorist violence. The third requirement is the use of primary sources that allow the researcher to acquire detailed, reliable, and new information on the involvement process. By applying these elements to a study of the Dutch Hofstadgroup, this book has aimed to make a contribution to a better understanding of this particular typology of terrorism. Hopefully, future studies on involvement in homegrown jihadism will similarly be able to utilize primary sources and thereby gradually but finally help overcome one of the oldest obstacles to progress in research on terrorism.

Abbreviations

AIVD	General Intelligence and Security Service
CTIVD	Review Committee on the Intelligence and Security Services
FBI	Federal Bureau of Investigation
IED	Improvised Explosive Device
KLPD	National Police Services Agency
NCTV	National Coordinator for Security and Counterterrorism
PBC	Pieter Baan Center
RPG	Rocket Propelled Grenade
SCP	Netherlands Institute for Social Research

Bibliography

Archival documents

Dienst Nationale Recherche. 'Piranha'. Korps Landelijke Politiediensten, 2005.
—. 'RL8026'. Korps Landelijke Politiediensten, 2005.

Primary sources

A[.], Samir. 'Deurwaarders'. 1-24, 2004.
—. 'Deurwaarders Van Allah'. 1-100, 2004/2005.
Donner, J.P.H. 'Wet Van 24 Juni 2004 Tot Wijziging En Aanvulling Van Het Wetboek Van Strafrecht En Enige Andere Wetten in Verband Met Terroristische Misdrijven (Wet Terroristische Misdrijven)'. In *Staatsblad 2004, 290*, 1-9. The Hague: Sdu Uitgevers, 2004.
Donner, J.P.H., and J.W. Remkes. 'Kamerstukken 2, 2004-2005, 29854, Nr. 1'. 1-3. The Hague: Sdu Publishers, 2004.
—. 'Kamerstukken 2, 2004-2005, 29854, Nr. 3'. 1-3. The Hague: Sdu Publishers, 2004.
Meijer, Roel. 'Inhoud Van De Religieuze En Ideologische Documenten Aangetroffen in Het Beslag Van Verdachten in Het Piranha-Onderzoek'. 1-74.
NOS. 'Verklaring Mohammed B. In Tekst'. 2005.
NOVA. 'Chatgesprekken Jason W.' NOVA, http://www.novatv.nl/page/detail/nieuws/516.
—. 'Informatie AIVD En Politie Uit Strafdossier'. http://www.novatv.nl/page/detail/nieuws/8239/Informatie+AIVD+en+politie+uit+strafdossier.
—. 'Videotestament Samir A. – Vertaling NOVA'. NOVA, http://www.novatv.nl/page/detail/nieuws/8887/Videotestament+Samir+A.+-+vertaling+NOVA.
Peters, Ruud. 'De Ideologische En Religieuze Ontwikkeling Van Mohammed B.', 1-87, 2005.
Remkes, J.W. 'Kamerstukken 2, 2004-2005, 29754, Nr. 22.' 1-3. The Hague: Sdu Publishers, 2005.
Ayaan Hirsi Ali and Theo van Gogh. 'Submission: Part 1'. YouTube, https://www.youtube.com/watch?v=G6bFR4_Ppk8.

Court documents

Amsterdam Court of Appeal. 'GHAMS:2014:905'. (25 March 2014): 1-21.
—. 'GHAMS:2014:914.' (25 March 2014): 1-23.
—. 'LJN BO7690'. (17 December 2010): 1-40.
—. 'LJN BO8032'. (17 December 2010): 1-43.
—. 'LJN BO9014'. (17 December 2010): 1-43.
—. 'LJN BO9015'. (17 December 2010): 1-44.
—. 'LJN BO9016'. (17 December 2010): 1-39.
—. 'LJN BO9017'. (17 December 2010): 1-42.
—. 'LJN BO9018'. (17 December 2010): 1-45.
Amsterdam District Court. 'LJN AU0025'. (26 July 2005): 1-22.
Den Hartigh, Bart, and Alexander Van Dam. 'Requisitoir "Piranha" Deel 1'. 1-87, 2006.
Rotterdam District Court. 'LJN AV5108'. (10 March 2006): 1-45.

—. 'LJN AZ3589'. (1 December 2006): 1-50.
Supreme Court of the Netherlands. 'LJN Bk5175'. (2 February 2010): 1-33.
The Hague Court of Appeal. 'LJN BC2576'. (23 January 2008): 1-36.
—. 'LJN BC4129'. (23 January 2008): 1-36.
—. 'LJN BC4171'. (23 January 2008): 1-31.
—. 'LJN BC4177'. (23 January 2008): 1-4.
—. 'LJN BC4178'. (23 January 2008): 1-5.
—. 'LJN BC4182'. (23 January 2008): 1-4.
—. 'LJN BC4183'. (23 January 2008): 1-7.
—. 'LJN BF3987'. (2 October 2008): 1-38.
Van Straelen, Frits. 'Requisitoir in De Strafzaak Tegen Mohammed B.', 1-45. Parketnr 129227-04: District Court Amsterdam, 2005.

Interviews

AIVD Employee 1. 'Personal Interview 1'. 1-3. The Hague, 2013.
Community Policing Officer 1. 'Personal Interview 1'. 1-3. Amsterdam, 2012.
Former Hofstadgroup Participant 1. 'Personal Interview 1'. 1-7. Amsterdam, 2012.
—. 'Personal Interview 2'. 1-45. Amsterdam, 2012.
—. 'Personal Interview 3'. 1-3. Amsterdam, 2012.
Former Hofstadgroup Participant 2. 'Personal Interview 1'. 1-7. The Hague, 2012.
Former Hofstadgroup Participant 3. 'Personal Interview 1'. 1-12. Leiden, 2013.
Former Hofstadgroup Participant 4. 'Personal Interview 1'. 1-2. The Hague, 2014.
—. 'Personal Interview 2'. 1-5. The Hague, 2015.
Former Hofstadgroup Participant 5. 'Personal Interview 1'. 1-5. Nieuwegein, 2015.
NCTV Employee 1. 'Personal Interview 1'. 1-7. The Hague, 2012.
—. 'Personal Interview 2'. 1-3. The Hague, 2012.
Police Investigator 1. 'Personal Interview 3'. 1-2. Houten, 2011.
—. 'Personal Interview 6'. 1-4. Houten, 2012.
Police Investigator 2. 'Personal Interview 1'. 1-6. Amsterdam, 2012.
Public Prosecutor 1. 'Personal Interview 1'. 1-52. The Hague, 2012.
Public Prosecutor 2. 'Personal Interview 1'. 1-5. Amsterdam, 2012.

Secondary sources

Aarts, Paul, and Fadi Hirzalla. 'Lions of Tawhid in the Polder'. *Middle East Report*, no. 235 (Summer 2005): 18-23.
Abels, Paul. '"Je Wilt Niet Geloven Dat Zoiets Kan!" Het Nederlandse Contraterrorismebeleid Sinds 1973'. In *Terroristen En Hun Bestrijders: Vroeger En Nu*, edited by Isabelle Duyvesteyn and Beatrice De Graaf, 121-28. Amsterdam: Boom, 2007.
Abrahms, Max. 'The Credibility Paradox: Violence as a Double-Edged Sword in International Politics'. *International Studies Quarterly* 57, no. 4 (December 2013): 660-71.
—. 'The Political Effectiveness of Terrorism Revisited'. *Comparative Political Studies* 45, no. 3 (February 2012): 366-93.
—. 'What Terrorists Really Want: Terrorist Motives and Counterterrorism Strategy'. *International Security* 32, no. 4 (Spring 2008): 78-105.
—. 'Why Terrorism Does Not Work'. *International Security* 31, no. 2 (Fall 2006): 42-78.

'AIVD Geeft Verkeerd Taxeren Van B. Toe'. *NRC Handelsblad*, 2 May 2005.
Akers, Ronald L., and Adam L. Silverman. 'Toward a Social Learning Model of Violence and Terrorism'. In *Violence: From Theory to Research*, edited by Margaret A. Zahn, Henry H. Brownstein and Shelly L. Jackson, 19-36. Newark: LexisNexis Anderson, 2004.
Al Raffie, Dina. 'Social Identity Theory for Investigating Islamic Extremism in the Diaspora'. *Journal of Strategic Security* 6, no. 4 (2013): 67-91.
Alberts, Jaco, Jutta Chorus, Steven Derix, and Ahmet Olgun. 'De Wereld Van Mohammed B.' *NRC Handelsblad*, 9 July 2005.
Alberts, Jaco, and Steven Derix. 'AIVD-Stuk Lekte Uit Naar Extremisten'. *NRC Handelsblad*, 9 November 2004.
—. 'Balkenende in 2003 Al Op Dodenlijst Jason W.' *NRC Handelsblad*, 28 January 2005.
—. 'Het Mysterie Van De Onbekende Extremist'. *NRC Handelsblad*, 29 October 2005.
—. 'Mohammed B. Schreef Meerdere Afscheidsbrieven'. *NRC Handelsblad*, 30 April 2005.
Alderdice, J.T. 'The Individual, the Group and the Psychology of Terrorism'. *International Review of Psychiatry* 19, no. 3 (June 2007): 201-09.
Algemene Inlichtingen- en Veiligheidsdienst. 'Jaarverslag 2002'. 1-140. The Hague: AIVD, 2003.
—. 'Jaarverslag 2014'. 1-43. The Hague: AIVD, 2015.
—. 'Jihadistisch Terrorisme in Nederland: Dreiging En Bestrijding'. In *Terrorisme: Studies over Terrorisme En Terrorismebestrijding*, edited by E.R. Muller, U. Rosenthal and R. De Wijk, 55-95. Deventer: Kluwer, 2008.
Aly, Anne, and Jason-Leigh Striegher. 'Examining the Role of Religion in Radicalization to Violent Islamist Extremism'. *Studies in Conflict & Terrorism* 35, no. 12 (2012): 849-62.
Andriessen, Iris, Eline Nievers, Laila Faulk, and Jaco Dagevos. *Liever Mark Dan Mohammed? Onderzoek Naar Arbeidsmarktdiscriminatie Van Niet-Westerse Migranten Via Praktijktests*. The Hague: Sociaal en Cultureel Planbureau, 2010.
Arena, Michael P., and Bruce A. Arrigo. *The Terrorist Identity: Explaining the Terrorist Threat*. New York/London: New York University Press, 2006.
Asal, Victor, Paul Gill, R. Karl Rethemeyer, and John Horgan. 'Killing Range: Explaining Lethality Variance within a Terrorist Organization'. *Journal of Conflict Resolution* 59, no. 3 (April 2015): 401-27.
Asal, Victor, and R. Karl Rethemeyer. 'The Nature of the Beast: Organizational Structures and the Lethality of Terrorist Attacks'. *The Journal of Politics* 70, no. 2 (2008): 437-49.
Asch, Solomon E. 'Opinions and Social Pressure'. *Scientific American* 193, no. 5 (November 1955): 31-35.
—. 'Studies of Independence and Conformity: 1. A Minority of One against a Unanimous Majority'. *Psychological Monographs: General and Applied* 70, no. 9 (1956): 1-70.

Bakker, Edwin. 'Characteristics of Jihadi Terrorists in Europe (2001-2009)'. In *Jihadi Terrorism and the Radicalisation Challenge*, edited by Rik Coolsaet, 131-44. Farnham/Burlington: Ashgate, 2011.
—. 'Islamism, Radicalisation and Jihadism in the Netherlands: Main Developments and Counter-Measures'. In *Understanding Violent Radicalisation: Terrorist and Jihadist Movements in Europe*, edited by Magnus Ranstorp, 168-90. London/New York: Routledge, 2010.
—. 'Zin En Onzin Van De Zoektocht Naar Oorzaken Van Terrorisme'. *Internationale Spectator* 58, no. 2 (November 2004): 542-47.
Bandura, Albert. 'Mechanisms of Moral Disengagement in Terrorism'. In *Origins of Terrorism: Psychologies, Ideologies, Theologies, States of Mind*, edited by Walter Reich, 161-91. Cambridge: Cambridge University Press, 1990.

—. *Social Learning Theory*. New York: General Learning Press, 1971.
Barnes, Collin D., Ryan P. Brown, Joshua Lenes, Jennifer Bosson, and Mauricio Carvallo. 'My Country, My Self: Honor, Identity, and Defensive Responses to National Threats'. *Self and Identity* 13, no. 6 (2014): 638-62.
Barros, Carlos Pestana, João Ricardo Faria, and Luis A. Gil-Alana. 'Terrorism against American Citizens in Africa: Related to Poverty?' *Journal of Policy Modeling* 30, no. 1 (January-February 2008): 55-69.
Bartels, Edien, and Martijn De Koning. 'Submission and a Ritual Murder. The Transnational Aspects of a Local Conflict and Protest'. In *Local Battles, Global Stakes: The Globalization of Local Conflicts and the Localization of Global Interests*, edited by Ton Salman and Marjo De Theije, 21-40. Amsterdam: VU University Press, 2011.
Bartlett, Jamie, and Carl Miller. 'The Edge of Violence: Towards Telling the Difference between Violent and Non-Violent Radicalization'. *Terrorism and Political Violence* 24, no. 1 (2012): 1-21.
Bartolo, Romain. 'Decentralised Leadership in Contemporary Jihadism: Towards a Global Social Movement'. *Journal of Terrorism Research* 2, no. 1 (June 2011): 44-61.
Beck, Aaron T. 'Prisoners of Hate'. *Behaviour Research and Therapy* 40, no. 3 (March 2002): 209-16.
Beck, Colin J. 'The Contribution of Social Movement Theory to Understanding Terrorism'. *Sociology Compass* 2, no. 5 (September 2008): 1565-81.
Beentjes, Mireille. 'Zaken Terreurverdachten Moeten Over'. *Hoge Raad Der Nederlanden*, 6 December 2011.
Benschop, Albert. 'Chronicle of a Political Murder Foretold'. Sociosite, http://www.sociosite.org/jihad_nl_en.php.
Bergen, Peter L. *Holy War: Inside the Secret World of Osama Bin Laden*. New York: The Free Press, 2001.
Berkowitz, Leonard. 'Frustration-Aggression Hypothesis: Examination and Reformulation'. *Psychological Bulletin* 106, no. 1 (July 1989): 59-73.
Berman, Eli, and David D. Laitin. 'Hard Targets: Theory and Evidence on Suicide Attacks'. 1-45. Stanford: Stanford University, 2006.
Berrebi, Claude. 'The Economics of Terrorism and Counterterrorism: What Matters and Is Rational-Choice Theory Helpful?' In *Social Science for Counterterrorism: Putting the Pieces Together*, edited by Paul K. Davis and Kim Cragin, 151-208. Santa Monica: RAND, 2009.
—. 'Evidence About the Link between Education, Poverty and Terrorism among Palestinians'. *Peace Economics, Peace Science and Public Policy* 13, no. 1 (2007): 1-36.
Bjørgo, Tore. 'Conclusions'. In *Root Causes of Terrorism: Myths, Reality and Ways Forward*, edited by Tore Bjørgo, 256-64. London/New York: Routledge, 2005.
Blazak, Randy. "White Boys to Terrorist Men: Target Recruitment of Nazi Skinheads." *American Behavioral Scientist* 44, no. 6 (2001): 982-1000.
Bloom, Mia. *Dying to Kill: The Allure of Suicide Terror*. New York: Columbia University Press, 2005.
Bloom, Mia, Paul Gill, and John Horgan. 'Tiocfaid Ár Mná: Women in the Provisional Irish Republican Army'. *Behavioral Sciences of Terrorism and Political Aggression* 4, no. 1 (January 2012): 60-76.
Borum, Randy. *Psychology of Terrorism*. Tampa: University of South Florida, 2004.
—. 'Radicalization into Violent Extremism I: A Review of Social Science Theories'. *Journal of Strategic Security* 4, no. 4 (Winter 2011): 7-36.
—. 'Radicalization into Violent Extremism II: A Review of Conceptual Models and Empirical Research'. *Journal of Strategic Security* 4, no. 4 (Winter 2011): 37-62.
—. 'Rethinking Radicalization'. *Journal of Strategic Security* 4, no. 4 (Winter 2011): 1-6.

—. 'Understanding the Terrorist Mindset'. *FBI Law Enforcement Bulletin* 72, no. 7 (January 2003): 7-10.
Bowie, Neil G., and Alex P. Schmid. 'Databases on Terrorism'. In *The Routledge Handbook of Terrorism Research*, edited by Alex P. Schmid, 294-340. London/New York: Routledge, 2011.
Bravo, Ana Bela Santos, and Carlos Manuel Mendes Dias. 'An Empirical Analysis of Terrorism: Deprivation, Islamism and Geopolitical Factors'. *Defence and Peace Economics* 17, no. 4 (August 2006): 329-41.
Brooke, Steven. 'Jihadist Strategic Debates before 9/11'. *Studies in Conflict & Terrorism* 31, no. 3 (2008): 201-26.
Bryan, Dominic, Liam Kelly, and Sara Templer. 'The Failed Paradigm of "Terrorism"'. *Behavioral Sciences of Terrorism and Political Aggression* 3, no. 2 (2011): 80-96.
Buijs, F.J., and F. Demant. 'Extremisme En Radicalisering'. In *Terrorisme: Studies over Terrorisme En Terrorismebestrijding*, edited by E.R. Muller, U. Rosenthal and R. De Wijk, 169-91. Deventer: Kluwer, 2008.
Buijs, Frank J., Froukje Demant, and Atef Hamdy. *Strijders Van Eigen Bodem*. Amsterdam: Amsterdam University Press, 2006.
Burke, Jason. *Al-Qaeda: Casting a Shadow of Terror*. London: I.B. Tauris, 2003.
Buruma, Ian. *Murder in Amsterdam: The Death of Theo Van Gogh and the Limits of Tolerance*. London: Atlantic Books, 2007.

Calis, Mayke. '"Iedereen Wil Martelaar Zijn"; Het Avontuur Van De Amsterdamse Moslim Mo (16)'. *Rotterdams Dagblad*, 29 March 2003, 807.
Caplan, Bryan. 'Terrorism: The Relevance of the Rational Choice Model'. *Public Choice* 128, no. 1-2 (July 2006): 91-107.
Carle, Robert. 'Demise of Dutch Multiculturalism'. *Society* 43, no. 3 (March/April 2006): 68-74.
Chorus, Jutta, and Ahmet Olgun. *Broeders: Tien Jaar Na De Moord Op Theo Van Gogh*. Amsterdam/Antwerp: Atlas Contact, 2014.
—. *In Godsnaam: Het Jaar Van Theo Van Gogh*. Amsterdam: Contact, 2005.
—. 'Op De Thee Bij De Jongens Van De Hofstadgroep'. *NRC Handelsblad*, 10 September 2011, 1-8.
Clauset, Aaron, Lindsay Heger, Maxwell Young, and Kristian Skrede Gleditsch. 'The Strategic Calculus of Terrorism: Substitution and Competition in the Israel-Palestine Conflict'. *Cooperation and Conflict* 45, no. 1 (March 2010): 6-33.
Cliteur, P. 'Waarom Terrorisme Werkt'. In *Terrorisme: Studies over Terrorisme En Terrorismebestrijding*, edited by E.R. Muller, U. Rosenthal and R. De Wijk, 307-45. Deventer: Kluwer, 2008.
Cliteur, Paul. 'De "Eigen-Schuldtheorie" En De Betekenis Van 10 November 2004'. *Ethische Perspectieven* 15, no. 3 (2005): 185-97.
—. 'Religieus Terrorisme En De Lankmoedige Elite'. In *Gaat De Elite Ons Redden? De Nieuwe Rol Van De Bovenlaag in Onze Samenleving*, edited by Krijn Van Beek and Marcel Van Ham, 207-35. Amsterdam: Van Gennep, 2007.
Collier, Paul, and Anke Hoeffler. 'Greed and Grievance in Civil War'. *Oxford Economic Papers* 56, no. 4 (August 2004): 563-95.
Commissie Evaluatie Antiterrorismebeleid. 'Naar Een Integrale Evaluatie Van Antiterrorismemaatregelen'. 1-120. The Hague: Rijksoverheid, 2009.
Commissie van Toezicht betreffende de Inlichtingen- en Veiligheidsdiensten. 'Toezichtsrapport Inzake De Afwegingsprocessen Van De AIVD Met Betrekking Tot Mohammed B.', 1-47. The Hague: CTIVD, 2008.
—. 'Toezichtsrapport over Eventuele Handlangers Van Mohammed B.', 1-41. The Hague: CTIVD, 2015.

Conrad, Justin, and Daniel Milton. 'Unpacking the Connection between Terror and Islam'. *Studies in Conflict & Terrorism* 36, no. 4 (2013): 315-36.

Coolsaet, Rik. 'EU Counterterrorism Strategy: Value Added or Chimera?' *International Affairs* 86, no. 4 (July 2010): 857-73.

Corner, Emily, Paul Gill, and Oliver Mason. 'Mental Health Disorders and the Terrorist: A Research Note Probing Selection Effects and Disorder Prevalance'. *Studies in Conflict & Terrorism* 39, no. 6 (2016): 560-68.

Corrado, Raymond R. 'A Critique of the Mental Disorder Perspective of Political Terrorism'. *International Journal of Law and Psychiatry* 4, no. 3-4 (1981): 293-309.

Cottee, Simon. 'Jihadism as a Subcultural Response to Social Strain: Extending Marc Sageman's "Bunch of Guys" Thesis'. *Terrorism and Political Violence* 23, no. 5 (2011): 730-51.

Cottee, Simon, and Keith Hayward. 'Terrorist (E)Motives: The Existential Attractions of Terrorism'. *Studies in Conflict & Terrorism* 34, no. 12 (2011): 963-86.

Cozzens, Jeffrey B. 'Al-Takfir Wa'l Hijra: Unpacking an Enigma'. *Studies in Conflict & Terrorism* 32, no. 6 (2009): 489-510.

Crenshaw, Martha. 'The Causes of Terrorism'. *Comparative Politics* 13, no. 4 (July 1981): 379-99.

—. *Explaining Terrorism: Causes, Processes and Consequences*. New York/Abingdon: Routledge, 2011.

—. 'The Logic of Terrorism: Terrorist Behavior as a Product of Strategic Choice'. In *Psychology of Terrorism: Classic and Contemporary Insights*, edited by Jeff Victoroff and Arie W. Kruglanski, 371-82. New York/Hove: Psychology Press, 2009.

—. 'The Psychology of Political Terrorism'. In *Political Psychology*, edited by Margaret G. Hermann, 379-413. San Francisco: Jossey-Bass Publishers, 1986.

—. 'Questions to Be Answered, Research to Be Done, Knowledge to Be Applied'. In *Origins of Terrorism: Psychologies, Ideologies, Theologies, States of Mind*, edited by Walter Reich, 247-60. Washington, D.C.: Woodrow Wilson Center Press, 1990.

—. 'Terrorism Research: The Record'. *International Interactions* 40, no. 4 (2014): 556-67.

—. 'Theories of Terrorism: Instrumental and Organizational Approaches'. *Journal of Strategic Studies* 10, no. 4 (December 1987): 13-31.

Crone, Manni. 'Radicalization Revisited: Violence, Politics and the Skills of the Body'. *International Affairs* 92, no. 3 (2016): 587-604.

—. 'Religion and Violence: Governing Muslim Militancy through Aesthetic Assemblages'. *Millennium – Journal of International Studies* 43, no. 1 (September 2014): 291-307.

Crone, Manni, and Martin Harrow. 'Homegrown Terrorism in the West'. *Terrorism and Political Violence* 23, no. 4 (2011): 521-36.

Cronin, Audrey Kurth. *How Terrorism Ends: Understanding the Decline and Demise of Terrorist Campaigns*. Princeton/Oxford: Princeton University Press, 2009.

Dalgaard-Nielsen, Anja. 'Violent Radicalization in Europe: What We Know and What We Do Not Know'. *Studies in Conflict & Terrorism* 33, no. 9 (2010): 797-814.

Davis, Paul K., and Kim Cragin, eds. *Social Science for Counterterrorism: Putting the Pieces Together*. Santa Monica: RAND, 2009.

Dawson, Lorne L. 'The Study of New Religious Movements and the Radicalization of Home-Grown Terrorists: Opening a Dialogue'. *Terrorism and Political Violence* 22, no. 1 (2009): 1-21.

De Bie, Jasper L., Christianne J. De Poot, and Joanne P. Van der Leun. 'Shifting Modus Operandi of Jihadist Foreign Fighters from the Netherlands between 2000 and 2013: A Crime Script Analysis'. *Terrorism and Political Violence* 27, no. 3 (2015): 416-40.

De Goede, Marieke, and Beatrice De Graaf. 'Sentencing Risk: Temporality and Precaution in Terrorism Trials'. *International Political Sociology* 7, no. 3 (September 2013): 313-31.

De Graaf, Beatrice. *Gevaarlijke Vrouwen: Tien Militante Vrouwen in Het Vizier*. Amsterdam: Boom, 2012.

—. 'The Nexus between Salafism and Jihadism in the Netherlands'. *CTC Sentinel* 3, no. 3 (March 2010): 17-22.

—. 'The Van Gogh Murder and Beyond'. In *The Evolution of the Global Terrorist Threat: From 9/11 to Osama Bin Laden's Death*, edited by Bruce Hoffman and Fernando Reinares, 101-42. New York: Columbia University Press, 2014.

De Graaf, Beatrice, and Quirine Eijkman. 'Terrorismebestrijding En Securitisering: Een Rechtssociologische Verkenning Van De Neveneffecten'. *Justitiële Verkenningen* 37, no. 8 (December 2011): 33-52.

De Koning, Martijn. 'Changing Worldviews and Friendship: An Exploration of the Life Stories of Two Female Salafists in the Netherlands'. In *Global Salafism: Islam's New Religious Movement*, edited by Roel Meijer, 372-92. London/New York: Hurst, 2009.

—. '"Moge Hij Onze Ogen Openen": De Radicale Utopie Van Het "Salafisme"'. *Tijdschrift voor Religie, Recht en Beleid* 2, no. 2 (2011): 47-61.

—. '"We Reject You"' – "Counter Conduct" and Radicalisation of the Dutch Hofstad Network'. In *Radikaler Islam Im Jugendalter: Erscheinungsformen, Ursachen Und Kontexte*, edited by Maruta Herding, 92-109. Halle: Deutsches Jugendinstitut, 2013.

De Koning, Martijn, and Roel Meijer. 'Going All the Way: Politicization and Radicalization of the Hofstad Network in the Netherlands'. In *Identity and Participation in Culturally Diverse Societies*, edited by Assaad E. Azzi, Xenia Chryssochou, Bert Klandermans and Bernd Simon, 220-38. Chichester: Wiley-Blackwell, 2011.

De Poot, C.J., A. Sonnenschein, M.R.J. Soudijn, J.G.M. Bijen, and M.W. Verkeulen. *Jihadi Terrorism in the Netherlands: A Description Based on Closed Criminal Investigations*. The Hague: Boom Juridische Uitgevers/Wetenschappelijk Onderzoek- en Documentatiecentrum, 2011.

De Weger, M.J. 'Continuïteit En Verandering: Het Nederlandse Stelsel Van Antiterreureenheden Sinds Zijn Oprichting'. In *Terrorisme: Studies over Terrorisme En Terrorismebestrijding*, edited by E.R. Muller, U. Rosenthal and R. De Wijk, 613-40. Deventer: Kluwer, 2008.

Dechesne, Mark, Tom Pyszczynski, Jamie Arndt, Sean Ransom, Kennon M. Sheldon, Ad Van Knippenberg, and Jacques Janssen. 'Literal and Symbolic Immortality: The Effect of Evidence of Literal Immortality on Self-Esteem Striving in Response to Mortality Salience'. *Journal of Personality and Social Psychology* 84, no. 4 (April 2003): 722-37.

Della Porta, Donatella. 'Recruitment Processes in Clandestine Political Organizations: Italian Left-Wing Terrorism'. In *Psychology of Terrorism: Classic and Contemporary Insights*, edited by Jeff Victoroff and Arie W. Kruglanski, 307-16. New York/Hove: Psychology Press, 2009.

—. *Social Movements, Political Violence, and the State*. Cambridge: Cambridge University Press, 1995.

Della Porta, Donatella, and Gary LaFree. 'Guest Editorial: Processes of Radicalization and De-Radicalization'. *International Journal of Conflict and Violence* 6, no. 1 (2012): 4-10.

Demant, Froukje, Marieke Slootman, Frank Buijs, and Jean Tillie. 'Decline and Disengagement: An Analysis of Processes of Deradicalisation'. In *IMES Reports Series*, 1-208. Amsterdam: Institute for Migration and Ethnic Studies, 2008.

Derix, Steven. 'Hoe Kwam Toch Die Vingerafdruk Op B.'S Brief?' *NRC Handelsblad*, 27 July 2005, 3.

—. 'Volgelingen Syriër "Opgefokt En Gehersenspoeld"'. *NRC Handelsblad*, 29 April 2005.

Dolnik, Adam. 'Conducting Field Research on Terrorism: A Brief Primer'. *Perspectives on Terrorism* 5, no. 2 (May 2011): 3-35.

—, ed. *Conducting Terrorism Field Research: A Guide*. London/New York: Routledge, 2013.
Doosje, Bertjan, Annemarie Loseman, and Kees Van den Bos. 'Determinants of Radicalization of Islamic Youth in the Netherlands: Personal Uncertainty, Perceived Injustice, and Perceived Group Threat'. *Journal of Social Issues* 69, no. 3 (September 2013): 586-604.
Douwes, Dick. 'Richtingen En Stromingen'. In *In Het Huis Van De Islam*, edited by Henk Driessen, 162-81. Nijmegen: SUN, 2001.
Downs, William M. *Political Extremism in Democracies: Combating Intolerance*. New York: Palgrave Macmillan, 2012.
'Drie Jaar Cel Soumaya S. In Oude Terreurzaak'. *Het Parool*, 25 March 2014.
Dugan, Laura, Gary LaFree, and Alex R. Piquero. 'Testing a Rational Choice Model of Airline Hijackings'. In *Intelligence and Security Informatics*, edited by Paul Kantor, Gheorghe Muresan, Fred Roberts, Daniel D. Zeng, Fei-Yue Wang, Hsinchun Chen and Ralph C. Merkle, 340-61. Berlin/Heidelberg: Springer, 2005.
Duyvesteyn, Isabelle. 'The Role of History and Continuity in Terrorism Research'. In *Mapping Terrorism Research: State of the Art, Gaps and Future Directions*, edited by Magnus Ranstorp, 51-75. New York/Abingdon: Routledge, 2007.
Duyvesteyn, Isabelle, and Mario Fumerton. 'Insurgency and Terrorism: Is There a Difference?' In *The Character of War in the 21st Century*, edited by Caroline Holmqvist-Jonsäter and Christopher Coker, 27-41. London: Routledge, 2009.
Duyvesteyn, Isabelle, and Bart Schuurman. '(Counter) Terrorism and Public Support'. In *Routledge Handbook of Terrorism and Counter-Terrorism*, edited by Andrew Silke. London/New York: Routledge, 2018.

Edwards, Aaron. 'When Terrorism as Strategy Fails: Dissident Irish Republicans and the Threat to British Security'. *Studies in Conflict & Terrorism* 34, no. 4 (2011): 318-36.
Egerton, Frazer. 'The Internet and Militant Jihadism: Global to Local Re-Imaginings'. In *Cyber-Conflict and Global Politics*, edited by Athina Karatzogianni, 115-27. Abingdon/New York: Routledge, 2008.
—. *Jihad in the West: The Rise of Militant Salafism*. Cambridge: Cambridge University Press, 2011.
Eijkman, Quirine. 'Has the Genie Been Let out of the Bottle? Ethnic Profiling in the Netherlands'. *Public Space: The Journal of Law and Social Justice* 5, no. 2 (2010): 1-21.
Eijkman, Quirine, and Bibi Van Ginkel. 'Compatible or Incompatible? Intelligence and Human Rights in Terrorist Trials'. *Amsterdam Law Forum* 3, no. 4 (2011): 3-16.
Eikelenboom, Siem. *Niet Bang Om Te Sterven: Dertig Jaar Terrorisme in Nederland*. Amsterdam: Nieuw Amsterdam, 2007.
Ellemers, Naomi, Russell Spears, and Bertjan Doosje. 'Self and Social Identity'. *Annual Review of Psychology* 53 (2002): 161-86.
Ellis, B. Heidi, Saida M. Abdi, John Horgan, Alisa B. Miller, Glenn N. Saxe, and Emily Blood. 'Trauma and Openness to Legal and Illegal Activism among Somali Refugees'. *Terrorism and Political Violence* 27, no. 5 (2015): 857-83.
Erkel, Arjan. *Samir*. Amsterdam: Uitgeverij Balans, 2007.
Esman, Abigail R. *Radical State: How Jihad Is Winning over Democracy in the West*. Santa Barbara: Praeger, 2010.
Esposito, John L. *Islam: The Straight Path*. New York/Oxford: Oxford University Press, 2011.
Eubank, William, and Leonard Weinberg. 'Terrorism and Democracy: Perpetrators and Victims'. *Terrorism and Political Violence* 13, no. 1 (2001): 155-64.
EUROPOL. *TE-SAT 2014: European Union Terrorism Situation and Trend Report 2014*. 's-Gravenzande: Drukkerij van Deventer, 2014.

Eyerman, Joe. 'Terrorism and Democratic States: Soft Targets or Accessible Systems'. *International Interactions* 24, no. 2 (1998): 151-70.
Eyerman, Ron. *The Assassination of Theo Van Gogh: From Social Drama to Cultural Trauma*. Durham/London: Duke University Press, 2008.
Eysenck, Michael W., and Mark T. Keane. *Cognitive Psychology: A Student's Handbook*. London/New York: Psychology Press, 2015.

Fair, C. Christine, and Bryan Shepherd. 'Who Supports Terrorism? Evidence from Fourteen Muslim Countries'. *Studies in Conflict & Terrorism* 29, no. 1 (2006): 51-74.
Fearon, James D., and David D. Laitin. 'Ethnicity, Insurgency, and Civil War'. *American Political Science Review* 97, no. 1 (February 2003): 75-90.
Feridun, Mete, and Selami Sezgin. 'Regional Underdevelopment and Terrorism: The Cause of South Eastern Turkey'. *Defence and Peace Economics* 19, no. 3 (2008): 225-33.
Festinger, Leon. *A Theory of Cognitive Dissonance*. Stanford: Stanford University Press, 1957.
Fish, M. Steven, Francesca R. Jensenius, and Katherine E. Michel. 'Islam and Large-Scale Political Violence: Is There a Connection?' *Comparative Political Studies* 43, no. 11 (2010): 1327-62.
Forest, James J.F. 'Exploring Root Causes of Terrorism: An Introduction'. In *The Making of a Terrorist, Volume III: Root Causes*, edited by James J.F. Forest, 1-14. Westport/London: Praeger Security International, 2005.
Franzosi, Roberto. 'The Press as a Source of Socio-Historical Data: Issues in the Methodology of Data Collection from Newspapers'. *Historical Methods* 20, no. 1 (Winter 1987): 5-16.
Frost, Robin M. 'Terrorist Psychology, Motivation and Strategy'. *The Adelphi Papers* 45, no. 378 (2005): 41-62.

Garnett, John. 'The Causes of War and the Conditions of Peace'. In *Strategy in the Contemporary World: An Introduction to Strategic Studies*, edited by John Baylis, James Wirtz, Eliot Cohen and Colin S. Gray, 66-87. New York: Oxford University Press, 2005.
Geelhoed, Fiore. *Purification and Resistance: Glocal Meanings of Islamic Fundamentalism in the Netherlands*. PhD Thesis, Rotterdam: Erasmus University, 2012.
General Intelligence and Security Service. 'From Dawa to Jihad: The Various Threats from Radical Islam to the Democratic Legal Order'. 1-58. The Hague: General Intelligence and Security Service, 2004.
—. 'The Transformation of Jihadism in the Netherlands: Swarm Dynamics and New Strength'. 1-55. The Hague: AIVD, 2014.
—. 'Violent Jihad in the Netherlands: Current Trends in the Islamist Terrorist Threat'. 1-65. The Hague: General Intelligence and Security Service, 2006.
Genkin, Michael, and Alexander Gutfraind. 'How Do Terrorist Cells Self-Assemble: Insights from an Agent-Based Model of Radicalization'. In *Social Science Research Network Working Paper Series*, 1-47. Rochester, NY: Social Science Research Network, 2011.
'Getuige Piranha-Zaak Zelf Radicaal'. *de Volkskrant*, 28 October 2006.
Gielen, Amy-Jane. *Radicalisering En Identiteit: Radicale Rechtse En Moslimjongeren Vergeleken*. Amsterdam: Aksant, 2008.
Gill, Paul, and Emily Corner. 'There and Back Again: The Study of Mental Disorder and Terrorist Involvement'. *American Psychologist* 72, no. 3 (2017): 231-41.
Gill, Paul, and John Horgan. 'Who Were the Volunteers? The Shifting Sociological and Operational Profile of 1240 Provisional Irish Republican Army Members'. *Terrorism and Political Violence* 25, no. 3 (2013): 435-56.

Gould, Eric D., and Esteban F. Klor. 'Does Terrorism Work?' *The Quarterly Journal of Economics* 125, no. 4 (2010): 1459-510.

Groen, Janny. 'Saleh B. Blijft Leveren Granaat Ontkennen'. *de Volkskrant*, 13 December 2005, 2.

Groen, Janny, and Annieke Kranenberg. '"Saleh B. Wel Terroristisch Actief"'. *de Volkskrant*, 2 June 2007, 1.

—. 'Samir A. In Afgesplitste Terreurgroep'. *de Volkskrant*, 28 January 2006.

—. *Women Warriors for Allah: An Islamist Network in the Netherlands*. Philadelphia: University of Pennsylvania Press, 2010.

Groen, Janny, Annieke Kranenberg, and Weert Schenk. 'Bilal B. Was Bekende Van Hofstadgroep'. *de Volkskrant*, 16 October 2007.

Groot Koerkamp, Sanne, and Marije Veerman. *Het Slapende Leger: Een Zoektocht Naar Jonge Jihad-Sympathisanten in Nederland*. Amsterdam: Rothschild & Bach, 2006.

Gurr, Ted Robert. *Why Men Rebel*. Boulder/London: Paradigm Publishers, 2011.

—. 'Why Minorities Rebel: A Global Analysis of Communal Mobilization and Conflict since 1945'. *International Political Science Review* 14, no. 2 (1993): 161-201.

Hafez, Mohammed M. 'Rationality, Culture, and Structure in the Making of Suicide Bombers: A Preliminary Theoretical Synthesis and Illustrative Case Study'. *Studies in Conflict & Terrorism* 29, no. 2 (2006): 165-85.

Hannah, Greg, Lindsay Clutterbuck, and Jennifer Rubin. 'Radicalization or Rehabilitation: Understanding the Challenge of Extremist and Radicalized Prisoners'. 1-70. Santa Monica: RAND, 2008.

Harris-Hogan, Shandon. 'Australian Neo-Jihadist Terrorism: Mapping the Network and Cell Analysis Using Wiretap Evidence'. *Studies in Conflict & Terrorism* 35, no. 4 (2012): 298-314.

Hemmingsen, Ann-Sophie. 'The Attractions of Jihadism: An Identity Approach to Three Danish Terrorism Cases and the Gallery of Characters around Them'. PhD Thesis, University of Copenhagen, 2011.

Hewitt, Christopher. 'Terrorism and Public Opinion: A Five Country Comparison'. *Terrorism and Political Violence* 2, no. 2 (1990): 145-70.

'"Hirsi Ali Zoekt Tegenstanders Voor Haar Wedstrijd"'. *de Volkskrant*, 30 August 2004.

Hoffman, Bruce. *Inside Terrorism*. New York: Columbia University Press, 2006.

—. 'The Rationality of Terrorism and Other Forms of Political Violence: Lessons from the Jewish Campaign in Palestine, 1939-1947'. *Small Wars & Insurgencies* 22, no. 2 (May 2011): 258-72.

Hoffman, Bruce, and Gordon H. McCormick. 'Terrorism, Signaling, and Suicide Attack'. *Studies in Conflict & Terrorism* 27, no. 4 (2004): 243-81.

Hofmann, David C., and Lorne L. Dawson. 'The Neglected Role of Charismatic Authority in the Study of Terrorist Groups and Radicalization'. *Studies in Conflict & Terrorism* 37, no. 4 (2014): 348-68.

'Hoge Raad Vernietigt Veroordeling Soumaya S.' *de Volkskrant*, 15 November 2011.

Horgan, John. 'The Case for Firsthand Research'. In *Research on Terrorism: Trends, Achievements and Failures*, edited by Andrew Silke, 30-56. London/New York: Frank Cass, 2004.

—. *Divided We Stand: The Strategy and Psychology of Ireland's Dissident Terrorists*. Oxford/New York: Oxford University Press, 2013.

—. 'From Profiles to Pathways and Roots to Routes: Perspectives from Psychology on Radicalization into Terrorism'. *The Annals of the American Academy of Political and Social Science* 618, no. 1 (July 2008): 80-94.

—. 'Interviewing the Terrorists: Reflections on Fieldwork and Implications for Psychological Research'. *Behavioral Sciences of Terrorism and Political Aggression* 4, no. 3 (2012): 195-211.

—. 'Issues in Terrorism Research'. *The Police Journal* 70, no. 3 (July 1997): 193-202.
—. 'Psychology of Terrorism: Introduction to the Special Issue'. *American Psychologist* 72, no. 3 (2017): 199-204.
—. *The Psychology of Terrorism*. London/New York: Routledge, 2014.
—. 'Understanding Terrorist Motivation: A Socio-Psychological Perspective'. In *Mapping Terrorism Research: State of the Art, Gaps and Future Directions*, edited by Magnus Ranstorp, 106-26. New York/Abingdon: Routledge, 2007.
—. *Walking Away from Terrorism: Accounts of Disengagement from Radical and Extremist Movements*. New York: Routledge, 2009.
Horgan, John, and Michael J. Boyle. 'A Case against "Critical Terrorism Studies"'. *Critical Studies on Terrorism* 1, no. 1 (April 2008): 51-64.
Horne, Cale, and John Horgan. 'Methodological Triangulation in the Analysis of Terrorist Networks'. *Studies in Conflict & Terrorism* 35, no. 2 (2012): 182-92.
Hudson, Rex A. 'The Sociology and Psychology of Terrorism: Who Becomes a Terrorist and Why?', 1-178. Washington, D.C.: Library of Congress, 1999.
Huntington, Samuel P. 'The Clash of Civilizations?' *Foreign Affairs* 72, no. 3 (Summer 1993): 22-49.

Ilardi, Gaetano Joe. 'Interviews with Canadian Radicals'. *Studies in Conflict & Terrorism* 36, no. 9 (2013): 713-38.

Jaarrapport Integratie 2005. The Hague: SCP, WODC, CBS, 2005.
Jackson, Brian A. 'Organizational Decisionmaking by Terrorist Groups'. In *Social Science for Counterterrorism: Putting the Pieces Together*, edited by Paul K. Davis and Kim Cragin, 209-56. Santa Monica: RAND, 2009.
Jackson, Richard. 'The Core Commitments of Critical Terrorism Studies'. *European Political Science* 6, no. 3 (September 2007): 244-51.
Jackson, Richard, Marie Breen Smyth, and Jeroen Gunning, eds. *Critical Terrorism Studies: A New Research Agenda*. New York/Abingdon: Routledge, 2009.
Jacobson, Michael. *The West at War: U.S. And European Counterterrorism Efforts, Post September 11*. Washington, D.C.: Washington Institute for Near East Policy, 2006.
Janis, Irving L. 'Groupthink'. *Psychology Today*, November 1971, 84-90.
Juergensmeyer, Mark. *Terror in the Mind of God: The Global Rise of Religious Violence*. Berkeley/Los Angeles/London: University of California Press, 2003.

'Kabinet Bindt Strijd Aan Met Moslimterreur'. *Het Financieele Dagblad*, 5 November 2004, 1.
Kacou, Amien. 'Five Arguments on the Rationality of Suicide Terrorists'. *Aggression and Violent Behavior* 18, no. 5 (September-October 2013): 539-47.
Kaddouri, Yehya. *Lach Met De Duivel: Autobiografie Van Een 'Rotte Appel'-Marokkaan*. Amsterdam: Van Gennep, 2011.
Kennedy-Pipe, Caroline. *The Origins of the Present Troubles in Northern Ireland*. New York: Longman, 1997.
Khalil, James. 'Radical Beliefs and Violent Actions Are Not Synonymous: How to Place the Key Disjuncture between Attitudes and Behaviors at the Heart of Our Research into Political Violence'. *Studies in Conflict & Terrorism* 37, no. 2 (2014): 198-211.
Kilcullen, David J. 'Subversion and Countersubversion in the Campaign against Terrorism in Europe'. *Studies in Conflict & Terrorism* 30, no. 8 (2007): 647-66.

King, Michael, and Donald M. Taylor. 'The Radicalization of Homegrown Jihadists: A Review of Theoretical Models and Social Psychological Evidence'. *Terrorism and Political Violence* 23, no. 4 (2011): 602-22.

Kiras, James D. 'Terrorism and Irregular Warfare'. In *Strategy in the Contemporary World: An Introduction to Strategic Studies*, edited by John Baylis, James Wirtz, Eliot Cohen and Colin S. Gray. New York: Oxford University Press, 2005.

Kirby, Aidan. 'The London Bombers as "Self-Starters": A Case Study in Indigenous Radicalization and the Emergence of Autonomous Cliques'. *Studies in Conflict & Terrorism* 30, no. 5 (2007): 415-28.

Kleinmann, Scott Matthew. 'Radicalization of Homegrown Sunni Militants in the United States: Comparing Converts and Non-Converts'. *Studies in Conflict & Terrorism* 35, no. 4 (2012): 278-97.

Kliot, Nurit, and Igal Charney. 'The Geography of Suicide Terrorism in Israel'. *GeoJournal* 66, no. 4 (2006): 353-73.

Knapp, Michael G. 'The Concept and Practice of Jihad in Islam'. *Parameters* 33, no. 1 (Spring 2003): 82-94.

Knefel, John. 'Everything You've Been Told About Radicalization Is Wrong'. *Rolling Stone*, 6 May 2013.

Koehler, Daniel. *Understanding Deradicalization: Methods, Tools and Programs for Countering Extremism*. London /New York: Routledge, 2017.

Koopmans, Ruud. 'Religious Fundamentalism and Hostility against out-Groups: A Comparison of Muslims and Christians in Western Europe'. *Journal of Ethnic and Migration Studies* 41, no. 1 (2015): 33-57.

Kranenberg, Annieke. 'De Zachte Krachten Achter Mohammed B.' *de Volkskrant*, 20 November 2004.

Kranenberg, Annieke, and Janny Groen. 'Kroongetuigen Vallen in Eigen Kuil'. *de Volkskrant*, 2 December 2006.

Krause, Peter. 'The Political Effectiveness of Non-State Violence: A Two-Level Framework to Transform a Deceptive Debate'. *Security Studies* 22, no. 2 (2013): 259-94.

Krueger, Alan B., and Jitka Malečková. 'Education, Poverty and Terrorism: Is There a Causal Connection?' *Journal of Economic Perspectives* 17, no. 4 (Fall 2003): 119-44.

Kruglanski, Arie. 'Inside the Terrorist Mind: The Relevance of Ideology'. *Estudios de Psicología: Studies in Psychology* 27, no. 3 (2006): 271-77.

Kruglanski, Arie, Xiaoyan Chen, and Agnieszka Golec. 'Individual Motivations, the Group Process and Organisational Strategies in Suicide Terrorism'. *Journal of Policing, Intelligence and Counter Terrorism* 3, no. 1 (2011): 70-84.

Kruglanski, Arie W., Xiaoyan Chen, Mark Dechesne, Shira Fishman, and Edward Orehek. 'Fully Committed: Suicide Bombers' Motivation and the Quest for Personal Significance'. *Political Psychology* 30, no. 3 (2009): 331-57.

Kruglanski, Arie W., and Shira Fishman. 'Psychological Factors in Terrorism and Counterterrorism: Individual, Group, and Organizational Levels of Analysis'. *Social Issues and Policy Review* 3, no. 1 (December 2009): 1-44.

—. 'The Psychology of Terrorism: "Syndrome" Versus "Tool" Perspectives'. *Terrorism and Political Violence* 18, no. 2 (2006): 193-215.

—. 'What Makes Terrorism Tick? Its Individual, Group and Organizational Aspects'. *Revista de Psicología Social: International Journal of Social Psychology* 24, no. 2 (2009): 139-62.

Kruglanski, Arie W., Michele J. Gelfand, Jocelyn J. Bélanger, Anna Sheveland, Malkanthi Hetiarachchi, and Rohan Gunaratna. 'The Psychology of Radicalization and Deradicalization:

How Significance Quest Impacts Violent Extremism'. *Advances in Political Psychology* 35, no. Supplement S1 (February 2014): 69-93.

Kruglanski, Arie W., and Edward Orehek. 'The Role of the Quest for Personal Significance in Motivating Terrorism'. In *The Psychology of Social Conflict and Aggression*, edited by Joseph P. Forgas, Arie W. Kruglanski and Kipling D. Williams, 153-66. New York/London: Psychology Press, 2011.

Kühle, Lene, and Lasse Lindekilde. *Radicalization among Young Muslims in Aarhus*. Aarhus: Aarhus University, 2010.

Kundnani, Arun. 'Radicalisation: The Journey of a Concept'. *Race & Class* 54, no. 2 (2012): 3-25.

Kydd, Andrew H., and Barbara F. Walter. 'The Strategies of Terrorism'. *International Security* 31, no. 1 (Summer 2006): 49-80.

'Laatste Woord Mohammed B.' *de Volkskrant*, 9 August 2005.

LaFree, Gary, and Gary Ackerman. 'The Empirical Study of Terrorism: Social and Legal Research'. *Annual Review of Law and Social Science* 5 (2009): 347-74.

LaFree, Gary, Laura Dugan, Min Xie, and Piyusha Singh. 'Spatial and Temporal Patterns of Terrorist Attacks by Eta 1970 to 2007'. *Journal of Quantitative Criminology* 28, no. 1 (March 2012): 7-29.

Lake, David A. 'Rational Extremism: Understanding Terrorism in the Twenty-First Century'. *Dialogue IO* 1, no. 1 (January 2002): 15-29.

Lankford, Adam. 'Précis of the Myth of Martyrdom: What Really Drives Suicide Bombers, Rampage Shooters, and Other Self-Destructive Killers'. *Behavioral and Brain Sciences* 37, no. 4 (August 2014): 351-62.

———. 'Promoting Aggression and Violence at Abu Ghraib: The U.S. Military's Transformation of Ordinary People into Torturers'. *Aggression and Violent Behavior* 14, no. 5 (September-October 2009): 388-95.

Leiken, Robert S. 'Europe's Angry Muslims'. *Foreign Affairs* 84, no. 4 (July/August 2005): 120-35.

———. 'Europe's Mujahideen: Where Mass Immigration Meets Global Terrorism'. 1-20: Center for Immigration Studies, 2005.

Lentini, Pete. '"If They Know Who Put the Sugar It Means They Know Everything": Understanding Terrorist Activity Using Operation Pendennis Wiretap (Listening Device and Telephone Intercept) Transcripts'. In *ARC Linkage Project on Radicalisation*, 1-35. Monash University, Melbourne, Australia: Monash University, 2010.

Levin, Shana, P.J. Henry, Felicia Pratto, and Jim Sidanius. 'Social Dominance and Social Identity in Lebanon: Implications for Support of Violence Agains the West'. In *Psychology of Terrorism: Classic and Contemporary Insights*, edited by Jeff Victoroff and Arie W. Kruglanski, 253-68. New York/Hove: Psychology Press, 2009.

Li, Quan. 'Does Democracy Promote or Reduce Transnational Terrorist Incidents?' *Journal of Conflict Resolution* 49, no. 2 (April 2005): 278-97.

Li, Quan, and Drew Schaub. 'Economic Globalization and Transnational Terrorism: A Pooled Time-Series Analysis'. *Journal of Conflict Resolution* 48, no. 2 (April 2004): 230-58.

Lia, Brynjar, and Katja H-W Skjølberg. 'Causes of Terrorism: An Expanded and Updated Review of the Literature'. 1-82. Kjeller: Norwegian Defense Research Establishment, 2004.

———. 'Why Terrorism Occurs – a Survey of Theories and Hypotheses on the Causes of Terrorism'. 1-43. Kjeller: Norwegian Defense Research Establishment, 2000.

Ligon, Gina Scott, Pete Simi, Mackenzie Harms, and Daniel J. Harris. 'Putting the "O" in VEOs: What Makes an Organization?' *Dynamics of Asymmetric Conflict* 6, no. 1-3 (2013): 110-34.

Likar, Lawrence E. *Eco-Warriors, Nihilistic Terrorists, and the Environment*. Santa Barbara: Praeger, 2011.
Locicero, Alice, and Samuel J. Sinclair. 'Terrorism and Terrorist Leaders: Insights from Developmental and Ecological Psychology'. *Studies in Conflict & Terrorism* 31, no. 3 (2008): 227-50.
Lofland, John, and Rodney Stark. 'Becoming a World-Saver: A Theory of Conversion to a Deviant Perspective'. *American Sociological Review* 30, no. 6 (December 1965): 862-75.
Loza, Wagdy. 'The Psychology of Extremism and Terrorism: A Middle-Eastern Perspective'. *Aggression and Violent Behavior* 12, no. 2 (March-April 2007): 141-55.
Lum, Cynthia, Leslie W. Kennedy, and Alison J. Sherley. 'The Effectiveness of Counter-Terrorism Strategies'. *Campbell Systematic Reviews*, no. 2 (January 2006): 1-50.
Lustick, Ian S. 'Terrorism in the Arab-Israeli Conflict: Targets and Audiences'. In *Terrorism in Context*, edited by Martha Crenshaw, 514-52. University Park: Pennsylvania State University Press, 1995.

MacCulloch, Robert. 'The Impact of Income on the Taste for Revolt'. *American Journal of Political Science* 48, no. 4 (2004): 830-48.
Maher, Shiraz. *Salafi-Jihadism: The History of an Idea*. London: Hurst, 2016. Salafi-Jihadism.
Maikovich, Andrea Kohn. 'A New Understanding of Terrorism Using Cognitive Dissonance Principles'. *Journal for the Theory of Social Behaviour* 35, no. 4 (December 2005): 373-97.
Mak, Geert. *Gedoemd Tot Kwetsbaarheid*. Amsterdam/Antwerp: Atlas, 2005.
—. *Nagekomen Flessenpost*. Amsterdam/Antwerp: Atlas, 2005.
Maliepaard, Mieke, and Mérove Gijsberts. 'Moslim in Nederland 2012'. 1-203. The Hague: Sociaal en Cultureel Planbureau, 2012.
Mandel, David R. 'The Role of Instigators in Radicalization to Violent Extremism'. In *Psychosocial, Organizational and Cultural Aspects of Terrorism*, edited by Anne Speckhard, 1-6. Neuilly-Sur-Sein: NATO, 2011.
Marcus, Jon. 'Oral History: Where Next after the Belfast Project?' *Times Higher Education*, 5 June 2014.
Marsden, Sarah V. 'Successful Terrorism: Framework and Review'. *Behavioral Sciences of Terrorism and Political Aggression* 4, no. 2 (May 2012): 134-50.
Martin, Gus. *Understanding Terrorism: Challenges, Perspectives, and Issues*. Thousand Oaks: Sage Publications, 2003.
Maynard, Jonathan Leader. 'Rethinking the Role of Ideology in Mass Atrocities'. *Terrorism and Political Violence* 26, no. 5 (2014): 821-41.
McAllister, Bradley, and Alex P. Schmid. 'Theories of Terrorism'. In *The Routledge Handbook of Terrorism Research*, edited by Alex P. Schmid, 201-62. Abingdon/New York: Routledge, 2011.
McBride, Megan K. 'The Logic of Terrorism: Existential Anxiety, the Search for Meaning, and Terrorist Ideologies'. *Terrorism and Political Violence* 23, no. 4 (2011): 560-81.
McCauley, Clark. 'Psychological Issues in Understanding Terrorism and the Response to Terrorism'. In *The Psychology of Terrorism: Volume Iii, Theoretical Understandings and Perspectives*, edited by Chris E. Stout, 3-29. Westport/London: Praeger, 2002.
—. 'Testing Theories of Radicalization in Polls of U.S. Muslims'. *Analyses of Social Issues and Public Policy* 12, no. 1 (December 2012): 296-311.
McCauley, Clark, and Sophia Moskalenko. *Friction: How Radicalization Happens to Them and Us*. New York: Oxford University Press, 2011.
—. 'Mechanisms of Political Radicalization: Pathways toward Terrorism'. *Terrorism and Political Violence* 20, no. 3 (2008): 415-33.

—. 'Some Things We Think We've Learned since 9/11: A Commentary on Marc Sageman's "the Stagnation in Terrorism Research"'. *Terrorism and Political Violence* 26, no. 4 (2014): 601-08.
McCauley, Clark, and Mary E. Segal. 'Social Psychology of Terrorist Groups'. In *Psychology of Terrorism: Classic and Contemporary Insights*, edited by Jeff Victoroff and Arie W. Kruglanski, 331-46. New York/Hove: Psychology Press, 2009.
McCormick, Gordon H. 'Terrorist Decision Making'. *Annual Review of Political Science* 6 (June 2003): 473-507.
Merari, Ariel. 'Psychological Aspects of Suicide Terrorism'. In *Psychology of Terrorism*, edited by Bruce Bongar, Lisa M. Brown, Larry E. Beutler, James N. Breckenridge and Philip G. Zimbardo, 101-15. Oxford/New York: Oxford University Press, 2007.
—. 'Social, Organizational and Psychological Factors in Suicide Terrorism'. In *Root Causes of Terrorism: Myths, Reality and Ways Forward*, edited by Tore Bjørgo, 70-86. London/New York: Routledge, 2005.
—. 'Terrorism as a Strategy of Insurgency'. *Terrorism and Political Violence* 5, no. 4 (1993): 213-51.
Merari, Ariel, Ilan Diamant, Arie Bibi, Yoav Broshi, and Giora Zakin. 'Personality Characteristics of "Self Martyrs"/"Suicide Bombers" and Organizers of Suicide Attacks'. *Terrorism and Political Violence* 22, no. 1 (2009): 87-101.
Merari, Ariel, Jonathan Fighel, Boaz Ganor, Ephraim Lavie, Yohanan Tzoreff, and Arie Livne. 'Making Palestinian "Martyrdom Operations"/"Suicide Attacks": Interviews with Would-Be Perpetrators and Organizers'. *Terrorism and Political Violence* 22, no. 1 (2009): 102-19.
Merkle, Peter H. 'West German Left-Wing Terrorism'. In *Terrorism in Context*, edited by Martha Crenshaw, 160-210. University Park: The Pennsylvania State University Press, 2007.
Milgram, Stanley. 'Behavioral Study of Obedience'. *Journal of Abnormal and Social Psychology* 67, no. 4 (1963): 371-78.
Milla, Mira Noor, Faturochman, and Djamaludin Ancok. 'The Impact of Leader-Follower Interactions on the Radicalization of Terrorists: A Case Study of the Bali Bombers'. *Asian Journal of Social Psychology* 16, no. 2 (June 2013): 92-100.
Miller, Gregory D. 'Rationality, Decision-Making and the Levels of Analysis Problem in Terrorism Studies'. In *ISA's 50th Annual Convention 'Exploring the past, anticipating the future'*, 1-21. New York: International Studies Association, 2009.
—. 'Terrorist Decision Making and the Deterrence Problem'. *Studies in Conflict & Terrorism* 36, no. 2 (2013): 132-51.
Moghadam, Assaf. 'Mayhem, Myths, and Martyrdom: The Shi'a Conception of Jihad'. *Terrorism and Political Violence* 19, no. 1 (2007): 125-43.
Moghaddam, Fathali M. 'The Staircase to Terrorism: A Psychological Exploration'. *American Psychologist* 60, no. 2 (February-March 2005): 161-69.
'Mohammed Bleef Gesloten Boek in Observatiekliniek'. *de Volkskrant*, 11 July 2005.
Mullins, Sam. 'Iraq Versus Lack of Integration: Understanding the Motivations of Contemporary Islamist Terrorists in Western Countries'. *Behavioral Sciences of Terrorism and Political Aggression* 4, no. 2 (May 2012): 110-33.
—. 'Radical Attitudes and Jihad: A Commentary on the Article by Clark Mccauley (2012) Testing Theories of Radicalization in Polls of U.S. Muslims'. *Analyses of Social Issues and Public Policy* 12, no. 1 (December 2012): 312-15.
Munson, Ziad W. *The Making of Pro-Life Activists*. Chicago/London: The University of Chicago Press, 2008.
Murshed, S. Mansoob, and Scott Gates. 'Spatial-Horizontal Inequality and the Maoist Insurgency in Nepal'. *Review of Development Economics* 9, no. 1 (February 2005): 121-34.

Nalbandov, Robert. 'Irrational Rationality of Terrorism'. *Journal of Strategic Security* 6, no. 4 (2013): 92-102.
National Coordinator for Security and Counterterrorism. 'Jihadists and the Internet: 2009 Update'. 1-96. The Hague: NCTV, 2010.
Nesser, Petter. 'Chronology of Jihadism in Western Europe 1994-2007: Planned, Prepared, and Executed Terrorist Attacks'. *Studies in Conflict & Terrorism* 31, no. 10 (2008): 924-46.
—. 'How Did Europe's Global Jihadis Obtain Training for Their Militant Causes?' *Terrorism and Political Violence* 20, no. 2 (2008): 234-56.
—. *Jihad in Europe: Patterns in Islamist Terrorist Cell Formation and Behaviour, 1995-2010*. Oslo: University of Oslo, 2012.
—. 'Jihadism in Western Europe after the Invasion of Iraq: Tracing Motivational Influences from the Iraq War on Jihadist Terrorism in Western Europe'. *Studies in Conflict & Terrorism* 29, no. 4 (September 2006): 323-42.
—. 'Joining Jihadi Terrorist Cells in Europe: Exploring Motivational Aspects of Recruitment and Radicalization'. In *Understanding Violent Radicalisation: Terrorist and Jihadist Movements in Europe*, edited by Magnus Ranstorp, 87-114. London/New York: Routledge, 2010.
—. 'Lessons Learned from the September 2007 German Terrorist Plot.' *CTC Sentinel* 1, no. 4 (2008): 1-3.
—. 'The Slaying of the Dutch Filmmaker – Religiously Motivated Violence or Islamist Terrorism in the Name of Global Jihad?', 1-35. Kjeller: Norwegian Defense Research Establishment, 2005.
—. 'Toward an Increasingly Heterogeneous Threat: A Chronology of Jihadist Terrorism in Europe 2008-2013'. *Studies in Conflict & Terrorism* 37, no. 5 (2014): 440-56.
Neumann, Peter, and Scott Kleinmann. 'How Rigorous Is Radicalization Research?' *Democracy and Security* 9, no. 4 (2013): 360-82.
Neumann, Peter R. 'Chapter Four: The Message'. *The Adelphi Papers* 48, no. 399 (2008): 43-52.
—. 'Foreign Fighter Total in Syria/Iraq Now Exceeds 20,000; Surpasses Afghanistan Conflict in the 1980s'. International Centre for the Study of Radicalisation, icsr.info/2015/01/foreign-fighter-total-syriairaq-now-exceeds-20000-surpasses-afghanistan-conflict-1980s/.
—. 'Prisons and Terrorism: Radicalisation and De-Radicalisation in 15 Countries'. 1-64. London: The International Centre for the Study of Radicalisation and Political Violence, 2010.
—. 'The Trouble with Radicalization'. *International Affairs* 89, no. 4 (July 2013): 873-93.
Neumann, Peter R., and M.L.R. Smith. 'Strategic Terrorism: The Framework and Its Fallacies'. *Journal of Strategic Studies* 28, no. 4 (2005): 571-95.
—. *The Strategy of Terrorism: How It Works, and Why It Fails*. London/New York: Routledge, 2008.
Newman, Edward. 'Exploring the "Root Causes" of Terrorism'. *Studies in Conflict & Terrorism* 29, no. 8 (2006): 749-72.
Noivo, Diogo. 'Jihadism in Portugal: Grasping a Nebulous Reality'. 1-9. Madrid: Real Instituto Elcano, 2010.

Oleson, Thomas, and Fahrad Khosrokhavar. *Islamism as Social Movement*. Aarhus: The Centre for Studies in Islamism and Radicalisation, 2009.
Ongering, Lidewijde. 'Home-Grown Terrorism and Radicalisation in the Netherlands: Experiences, Explanations and Approaches'. In *Testimony to the U.S. Senate Homeland Security and Governmental Affairs Committee*, 1-10. Washington, DC: U.S. Senate Homeland Security and Governmental Affairs Committee, 2007.
Oostveen, Margriet. 'De Knip-En-Plak-Islam; Hoe Jonge Moslims in Nederland Hun Radicale Wereldbeeld Samenstellen'. *NRC Handelsblad*, 27 November 2004, 1-5.

Orsini, Alessandro. 'A Day among the Diehard Terrorists: The Psychological Costs of Doing Ethnographic Research'. *Studies in Conflict & Terrorism* 36, no. 4 (2013): 337-51.

Ozer, Murat. 'The Impact of Group Dynamics on Terrorist Decision Making'. In *Understanding Terrorism: Analysis of Sociological and Psychological Aspects*, edited by Suleyman Ozeren, Ismail Dincer Gunes and Diab M. Al-Badayneh, 63-75. Amsterdam: IOS Press, 2007.

Pape, Robert A. *Dying to Win: The Strategic Logic of Suicide Terrorism*. New York: Random House, 2006.

—. 'The Strategic Logic of Suicide Terrorism'. *American Political Science Review* 97, no. 3 (August 2003): 1-19.

Patel, Faiza. 'Rethinking Radicalization'. 1-55. New York: Brennan Center for Justice, 2011.

Pauwels, Lieven, and Nele Schils. 'Differential Online Exposure to Extremist Content and Political Violence: Testing the Relative Strength of Social Learning and Competing Perspectives'. *Terrorism and Political Violence* 28, no. 1 (2016): 1-29.

Pearce, Susanna. 'Religious Sources of Violence'. In *The Making of a Terrorist: Recruitment, Training and Root Causes, Volume Three, Root Causes*, edited by James J.F. Forest, 109-25. Westport/London: Praeger Security International, 2006.

Pedahzur, Ami. *Suicide Terrorism*. Cambridge/Malden: Polity Press, 2005.

Pedahzur, Ami, Arie Perliger, and Leonard Weinberg. 'Altruism and Fatalism: The Characteristics of Palestinian Suicide Terrorists'. *Deviant Behavior* 24, no. 4 (2003): 405-23.

Peters, Ruud. 'Dutch Extremist Islamism: Van Gogh's Murderer and His Ideas'. In *Jihadi Terrorism and the Radicalisation Challenge: European and American Experiences*, edited by Rik Coolsaet, 145-59. Farnham/Burlington: Ashgate, 2011.

Petraeus, David H., and James F. Amos. 'FM 3-24: Counterinsurgency'. Washington, D.C.: Headquarters Department of the Army, 2006.

Phalet, Karen, Jessika Ter Wal, and Carlo Van Praag. 'Moslim in Nederland: Een Onderzoek Naar De Religieuze Betrokkenheid Van Turken En Marokkanen'. 1-50. The Hague: Sociaal en Cultureel Planbureau, 2004.

Piazza, James A. 'Do Democracy and Free Markets Protect Us from Terrorism?' *International Politics* 45, no. 1 (2008): 72-91.

—. 'Draining the Swamp: Democracy Promotion, State Failure, and Terrorism in 19 Middle Eastern Countries'. *Studies in Conflict & Terrorism* 30, no. 6 (June 2007): 521-39.

—. 'Poverty, Minority Economic Discrimination, and Domestic Terrorism'. *Journal of Peace Research* 48, no. 3 (2011): 339-53.

—. 'Rooted in Poverty?: Terrorism, Poor Economic Development, and Social Cleavages'. *Terrorism and Political Violence* 18, no. 1 (2006): 159-77.

Porter, Louise E., and Mark R. Kebbell. 'Radicalization in Australia: Examining Australia's Convicted Terrorists'. *Psychiatry, Psychology and Law* 18, no. 2 (May 2011): 212-31.

Post, Jerrold M. 'The Socio-Cultural Underpinnings of Terrorist Psychology: When Hatred Is Bred in the Bone'. In *Root Causes of Terrorism: Myths, Reality and Ways Forward*, edited by Tore Bjørgo, 54-69. London/New York: Routledge, 2005.

—. 'Terrorist Psycho-Logic: Terrorist Behavior as a Product of Psychological Forces'. In *Origins of Terrorism: Psychologies, Ideologies, Theologies, States of Mind*, edited by Walter Reich, 25-40. Washington, D.C.: Woodrow Wilson Center Press, 1990.

Post, Jerrold M., and Anat Berko. 'Talking with Terrorists'. *Democracy and Security* 5, no. 2 (2009): 145-48.

Post, Jerrold, Ehud Sprinzak, and Laurita Denny. 'The Terrorists in Their Own Words: Interviews with 35 Incarcerated Middle Eastern Terrorists'. *Terrorism and Political Violence* 15, no. 1 (2003): 171-84.

Postmes, Tom, and Russell Spears. 'Deindividuation and Antinormative Behavior: A Meta-Analysis'. *Psychological Bulletin* 123, no. 3 (May 1998): 238-59.

Pratto, Felicia, Jim Sidanius, Lisa M. Stallworth, and Bertram F. Malle. 'Social Dominance Orientation: A Personality Variable Predicting Social and Political Attitudes'. *Journal of Personality and Social Psychology* 67, no. 4 (1994): 741-63.

'Psychisch Onderzoek Naar Samir A. Levert Niets Op'. *de Volkskrant*, 13 December 2004.

Pynchon, Marisa Reddy, and Randy Borum. 'Assessing Threats of Targeted Group Violence: Contributions from Social Psychology'. *Behavioral Sciences and the Law* 17, no. 3 (July/September 1999): 339-55.

Pyszczynski, Tom, Matt Motyl, and Abdolhossein Abdollahi. 'Righteous Violence: Killing for God, Country, Freedom and Justice'. *Behavioral Sciences of Terrorism and Political Aggression* 1, no. 1 (2009): 12-39.

Quiggin, Tom. 'Words Matter: Peer Review as a Failing Safeguard'. *Perspectives on Terrorism* 7, no. 2 (April 2013): 71-81.

Rabasa, Angel, and Cheryl Benard. *Eurojihad: Patterns of Islamist Radicalization and Terrorism in Europe*. New York: Cambridge University Press, 2015.

Ranstorp, Magnus. 'Mapping Terrorism Studies after 9/11: An Academic Field of Old Problems and New Prospects'. In *Critical Terrorism Studies: A New Research Agenda*, edited by Richard Jackson, Marie Breen Smyth and Jeroen Gunning, 13-33. New York/Abingdon: Routledge, 2009.

'Rechter Wil Meer Getuigen, Zaak Samir A. Vertraagd'. *NRC Handelsblad*, 25 February 2005.

Reich, Walter. 'Understanding Terrorist Behavior: The Limits and Opportunities of Psychological Inquiry'. In *Origins of Terrorism: Psychologies, Ideologies, Theologies, States of Mind*, edited by Walter Reich, 261-79. Washington, D.C.: Woodrow Wilson Center Press, 1990.

Reicher, Stephen. 'The Psychology of Crowd Dynamics'. In *Blackwell Handbook of Social Psychology: Group Processes*, edited by Michael A. Hogg and R. Scott Tindale, 182-208. Malden/Oxford: Blackwell Publishers, 2001.

Reid, Edna F., and Hsinchun Chen. 'Mapping the Contemporary Terrorism Research Domain'. *International Journal of Human-Computer Studies* 65, no. 1 (January 2007): 42-56.

Robison, Kristopher K., Edward M. Crenshaw, and J. Craig Jenkins. 'Ideologies of Violence: The Social Origins of Islamist and Leftist Transnational Terrorism'. *Social Forces* 84, no. 4 (June 2006): 2009-26.

Roex, Ineke, Sjef Van Stiphout, and Jean Tillie. 'Salafisme in Nederland: Aard, Omvang En Dreiging'. 1-415. Amsterdam: Institute for Migration & Ethnic Studies, University of Amsterdam, 2010.

Rogers, Brooke. 'The Psychology of Violent Radicalisation'. In *The Psychology of Counter-Terrorism*, edited by Andrew Silke, 34-47. London/New York: Routledge, 2011.

Rose, William, Rysia Murphy, and Max Abrahms. 'Does Terrorism Ever Work? The 2004 Madrid Train Bombings'. *International Security* 32, no. 1 (Summer 2007): 185-92.

Ross, Jeffrey Ian. 'A Model of the Psychological Causes of Oppositional Political Terrorism'. *Peace and Conflict* 2, no. 2 (1996): 129-41.

———. 'Structural Causes of Oppositional Political Terrorism: Towards a Causal Model'. *Journal of Peace Research* 30, no. 3 (August 1993): 317-29.

Rourke, John T. *International Politics on the World Stage*. Boston: McGraw-Hill, 2008.

Roy, Olivier. 'Al-Qaeda: A True Global Movement'. In *Jihadi Terrorism and the Radicalisation Challenge: European and American Experiences*, edited by Rik Coolsaet, 19-26. Farnham/Burlington: Ashgate, 2011.

—. 'Euro-Islam: De Jihad Van Binnenuit?' *Justitiële Verkenningen* 31, no. 2 (2005): 28-46.

Royal Netherlands Academy of Arts and Sciences. *Gedragscode Voor Gebruik Van Persoonsgegevens in Wetenschappelijk Onderzoek*. Amsterdam: Royal Netherlands Academy of Arts and Sciences, 2003.

Ruby, Charles L. 'Are Terrorists Mentally Deranged?' *Analyses of Social Issues and Public Policy* 2, no. 1 (November 2002): 15-26.

Russell, Gordon W. 'Sport Riots: A Social-Psychological Review'. *Aggression and Violent Behavior* 9, no. 4 (July 2004): 353-78.

Sageman, Marc. 'Confronting Al-Qaeda: Understanding the Threat in Afghanistan'. *Perspectives on Terrorism* 3, no. 4 (December 2009): 4-25.

—. *Leaderless Jihad: Terror Networks in the Twenty-First Century*. Philadelphia: University of Pennsylvania Press, 2008.

—. 'Low Return on Investment'. *Terrorism and Political Violence* 26, no. 4 (2014): 614-20.

—. 'The Next Generation of Terror'. *Foreign Policy*, no. 165 (March/April 2008): 37-42.

—. 'The Stagnation in Terrorism Research'. *Terrorism and Political Violence* 26, no. 4 (2014): 565-80.

—. 'The Turn to Political Violence in the West'. In *Jihadi Terrorism and the Radicalisation Challenge: European and American Experiences*, edited by Rik Coolsaet, 117-29. Farnham/Burlington: Ashgate, 2011.

—. *Turning to Political Violence: The Emergence of Terrorism*. Philadelphia: University of Pennsylvania Press, 2017.

—. *Understanding Terror Networks*. Philadelphia: University of Pennsylvania Press, 2004.

'Saleh B. Niet Meer Verdacht Van Terroristische Daden'. *NRC Handelsbad*, 9 March 2006, 2.

Sánchez-Cuenca, Ignacio. 'Why Do We Know So Little About Terrorism?' *International Interactions* 40, no. 4 (2014): 590-601.

Sandler, Todd, and Walter Enders. 'An Economic Perspective on Transnational Terrorism'. *European Journal of Political Economy* 20, no. 2 (June 2004): 301-16.

Savun, Burcu, and Brian J. Phillips. 'Democracy, Foreign Policy, and Terrorism'. *Journal of Conflict Resolution* 53, no. 6 (December 2009): 878-904.

Schanzer, David H. 'No Easy Day: Government Roadblocks and the Unsolvable Problem of Political Violence: A Response to Marc Sageman's "the Stagnation in Terrorism Research"'. *Terrorism and Political Violence* 26, no. 4 (2014): 596-600.

Schbley, Ayla. 'Torn between God, Family, and Money: The Changing Profile of Lebanon's Religious Terrorists'. *Studies in Conflict & Terrorism* 23, no. 3 (2000): 175-96.

Schmid, Alex P. 'The Definition of Terrorism'. In *The Routledge Handbook of Terrorism Research*, edited by Alex P. Schmid, 39-98. London/New York: Routledge, 2011.

—. 'The Literature on Terrorism'. Chapter 8 In *The Routledge Handbook of Terrorism Research*, edited by Alex P. Schmid, 457-74. London/New York: Routledge, 2011.

—. 'Radicalisation, De-Radicalisation, Counter-Radicalisation: A Conceptual Discussion and Literature Review'. In *ICCT Research Paper*, 1-91. The Hague: International Centre for Counter-Terrorism, 2013.

—. 'Terrorism as Psychological Warfare'. *Democracy and Security* 1, no. 2 (2005): 137-46.

Schmid, Alex P., and Albert J. Jongman. *Political Terrorism: A New Guide to Actors, Authors, Concepts, Data Bases, Theories, and Literature*. New Brunswick: Transaction Books, 1988.

Schulze, Frederick. 'Breaking the Cycle: Empirical Research and Postgraduate Studies on Terrorism'. In *Research on Terrorism: Trends, Achievements and Failures*, edited by Andrew Silke, 161-85. London/New York: Frank Cass, 2004.

Schuurman, Bart. 'Defeated by Popular Demand: Public Support and Counterterrorism in Three Western Democracies, 1963-1998'. *Studies in Conflict & Terrorism* 36, no. 2 (2013): 152-75.

Schuurman, Bart, Edwin Bakker, and Quirine Eijkman. 'Structural Influences on Involvement in European Homegrown Jihadism: A Case Study'. *Terrorism and Political Violence* 30, no. 1 (2018): 97-115.

Schuurman, Bart, and Quirine Eijkman. 'Moving Terrorism Research Forward: The Crucial Role of Primary Sources'. In *ICCT Background Note*, 1-13. The Hague: International Centre for Counter-Terrorism, 2013.

Schuurman, Bart, Quirine Eijkman, and Edwin Bakker. 'A History of the Hofstadgroup'. *Perspectives on Terrorism* 8, no. 3 (June 2014): 65-81.

—. 'The Hofstadgroup Revisited: Questioning Its Status as a "Quintessential" Homegrown Jihadist Network'. *Terrorism and Political Violence* 27, no. 5 (2015): 906-25.

Schuurman, Bart, and John G. Horgan. 'Rationales for Terrorist Violence in Homegrown Jihadist Groups: A Case Study from the Netherlands'. *Aggression and Violent Behavior* 27 (March-April 2016): 55-63.

Schwartz, Seth J., Curtis S. Dunkel, and Alan S. Waterman. 'Terrorism: An Identity Theory Perspective'. *Studies in Conflict & Terrorism* 32, no. 6 (2009): 537-59.

Scott, John. 'Rational Choice Theory'. In *Understanding Contemporary Society: Theories of the Present*, edited by Gary Browning, Abigail Halcli and Frank Webster, 126-38. London: Sage, 2000.

Sedgwick, Mark. 'The Concept of Radicalization as a Source of Confusion'. *Terrorism and Political Violence* 22, no. 4 (2010): 479-94.

Sellers, Christine S., John K. Cochran, and L. Thomas. Winfree, Jr. 'Social Learning Theory and Courtship Violence: An Empirical Test'. In *Social Learning Theory and the Explanation of Crime*, edited by Ronald L. Akers and Gary F. Jensen, 109-28. New Brunswick: Transaction Publishers, 2007.

Senechal de la Roche, Roberta. 'Collective Violence as Social Control'. *Sociological Forum* 11, no. 1 (March 1996): 97-128.

Shapiro, Jacob N. 'Terrorist Decision Making: Insights from Economics and Political Science'. *Perspectives on Terrorism* 6, no. 4-5 (October 2012): 5-20.

Shughart, William F., II. 'Terrorism in Rational Choice Perspective'. In *The Handbook on the Political Economy of War*, edited by Christopher J. Coyne and Rachel L. Mathers, 126-53. Cheltenham/Northampton: Edward Elgar, 2011.

Silber, Mitchell D. *The Al Qaeda Factor: Plots against the West*. Philadelphia: University of Pennsylvania Press, 2012.

Silber, Mitchell D., and Arvin Bhatt. 'Radicalization in the West: The Homegrown Threat'. 1-90. New York: New York Police Department, 2007.

Silke, Andrew. 'Cheshire-Cat Logic: The Recurring Theme of Terrorist Abnormality in Psychological Research'. *Psychology, Crime & Law* 4, no. 1 (1998): 51-69.

—. 'Contemporary Terrorism Studies: Issues in Research'. In *Critical Terrorism Studies: A New Research Agenda*, edited by Richard Jackson, Marie Breen Smyth and Jeroen Gunning, 34-48. New York/Abingdon: Routledge, 2009.

—. 'Deindividuation, Anonymity, and Violence: Findings from Northern Ireland'. *The Journal of Social Psychology* 143, no. 4 (2003): 493-99.

—. 'The Devil You Know: Continuing Problems with Research on Terrorism'. *Terrorism and Political Violence* 13, no. 4 (December 2001): 1-14.
—. 'Holy Warriors: Exploring the Psychological Processes of Jihadi Radicalization'. *European Journal of Criminology* 5, no. 1 (2008): 99-123.
—. 'The Impact of 9/11 on Research on Terrorism'. In *Mapping Terrorism Research: State of the Art, Gaps and Future Directions*, edited by Magnus Ranstorp, 76-93. New York/Abingdon: Routledge, 2007.
—. 'The Internet & Terrorist Radicalisation: The Psychological Dimension'. In *Terrorism and the Internet: Threats – Target Groups – Deradicalisation Strategies*, edited by Hans-Liudger Dienel, Yair Sharan, Christian Rapp and Niv Ahituv, 27-40. Amsterdam: IOS Press, 2010.
—. 'An Introduction to Terrorism Research'. In *Research on Terrorism: Trends, Achievements and Failures*, edited by Andrew Silke, 1-29. London/New York: Frank Cass, 2004.
—. *Terrorism: All That Matters*. London: Hodder & Stoughton, 2014.
Simon, Herbert A. 'Rationality in Political Behavior'. *Political Psychology* 16, no. 1 (March 1995): 45-61.
Sinai, Joshua. 'New Trends in Terrorism Studies: Strengths and Weaknesses'. In *Mapping Terrorism Research: State of the Art, Gaps and Future Directions*, edited by Magnus Ranstorp, 31-50. New York/Abingdon: Routledge, 2007.
Slootman, Marieke, and Jean Tillie. 'Processen Van Radicalisering: Waarom Sommige Amsterdamse Moslims Radicaal Worden'. 1-136. Amsterdam: Institute for Migration & Ethnic Studies, University of Amsterdam, 2006.
Sluka, Jeffrey A. *Hearts and Minds, Water and Fish: Support for the Ira and the Inla in a Northern Irish Ghetto*. Greenwich/London: JAI Press, 1989.
Smith, M.L.R. 'William of Ockham, Where Are You When We Need You? Reviewing Modern Terrorism Studies'. *Journal of Contemporary History* 44, no. 2 (2009): 319-34.
Spaaij, Ramón. 'The Enigma of Lone Wolf Terrorism: An Assessment'. *Studies in Conflict & Terrorism* 33, no. 9 (2010): 854-70.
'Spanje Ziet Band Met Nederland'. *NRC Handelsblad*, 17 November 2004.
Sprinzak, Ehud. 'The Process of Delegitimation: Towards a Linkage Theory of Political Terrorism'. *Terrorism and Political Violence* 3, no. 1 (1991): 50-68.
Spruyt, Bart Jan. '"Can't We Discuss This?" Liberalism and the Challenge of Islam in the Netherlands'. *Orbis* 51, no. 2 (2007): 313-30.
Stampnitzky, Lisa. *Disciplining Terror: How Experts Invented 'Terrorism'*. Cambridge: Cambridge University Press, 2014.
Stenersen, Anne. 'The Internet: A Virtual Training Camp?' *Terrorism and Political Violence* 20, no. 2 (2008): 215-33.
Stern, Jessica. 'Response to Marc Sageman's "the Stagnation in Terrorism Research"' *Terrorism and Political Violence* 26, no. 4 (2014): 607-13.
Stewart, David W., and Michael A. Kamins. 'Evaluating Secondary Sources'. In *Secondary Research: Information Sources and Methods*, edited by David W. Stewart and Michael A. Kamins, 17-32. Thousand Oaks: Sage, 1993.
Stewart, Frances. 'Crisis Prevention: Tackling Horizontal Inequalities'. *Oxford Development Studies* 28, no. 3 (2000): 245-62.

't Sas, Sander, and Jan Born. 'Hoofdofficier: Mohammed Bouyeri Handelde Niet Alleen'. In *EenVandaag*, 2014.
Tajfel, Henri. 'Social Identity and Intergroup Behaviour'. *Social Science Information* 13, no. 2 (1974): 65-93.

Tajfel, Henri, and John Turner. 'An Integrative Theory of Intergroup Conflict'. In *The Social Psychology of Intergroup Relations*, edited by W.G. Austin and S. Worchel, 33-47. Monterey: Brooks-Cole, 1979.

Tansey, Oisín. 'Process Tracing and Elite Interviewing: A Case for Non-Probability Sampling'. *Political Science & Politics* 40, no. 4 (October 2007): 765-72.

Tarrow, Sidney. *Power in Movement: Social Movements and Contentious Politics*. Cambridge: Cambridge University Press, 1998.

Taylor, Max. 'Conflict Resolution and Counter Radicalization: Where Do We Go from Here?' In *DIIS Religion and Violence*, 1-5. Copenhagen: Danish Institution for International Studies, 2012.

—. 'If I Were You, I Wouldn't Start from Here: Response to Marc Sageman's "the Stagnation in Terrorism Research"'. *Terrorism and Political Violence* 26, no. 4 (2014): 581-86.

—. 'Is Terrorism a Group Phenomenon?' *Aggression and Violent Behavior* 15, no. 2 (2010): 121-29.

Taylor, Max, and John Horgan. 'A Conceptual Framework for Addressing Psychological Process in the Development of the Terrorist'. *Terrorism and Political Violence* 18, no. 4 (2006): 585-601.

—. 'The Psychological and Behavioural Bases of Islamic Fundamentalism'. *Terrorism and Political Violence* 13, no. 4 (Winter 2001): 37-71.

Taylor, Maxwell. *The Fanatics: A Behavioural Approach to Political Violence*. London: Brassey's, 1991.

Taylor, Maxwell, and Ethel Quayle. *Terrorist Lives*. London: Brassey's, 1994.

'Terreurverdachten Hofstadgroep Na Tien Jaar Vrijgesproken'. *NRC Handelsblad*, 17 June 2015.

Testas, Abdelaziz. 'Determinants of Terrorism in the Muslim World: An Empirical Cross-Sectional Analysis'. *Terrorism and Political Violence* 16, no. 2 (2004): 253-73.

Tilly, Charles. *The Politics of Collective Violence*. Cambridge: Cambridge University Press, 2007.

Toros, Harmonie. 'Terrorists, Scholars and Ordinary People: Confronting Terrorism Studies with Field Experiences'. *Critical Studies on Terrorism* 1, no. 2 (2008): 272-92.

—. '"We Don't Negotiate with Terrorists!": Legitimacy and Complexity in Terrorist Conflicts'. *Security Dialogue* 39, no. 4 (August 2008): 407-26.

Tosini, Domenico. 'Calculated, Passionate, Pious Extremism: Beyond a Rational Choice Theory of Suicide Terrorism'. *Asian Journal of Social Science* 38, no. 3 (2010): 394-415.

Transnational Terrorism Security & the Rule of Law Project. 'The "Hofstadgroep"'. In *TTSRL Contextual Papers*, 1-20. The Hague: TTSRL, 2008.

Tse-Tung, Mao. *On Guerrilla Warfare*. edited by Samuel B. Griffith Mineola: Dover, 2005.

Tsintsadze-Maass, Eteri, and Richard M. Maass. 'Groupthink and Terrorist Radicalization'. *Terrorism and Political Violence* 26, no. 5 (2014): 735-58.

Turk, Austin T. 'Sociology of Terrorism'. *Annual Review of Sociology* 30 (August 2004): 271-86.

Turner, John. 'From Cottage Industry to International Organisation: The Evolution of Salafi-Jihadism and the Emergence of the Al Qaeda Ideology'. *Terrorism and Political Violence* 22, no. 4 (2010): 541-58.

'"U Wilt Misschien Wel Dat Wilders Doodgaat?"'. *NRC Handelsblad*, 24 November 2004.

Van der Hulst, Renée. 'Terroristische Netwerken En Intelligence: Een Sociale Netwerkanalyse Van De Hofstadgroep'. *Tijdschrift voor Veiligheid* 8, no. 2 (June 2009): 8-27.

Van der Laan, Cees. 'Donners Rigoureuze Maatregelen'. *Trouw*, 11 September 2003.

Van der Veen, Casper. 'Kijken: 10 Jaar Na De Aanslagen Van 7/7 in Londen Kijken Overlevenden Terug'. *NRC Handelsblad*, 7 July 2015.

Van der Woude, M.A.H. *Wetgeving in Een Veiligheidscultuur: Totstandkoming Van Antiterrorismewetgeving in Nederland Bezien Vanuit Maatschappelijke En (Rechts)Politieke Context*. The Hague: Boom Juridische Uitgevers, 2010.

Van San, Marion, Stijn Sieckelinck, and Micha De Winter. *Idealen Op Drift: Een Pedagogische Kijk Op Radicaliserende Jongeren*. The Hague: Boom, 2010.

Van Um, Eric. 'Discussing Concepts of Terrorist Rationality: Implications for Counterterrorism Policy'. *Defence and Peace Economics* 22, no. 2 (April 2011): 161-79.

Veldhuis, Tinka, and Edwin Bakker. 'Causale Factoren Van Radicalisering En Hun Onderlinge Samenhang'. *Vrede en Veiligheid* 36, no. 4 (2007): 447-70.

Veldhuis, Tinka, and Jørgen Staun. *Islamist Radicalisation: A Root Cause Model*. The Hague: Netherlands Institute of International Relations Clingendael, 2009.

Venhaus, John M. 'Why Youth Join Al-Qaeda'. In *Special Report 236*, 1-20. Washington, D.C.: United States Institute of Peace, 2010.

Vermaat, Emerson. *De Hofstadgroep: Portret Van Een Radicaal-Islamitisch Netwerk*. Soesterberg: Aspekt, 2005.

—. *Nederlandse Jihad: Het Proces Tegen De Hofstadgroep*. Soesterberg: Aspekt, 2006.

Victoroff, Jeff. 'The Mind of the Terrorist: A Review and Critique of Psychological Approaches'. *Journal of Conflict Resolution* 49, no. 1 (February 2005): 3-42.

Vidino, Lorenzo. *Al Qaeda in Europe: The New Battleground of International Jihad*. New York: Prometheus Books, 2006.

—. 'European Foreign Fighters in Syria: Dynamics and Responses'. *European View* 13, no. 2 (December 2014): 217-24.

—. 'The Hofstad Group: The New Face Terrorist Networks in Europe'. *Studies in Conflict & Terrorism* 30, no. 7 (2007): 579-92.

—. 'Radicalization, Linkage, and Diversity: Current Trends in Terrorism in Europe'. 1-49. Santa Monica: RAND Corporation, 2011.

Vidino, Lorenzo, and James Brandon. 'Countering Radicalization in Europe'. 1-80. London: The International Centre for the Study of Radicalisation and Political Violence, 2012.

Von Clausewitz, Carl. *On War*. New York: Everyman's Library, 1993.

Von Hippel, Karin. 'The Roots of Terrorism: Probing the Myths'. *The Political Quarterly* 73, no. Supplement 1 (August 2002): 25-39.

Von Knop, Katharina. 'The Female Jihad: Al Qaeda's Women'. *Studies in Conflict & Terrorism* 30, no. 5 (2007): 397-414.

Weenink, Anton, and Shuki Cohen. 'Trends in Terrorisme. Een Onderzoek Naar De Betrouwbaarheid Van De Global Terrorism Database'. In *NVC Congres 2014*. Leiden: Nederlandse Vereniging voor Criminologie, 2014.

Weenink, Anton W. 'Behavioral Problems and Disorders among Radicals in Police Files'. *Perspectives on Terrorism* 9, no. 2 (April 2015): 17-33.

Weinberg, Leonard. 'The Red Brigades'. In *Democracy and Counterterrorism: Lessons from the Past*, edited by Robert J. Art and Louise Richardson, 25-62. Washington, D.C.: United States Institute of Peace Press, 2007.

Weinberg, Leonard, Ami Pedahzur, and Sivan Hirsch-Hoefler. 'The Challenges of Conceptualizing Terrorism'. *Terrorism and Political Violence* 16, no. 4 (2004): 777-94.

Wessels, M. *De Radicaal-Islamitische Ideologie Van De Hofstadgroep: De Inhoud En De Bronnen*. The Hague: Teldersstichting, 2006.

Wiktorowicz, Quintan. 'Anatomy of the Salafi Movement'. *Studies in Conflict & Terrorism* 29, no. 3 (2006): 207-39.

—. 'Joining the Cause: Al-Muhajiroun and Radical Islam'. In *The Roots of Islamic Radicalism*, 1-29. Yale University, United States 2004.

Wilkinson, Paul. 'International Terrorism: The Changing Threat and the EU's Response'. In *Chaillot Papers*, 1-57: European Union Institute for Security Studies, 2005.

Willems, Marije. 'Zaak Tegen Terrorismeverdachte Soumaya S. Moet Over'. *NRC Handelsblad*, 15 November 2011.

Wilner, Alex S., and Claire-Jehanne Dubouloz. 'Transformative Radicalization: Applying Learning Theory to Islamist Radicalization'. *Studies in Conflict & Terrorism* 34, no. 5 (2011): 418-38.

Winston, Bruce E., and Kathleen Patterson. 'An Integrative Definition of Leadership'. *International Journal of Leadership Studies* 1, no. 2 (2006): 6-66.

Wubbels, Eline. 'Mohammed B. Strijdt Verder'. http://www.kennislink.nl/publicaties/mohammed-b-strijdt-verder.

Zhang, Yan, and Barbara M. Wildemuth. 'Unstructured Interviews'. In *Applications of Social Research Methods to Questions in Information and Library Science*, edited by Barbara M. Wildemuth, 222-31. Westport, CT: Libraries Unlimited, 2009.

Index

2000
    June, arrest of Van Gogh's future murderer for fighting 207

2001
    9/11 attacks 15, 37, 55, 78, 116, 169, 182, 219
    December, mother of Van Gogh's future murderer dies 180, 183
    July, Van Gogh's future murderer imprisoned for violence 183
    July, Van Gogh's future murderer stabs police officer 183, 207

2002
    first signs of Hofstadgroup 56
    Hofstadgroup participant supports mass-casualty bombing 57

2003
    attempted travel to Afghanistan 57, 59
    attempted travel to Chechnya 57
    ideological radicalization murderer of Van Gogh 59-60
    October arrests 13, 59-60, 79, 84, 111
    October, future murderer of Van Gogh travels to Denmark 60
    October, surreptitious telephone conversations 58-59, 79
    October, travel to Belgium 58
    October, travel to Spain for meeting with potential GICM member 58
    overseas connections emerge 58, 79
    Ramadan as potential time for an attack 58
    recruitment activities 59, 79
    September, AIVD designates Hofstadgroup 56

2004
    absence of communal activities 60
    April, supermarket robbery Rotterdam 61, 109
    August, broadcast of *Submission, part 1* 63, 86, 108, 115, 120, 211
    August, online threats against Hirsi Ali & Van Gogh 63-64, 120
    June, AIVD mole begins leaking to group 63
    June, arrest of Hofstadgroup ringleader 61-62, 92
    June, inquiries into buying fertilizer 62, 92
    June, Portugal traveler warns police of takfiri friend 62
    May, Van Gogh's future murderer threatens social services employee 207
    mother of participants feels threatened 62-63
    November, arrest for threatening Geert Wilders online 64
    November, arrest of Van Gogh's murderer 13, 65
    November, arrests of suspected Hofstadgroup members 66
    November, hand grenade incident 14, 67, 92-93
    November, murder of Van Gogh 13, 64-65
    November, participant evades arrest 66
    Return from attempted travel to Afghanistan 59
    September, arrest of author of online threats 64
    September, arrest of Yehya Kaddouri 22, 203
    September, Van Gogh's future murderer arrested on public transport 207

2005
    April, emergence Piranha group 68
    April, release from prison of Hofstadgroup ringleader 68
    July, potential explosives test 71
    July, trial against Van Gogh's murderer concludes 74
    May, signs of renewed interest terrorist attacks 69
    October, arrests of Piranha suspects 73
    October, attempted weapons deal 72-73
    October, videotaped will / threats 73, 143, 158, 162, 189
    September, meeting with Belgian national who allegedly offered suicide bombers 104-105

2006
    March, first verdict against Hofstadgroup suspects 74
    verdict in Piranha case 75

2008
    acquittal of several suspects 74
    October, appeals hearing Piranha case 75

2010
    December, verdicts in Hofstadgroup case 74
    February, Supreme Court orders retrial 74

2011
    Supreme Court orders retrials in Piranha case 75

2014
    March, convictions in Piranha case 75

2015
    June, verdicts in Hofstadgroup case 75

Abu Khaled 31, 56, 59-60, 66, 78, 82, 85, 89, 128, 140, 151, 166, 174-175, 183, 223
    alleged ties to al-Qaeda 103
    as asylum seeker in Germany 78
    involvement in murder of Van Gogh 66, 151
    position within the group 89-90, 151, 175
    teachings 85, 128, 151
    travel to Syria 66
adventure *see* involvement in terrorism

Afghanistan 15, 55, 57-58, 79, 84, 98, 100-101, 104-105, 110, 115, 117-118, 126-127, 134, 158, 162, 203, 208, 219
    jihadi veterans 55
Agram 2000 see weapons
AIVD 13-14, 23-24, 28-29, 57-58, 61-63, 66, 68-69, 71- 73, 87, 91-93, 103, 105, 108-109, 118, 121, 135, 164, 175, 211
    as potential target 61, 92, 164, 210-211
    assessment of Van Gogh's murderer 13, 24, 66, 108, 121
    informants (alleged) 61, 73, 104, 109
    investigation into Hofstadgroup 23-24, 56, 110-111
    leaks to Hofstadgroup 63
    tip to Portuguese authorities 62
al-Durrah, Muhammad 182
al-Qaeda 15, 21, 37, 53, 55, 78, 81-82, 103, 126, 201
al-Qaeda in Iraq (AQI) 83, 138
al-Shuebi, Hamoud al-Aqla 116
al-Zarqawi, Abu Musab 83, 138, 141, 145, 153, 165, 189
al-Zawahiri, Ayman 189
Amsterdam 13, 15, 23, 56, 58, 60, 63-64, 70-72, 74-75, 88, 93, 108, 180, 207
    shooting practice 70
Amsterdam Lelylaan arrests (2005)
    See Hofstadgroup: arrests
anonymization see methodology
Ansar al-Islam see 2003: October, travel to Spain for meeting with potential GICM member
apostasy 62-63, 81-82, 102, 191, 213
Arab European League (AEL) 111
Article 140a (Dutch Criminal Code) 74
Asal, Victor 148
Asch, Solomon E. 142
as-Soennah mosque (The Hague)
    sermon on Van Gogh & Hirsi Ali 153

Bakker, Edwin 112, 204-205
Bandura, Albert 186
Barcelona 58
Barroso, José 21, 62
BBE-SIE see special forces deployment
Beck, Colin J. 48
Belgium 58, 66, 72, 110
    2005 suicide terrorism plot see Hofstadgroup
    Brussels 66
    Brussels safe house 69, 90
Berkowitz, Leonard 209-210
Bhatt, Arvin 172
bin Laden, Osama 15, 83, 85, 103, 115, 138, 141, 145, 153, 162, 165-166, 189
biographical availability 182
blaming the victims 187
Blazak, Randy 125
blood price (of involvement in terrorism) 142
Borssele (the Netherlands)
    nuclear reactor 61

Borum, Randy 41, 141, 149, 169
Bosnia
    jihadi veterans 55
Boston College controversy 39
bottom-up group formation 125-126
bounded rationality 154
Brigades of the Islamic Jihad 89
Buijs, Frank 23, 171
bulletproof vest 61, 65
Bunch of Guys (concept) see Sageman, Marc
Bush, George W. 183, 189

Casablanca bombings see terrorism
Chechnya 57-58, 61-62, 78, 84-85, 117, 138, 158, 175-176, 179, 182, 188, 201, 210, 212-215
clash of civilizations 118
Cliteur, Paul 22
coercion by Hofstadgroup participants
    See Hofstadgroup: recruitment activities
cognition 170
cognitive dissonance see involvement in terrorism
cognitive openings see involvement in terrorism
competition of piety 132
copycat behavior 163
Corner, Emily 197
cost-benefit analysis 157
counterterrorism 21, 39, 74, 107-109, 126
    impact on Hofstadgroup 163
    measures taken by Dutch authorities 21, 60
court cases 74-75
    hearing of alleged AIVD informant 109
    key witnesses for the prosecution 69, 128
Crenshaw, Martha 35, 42-44, 46, 87, 91, 97-98, 107, 120, 124, 14- 142, 169
Crimes of Terrorism Act (2004) 74, 163-164
crime-terror nexus 98
critical terrorism studies see terrorism research
Crone, Manni 53, 78
CTIVD 23-24, 66, 108
cut-and-paste Islam 130

Daesh see Islamic State
Dalgaard-Nielsen, Anja 129, 172
declaration of war on terrorism by Dutch Prime Minister (2004) 164
defining terrorist organizations 87
Definition of terrorism see terrorism research
    dehumanization 187, 190, 192, 221
De Koning, Martijn 20, 132, 165
Della Porta, Donatella 41, 125, 132, 161, 205, 224
Demant, Froukje 171
Denmark 60
    Syrian preacher affiliated with Hofstadgroup 60
De Poot, Christianne 22
differential association 136
discrimination see involvement in terrorism
Doosje, Bertjan 206

effects of imprisonment 163
Egypt 82, 85
El-Al airline plot *see* Hofstadgroup: terrorist plots
essentialist thinking 187
ethics (research) 31
Europe 15-18, 21, 24, 26, 62, 85, 106, 112, 117-118, 126, 138, 204, 210, 217-218, 222, 224, 226-228, 231
  immigration policies 21
European soccer championships (2004) 62
execution videos 138
expressionist tradition of terrorism 203
extremity shift 142-143, 146

Fair, C. Christine 112
Fanaticism (concept) *see* involvement in terrorism
far enemy 81
FBI 78, 103
Fearon, James D. 118
foreign fighters 16, 57, 84, 90, 95, 105, 111, 121, 126, 218-219
  2002 deaths of two Dutch men in Kashmir 56
  Hofstadgroup attempts to travel abroad 84, 105, 117-118
  returnees (threat of) 16
Fortuyn, Pim 55, 114
Freud, Sigmund 198

General Intelligence and Security Service *see* AIVD
GICM 58
Gill, Paul 197
governmentality 20
Groen, Janny 19, 72, 163, 202
groupthink *see* involvement in terrorism
Guantanamo Bay 103
Gurr, Ted Robert 113, 209

Hamas 156, 201
hand grenades *see* weapons
Harrow, Martin 53, 78
Hirsi Ali, Ayaan 13, 63-64, 68, 70, 74, 86, 104, 108, 116, 153, 201, 211
  as target of 2005 plot 68, 70
  online threats 63-64, 120
  Zomergasten (TV program) 63
Hofstadgroup
  2005 offer of assistance with suicide plot (Belgian connection) 104-105
  activities, overview of 55-76
  anger & frustration (roles of) 212
  arrests of 13, 28, 58, 60-62, 66, 70, 84, 111
  as clash of value systems 118-119
  as homegrown jihadist group 78-79
  attitudes towards Van Gogh 86, 115-116, 120
  benefits group membership (social identity) 131
  cognitive dissonance 188

converts 119, 183, 202, 208
costs of involvement 188
criminal connections 71
democracy (views on) 101, 111, 119, 143, 190
discrimination 114-115, 121, 163, 220, 223
Dutch debate on Islam 115, 165
Dutch foreign policy 55, 73, 84, 86, 118
emir (from Pakistan / Afghanistan) 58-59, 79, 104, 152
emulation of role models 138-139, 141, 145, 154, 158, 162, 166, 219-220, 224
existing literature on 18-24, 55
geopolitical factors 182, 190, 210
group formation 100-101, 126-128
ideological materials 61, 82, 138
ideology 14, 64, 82-87, 130, 132-133, 149
injustice 101, 116, 118, 158, 189, 201-202, 208, 210-211, 214-215, 221-222, 224, 229
Internet (role of) 100-101, 110, 121, 127, 138-139, 153, 182-183, 201, 219
intimidation 144
journalistic accounts 18-19
justifications for violence 86-87, 132-133, 145, 151-153, 182, 189, 202
leaders 23-24, 89-90, 151-153, 187, 220
meetings 56, 58, 71-72, 90, 137-139, 144
mental health evaluations 197-198
name, origins of 13, 56
number of participants 77
operational security 72, 131
organizational rationales for terrorism 161-166
paramilitary training 59, 105, 148, 158-159
paranoia 60, 111, 135
personal motives for terrorism 69, 162, 164, 175, 211
Piranha case 15, 68-74, 86
primary-sources based research 19-20
protests, involvement in 111
radicalization 174-177
recruitment activities 59, 69-70, 79, 100-101, 104, 144
relation with Dutch Salafism 212
relevance as case study 17-18, 218
sect-like qualities 85-87, 144, 225
sex and relationships 131
Shiism (views on) 111
social / cultural facilitation of violence 106-107
societal impact 14
takfir 62, 85, 87, 101, 144, 176
terrorist plots 21, 57, 61, 64-65, 69-70, 92-94
ties to Casablanca bombings suspect 58, 104
ties to foreign extremists 78-79, 103-105
ties to radical Dutch convert preacher 152-153
travel abroad 57-58, 79, 84, 105, 110
vicarious deprivation 116, 118, 182, 210, 212, 219

videotaped will / threats (2005) 73, 84, 86, 143, 158, 162, 179-180, 201
wills 14, 59, 61, 67
women (roles of) 19, 144-145, 202
homegrown jihadism *see* jihad
hooliganism 149
Horgan, John 44, 124, 147, 171-172, 199, 206
House of Representatives 61, 64
Huntington, Samuel P. 118

ibn Abd al-Wahhab, Muhammad 138
ibn Taymiyya, Ahmad 64, 82, 86, 153
identity-related alienation *see* involvement in terrorism
ideology *see* involvement in terrorism idolatry 81, 191
Internet, role of *see* involvement in terrorism
interview *see* methodology
intifada 126, 182
involvement in terrorism
 adventurism 159, 208, 214, 222
 authorization of violence 150-154
 benefits group membership (social identity) 129-131
 clash of value systems 118-119
 cognitive dissonance 185-189
 cognitive openings 181-185
 diffusion of responsibility 149-150
 discrimination 23, 114-115
 emotions (role of) 209-212
 external assistance 102-105
 facilitating and motivating conditions 42-43, 97-98
 Fanaticism (concept) 177-181
 frustration-aggression theory 209-210
 geopolitical factors 116-118
 group formation 125-128
 group influences that lower barriers to violence 149-154
 groupthink 159-160
 identity-related alienation 200-203
 ideology 79-82
 Internet 99-101
 involvement versus event decisions 25, 44-45, 124, 147, 224-225
 justification of violence 81, 186-191
 leaders 139-141, 150-154
 moral disengagement 185-190
 mortality salience 212-214
 narcissism-aggression theory 198
 omitted explanations *see* methodology
 peer pressures 141, 145
 political grievances 116-118
 political opportunity structure 109-112
 popular support 101-102
 precipitants 43, 98, 120

 profiles / personality characteristics 204-209
 psychoanalysis 198-199
 psychopathology 196-198
 (relative) deprivation 112-116
 role models 136-137
 significance quest 200-204
 slippery-slope mechanism 186
 social / cultural facilitation of violence 106-107
 socialization into violence 132-133
 social learning theory 136-139
 social solidarity 23
 social ties (role in involvement) 125-128
 socioeconomics 22, 42, 112-113, 121, 204-205, 219, 228
 spillover 98
 underground existence 133-136
 unfreezing 181-185, 192, 221
 urbanization 98
 vicarious deprivation 116, 118, 182, 210, 212
Iraq 15, 21, 58, 73, 83-86, 98, 100, 111, 114, 118, 126, 138, 158, 217-218
Islamic State (group) 15-16, 217-218
Israel 118
Israeli-Palestinian conflict 100, 116, 158, 175, 182, 184, 210, 223
Italy
 Red Brigades 102

jihad
 defensive jihad 84, 87, 117, 162
 definition of 52-53
 homegrown jihadism 15-17, 53, 55, 78, 112, 118, 217-218, 222, 227, 231
 international terrorist threat 15
 jihadist networks in the Netherlands 22
 lesser and greater jihad 53
 offensive jihad 84, 87
 ongoing threat 15-16, 217
Jongman, Berto 35-36

Kaddouri, Yehya 22, 203
Kashmir 56, 165
Kleinmann, Scott Matthew 123, 196
KLPD 27
Koopmans, Ruud 106-107
Kranenberg, Annieke 19, 72, 163, 202
Kruglanski, Arie 171, 200, 202
kuffar 190
Kundnani, Arun 173

Laitin, David D. 118
Lankford, Adam 196
Leaderless jihad (book) 123
Leidschendam 61
Leiken, Robert S. 102

levels of analysis 17, 20, 25-27, 32, 40-41, 97, 217, 223, 231
    group-level explanations 44-45, 123, 167
    individual-level explanations 45-47, 169-215
    rationale for multicausal approach 39-42, 47
    structural-level explanations 42-43, 97-121
Ligon, Gina Scott 88, 94
'Lions of Tawheed' 89
living room meetings see Hofstadgroup: meetings
Luxembourg 66

Madrid attacks (2004) see terrorism
Maikovich, Andrea Kohn 185
majority effect 142-143
martyrdom 13-14, 59, 65, 67, 69, 138-139, 162, 200
Maynard, Jonathan Leader 79
McCauley, Clark 142, 171, 181, 187, 204
McCormick, Gordon H. 203
Meijer, Roel 165
Merari, Ariel 199
methodology 25-27, 217-218
    anonymization 31
    case study research 17
    interviews 25, 27-31
    limitations 26, 47-48
    omitted explanations 46, 98-99
    police files 27-29, 31, 218
    transparency, issues with 29
    use of existing insights involvement in terrorism 26
Milgram, Stanley 150-151
millenarianism see Fanaticism (concept)
Ministry of Defense 61
Moghadam, Assaf 53
Moghaddam, Fathali M. 171
moral disengagement see involvement in terrorism
Moroccan Islamic Combatant Group see GICM
Morocco 62, 66, 72, 78, 107, 131, 184
    Al Hoceima 63
mortad 64, 190
mortality salience see involvement in terrorism
Moskalenko, Sophia 171, 181, 187
mujahedeen 85, 88
multiculturalism 15, 22, 114
munafiq 190
Munson, Ziad W. 182
murderer of Van Gogh
    as fanatic 179-181
    as role model 163
    attack planning and preparation 65
    changes in appearance 59-60
    Chechnyan connections 78-79, 103-104
    death of mother 162, 174, 180, 183, 201, 223
    history of violent behavior 207
    isolation 59, 180
    letter on body of Van Gogh 14, 64
    letter to family 161-162, 183, 189, 201
    mental health assessment 197-198, 207
    motives 21, 43, 60, 66, 86, 115, 151, 157-158, 161-162, 211
    November 2004 arrest 65
    open letters 65, 157, 165-166
    position within the group 89, 140
    radicalization 174
    shootout with police 64-65
    statement in court 157
    'Taliban' nickname 59-60
    teachings 140
    trial 74
    volunteer work 59
    will 14
    writings 86, 115, 151, 157
mushrik 190
Muslim Brotherhood 78, 82, 85, 103
Muwahhidin Brigade see Hirsi Ali, Ayaan: online threats

narcissism see involvement in terrorism
NCTV 23-24, 29
near enemy 81
Nesser, Petter 126, 205
network (jihadist) 87-88
Neumann, Peter 171-172
night-vision goggles 61

organizational rationales for terrorism 159-166
organizational structure and lethality 148-149

Pakistan 57-60, 79, 84, 101, 104-105, 110, 117, 127, 134, 152, 158, 162, 203, 208
Pape, Robert 156
paranoia see Hofstadgroup
Pedahzur, Ami 206
peer pressure see involvement in terrorism
Peters, Ruud 19, 60
Piazza, James 112
Pieter Baan Centre (PBC) 197, 207
Piranha group / case see Hofstadgroup
Polder Mujahideen 88
Police 13, 27, 57, 59
    injuries sustained during November 2004 arrests 14
    November 2004 attempted arrest in The Hague 67
police files see methodology
political access school (political opportunity structure) see involvement in terrorism
political correctness 22
politicos, purists, jihadists (Salafism) 81
Portugal 21, 62, 66
Post, Jerrold 199
Postmes, Tom 150

prank call to emergency services 67
precipitants *see* involvement in terrorism
primary sources *see* terrorism research
profiles (of terrorists) *see* involvement in terrorism
Prosecutor General (Dutch) 27
psychopathology *see* involvement in terrorism
Public Prosecution Service (Dutch) 58
Pynchon, Marisa Reddy 141

Qutb, Sayyid 82, 138

radicalism
    definition of 51-52
radicalization 46, 171-177
rational choice theory 154-156
rationality of terrorism 154
recruitment *see* Hofstadgroup
Reich, Walter 35
relevant arguments 142
Roex, Ineke 23
Roosendaal 61
Rotterdam 74-75
    April 2004 supermarket robbery 61, 109
Russia 57

Sageman, Marc 16, 36-37, 80, 87, 94, 112, 123, 205
    Bunch of Guys (concept) 226
Salafi-Jihadism 80-87, 107, 119, 175, 179, 182, 187, 225
Salafism 64, 80-83, 89
    in the Netherlands 20, 23, 55, 83, 165
Saudi Arabia 83, 104, 165
Schiedam 56
Schiphol airport 61-62, 71, 93
Schmid, Alex 35-36, 51-52, 65
    revised academic consensus definition of terrorism 50
sects *see* Hofstadgroup
Segal, Mary E. 142, 204
Senechal de la Roche, Roberta 118
Sharia 132, 191
Shepherd, Bryan 112
significance quest *see* involvement in terrorism
Silber, Mitchell D. 19, 172
Silke, Andrew 37, 150, 199
Skorpion submachine gun *see* weapons
slippery slope *see* involvement in terrorism
Slootman, Marieke 23, 171
social comparison 142
social identity theory *see* involvement in terrorism: benefits of group membership
social learning theory *see* involvement in terrorism
social movement theory 20, 47-48
social reality value 133

Spain 58-59, 75, 79, 104, 110, 152
    withdrawal of troops from Iraq 138
Spears, Russell 150
special forces deployment 67
Stern, Jessica 41
strategic school (political opportunity structure) *see* involvement in terrorism
strategy (terrorism) 156-159
Submission, part 1 43, 63, 86, 108, 115, 120-121, 211, 215, 219
suicide terrorism 155, 173, 206
sunk cost fallacy 186
Syria 15, 31, 56, 59-60, 66, 78, 82, 89, 103, 127-128, 151, 217-218
    civil war, 2011-present 15-16, 217-218

taghut 191
takfir 62, 81-82, 85-87, 101, 133, 144-146, 176
Takfir wal Hijra 85
Tarrow, Sidney 47
tawhid 80-83, 101, 133, 143, 146
Taylor, Max 44, 124, 147, 177-180, 227
terrorism
    2003 Casablanca bombings 58, 104
    2004 Madrid attacks 15, 84, 138, 217
    2004 murder of Van Gogh *see* Van Gogh, Theo
    2005 London attacks 15, 217
    2015 Paris attacks 217
    as communication 51, 65
    defining terrorism 49-51, 65
terrorism research
    critical terrorism studies 35
    databases 39
    defining terrorism 49-51
    enduring issues 16-17, 35-39
    fieldwork 23, 39
    media sources, use of 18-19, 21, 36-38
    overreliance on secondary sources 17-18, 36-38
    primary sources 21, 37-39
    societal relevance 17, 217-218
    theoretical perspectives 39-47
Terror Management Theory 212
The Hague 13-14, 56, 64, 67, 70, 72, 74-75, 88, 105, 153
    potential explosives test in park (2005) 71
Tillie, Jean 23, 171
top-down group formation 125
training (paramilitary) *see* Hofstadgroup
Turkey 66

ummah 52, 81, 87, 117-118, 190, 203
unfreezing *see* involvement in terrorism
United States 15, 81-82, 84, 100, 117-118, 123, 182

Van Gogh, Theo 13-15, 48, 60, 63-66, 77, 86, 89, 92-93, 97, 103-104, 108, 114-116, 120-121, 131, 138, 140, 149-153, 163-164, 167, 174-176, 179, 181, 190, 201-202, 211, 215, 219, 221, 223
    criticism of Islam and Muslims 60, 114
    director of Submission, part 1 63
    murderer of *see* Murderer of Van Gogh
    murder, involvement wider Hofstadgroup 65-66
    online threats 63-64
    refusal of personal protection 108
variance decrease 142-144
Verdonk, Rita 114
Vermaat, Emerson 19
vicarious deprivation *see* involvement in terrorism
Victoroff, Jeff 170, 204
war against Islam (presumed) 20, 23, 117, 121, 149, 180, 183, 229
War on Terror 55, 117, 121, 219, 227
weapons
    2004 Portugal trip 62
    explosives 59, 61, 67, 71, 84, 92-93, 99, 121, 139, 149
    firearms 13, 61, 64, 68-70, 72-73
    firearms (fake) 67
    handbooks on explosives / jihad 61, 100
    hand grenades 14, 67, 92, 104-105, 109, 150, 152
    knives 13, 64, 67, 144, 183, 207
    magazines 61
    pre-cursor components explosive device 61, 92
    RPG 71, 93
    silencer 61, 70
    suicide vest 69, 72
Weenink, Anton 196-197
Welkoop (store) 62, 92
Wiktorowicz, Quintan 81, 181
Wilders, Geert 55, 85, 114, 153
    online threats 64
women in Hofstadgroup *see* Hofstadgroup

zindiq 190